SAT

DeMYSTiFieD®

DeMYSTiFieD® Series

Accounting Demystified
ACT Demystified
Advanced Calculus Demystified
Advanced Physics Demystified
Advanced Statistics Demystified
Algebra Demystified
Alternative Energy Demystified
Anatomy Demystified
Astronomy Demystified
Audio Demystified
Biology Demystified
Biophysics Demystified
Biotechnology Demystified
Business Calculus Demystified
Business Math Demystified
Business Statistics Demystified
C++ Demystified
Calculus Demystified
Chemistry Demystified
Circuit Analysis Demystified
College Algebra Demystified
Corporate Finance Demystified
Data Structures Demystified
Databases Demystified
Differential Equations Demystified
Digital Electronics Demystified
Earth Science Demystified
Electricity Demystified
Electronics Demystified
Engineering Statistics Demystified
Environmental Science Demystified
Everyday Math Demystified
Financial Planning Demystified
Forensics Demystified
French Demystified
Genetics Demystified
Geometry Demystified
German Demystified
Home Networking Demystified
Investing Demystified
Italian Demystified
Java Demystified
JavaScript Demystified
Lean Six Sigma Demystified
Linear Algebra Demystified
Logic Demystified

Macroeconomics Demystified
Management Accounting Demystified
Math Proofs Demystified
Math Word Problems Demystified
MATLAB® Demystified
Medical Billing and Coding Demystified
Medical Terminology Demystified
Meteorology Demystified
Microbiology Demystified
Microeconomics Demystified
Minitab Demystified
Nanotechnology Demystified
Nurse Management Demystified
OOP Demystified
Options Demystified
Organic Chemistry Demystified
Personal Computing Demystified
Pharmacology Demystified
Philosophy Demystified
Physics Demystified
Physiology Demystified
Pre-Algebra Demystified
Precalculus Demystified
Probability Demystified
Project Management Demystified
Psychology Demystified
Quality Management Demystified
Quantum Mechanics Demystified
Real Estate Math Demystified
Relativity Demystified
Robotics Demystified
SAT Demystified
Signals and Systems Demystified
Six Sigma Demystified
Spanish Demystified
SQL Demystified
Statics and Dynamics Demystified
Statistical Process Control Demystified
Statistics Demystified
Technical Analysis Demystified
Technical Math Demystified
Trigonometry Demystified
UML Demystified
Visual Basic 2005 Demystified
Visual C# 2005 Demystified
XML Demystified

SAT
DeMYSTiFieD®

Alexandra Mayzler and Joseph Daniele

New York   Chicago   San Francisco   Lisbon   London   Madrid   Mexico City
Milan   New Delhi   San Juan   Seoul   Singapore   Sydney   Toronto

1 2 3 4 5 6 7 8 9 10 11 12 13 14 15   DOC/DOC   1 9 8 7 6 5 4 3 2 1

ISBN 978-0-07-175295-4
MHID 0-07-175295-1

e-ISBN 978-0-07-175296-1
e-MHID 0-07-175296-X

LOC Control Number 2010941615

Contents

Part I

Introduction

Congratulations on taking the first step toward preparing for the SAT. In this section, you'll find answers to questions like "Why this book?", "What can you expect to learn?", and "How do I create a study schedule?" We recommend you read through this section carefully to familiarize yourself with the DeMYSTiFeD prep.

chapter 1

About the Book

Why This Book?

There are many resources available for test preparation. A stroll through the neighborhood bookstore or library will yield a plethora of materials that can be used to prepare for the SAT. Selecting a prep book can be an overwhelming experience; the ability to distinguish one guide from another can be a murky process. With *SAT DeMYSTiFieD*, we present one option for helping you get ready for the test. Our inspiration in writing this manual came from many years of working with students and our own personal experiences as test takers. We have also spent years dissecting and practicing the SAT and have learned a thing or two along the way. Rather than just write a long book with extensive practice questions, we wanted to put together a resource that would guide students through the prep process. This workbook serves not just to communicate the strategies we've come up with to beat the test but a hands-on experience to help you get ready for the SAT. We love working one-on-one with students, and although we cannot sit at every kitchen table with each of you, we hope that we'll come close with *SAT DeMYSTiFieD*.

What's in the Book and How to Use It

Before you jump into prepping for your SAT, we would like you to flip through the book in order to get an understanding of the layout. You'll notice that it is divided into five sections: Verbal, Math, Writing, Practice Tests, and the

Appendix. In each of the Verbal, Math, and Writing sections, we will intro-duce an approach and a strategy for tackling that type of SAT problem. These chapters serve to "zoom-in" on various types of SAT tasks and teach methods that improve the way you think about problems in those specific sections. The introduction to each strategy is given in a "Steps" box followed by an explana-tion of each of the steps. It looks something like this:

Steps

Step 1:
Step 2:
Step 3:
Step 4:
Step 5:
Step 6:

We encourage you to memorize the steps as well as learn the actual process. The reason for this dual approach is that while we would like you to master our process, we also realize that during stressful times—such as during the actual test—you might feel flustered and confused about your process. However, chances are that you'll be able to remember a few keywords. By keeping the steps in mind, you will have an easier time recalling the process—it's like a cheat sheet for your brain.

Once you've understood the steps, can recall them easily, and have read over the process you should put everything into practice. Following each section we provide you with a few guided practice problems. With these problems, we lead you through our process step-by-step. Try not to jump ahead and solve the prob-lems on your own; instead, focus on how to apply the steps to find the solution.

Finally, you'll encounter the Drill/Quiz portion of the section. Here your goal is to apply the steps and process to SAT-like questions. We urge you to work through these problems carefully with an awareness of the process. If you notice that you're struggling with a particular type of problem then make sure to plan on doing additional practice. Again, the most important aspect of these practice problems is to rehearse the steps!

Once you've worked through the Verbal, Math, and Writing sections, you will have learned the ins and outs of the exam. It will then be time to put everything together. The SAT is difficult because it is a long exam that has you move between different sections. You not only need to know how to solve all the problems, but also be comfortable navigating from section to section, all under major time constraints. Therefore, practicing the test as a whole is extremely important. In the Practice Tests section, we provide you with three full-length tests. The purpose of these tests is to give you the opportunity to practice and to hone your full-length test-taking strategies. The first test serves as a "Test Taker's Compass"—you'll complete an example and follow a guide to determine what type of strategies you should use. Study these strategies carefully and adapt the appropriate methods to your test-taking style. Then, once you feel confident about your personal "Compass," practice the next two tests. Remember to create a test-like environment—wake up early, select a quiet space, and time yourself.

The final section of the book is the Appendix. Here you'll find some reminders from us as well as pages to write reminders to yourself. Our reminders, along with the Keep in Mind blurbs, are essentially lists of the errors that students make most frequently. Read our Keep in Minds so that you can avoid falling for common SAT traps. The pages designated to fill in with your personal strategy should be used to make final notes to yourself. This is not the area to take notes on the book. Instead, use the Appendix pages as the space to write any ideas, suggestions, and strategies that you'll want to look over before the test—anything important that keeps slipping your mind, a mistake you make frequently that you want to avoid, or a helpful tip or mnemonic.

What This Book Won't Do

This book will not serve as a magical panacea for test prep. Unfortunately, we aren't going to reveal a secret path to acing the exam or sprinkle "perfect score" pixie dust. However, what we will do is provide a comprehensive preparation, review all the content required for the test, and introduce strategies to achieve your personal best score. By following the course of study carefully and dedicating the necessary amount of time, you will be ready for the test. Leisurely flipping through the pages of the book doesn't count as preparation. Read the chapters meticulously, complete the practice problems, and spend time on the mock tests. If you feel that you're stuck, remember to ask for help. Set aside time to meet with a teacher or seek assistance from a tutor.

Think about this book as a prep that can teach you critical thinking skills—the number one skill you need to rock the SAT. So go in, go hard, and always go for the gold!

Creating a Schedule

Now that you are familiar with the book, let's turn our attention to getting started and creating a schedule. Before delving into the approaches and practicing problems, you should think about how much time you will need to prepare for the test. The best way to prep is slowly and gradually. Because it takes your brain time to learn and master new material, you want to allow yourself several months to prepare. Making a schedule will also help you stay on track and hold yourself accountable for your prep.

We suggest that you set aside 11 weeks to work through the book and thus get ready for the test. If you feel that you need to move through the preparation more slowly, add on a few extra weeks. You'll also notice that we left a few "flexible" weeks in the event that you need to make an adjustment. If you find that you have a particularly tough week at school or you need an extra few days to go over some material, you don't need to get off track.

On a weekly basis, you will need to spend about 1 hour each on learning the steps and processes for each section (so, approximately 2 hours total—1 hour for English [verbal and writing] and 1 hour for Math). We suggest setting aside an English day and a Math day and planning on reading, memorizing, understanding, and practicing the steps for each section. We recommend that you designate an SAT time that does not vary from week to week. Block out the time on your calendar and plan for it the same way you do for sports practice, school commitments, and extracurricular activities. If you set aside a consistent time each week, you won't feel like you have to cram SAT prep into your schedule and you'll be able to better focus on doing the necessary work. Then you will need anywhere from 1 to 4 hours a week to complete the homework. The time that you will spend practicing will vary based on the topic and your work speed. For example, the homework following the first lesson may be more of a review and thus take less time than the homework you will be doing at the end of the guide which involves taking a full-length test. Do the practice problems carefully and thoroughly—remember, if you rush through the homework, you will only be cheating yourself.

Use the chart included here to help you plan out a calendar. We've divided up the chapters in the book. Keeping in mind when your test date will be, fill in the dates for the corresponding lessons and homeworks.

Date	Chapter to Study	Homework	Notes
	Intro	Make your schedule	
	Math: Numbers	Quiz: Numbers	
	Math: Algebra	Quiz: Algebra	
	Math: Measure of central tendency, probability, and sequences	Quiz: Measure of central tendency, probability, and sequences	
	Math: Coordinate geometry	Quiz: Coordinate geometry	
	Math: Geometry	Quiz: Geometry	
	Math: Proportions	Quiz: Proportions	
	Math: Functions	Quiz: Functions	
	Verbal: Sentence completion	Quiz: Sentence completion	
	Verbal: Reading comprehension	Quiz: Reading comprehension	
	Writing: Grammar review	Grammar review	
	Writing: Essay	Practice Essays	
	Writing: Identifying sentence errors	Quiz: Identifying sentence errors	
	Writing: Improving sentences	Quiz: Improving sentences	
	Writing: Improving paragraphs	Quiz: Improving paragraphs	
	Review	Compass Test	
	Review Compass Test and Personalized Strategies	Test 2	
	Grade and Review Test 2	Test 3	
	Grade and Review Test 3	Go over Appendix Reminders	
Test Date: _____			Good Luck!

chapter 2

About the Test

Layout of the Test

The test is divided up into three sections—Critical Reading, Math, and Writing. The chart explains what you can expect from each section.

Critical Reading Section	
Time	Two 25-minute sections, one 20-minute section
Total Points	200–800
Format	• Sentence completion • Two short passages • Four long passages
Question Types	• Sentence completion • Reading comprehension

Writing Section	
Time	Two 25-minute sections, one 10-minute section
Total Points	200–800
Format	• Improving sentences • Identifying sentence errors • Improving paragraphs • Essay
Topics Tested	• Grammar • Writing

Math Section	
Time	Two 25-minute sections, one 20-minute section
Total Points	200–800
Format	• 10 Grid-in Questions • 44 Multiple-choice Questions
Topics Tested	• Arithmetic (basic math functions) • Algebra • Geometry • Probability • Central Tendency • Functions
Question Types	• Multiple choice • Grid-ins

SAT Ground Rules

Understanding the exam and knowing the general strategy are the first steps in your preparation. As you go through each section of the review you will learn how to apply these, and more specific strategies, to the test. For now, the ground rules:

Time Management Tactics

The most challenging thing about the SAT is the time limitations. You are not just tested on how well you know Math and English, but also on your ability to manage time. On most tests you take in school, you start with question number 1, work through the question, go on to number 2, and so on. This method won't work for the SAT. Your goal is to answer as many questions correctly as you can. Because of the limited time on the exam, you must skip around and secure points.

Grouping

For the SAT, you need to use a technique we call *grouping*. Scan the questions for each section and start with the questions you find easiest. Complete all the easy items first, skip and circle anything that seems difficult, then go back and do all the medium questions, and finally attempt the hard questions.

The questions in sentence completion and multiple-choice Math sections are set up in order of difficulty, whereas the other sections mix and match. However, what matters most is *your* order of difficulty.

Time Investment

As we have discussed, this test is part knowledge and part time management. In answering the questions, you want to work based on your level of difficulty. You should also consider time investment per question. Let's look at a typical Verbal section:

- 10 sentence completions
- 2 short passages
- 1 long passage

Complete the sections that take the least amount of time per question. Do all of the sentence completions first. Move on to the short reading passages. Finally, tackle the long reading passage.

Confidence

Answering questions that are "easy" builds your confidence—not a point to take lightly. Once you've answered the easier questions, you will feel more comfortable about your skills and get into a helpful test-taking rhythm. Also remember that "easy" can be subjective. The last problem, while usually considered "difficult," could be easy for you. Different topics appeal to different people.

Cutting Your Losses

Each question on the test is worth one point. That means the easy questions and the hard questions are all worth the same number of points. You will not get bonus points for spending 5 minutes on a difficult question.

You should spend 1 to 2 minutes on each question. Some of the easy questions might only take 30 seconds, buying you time for the harder ones. Don't worry about keeping a timer—just keep track of time in the back of your mind. If you feel like you have spent more than 2 minutes on a question, consider cutting your losses by:

- Skipping the question and coming back to it later (time permitting)
- Eliminating impossible answers and guessing (depending on the section)

Basic Strategy

Now that you have learned to manage your time efficiently, let's look at the other part of the equation: accuracy.

Answer the Question Before You Answer the Question

Multiple-choice answers have built-in tricks. For every five answer choices, four are distracters. These menaces are meant to sound good—really good—so that the answer options guide your choices. Don't fall into the trap! Make sure to answer the questions before looking at the choices. We will work on steps to make this concept easier for you.

Educated Guessing

You are probably thinking about all those times you made bad guesses. The SAT does not have a guessing penalty—it has a wrong-answer penalty. The exam doesn't expect you to know the answer to every single question. What it does expect is that you make educated decisions.

For the Verbal and Writing sections, educated guessing can earn you a heck of a lot of points. Every time you eliminate even *one* answer choice and guess from the remaining, you are raising your score. Without even knowing the correct answer you can eliminate incorrect choices, guess, and rack up the points. By not guessing, you put a ceiling on your score potential. We will give you specific omitting and guessing strategies for each of the sections. However, the most important thing is to keep track of how well you are able to make an educated guess.

For the Math section problems, it is not in your favor to guess! You can make an educated guess on one or two problems, but no more. For the math component, students who boil the choices down to two possibilities usually have an equal argument for choosing both solutions. In that case, educated guessing becomes simple guessing, which is definitely not beneficial.

Target Score

As we said in the past, your strategy will be personalized as you work through the prep. We know you are different from the next student over. However, your target score does impact your overall strategy. Depending on your goal, the approach method will be different. The chart below illustrates approximately how many questions you need to answer to reach various target scores.

Target Score	Number You Should Leave Blank per Section
750–800	0–1
700–750	0–2
650–700	1–3
600–650	2–5
550–600	4–8
500–550	7–12
450–500	10–16
400–450	14–20

Part II

Verbal Section

The Verbal section is composed of two parts: Sentence Completion and Reading Comprehension. We will introduce specific strategies for tackling these sections. Although sentence completion and reading comprehension are parts of one section, each task requires a distinct strategy. Master one subsection before moving on to the next one.

chapter 3

Sentence Completion

What's Being Tested?

Sentence completion questions test your knowledge of word meanings and your ability to understand sentence structure. Each sentence completion consists of a statement with one or two blanks. Your task is to use the statement to figure out the word(s) that best fit(s) into the blank(s).

Dissecting Sentences

Most students tackle the sentence completion section by reading the sentence and intuitively thinking of a word that fits into the blank(s). While this system works it does not always work well and is not effective for harder questions. We will teach you to think of sentence completions in a new way. Our process may seem laborious at first glance, but with practice it'll become easier and your accuracy will improve.

 Think of each question as a dictionary in reverse. Usually you are given a word followed by a definition. Here you will find the definition and then look for the word that fits that definition. The definition will be part of the sentence. Your job is to find the definition in the sentence and select the word that fits the definition.

We've developed a six-step method to help you dissect and find the answer choice that best fits in the blank.

Let's go over the six steps:

Sentence Completion Steps

Step 1: Read
Step 2: Find the definition
Step 3: Positive/negative/neutral
Step 4: Fill in the blank
Step 5: Eliminate
Step 6: Plug it in

Step 1: Read

Carefully read the question and cover up the answer choices.

Step 2: Find the Definition

Find the definition or group of defining "clue" words for the blank. These are the words that explain what the word means. Underline the defining words.

Step 3: Positive/Negative/Neutral

Determine whether the missing word is positive, negative, or neutral. Keep in mind that not all blanks will have a positive or negative tone. Some of the blanks will be neutral. Be on the lookout for negatives and trap words that seem negative but really are not. These traps have prefixes such as:

- no, not, none, non-, un-, in-

Step 4: Fill in the Blank

Using your own words, fill in the blank. Use the definition you underlined in Step 2 to establish the meaning of the missing word. Coming up with your own answer will force you to stick with the steps, which will prevent you from falling for the "easy trap answer." You don't need to worry about thinking of a "perfect" word to fill in the blank because that is a waste of time. Instead, think of the first word(s) that come to mind that explains to you the meaning of the blank.

Step 5: Eliminate

Once you've used the information in the sentence to build your own answer, then you can see which answer choice matches yours. Eliminate answers that don't fit your definition and feeling of the word (positive/negative). Keep any words that you don't know as open options. Compare your answer to the choices. The next step will help determine the final answer.

Step 6: Plug It In

Now that you have narrowed down your choices to one or two, plug in the answer choice (or choices) you've selected to make sure your choice works in the sentence.

Examples

Let's look at some sample questions to see what's involved. Here's our sentence. We're not looking at the answer choices yet. Remember to keep the choices covered, so that we can concentrate on the sentence.

> *Madison was a/an _____ person and thus made few public addresses, but those he made were memorable, filled with noble phrases.*

Now let's look for the definition or the words that help define the blank.

> Madison was a/an _____ person and <u>thus made few public addresses</u>, but those he made were memorable, filled with noble phrases.

(A) reticent
(B) stately
(C) inspiring
(D) introspective
(E) communicative

Here are our steps:

Step 1: Read

Step 2: Find the definition: <u>made few public addresses</u>

Step 3: Positive/negative/neutral: neutral

Step 4: Fill in the blank: someone who doesn't like to talk in public
[Notice that we're not thinking of a "perfect word" to fit the blank. Instead, we're using the words that make sense to us.]

Step 5: Eliminate: cross off any words that are too positive or too negative. Then look at the answer choices that fit your definition

Step 6: Plug it in: Madison was a *reticent* person and thus made few public addresses, but those he made were memorable, filled with noble phrases

---

Now it is your turn.

Take a look a look at the sentence. We'll give you the steps so that you can practice the process.

It is possible to analyze an email to death, _____ what should be an improvised communication as if it were a laboratory specimen.

(A) questioning
(B) dissecting
(C) amending
(D) nurturing
(E) reviving

> **Step 1:** Read
> **Step 2:** Find the definition:
> **Step 3:** Positive/negative/neutral:
> **Step 4:** Fill in the blank:
> **Step 5:** Eliminate:
> **Step 6:** Plug it in:

The correct answer is B.

Here's another example.

Look over the following sentence and use our six steps to find the correct answer. Use the workspace to go through the steps.

Given the ability of technology to ____ the environment, it is clear that, if we are not careful, many of the species roaming the earth today may soon be as extinct as a dinosaur.

(A) enhance
(B) destroy
(C) analyze
(D) repair
(E) nurture

> Step 1:
> Step 2:
> Step 3:
> Step 4:
> Step 5:
> Step 6:

The correct answer is B.

Sentence Completion With Two Blanks

Working with two blanks is similar to working with one blank. Include one extra step to help you find the answer choice that best fills the blank. Take one blank at a time.

> ### Sentence Completion Two-Blanks Steps
> **Step 1:** Read
> **Step 2:** Definition
> **Step 3:** Positive/negative/neutral
> **Step 4:** Fill in the blank
> **Step 5:** Establish a relationship between the two blanks (synonyms or antonyms)
> **Step 6:** Eliminate
> **Step 7:** Plug it in

Let's take a look at the question: First read the sentence and then let's look at the steps together.

Trilobites, a type of segmented animal with jointed appendages of the prehistoric times, were one of the most _____ forms of life on the planet: thousands of species have been _____ for fossil records.

Trilobites, a type of segmented animal with jointed appendages of the prehistoric times, were one of the most ____ forms of life on the planet: <u>thousands of species</u> have been ____ for fossil <u>records</u>.

(A)   abundant…subtracted
(B)   elaborate…recovered
(C)   multifarious…catalogued
(D)   limited…extracted
(E)   anachronistic…extrapolated

Blank One

Step 1: Read
Step 2: Definition: <u>thousands of species</u>
Step 3: Positive/negative/neutral: neutral
Step 4: Fill in the blank: *there were a lot of these animals*
Step 5: Eliminate: cross out any word that's too positive or negative and find the one that means "a lot of"

Blank Two

Step 1: Read
Step 2: Definition: <u>records</u>
Step 3: Positive/negative/neutral: neutral
Step 4: Fill in the blank: filed or recorded
Step 5: Establish a relationship between the words: no relationship
Step 6: Eliminate: cross out any word that's too positive or negative and find the one that means "filed" or "recorded"
Step 7: Plug it in: Trilobites, a type of segmented animal with jointed appendages of the prehistoric times, were one of the most <u>multifarious</u> forms of life on the planet: thousands of species have been <u>catalogued</u> for fossil records

The correct answer is C.

Practice the Process

Although special effects have existed in cinema for decades, today's special effects engineers have access to _____ that would have _____ their counterparts in years past.

(A)   technology…amazed
(B)   knowledge…regaled
(C)   creativity…altered
(D)   largesse…instigated
(E)   profits…amused

> **Step 1:** Read
> **Step 2:** Definition:
> **Step 3:** Positive/negative/neutral:
> **Step 4:** Fill in the blank:
> **Step 5:** Establish a relationship between the words (are they synonyms or antonyms):
> **Step 6:** Eliminate:
> **Step 7:** Plug it in:

The correct answer is A.

Keep in Mind

- Sentence completion questions are generally arranged in order of difficulty, from easiest to hardest.
- Clue words, such as *and, but, however, although,* etc., can indicate the direction the sentence is heading.
- Make sure to read the entire sentence because a single word can change the meaning of the sentence.
- Do not eliminate a word if you do not know the definition. Leave it as an option and try to eliminate the other choices.
- Just because you do not know the definition of the word does not mean that the word isn't the best fit. If you've eliminated all the other choices and are faced with an unfamiliar word, assume that you are correct.

Sentence Completion Drills

Directions: For each question in this section, select the best answer from among the answer choices given.

1. What are the steps for single-blank sentence completion?

   Step 1:
   Step 2:
   Step 3:
   Step 4:
   Step 5:
   Step 6:

2. What are the steps for double-blank sentence completion?

   Step 1:
   Step 2:
   Step 3:
   Step 4:
   Step 5:
   Step 6:
   Step 7:

3. The band's playing was so _____ that singers couldn't be heard above the clamor.

   (A) subtle
   (B) poor
   (C) loud
   (D) energetic
   (E) fast

4. Some psychologists believe that children have less _____ today than in the past and no longer have an understanding of other people's feelings.

   (A) kindness
   (B) pity
   (C) empathy
   (D) enthusiasm
   (E) apathy

5. Gerry showed a/an ____ for science and therefore ____ his physics class over his English class.

    (A) aptitude…favored
    (B) enthusiasm…esteemed
    (C) choice….selected
    (D) dislike…preferred
    (E) interest…switched

6. Throughout his illustrious career, the artist's work has been ____, with years of prolific creativity interspersed with decades of meager production.

    (A) unparalleled
    (B) innovative
    (C) temporary
    (D) erratic
    (E) impracticable

7. As wild fish becomes less abundant, fisherman are ____ to more dangerous methods to retrieve the natural resource, ____ the potential for injuries.

    (A) swimming…lessening
    (B) resorting…increasing
    (C) removing…preventing
    (D) arriving…seeing
    (E) planning…creating

8. Emily Dickinson is known for her poetry and her ____ lifestyle; she was extremely introverted and lived most of her days in near isolation.

    (A) reclusive
    (B) miserable
    (C) hedonistic
    (D) unusual
    (E) exultant

9. The mother gave her child _____ directions, stating her expectations clearly and directly.

   (A) explicit
   (B) quiet
   (C) arcane
   (D) strict
   (E) circuitous

10. Lauren's friends often referred to her as stingy, but she preferred to think of herself as _____ and prudent.

    (A) poor
    (B) inflexible
    (C) frugal
    (D) concise
    (E) dynamic

11. The fruit stand owner, a particularly _____ and furtive man, often cheated his customers by manipulating the scales.

    (A) devious
    (B) sensitive
    (C) industrious
    (D) pugnacious
    (E) principled

12. Susanna prided herself on her _____ and _____ nature; she was painstakingly careful with every aspect of her life.

    (A) exacting…tiresome
    (B) meticulous…scrupulous
    (C) fussy…consciousness
    (D) sloppy…abrasive
    (E) productive…choosy

13. A discerning manager can ____ a promising employee from a mass of applicants, separating the excellent from the mediocre.

    (A) supplant
    (B) dramatize
    (C) overhaul
    (D) finagle
    (E) reject

14. Despite her general ____, Rachel could often be ____ with people when she felt stressed and tired.

    (A) affability...brusque
    (B) dependability...vague
    (C) happiness...relentless
    (D) softness...unpredictable
    (E) hostility...pleasant

15. Ms. Krasnow was surprised when her otherwise ____ students made careless mistakes on the final exam.

    (A) fastidious
    (B) hard-working
    (C) zealous
    (D) amiable
    (E) haphazard

16. Glen had a/an ____ for music: He started playing the piano when he was five, attended band camp during his teen years, and pursued a career as a guitarist.

    (A) congruency
    (B) aptitude
    (C) indifference
    (D) lyrical
    (E) cadence

17. The law professor's students respected him because he was both ____ and ____: candid with his expectations and fair in his judgments.

(A) lenient…prudent
(B) resourceful…tenacious
(C) honest…unbiased
(D) outspoken…inflexible
(E) judicious…austere

18. Although a surprise for many Van Gogh lovers, his fame and popularity were ____ posthumously.

(A) bolstered
(B) inspired
(C) decreed
(D) convalesced
(E) illuminated

19. The boy's speech was ____ as he mumbled a disjointed story in his sleep.

(A) imaginative
(B) inspiring
(C) slow
(D) incoherent
(E) opaque

20. Bob's mom ____ him for his exceptional achievement in the spelling bee.

(A) lauded
(B) appraised
(C) castigated
(D) mollified
(E) chastise

21. Charley ____ the altercation by berating his friend in the middle of the playground.

(A) instigated
(B) assuaged
(C) strengthened
(D) approved
(E) terminated

22. The ____ house had fifteen bedrooms, two kitchens, three pools, and a helicopter landing pad.

    (A) modest
    (B) grandiose
    (C) flagrant
    (D) garish
    (E) elegant

23. The scientist's study of evolutionary theory is ____: She begins with early ideas and ends with contemporary hypotheses.

    (A) comprehensive
    (B) thoughtful
    (C) idiosyncratic
    (D) chronological
    (E) disorganized

24. The players were ____ when the referee decided not to count the goal their teammate scored in overtime.

    (A) enervated
    (B) indignant
    (C) boisterous
    (D) ascetic
    (E) ecstatic

25. Ben's mom implored him to stop watching ____ television shows that were neither entertaining nor intellectually stimulating.

    (A) insipid
    (B) futile
    (C) convivial
    (D) random
    (E) ebullient

26. The philharmonic's program at the festival was ____, haphazardly incor-
porating pieces from many different composers and eras.

(A) melodious
(B) slapdash
(C) flawless
(D) eclectic
(E) baleful

27. Quentin's writing is considered ____ and ____ because it is direct and
does not digress from the thesis.

(A) concise...succinct
(B) vague...circuitous
(C) laconic...aggrandized
(D) economical...cautious
(E) didactic...obscure

chapter **4**

Reading Comprehension

What's Being Tested?

The Reading section of the SAT is no *Sports Illustrated* or latest beach read. The SAT contains two kinds of critical reading passages (from now on called CRs): long CRs with multiparagraph passages followed by a series of questions, and short CRs with a brief one-paragraph passage followed by two questions. We'll take a look at both types of CRs and introduce strategies to tackle this section.

What You'll Be up Against

The first two sections of the CR will have the following types of passages:

- Two short passages with two questions or one short passage with four questions
- Two long passages each followed by six or nine questions

The third section of the CR will have the longest and often most boring passage(s) followed by about 13 questions. You will probably encounter the Double Trouble passages here with two passages and questions about each individual passage followed by questions about both passages. We'll use a special strategy to deal with the Double Troubles.

Train Your Brain

How do you tackle the reading section? The answer is simple: read, read, read! And read some more. We suggest that you keep a log of your reading from this instant until the day you take the SAT. Write down a brief summary of the reading so that you can practice looking out for the main ideas. You will need to practice active reading, looking between the lines, and thinking about what you are reading, so that you can train your brain. While reading think about the following:

1. **What is the main point of the reading?** What are you reading about anyway? Is there a purpose to the article?

2. **What is the author's attitude?** Does the writer have a point of view? Is the writer supporting or opposing the topic?

3. **Is special language being used?** Does the writer use language, sentence structure, and paragraph structure to get his or her opinion across?

Those Pesky Literary Devices

The SAT asks you to recognize and analyze rhetorical devices in literature. If any of these doesn't look familiar, make flashcards and study the terms. This list contains the terms that are most likely to appear on the exam:

1. **Alliteration**—The repetition of similar sounds, usually consonants, at the beginning of words. "Sandy sold seashells" is an example of alliteration.

2. **Cliché/Colloquial**—A familiar expression that has been used and reused so many times that it has lost its expressive power. "It's raining cats and dogs" is an example of a cliché.

3. **Foreshadowing**—An author's deliberate use of hints or suggestions to give a preview of events or themes that do not develop until later in the narrative. Images such as a storm brewing or a crow landing on a fencepost often foreshadow ominous developments in a story.

4. **Hyperbole**—An excessive overstatement or exaggeration of fact. "I've told you that a million times already" is a hyperbolic statement.

5. **Imagery**—Language that brings to mind sensory impressions.

6. **Irony**—Usually emphasizes the contrast between the way things are expected to be and the way they actually are. You've heard people say, "Isn't that ironic?"

7. **Metaphor**—The comparison of one thing to another that does not use the terms *like* or *as*.

8. **Oxymoron**—The association of two terms that seem to contradict each other, as in the expression "jumbo shrimp."

9. **Personification**—The use of human characteristics to describe animals, things, or ideas. Using the word "babbling" to describe a brook is an example of personification.

10. **Rhetorical Question**—A question asked not to elicit an actual response but to make an impact or call attention to something.

11. **Simile**—A comparison of two things that uses the words *like* or *as*.

12. **Symbol**—An object, character, figure, place, or color used to represent an abstract idea or concept.

13. **Theme**—A fundamental and universal idea explored in a literary work.

14. **Tone**—The author's or narrator's attitude toward the story or the subject.

Types of Questions

The SAT reading passages are followed by questions ranging from easy to difficult. Unlike the sentence completion section, the questions in the CR do not always follow an increasing order of difficulty. Therefore, it is particularly important to know the types of questions that show up on this section and understand what types of questions are easier and more difficult for you to answer. Based on your personal scale of difficulty, you'll tackle the questions in an order that is appropriate for you.

The CR questions can be categorized into two groups:

1. General

   A. Main idea

   B. Theme

   C. Tone

   D. Implied information

2. Specific

   A. Most questions with quotation marks (" ")

   B. Technique

   C. Vocabulary in context

General Questions

These are the questions that you can answer after having skimmed the passage.

A. Main idea

Main idea questions test your comprehension of the passage: these are general questions and focus on the passage's primary purpose. Main idea questions include questions such as:

- What does this passage illustrate?
- What is the author trying to communicate?
- What is the purpose of this passage?

B. Theme

A theme is the recurring concept that the author uses to establish the main idea. Theme questions test your ability to find the underlying feelings about the main idea. The theme may be different from what the author is stating outright. You need to follow the flow of the concepts and arguments and come up with your own answer.

C. Tone

These questions test whether you understand the author's point of view. Does the author support or oppose the topic? What are the feelings involved in this passage?

D. Implied information

These questions ask you to fish for the underlying information that is not stated outright. Your job is to read between the lines and make an inference based on the information given. Remember that the SAT isn't asking for your opinion—it's asking for you to infer *based* on the information provided.

Specific Information Questions

These are questions that direct you back to the passage and that require close reading.

A. Questions with quotation marks

Any questions that quote the passage or refer you to specific lines of a passage. Your job is to carefully reread that area and answer the question based on close reading.

B. Technique

Technique questions test your ability to identify literary and rhetoric devices. These questions require you to identify a specific tool being used.

C. **Vocabulary in context**

These questions ask you to identify the meaning of the words in the context of the passage. The question directs you to a word as it appears. Answer these questions the way you would a sentence completion question.

What to Do?

The Short of It

Short CRs are just that: short, one-paragraph passages, followed by two questions. We already reviewed the questions that the SAT may ask, so let's look at the strategy we should use to conquer these shorter CRs. Because there isn't a lot of "fluff information" in these passages, we need to really hone our detective skills. The questions lead us to the focus point of the passage.

Let's look at the strategy:

> ### *Steps to Short Passages*
> **Step 1:** Read the questions
> **Step 2:** Read the passage
> **Step 3:** Answer before you answer
> **Step 4:** Find the answer

Step 1: Read the questions

Read the questions first without looking at the answer choices. Restate the questions to yourself so that you know what to look out for while reading the passage.

Step 2: Read the passage

Very carefully read the passage and keep the questions in mind. You should be able to find the answers to the questions as you are working through the passage.

Step 3: Answer before you answer

Reread the questions and answer each in your own words. It helps to jot down the answers or keywords in the workspace. Once you're confident of the answer, look at the choices.

Step 4: Find the answer

Match your answer to the best choice.

Let's Look at a Short CR

The literary reputation of Dr. Holmes will rest on the three great
books which have made his name famous on two continents.
Line   Thackeray had passed his 40th year before he produced his
magnificent novel. Holmes, too, was more than 40 when he began
5   that unique and original book, *The Autocrat of the Breakfast Table*, one
of the most thoughtful, graceful, and able investigations into
philosophy and culture ever written. We have the author in every
mood, playful and pathetic, witty and wise. ... At a bound *The Autocrat*
leaped into popular favor. The reading public could hardly wait for the
10   numbers.

1.   The reference to "the author in every mood" (lines 7–8) serves to suggest
that

(A)   Dr. Holmes had a diverse narrative ability
(B)   Many types of characters are introduced in *The Autocrat of the Breakfast Table*
(C)   The popularity of *The Autocrat of the Breakfast Table* resulted from the author's erratic behavior
(D)   Dr. Holmes could not settle on a tone for his writing
(E)   Dr. Holmes has a canny ability to understand behavior and mood

2.   It can be inferred from this passage that

(A)   Dr. Holmes completed his defining work by his 40th birthday
(B)   Writers blossom in or after midlife
(C)   The author holds Dr. Holmes in great esteem
(D)   Dr. Holmes emulated Thackeray in life and in writing
(E)   *The Autocrat of the Breakfast Table* is a nonfiction work that explores cultural trends and tensions

Use the space below to follow the steps:

Step 1: Read the questions.
   1. The reference to "the author in every mood" (lines 7–8) serves to suggest that

   2. It can be inferred from this passage that

Step 2: Read the passage.
Step 3: Answer before you answer.
   1. The reference to "the author in every mood" (lines 7–8) serves to suggest that

   2. It can be inferred from this passage that

Step 4: Find the answer.

The Long of It

The strategy for the long CRs is different from the short CRs because you will not have time to carefully read the entire passage and you also will not be able to keep all the details in mind. Instead, you'll be getting a basic idea of the reading so that you can quickly navigate the passage to find answers. Your goal isn't to *learn* the information (although that's a great bonus). You've just got to figure out the main point and be able to find details. We have created a four-step method to dealing with the CRs:

Critical Reading Steps
Step 1: Skim
Step 2: Summarize
Step 3: Answer general
Step 4: Answer specific

Step 1: Skim

You will not have time to do everyday reading during the SAT because of the time constraints. Normal, everyday *reading* means reading all the words of a passage at least once at a leisurely pace. Instead, you will learn how to skim.

Skimming means reading only some of the words in a passage and letting your eyes skip over across the rest.

Because skimming is something you probably rarely practice, we will dedicate some time and effort to practicing this fine art. The key to skimming is breaking the habit of reading a passage word-for-word and trying to thoroughly understand the content. You need to read only the skeleton of the passage and skip over anything that makes you pause.

Here's how you do it:

The Fine Art of Skimming

- Use your pencil to help you break the habit of reading every word. Move the tip of your pencil across the lines of text quickly enough to make it impossible for you to read every word. This action forces you to skip over some words and phrases.
- Every time you feel like you are **pausing**, underline the words/sentences and move on. Instead of stopping and thinking (even for just a second), just underline and keep going.
  - What to underline: specific information (dates, names), anything that is confusing to you (complex sentences or words you don't know), any place you feel yourself pausing, anything you feel like you need to reread.
  - Underlining should not bring your attention to a specific area—instead it should be the trigger that reminds you to keep going.

Step 2: Summarize

After you have finished skimming each paragraph, write down a few notes about what you read. Summarize the passage in your own words. You don't and should not spend too much time writing complete sentences. Concentrate on writing a few key words to look back on when you're doing the questions. Keep in mind the general questions the SAT may ask you:

- Author's goal
- Primary argument/point

Step 3: Answer general questions

General questions ask about broad aspects of the passage. You should be able to find the answer to these questions just by skimming the notes you took while reading. You should also use the information you summarized for yourself after the reading. Use the following steps in answering general questions:

1. Read the question.
2. Paraphrase the question for yourself.
3. Answer the question in your own words.
4. Find the answer that best matches yours.

Step 4: Answer specific questions

Tackle the specific questions after the general because answering specific questions will require close reading. These questions ask you to refer directly to lines or words in the reading. Follow these steps in answering specific questions:

1. Read the question.
2. Paraphrase the question for yourself.
3. Research the paragraph: read two lines above and below the specific reference area.
4. Answer the question in your own words.
5. Find the answer that best matches yours.

Let's Practice

We will try our hand first at skimming and summarizing a paragraph. We will then move on to skimming and answering questions.

First Just the Skimming

The study of federalism, as a system of government, has in recent times become a favorite subject for constitutional writers. At present
Line the United States and the Dominion of Canada on this continent, the newly constituted Australian Commonwealth at the Antipodes, and
5 in Europe the German Empire, the Austro-Hungarian Empire, and the Swiss Confederation are all examples of the application of the federal principle in its various phases. What makes all research into this branch of political learning particularly difficult, and perhaps for that reason also exceptionally fascinating, is the fact that federated

10   states seem forever oscillating between the two extremes of complete centralization and decentralization. The two forces, centripetal and centrifugal, seem to be always pulling against each other, and producing a new resultant which varies according to their proportionate intensity. One is almost tempted to say that there must be an ideal

15   state somewhere between these two extremes, some point of perfect balance, from which no nation can ever depart very far without either falling apart into anarchy or being consolidated into despotism. Whatever, therefore, can throw light upon these obscure forces is certainly entitled to our deepest interest.

20   But not all the different states mentioned above as representatives of federalism possess an equal value for us in our search after improvements in the art of self-government. The study of the constitutions of the German and Austro-Hungarian empires can only be of secondary importance to us Americans because these states are

25   founded upon monarchical principles, quite foreign to our body politic. To a limited extent, the same objection may be made to the Canadian and Australian constitutions, since the connection of those countries with the monarchical mother country has not been constitutionally severed. But there is another federated state in

30   existence, until lately almost ignored by 173 writers on political subjects, whose example can in reality be of the utmost use to us, for its general organization more nearly resembles our own in miniature than any other. This country is Switzerland. In her quiet fashion the unobtrusive little Confederation is working out some of the great

35   modern problems, and her citizens, with their natural aptitude for self-government, are presenting object lessons which we especially in America cannot afford to overlook. It is true that political analogies are sometimes a little perilous, for identical situations can never be reproduced in different countries, but if there be any virtue at all in

40   the study of comparative politics, a comparison between the Federal constitutions of Switzerland and the United States ought to throw into relief some features which can be of service to us.

Write down the summary or some key points about the reading. _____

_____

_____

_____

Now the Questions

Here are our steps:

```
Step 1:  Skim
Step 2:  Summarize
Step 3:  Answer general
Step 4:  Answer specific
```

Alexander the Great: Maker of History
Jacob Abbot

Alexander the Great died when he was quite young. He was but
32 years of age when he ended his career, and as he was about 20

Line when he commenced it, it was only for a period of 12 years that he
was actually engaged in performing the work of his life. Napoleon was

5   nearly three times as long on the great field of human action.

Notwithstanding the briefness of Alexander's career, he ran through,
during that short period, a very brilliant series of exploits, which were
so bold, so romantic, and which led him into such adventures in scenes
of the greatest magnificence and splendor, that all the world looked on

10 with astonishment then, and mankind have continued to read the
story since, from age to age, with the greatest interest and attention.

The secret of Alexander's success was his character. He possessed a
certain combination of mental and personal attractions, which in
every age gives to those who exhibit it a mysterious and almost

15 unbounded ascendency over all within their influence. Alexander was
characterized by these qualities in a very remarkable degree. He was
finely formed in person, and very prepossessing in his manners. He
was active, athletic, and full of ardor and enthusiasm in all that he did.
At the same time, he was calm, collected, and considerate in

20 emergencies requiring caution, and thoughtful and far-seeing in
respect to the bearings and consequences of his acts. He formed
strong attachments, was grateful for kindnesses shown to him,
considerate in respect to the feelings of all who were connected with
him in any way, faithful to his friends, and generous toward his foes.

25 In a word, he had a noble character, though he devoted its energies
unfortunately to conquest and war. He lived, in fact, in an age when

great personal and mental powers had scarcely any other field for
their exercise than this. He entered upon his career with great ardor,
and the position in which he was placed gave him the opportunity to
30   act in it with prodigious effect.

Let's take a look at the questions:

Identify the general questions and answer those first and follow the steps to
answering general questions.

1. Read the question.
2. Paraphrase the question for yourself.
3. Answer the question in your own words.
4. Find the answer that best matches yours.

When you've answered the general questions move to the specific questions.

1. Read the question.
2. Paraphrase the question for yourself.
3. Research the paragraph: read two lines above and below the specific reference area.
4. Answer the question in your own words.
5. Find the answer that best matches yours.

1. The passage suggests all of the following about Alexander the Great
    EXCEPT

    (A) Alexander was revered during his lifetime
    (B) There was more interest in Alexander during his life than in modern
         history
    (C) Alexander was passionate and enthusiastic about his career
    (D) Much is known about Alexander's life after his 20th birthday
    (E) Alexander was an honorable man

2. In line 4 "engaged" most nearly means

    (A) occupied

    (B) demanding

    (C) available

    (D) betrothed

    (E) active

3. The author introduces Napoleon in line 4 in order to

    (A) compare two great military leaders

    (B) emphasize Alexander's endeavors given his short life

    (C) introduce Napoleon's conquests

    (D) provide a historical reference point

    (E) suggest how much Alexander could have accomplished had he lived longer

4. The statement "he devoted its energies unfortunately" (lines 25–26) implies that the author believes that Alexander the Great

    (A) did not use his strengths in the best possible way

    (B) regretted his occupation

    (C) could have avoided engaging in battle

    (D) intended to purse altruistic activities

    (E) applied his skills in a way appropriate for the time

Double Trouble

The SAT contains double passages, or two separate passages that are somehow related. These usually come at the end of the exam and are the longest reading passages that you will encounter. You will see two passages followed by questions for passage one, questions for passage two, and questions that ask you to relate the two passages.

Ignore the layout. Deal with the passages as two separate entities. You don't want to get stuck having read two passages with no time left over for questions. Also, the questions that deal with both passages are usually the most difficult and should be left until the end when you've answered as many of the easier questions as possible. Use the following steps in tackling the dual passages:

1. Read the first passage.
2. Answer the questions for the first passage (as you would in a single CR).
3. Read the second passage.
4. Answer the questions for the second passage (as you would a single CR).
5. Answer the rest of the questions that deal with both passages.

Keep in Mind

Watch out for these types of incorrect answer choices:

- Too broad
- Too narrow
- Exaggerated/strong language (always, all, never)
- True but not given in passage
- If a passage seems too difficult to read, remember the skimming process. You don't need to read the entire passage.
- Answer before you answer!
- If you are running out of time, look for quick points. For example, some reading questions will ask you to identify something very specific in the passage (e.g. particular word). These questions can be done even if you haven't read the passage.
- Don't skip the context blurb.

Reading Comprehension Drills

> **Directions:** The passages below are followed by questions based on their content; questions follow a pair of related passages may also be based on the relationship between the paired passages. Answer the questions on the basis of what is <u>stated</u> or <u>implied</u> in the passage in any introductory material that may be provided.

1. What are the steps for short passages?

    Step 1:
    Step 2:
    Step 3:
    Step 4:

2. What are the steps for long passages?

    Step 1:
    Step 2:
    Step 3:
    Step 4:
    Step 5:

Passage 1
The following excerpt from a work on Babylonian and Assyrian law serves to acquaint a general audience on family organization and structure.

(M323) The Code is explicit that a woman was not a wife without "bonds."(257) This was a marriage-contract; of which the essentials
Line were that the names of the parties and their lineage were given, the proper consents obtained and the declaration of the man that he has
5   taken so–and–so to wife inserted. As a rule, stringent penalties are set down for a repudiation of the marriage–tie. In these bonds a man might be required to insert the clause that his wife was not to be held responsible for any debts he might have incurred before marriage. The Code enacts that such a clause shall be held to act both ways; if
10   it is inserted, then the man shall not be liable for his wife's debts before marriage. (258) But, if no such bond existed, the wedded pair

were one body as far as liability for debt was concerned, by whichever
it had been contracted and, in spite of such a bond, both were liable
together for all debts contracted after marriage.

15   (M324) The family relationship was of primary importance. Whatever
may be said about traces of matriarchy in Babylonia, we have no legal
documents which recognize the institution. The father is the head of
the family and possesses full power over his wife and family. But the
woman is not in that degraded condition in which marriage by

20   capture, or purchase, left her. She was a man's inferior in some
respects, but his helper and an honorable wife.

(M325) Not only was the family, which consisted of the wedded pair
and their dependents, a unit, but there was also a connection with
ancestors and posterity which enlarged the family to a clan or gens. In

25   this sense it often appears. The family thus constituted had definite
rights over its members. It was very important to a man to be sure of
his family connection. We may note the importance attached at all
epochs to a man's genealogy as distinguishing his individuality. His
family identified him. There was a very large number of well–marked

30   and distinguished families, which took their names from a remote
ancestor. So far as our evidence goes, these ancestors were by no
means mythical, but actually lived in the time of the first dynasty of
Babylon. To all appearances they date back "to the Conquest."
Unfortunately no attempt has yet been made to work out the family

35   histories. But men of such families were the mârbânê, or "sons of
ancestors," and had special privileges, which continually emerge into
notice. We may compare the hundred families of China and the
patricians of many nations. There were other families of scarcely less
antiquity and consideration. They do not name their ancestor, but

40   refer to him as a tradesman. They were sons of "the baker," of "the
measurer," et cetera, with which we may compare our proper names
Baker and Lemesurier. There was a court of ancestry, *bîtmârbânûti*,
which investigated questions arising from claims to belong to such
families and which doubtless preserved in its archives the genealogical

45   lists of these exclusive families. They must have registered the birth of
all fresh members and all adoptions; for men were adopted freely into
such families.

...

(M328) The importance of descent was not a sentimental matter
50   only. The laws of inheritance involved 61 Babylonian and Assyrian
Laws, Contracts and Letters careful distinction between proper heirs
and a variety of claimants. Hence it seems likely that there was a
registration of births, deaths, and marriages, at least covering the
patrician families.

3.   The primary purpose of the passage is to

(A)   explain the matrimony laws of Babylonia
(B)   outline inheritance guidelines for Babylonian families
(C)   discuss the family hierarchy of Babylonia
(D)   demonstrate the organization and purpose of familial structure in
        Babylon
(E)   illustrate early uses of birth, death, and marriage certificates

4.   Which of the following best describes a woman's position in a Babylonian
family?

(A)   on equal footing with her husband
(B)   equally responsible for her family's debt as is her husband
(C)   head and ruler of her family and descendants
(D)   responsible for all domestic activities and child rearing
(E)   purchased by her husband's family and clan

5.   In line 5, "stringent" is closest in meaning to

(A)   rigid
(B)   purposeful
(C)   clear
(D)   pliable
(E)   harsh

6.   In the sentence "Whatever may be said...recognize the institution"
(lines 15–17) the author

(A)   explores conflicting theories of familial organization
(B)   supports the possibility of patriarchy in Babylonia
(C)   dismisses a possible theory based on lack of evidence
(D)   introduces evidence that supports a popular theory
(E)   presents new theory on familial organization

7. The author suggests that a man's connection to his family

   (A) has little practical function
   (B) promotes Babylonian values
   (C) creates his identity in Babylonian society
   (D) is primarily shaped by his personal preferences
   (E) depends solely on his professional interests

8. The Babylonian laws of family structure and inheritance are

   (A) loosely shaped by Chinese customs and traditions
   (B) carefully documented and followed
   (C) reinforced by a belief in mythical ancestors
   (D) passed on through folk songs and oral stories
   (E) drafted by prominent Lemesuriers and lawyers

9. The author's description of the family organization in the Babylonian and Assyrian Laws, Contracts and Letters

   (A) suggests disapproval of the effort devoted to such an insignificant issue
   (B) indicates a well-organized and hierarchal system
   (C) expresses approval of the laws of inheritance
   (D) shows outrage at the lack of effort to modify unjust laws
   (E) implies that women of the era feared a change in the social order

Passage 2

The following excerpt from a student resource manual is intended to familiarize the reader with building and maintenance of rural highways.

Necessity for Planning—Sometimes highway improvement is the result of spasmodic and carelessly directed work carried out at odd
Line   times on various sections of a road, finally resulting in the worst places being at least temporarily bettered. The grade on the steepest
5   hills is probably reduced somewhat and some of the worst of the low lying sections are filled in and thereby raised. Short sections of surfacing such as gravel or broken stone may be placed here and there. From the standpoint of the responsible official, the road has been "improved," but too often such work does not produce an
10   improvement that lasts, and sometimes it is not even of any great

immediate benefit to those who use the roads. In nearly every instance such work costs more in money and labor that it is worth.

Lasting improvement of public highways can be brought about only through systematic and correlated construction carried on for a series
15 of years. In other words, there must be a road improvement policy which will be made effective through some agency that is so organized that its policies will be perpetuated and is clothed with enough authority to be capable of enforcing the essential features of good design and of securing the proper construction of improvements.

20 Details of highway construction and design must vary with many local conditions and types of surface. The limits of grades and the many other details of design may properly be adopted for a specific piece of work only after an adequate investigation of the local requirements and in the light of wide experience in supervising road
25 improvement.

New ideas are constantly being injected into the art of road building, but these are disseminated somewhat slowly, so that valuable devices and improvements in methods remain long unknown except to the comparatively few who have the means for informing themselves of
30 all such developments.

It follows then that the logical system of conducting road improvement is through an agency of continuing personnel which will supervise the preparation of suitable plans and direct the construction in accordance with the most recent experience.

35 Preliminary Investigation—The first step in road improvement is to secure an adequate idea of the existing conditions on the road or roads involved. The detail to which this information need go will depend entirely upon the purpose of the preliminary investigation, for before a definite plan is prepared, it may be necessary to choose
40 the best from among several available routes. For this purpose, it is not always necessary to make an actual instrument survey of the several routes. A hasty reconnaissance will usually be sufficient. This is made by walking or riding over the road and noting, in a suitable book or upon prepared blanks, the information needed. The items of
45 information recorded will usually be as follows: distances, grades, type

of soil on the road and nature of existing surface, character of drainage, location of bridges and culverts and the type of each with notes as to its condition, location of railway crossings and notes as to type, location of intersecting roads, farm entrances, and all similar features
50   that have a bearing on the choice of routes. These data can be obtained in a comparatively short time by a skilled observer who may drive over the road in a motor car. Sometimes it may be desirable to make a more careful study of some certain sections of road and this may be done by waking over the section in question in order to make a more
55   deliberate survey of the features to be considered than is possible when riding in a motor car.

10. The passage is primarily concerned with

(A)   contrasting various methods of road improvement
(B)   underscoring the importance of road survey and construction
(C)   demonstrating the deficits in existing methods and approaches
(D)   suggesting implementation of methodical approaches to road improvement
(E)   illustrating the necessity of road development

11. The author states that "From the standpoint of the responsible official, the road has been 'improved," (lines 8–9) in order to

(A)   explain an intense professional interest in the topic
(B)   introduce benefits of short-term building strategies
(C)   lend an air of authority to the discussion of road improvement
(D)   support current building strategies
(E)   emphasize the lack of rigorous standards in road maintenance

12. The author mentions all of the following as flawed conventions used in road planning EXCEPT

(A)   repair completed at irregular intervals
(B)   work standards that are intermittent and inconsistent
(C)   short-term solutions that are ultimately not cost efficient
(D)   road improvement is often a result of random assignment and lack of planning
(E)   prompt repair of significant problems leads to enduring road development

13. The primary purpose of surveying an area for road development and improvement is to

    (A) prepare a detailed and comprehensive report to serve as a foundation for planning

    (B) determine the types of motor vehicles that traverse the road

    (C) gain an understanding of the type of soil on the road

    (D) evaluate the current state of the area and any existing roads

    (E) methodically inspect the existing roads for erosion

14. The author would most likely agree with which of the following statements

    (A) A cursory understanding of existing roads and conditions suffices for road planning

    (B) A government agency should be created for the sole purpose of road survey

    (C) Engineers should volunteer to improve roads in their communities

    (D) A perfunctory approach to road improvement is necessary to achieve sustainable change

    (E) Quick-fix solutions create marginal and temporary results in road improvement

15. The author suggests all of the following in creating a continued road improvement system EXCEPT

    (A) proliferating new ideas on road design quickly and widely

    (B) increasing the standards of work in a consistent way

    (C) creating a government authority to manage road design and improvement

    (D) instituting strategies and procedures for road development

    (E) allowing for an understanding of local road needs and uses

16. In line 55 the word "deliberate" most closely means

    (A) cautious

    (B) methodical

    (C) thoughtful

    (D) unhurried

    (E) inadvertent

Passage 3

In the following excerpt from a report published by the U.S. Arms Control and Disarmament Agency, the Agency offers a pointed evaluation of the effects of nuclear war.

It has now been two decades since the introduction of thermonuclear fusion weapons into the military inventories of the great powers, and
Line   more than a decade since the United States, Great Britain, and the Soviet Union ceased to test nuclear weapons in the atmosphere. Today
5   our understanding of the technology of thermonuclear weapons seems highly advanced, but our knowledge of the physical and biological consequences of nuclear war is continuously evolving.

We have considered the problems of large-scale nuclear war from the standpoint of the countries not under direct attack, and the difficulties
10   they might encounter in postwar recovery. It is true that most of the horror and tragedy of nuclear war would be visited on the populations subject to direct attack, who would doubtless have to cope with extreme and perhaps insuperable obstacles in seeking to reestablish their own societies. It is no less apparent, however, that other nations,
15   including those remote from the combat, could suffer heavily because of damage to the global environment.

Finally, at least brief mention should be made of the global effects resulting from disruption of economic activities and communications. Since 1970, an increasing fraction of the human race has been losing
20   the battle for self-sufficiency in food, and must rely on heavy imports. A major disruption of agriculture and transportation in the grain-exporting and manufacturing countries could thus prove disastrous to countries importing food, farm machinery, and fertilizers—especially those which are already struggling with the threat of widespread
25   starvation. Moreover, virtually every economic area, from food and medicines to fuel and growth engendering industries, the less-developed countries would find they could not rely on the "undamaged" remainder of the developed world for trade essentials: in the wake of a nuclear war the industrial powers directly involved would themselves
30   have to compete for resources with those countries that today are described as "less-developed."

Similarly, the disruption of international communications—satellites, cables, and even high frequency radio links—could be a major obstacle to international recovery efforts.

35 In attempting to project the aftereffects of a major nuclear war, we have considered separately the various kinds of damage that could occur. It is also quite possible, however, that interactions might take place among these effects, so that one type of damage would couple with another to produce new and unexpected hazards. For

40 example, we can assess individually the consequences of heavy worldwide radiation fallout and increased solar ultraviolet, but we do not know whether the two acting together might significantly increase human, animal, or plant susceptibility to disease. We can conclude that massive dust injection into the stratosphere, even greater in scale

45 than Krakatoa, is unlikely by itself to produce significant climatic and environmental change, but we cannot rule out interactions with other phenomena, such as ozone depletion, which might produce utterly unexpected results.

We have come to realize that nuclear weapons can be as

50 unpredictable as they are deadly in their effects. Despite some 30 years of development and study, there is still much that we do not know. This is particularly true when we consider the global effects of a large-scale nuclear war.

17. The phrase "It has now been two decades since the introduction of ther-monuclear fusion weapons into the military inventories...atmosphere" (lines 1–4) is used by the author to

(A) suggest that only events experienced directly can be understood
(B) demonstrate the accumulated experience of the world with nuclear power
(C) introduce a timeline for nuclear development, use, and understanding
(D) explain that people have been living their whole lives with nuclear weapons possibilities
(E) convey how little is known about nuclear power

18. In line 4, the word "ceased" most nearly means

(A) terminate
(B) begin
(C) prepare
(D) initiate
(E) continue

19. The author would most likely agree with which of the following statements

(A) Nuclear power is an important source of energy
(B) Loyalty to one's country and its military agenda takes precedence over other matters in times of crisis
(C) Scientists and governments have fully considered consequences of nuclear use
(D) Nuclear weapons use will not result in environmental changes
(E) There remains knowledge to be gathered on the effects of nuclear war

20. The author states "an increasing fraction of the human race has been losing the battle for self-sufficiency in food, and must rely on heavy imports" (lines 19–20) to convey

(A) scorn for the global marketplace
(B) doubt in people's ability to survive on earth
(C) envy for nations that are able to produce a food supply
(D) presence of global interdependence
(E) frustration in new food production processes

21. In line 44 the word "injection" most closely means

(A) inoculation
(B) combination
(C) permeation
(D) distillation
(E) implantation

22. The passage suggests that our understanding of thermonuclear fusion is incomplete because

(A) the world has had limited experience with nuclear weapons

(B) scientists have not been able to derive evidence of biological damage from nuclear attacks

(C) 30 years is not enough time to produce scientifically sound conclusions

(D) nations have not cooperated in disclosing information about weapons development

(E) it has been impossible to predict the scientific and economic consequences of a large-scale nuclear event

Passage 4

The following passage is adapted from a series of stories published in 1906 by a famous American author.

The family consisted of four persons: Margaret Lester, widow, aged 36; Helen Lester, her daughter, aged 16; Mrs. Lester's maiden aunts,
Line   Hannah and Hester Gray, twins, aged 67. Waking and sleeping, the
three women spent their days and night in adoring the young girl; in
5   watching the movements of her sweet spirit in the mirror of her face;
in refreshing their souls with the vision of her bloom and beauty; in
listening to the music of her voice; in gratefully recognizing how rich
and fair for them was the world with this presence in it; in shuddering
to think how desolate it would be with this light gone out of it.

10   By nature—and inside—the aged aunts were utterly dear and lovable
and good, but in the matter of morals and conduct their training had
been so uncompromisingly strict that it had made them exteriorly
austere, not to say stern. Their influence was effective in the house;
so effective that the mother and the daughter conformed to its moral
15   and religious requirements cheerfully, contentedly, happily,
unquestionably. To do this was become second nature to them. And
so in this peaceful heaven there were no clashings, no irritations, no
fault-finding, no heart-burnings.

In it a lie had no place. In it a lie was unthinkable. In it speech was
20   restricted to absolute truth, iron-bound truth, implacable and
uncompromising truth, let the resulting consequences be what they
might. At last, one day, under stress of circumstances, the darling of

the house sullied her lips with a lie—and confessed it, with tears and
self-upbraidings. There are not any words that can paint the
25   consternation of the aunts. It was as if the sky had crumpled up and
collapsed and the earth had tumbled to ruin with a crash. They sat
side by side, white and stern, gazing speechless upon the culprit, who
was on her knees before them with her face buried first in one lap
and then the other, moaning and sobbing, and appealing for sympathy
30   and forgiveness and getting no response, humbly kissing the hand of
the one, then of the other, only to see it withdrawn as suffering
defilement by those soiled lips.

23.   The narrator's attitude toward the family can best be described as

   (A)   lethargic
   (B)   pragmatic
   (C)   charmed
   (D)   disillusioned
   (E)   apathetic

24.   In line 13 "austere" most nearly means

   (A)   fussy
   (B)   rigorous
   (C)   hedonistic
   (D)   serious
   (E)   humorless

25.   The phrase "To do this was become second nature to them" (line 16)
      emphasizes the family's

   (A)   annoyance with a common state of affairs
   (B)   regret about the particular habit
   (C)   uneasiness with the unexpected revelation
   (D)   disappointment at the aunts' actions
   (E)   compliance with an expectation

26. The phrase "the sky had crumpled up…with a crash" (lines 25–26) primarily emphasizes the aunts'

    (A) extreme displeasure
    (B) undisguised embarrassment
    (C) surprised disbelief
    (D) sense of urgency
    (E) feelings of regret

27. In line 27 "the culprit" refers to

    (A) Margaret Lester
    (B) the elderly aunts
    (C) the widowed mother
    (D) the narrator
    (E) the young girl

Verbal Section Answer Key

Sentence Completion Drills

1. Step 1: Read, Step 2: Find the definition, Step 3: Positive/negative/neutral, Step 4: Fill in the blank, Step 5: Eliminate, Step 6: Plug it in
2. Step 1: Read, Step 2: Find the definition, Step 3: Positive/negative/neutral, Step 4: Fill in the blank, Step 5: Establish a relation-ship, Step 6: Eliminate, Step 7: Plug it in
3. C
4. C
5. A
6. D
7. B
8. A
9. A
10. C
11. A
12. B
13. D
14. A
15. A
16. B
17. C
18. A
19. D
20. A
21. A
22. B
23. D
24. B
25. A
26. B
27. A

Reading Comprehension Drills

1. Step 1: Read the question, Step 2: Read the passage, Step 3: Answer before you answer, Step 4: Find the answer
2. Step 1: Skim, Step 2: Summarize, Step 3: Answer general, Step 4: Answer specific
3. D
4. B
5. A
6. C
7. C
8. B
9. B
10. D
11. E
12. E
13. D
14. E
15. C
16. B
17. C
18. A
19. E
20. D
21. C
22. E
23. E
24. D
25. E
26. A
27. E

Part III

Writing Section

The Writing section is divided into three parts: Identifying Sentence Errors, Improving Sentences, and Improving Paragraphs. All of these sections actually test the same skills and broad concepts:

- Verb tense
- Subject/verb agreement
- Noun/number agreement
- Pronoun/number agreement
- Ambiguous pronouns
- Comparisons and parallelism
- Word choice
- Active and passive voice
- Punctuation

chapter **5**

Grammar Review

Although grammar sometimes seems like the bane of our existence, we will try our best to go over important concepts for the Writing section. Focus on the concepts instead of the names and the grammar will make a lot more sense.

Once you are familiar with these concepts we will apply them to the three sections.

Punctuation

Unfortunately, the SAT people don't subscribe to the movement of retiring punctuation. They actually care that you know how to use the rules for period, commas, etc. Let's take a look at the basics.

Commas

Commas are used to do a few things:

- To write out a list within a sentence

  Lauren bought a shirt, skirt, and sunblock.

- To combine two independent clauses with the use of a conjunction (but, and, etc.)

  Ben wanted to play soccer outside, but it was raining.

- To separate a prepositional phrase from the rest of a sentence

  Upon my arrival, I was greeted by an ominous note.

- To set off an interjection, adverbial clause, or adverbial modifier from an independent clause

  Mark, who was the strongest candidate for student body president, lost theelection by two votes.

- To set off dependent clauses from main clause

  After studying all night for a test, Nancy was too tired to brush her teeth.

- To set off nonessential information

  Bobby Ray, the coolest boy in the grade, was voted class president.

Keep in Mind

Watch out for comma splices. Adding a comma to link two independent clauses is an illegal comma usage. Fix a comma splice by adding 1) a comma and conjunction, 2) a period and a capital letter, or 3) a semicolon.

The sentence: Lyn did a perfect cartwheel unfortunately the coach's back was turned.

The comma splice: Lyn did a perfect cartwheel, unfortunately the coach's back was turned.

1. The correct fix with a conjunction: Lyn did a perfect cartwheel, but the coach's back was turned.

2. The correct fix with a period: Lyn did a perfect cartwheel. Unfortunately, the coach's back was turned.

3. The correct fix with a semicolon: Lyn did a perfect cartwheel; unfortunately, the coach's back was turned.

Apostrophes

Apostrophes are usually used to show possession or in place of contractions.

- Possession and singular nouns

  Add an apostrophe and "s" to show procession

  Lauren's cat was sad.

- Possession and plural nouns

  Just add an apostrophe

  My teacher forgot the boys' tests.

- Possession and multiple nouns

  Apostrophe and "s" following the last of the series of names to show co-ownership

  Sid and Nancy's house.

  Apostrophe and "s" following each name to show individual possession

  Sid's and Nancy's dirty laundry.

- Possession and pronouns

  Unlike nouns, the possessive case for pronouns does not use an apostrophe. Instead, the pronoun changes to indicate possession.

Pronoun	Possessive Pronoun
I	my
you	your
she	her
he	his
we	our
they	their
it	its
who	whose

Semicolons

A semicolon is most often used to separate two related but independent clauses. A semicolon can be used instead of a period. However, use of a semicolon shows more relation between clauses. Here's an example: *Lauren needed milk to make cookies; she ran to the store.*

Keep in Mind

The SAT will not ask you to pick between a period and a semicolon.

Colons

Colons are usually used to introduce lists, explanations, and quotes. Basically the colon is a heads-up that you're about to get more info.

Here are some typical instances of colon use: ← (!)

The date had all the elements of romance: candles, flowers, and classical music.

The girl's exclamation summed up the date: "If only I'd liked candles, flowers, and classical music!"

Keep in Mind

There can only be one colon in a sentence, and the colon must always be preceded by an independent clause.

Grammarpalooza

Let's review basic grammar rules. We'll go through the rules that the SAT likes to test. However, the following is by no means an exhaustive grammar primer!

Verb Tense

Verbs—in case anyone has forgotten—are action words. For the SAT, you need to know the proper form each tense of the word takes.

Past Versus Present Perfect

Past tense: something has happened or existed in the past. This means that the event definitely occurred in the past.

   Example: She lived in New York.

Present-perfect tense: something began in the past and continues into the present or has bearing on the present. It is indicated by using has/have and –ed.

   Example: She has lived in New York for 5 years.

Past Versus Past Perfect

Past perfect: something that began and ended before something new began and all of this is in the past. In other words this tense is used to show what happened in the past before the past.

   Example: She had lived in Boston before she lived in New York.

If-clauses

Indicative mood: an if-clause in which something can/will actually happen.

   Example: If I have to do one more SAT practice, I will scream.

Subjunctive mood: an if-clause that states something imagined or existing in thought.

   Example: If I were Betty, I would not take the SAT at all.

Subject/Verb Agreement

Subject

The subject is the main thing (or things) in the sentence

Make sure that the subject and the verb are in agreement.

Correct: *Lauren is smart.*

Incorrect: *Lauren are smart.*

The tricky thing is to make sure you are identifying the correct subject.

Adjectives and Adverbs

Adjectives describe nouns, whereas adverbs describe verbs. Adverbs usually end in *–ly*. Don't confuse the two. Here's an example:

The smart (adjective) student (noun) studied (verb) efficiently (adverb).

Noun/Number Agreement

Nouns have to agree in number throughout the sentence.

Example: All students are very good at taking their test.

Here the nouns "students" and "test" don't match in number. The sentence should be: *All students are very good at taking their tests.*

Here's another example:

Kim and Bob are planning to sell their house and move to Bermuda in order to become a beach bum.

What is the problem with this sentence?

Pronoun/Noun Agreement

This one is tricky because often when we speak we use pronouns and nouns incorrectly. How often have you said, "Did everyone remember to bring their IDs with them?" when you should be saying, "Did everyone remember to bring his or her ID with him or her?"

Anytime you see a plural pronoun in the Writing section, check the noun or pronoun it refers to. Watch out for "pronoun shift":

Incorrect: *If you study for the exam, one will do well on it later.*

Correct: *If one studies for the exam, one will do well on it later.*

Ambiguous Pronouns

The case of ambiguous pronouns is probably the easiest pronoun concept to remember. An ambiguous pronoun lacks an obvious antecedent. In other words, if you don't know what the pronoun is referring to, you have a case of ambiguous pronouns.

Example: Tara visited Sue after her graduation.

In reading the pronoun "her" we don't know who graduated. Was it Tara or Sue? Doesn't matter—the sentence is grammatically incorrect.

Here's a harder example:

Lauren gave Joanne a gift that she used from that moment on.

It seems that the pronoun is clear. The "she" that used the present is Joanne, right? But what if Lauren gave Joanne a gift and then used it herself? Again, since it isn't clear who used the gift this sentence is grammatically incorrect.

And finally:

They say that the SAT is a really difficult test.

The problem here is that we don't have any idea who "they" are. This is yet another case of ambiguous pronouns.

Word Choice

The SAT might slip in words that are spelled incorrectly or have wrong definitions. For example: *The book had a powerful affect on me.* The correct usage is: The book had a powerful effect on me. Other examples are too, to, two or noisy and noisome. Take some time and think about the tricky pairs and triads we often use incorrectly.

Redundancy

Any words or phrases that are superfluous should be removed or corrected. The SAT strives for concise writing so watch out for too much redundancy, as well as repetition (does that sound good to you?).

Active Voice and Passive Voice

You are probably picturing your English teacher again telling you to stop using the passive voice. Well, what did she mean all those years?

Passive: structure that allows for evasion of responsibility.

> *Example: Lauren was not informed.*

Active: structure that attributes responsibility.

> *Example: Sue did not inform Lauren.*

> Here's another example:

> Passive: *The investigation of plagiarism alleged to have been committed by several students was being carried out by the English Department.*

> Active: *The English Department led an investigation of the students' alleged plagiarism.*

Modifier

A modifier is a word or phrase that provides additional information about another word or phrase. Common modifier errors are:

- A misplaced modifier is a word that is placed in an incorrect part of the sentence and thus does not qualify the appropriate word or phrase. If you're confused when reading a sentence, there's a good chance that the modifier is misplaced.

  I found a pen in the locker that doesn't belong to me. What doesn't belong to me…the pen or the locker?

- A dangling modifier is a word or phrase that describes something that isn't even in the sentence. A dangling modifier is usually the result of describing a subject that is not in the sentence.

Walking through the halls, the bells rang loudly. The bells didn't walk through the halls. The modifier assumes that the reader knows who is walking through the halls.

Sentence Structure

Lastly, the SAT will probably test you on sentence structure. Two favorite errors of the exam writers have to do with fragments vs. complete sentences and faulty parallelism. Let's take a look at the rules:

Complete Sentences

For starters, all sentences on the SAT should be complete sentences. A complete sentence is one that has a subject and a predicate. A fragment usually doesn't sound right and lacks the appropriate parts of a complete sentence. For example, *since you asked.*

Run-on Sentences

Run-ons are sentences with too much and/or unrelated information. To fix a run-on sentence you should identify where the sentence should be split and add words or punctuation. Let's take a look at an example:

Sarah likes to eat out at restaurants Bobby doesn't.

You can split the sentence into: "Sarah likes to eat out at restaurants" and "Bobby doesn't.

There are several ways to fix the run-on. Here are a few options:

Sarah likes to eat out at restaurants, but Bobby doesn't.

Sarah likes to eat out at restaurants; however, Bobby doesn't.

Comparisons and Parallelism

Sentences need to compare like with like. You cannot compare apples and oranges.

Incorrect: *Like mammals, digestive systems have evolved in some unicellular organisms.*

Correct: *Like mammals, some unicellular organisms have evolved digestive systems.*

Faulty comparisons can get tricky; they can involve so many distracters that you forget what is being compared. Read each sentence carefully. Here is an example of a tricky sentence:

I read so many books, but on the other hand, I read a lot of magazines.

Notice that in this sentence you are missing the *first hand*.

Watch out for words that must always go together:

neither/nor
either/or
not only/but also
the more/the more
the less/the less
both/and
if/then

Transitions (Words)

The SAT will often contain sentences that are missing connections. You will be responsible for adding appropriate transitions. Connecting words you should keep in mind are conjunctions (and, but, or, nor, for, yet) and transitional adverbs (however, also, consequently, nevertheless, thus, moreover, furthermore, etc.). The latter should be preceded by a semicolon and followed by a comma. If you see a transitional adverb followed by a comma, you should immediately know that there is an error.

Keep in Mind

Be careful with transitions. Don't link ideas that are not related.

chapter 6

Identifying Sentence Errors

What's Being Tested?

Identifying sentence errors is the second type of multiple-choice question you'll encounter on the writing section. Although these questions do not appear first, we'll cover the strategy first and build on the basics of identifying sentence errors for the other two sections. In the identifying sentence errors section, all you have to do is determine whether or not there is an error. You don't have to correct anything. If you know *something* is wrong but cannot quite pin it, eliminate choice E (no error) and start guessing.

What to Do?

Follow these steps in finding the mistake:

> ### Identifying Sentence Error Steps
>
> **Step 1:** Read the sentence
> **Step 2:** Look for common errors
> **Step 3:** Eliminate no-error choices
> **Step 4:** If everything looks good, select choice E

Step 1: Read the sentence

Carefully read the sentence. Try to read "aloud"—reading under your breath will allow you to hear the cadence of the sentence and make catching errors easier. Although you'll be in a classroom full of students and will not be able to read the sentence out loud, try to pronounce the words quietly to yourself.

Step 2: Look for common errors

Check to see whether or not any underlined part of the sentence is incorrect. If you've read the sentence and you didn't catch any problems, double- check for mistakes from the "common errors" list:

- Verb tense
- Subject/verb agreement
- Noun/number agreement
- Pronoun/number agreement
- Ambiguous pronouns
- Comparisons and parallelism
- Word choice
- Active and passive voice
- Punctuation

Look at the sentence to see whether or not one of the above errors is hiding in an "okay-sounding" sentence.

Step 3: Eliminate no-error choices

Cross off any parts of the sentence that sound right. Remember that you're only looking for errors in the underlined parts of the sentence.

Step 4: If everything looks good, select choice E

Don't forget choice E—no error. The SAT will throw in sentences that have no grammatical errors.

Let's take a look:

Lauren <u>is</u> one of the teachers who <u>parks</u> in the school lot <u>every morning</u>.
      A   B   C   D
<u>No error</u>.
     E

Here are our steps:

> **Step 1:** Read the sentence
> **Step 2:** Look for common errors
>
> *This sentence has an error with noun/number/
> pronoun agreement.*
>
> **Step 3:** Eliminate no-error choices
>
> *Since* who *refers to teachers, it is plural, and needs
> a plural noun.*
>
> **Step 4:** If everything looks good, select choice E

The correct answer is B.

Now It Is Your Turn

Take a look a look at this sentence. We'll give you the steps so that you can practice the process.

Kim and <u>I</u> ran as fast as we <u>could</u>, but we <u>missed</u> the bus, <u>which</u> made us
      A   B   C   D
late for school. <u>No error</u>.
                    E

> **Step 1:** Read the sentence
> **Step 2:** Look for common errors
>
> *What is the error in this sentence:*
>
> _____
>
> _____
>
> _____
>
> **Step 3:** Eliminate no-error choices
> **Step 4:** If everything looks good, select choice E

The correct answer is D.

Another Example

Look over the following sentence and use our six steps to find the correct answer. Use the workspace to go through the steps.

Although Sam was not in school on the day the senior class glued the
    A   B   C

doors shut, he was associated in the prank. No error.
                       D   E

> **Step 1:**
> **Step 2:**
> **Step 3:**
> **Step 4:**

The correct answer is D.

Identifying Sentence Errors Drills

> **Directions:** For each question in this section, select the best answer from among the answer choices given.

1. What are the steps for identifying sentence errors?

> **Step 1:**
> **Step 2:**
> **Step 3:**
> **Step 4:**

2. If we are going to win this game than we need to work as a team.
               A   B   C   D

  No error.
     E

3. Some researchers speculate that an early exposure to allergens such as
                                      A

peanuts and dairy products may cause children to develop severe
                             B   C

health issues later in life. No error.
               D   E

4. The Park Conservancy <u>is accepting</u> proposals <u>from several</u> architects
         A   B
with the hope <u>to gain</u> creative <u>ideas</u> for a new playground. <u>No error.</u>
     C   D   E

5. The cost of <u>safely</u> disposing of electronic parts <u>is</u> approximately
      A   B
<u>five times what</u> it costs to <u>purchase</u> the parts. <u>No error.</u>
   C   D   E

6. Fraud <u>has occurred</u> in many areas of science <u>from</u> biology to physics,
    A   B
<u>all of which</u> are <u>still</u> around today. <u>No error.</u>
  C   D   E

7. <u>Maintaining</u> a tough line, the school principal warned <u>that</u> bullies
  A   B
<u>taunting</u> other students <u>would be</u> punished by the disciplinary
  C   D
committee. <u>No error.</u>
     E

8. The report <u>suggest</u> that the estimated <u>number</u> of Asian carp in
     A   B
United States waters, particularly in the areas of the midwest, <u>is</u> grossly
                        C
<u>underestimated.</u> <u>No error.</u>
  D   E

9. <u>According to</u> a recent article, only 58 percent of high school graduates
  A
<u>from the</u> bottom quarter nationally, <u>as</u> ranked by family income,
  B   C
<u>went into</u> college in 2008. <u>No error.</u>
  D   E

10. We <u>arrived</u> at the <u>pool. Where</u> we <u>waited</u> for <u>our</u> teammates. <u>No error.</u>
   A   B   C D   E

11. Chimpanzees and bonobos <u>will voluntarily</u> offer a companion <u>access to</u>
                                        A   B
    food, even if <u>they</u> lose part of <u>them</u> in the process. <u>No error</u>.
                        C   D   E

12. The school <u>prohibited running</u> through the halls, <u>which</u> many students
                        A   B   C
    <u>resented</u>. <u>No error</u>.
         D   E

13. Transmitting phone signals by satellite <u>is a way</u> of overcoming the
                                                  A
    <u>problem of</u> overcrowding in Airways <u>and</u> limiting how <u>they</u> are used.
         B   C   D
    <u>No error</u>.
         E

14. The radio host <u>criticized</u> the <u>President's</u> policies <u>on</u> taxation,
                        A   B   C
    <u>the economy and security</u>. <u>No error</u>.
                D   E

15. <u>Each of</u> the kittens <u>thrived</u> in <u>their</u> <u>new homes</u>. <u>No error</u>.
         A   B   C   D   E

16. <u>Every student</u> must provide <u>his or her</u> own pencil, paper, textbook, and
         A   B
    calculator <u>for the</u> math <u>class</u>. <u>No error</u>.
                    C   D   E

17. The hikers <u>could</u> <u>find</u> the <u>direction of</u> the camp <u>with a compass</u>.
                    A   B   C   D
    <u>No error</u>.
         E

18. <u>The United</u> States <u>drop</u> a nuclear <u>bomb on</u> Hiroshima <u>in 1965</u>.
         A   B   C   D
    <u>No error</u>.
         E

19. <u>Lauren and I agreed</u> that we <u>would</u> meet <u>in</u> Hudson Street in
       A   B   C   D
    New York City. <u>No error</u>.
                        E

20. The team <u>randomly</u> changed <u>its</u> positions <u>to get</u> a varied athletic
                   A   B   C
    <u>experience</u>. <u>No error</u>.
        D   E

21. <u>Looking</u> down the sandy beach <u>we see</u> that people <u>are</u> <u>tanning</u>
       A   B   C   D
    themselves. <u>No error</u>.
                    E

22. Sam, <u>along with</u> her five classmates, <u>were</u> charged
              A   B
    <u>with the responsibility</u> of <u>distributing</u> cupcakes. <u>No error</u>.
              C   D   E

23. <u>Determined</u> to <u>do well on</u> the <u>project we</u> worked <u>all</u> weekend.
        A   B   C   D
    <u>No error</u>.
        E

24. <u>When</u> one first <u>sees</u> a painting by Van Gogh, <u>you are</u> impressed <u>by the</u>
        A   B   C   D
    vivid color and energetic brushwork. <u>No error</u>.
                                              E

25. The microbes <u>that cause</u> the common cold <u>are</u> <u>always evolving</u>, and it is
                     A   B   C
    unlikely that <u>they will</u> ever find a reliable vaccine. <u>No error</u>.
                       D   E

chapter 7

Improving Sentences

What's Being Tested?

Improving sentences is the first section that you will encounter in the Writing multiple-choice questions. Here you'll have to identify whether or not there is an error in the sentence. You will also correct the sentence in the case that there is an error. If there is no error, the answer is always A.

What to Do?

We'll be building on the steps from identifying sentence errors for the this section. Follow these steps to the right answer:

> *Improving Sentences Steps*
> **Step 1:** Read the sentence
> **Step 2:** Look for common errors
> **Step 3:** Self-correct the error
> **Step 4:** Plug it in

Step 1: Read the sentence

Carefully read the sentence. As with the error identification sentences, try to read "aloud"—reading under your breath will allow you to hear the cadence of the sentence and make catching errors easier.

Step 2: Look for common errors

Check to see whether or not the underlined part of the sentence is incorrect. If you've read the sentence and you didn't catch any problems, double-check for mistakes from the "common errors" list:

- Verb tense
- Subject/verb agreement
- Noun/number agreement
- Pronoun/number agreement
- Ambiguous pronouns
- Comparisons and parallelism
- Word choice
- Active and passive voice
- Punctuation

Look at the sentence to see whether or not one of the above errors is hiding in an "okay-sounding" sentence.

If there is no error, select Choice A.

Step 3: Self-correct the error

If something about the underlined part of the sentence doesn't sound right then you'll need to fix the sentence. Keep the answer choices covered and self-correct the underlined part of the sentence. Don't peek at the answer choices— just as with the reading comprehension, the SAT tries to trick the test taker with answer choices that sound correct (the "trap" choices). By correcting the error and finding a choice that matches your correction, you will be less likely to fall for the "trap" answer choice.

Step 4: Plug it in

Now that you have self-corrected and matched your response to the answer choices, plug in the answer you've selected to make sure your choice works in the sentence.

Let's take a look:

Dina and Eli are driving across the country and moving to Los Angeles <u>in order to pursue an acting career</u>.

(A)   in order to pursue an acting career
(B)   in order to pursue careers in acting
(C)   in pursuant of acting careers
(D)   in order to become an actor
(E)   for their careers in acting

Here are our steps:

Step 1: Read the sentence
Step 2: Look for the common errors

This sentence has an error with noun/number agreement.

Step 3: Self-correct the error

to pursue careers in acting

Step 4: Plug it in

The choice that most nearly matches our correction is B.

Now It Is Your Turn

Take a look at the sentence. We'll give you the steps so that you can practice the process.

Michael Phelps won his first Olympic Gold Medal <u>and he was 19 at the time</u>.

(A)   and he was 19 at the time
(B)   at the then age of 19
(C)   when he was 19 years old
(D)   on the 19 year
(E)   at age 19 years old

Step 1: Read the sentence

Step 2: Look for the common errors

What is the error in this sentence:

_____

_____

_____

Step 3: Self-correct the error

_____

_____

_____

Step 4: Plug it in

The answer best choice is C.

Here's another example.

Look over the following sentence and use our six steps to find the correct answer. Use the workspace to go through the steps.

Psychology, neuroscience, and biology are all <u>different, if interconnected, subjects</u>.

(A) different, if interconnected, subjects
(B) subjects that are different although interconnected
(C) subjects that are different and interconnected
(D) interconnected subjects that are different
(E) interconnected but at the same time different subjects

Step 1:
Step 2:
Step 3:
Step 4:

The correct answer is A.

Improving Sentences Drills

> **Directions:** For each question in this section, select the best answer from among the answer choices given.

1. What are the steps for improving sentences?

> **Step 1:**
> **Step 2:**
> **Step 3:**
> **Step 4:**

2. Since technological advances are essential to progress, <u>science and math studying deserves continuing academic attention</u>.

   (A) science and math studying deserves continuing academic attention
   (B) science and math studies deserve continuing academic attention
   (C) attention must be paid to have the study of science and math
   (D) payment of attention to science and math studies
   (E) continued study of science and math is deserved

3. Susan went to the <u>grocery store, forgot to buy the milk</u>.

   (A) grocery store, forgot to buy the milk
   (B) grocery store and forgotten to buy the milk
   (C) grocery store, and forgot to buy the milk
   (D) forgot to buy the milk at the grocery store
   (E) grocery store having forgotten to buy the milk

4. As a result of the 2008 incident, the CERN collider is <u>operating at only half the power for which it was designed</u>.

   (A) operating at only half the power for which it was designed
   (B) operational at only half the power that it was designed
   (C) operating not as it was designed, but at only half the power
   (D) designed for more than half the power it is currently operating on
   (E) operating, however, at only half the power for which it was designed

5. <u>Rachel is very precocious, she began reading when she was two years old</u>.

    (A) Rachel is very precocious, she began reading when she was two years old
    (B) Rachel is very precocious; and because of that she began reading when she was two years old
    (C) Rachel is very precocious; she began reading when she was two years old
    (D) Rachel is very precocious, and thusly she began reading when she was two years old
    (E) Rachel's precociousness resulted in her reading when she was two years old

6. <u>Although nearly finished, we left play practice early</u> because we needed to study for our science test.

    (A) Although nearly finished, we left play practice early
    (B) Although play practice was nearly finished, we left early
    (C) With play practice nearly finished we left early
    (D) Nearly finished with play practice, we left early
    (E) Play practice was nearly finished thus we left early

7. He was an electrical engineer <u>before he became a full-time science teacher</u>.

    (A) before he became a full-time science teacher
    (B) before becoming a full-time science teacher
    (C) and became a full-time science teacher after
    (D) and then became a full-time science teacher
    (E) before teaching science as a teacher full time

8. <u>It states in this article in the *Globe*</u> that runners are taking up the Boston Marathon in unprecedented numbers.

    (A) It states in this article in the *Globe*
    (B) The *Globe*'s article states
    (C) The *Globe* stated in the article
    (D) In this article the *Globe* states
    (E) In this article which is in the *Globe* states

9.   The colors at the top <u>of the painting were brighter</u>.

  (A) of the painting were brighter
  (B) were brighter in the painting
  (C) of the painting were brighter than those at the bottom of the painting
  (D) were brighter than the painting
  (E) were painted brighter

10.   A team of scientists <u>reported conclusively that the virus was derived from an early bacterium known as *Yersinia pestis*</u>.

  (A) reported conclusively that the virus was derived from an early bacterium known as *Yersinia pestis*
  (B) report conclusively that the virus was derived from an early bacterium known as *Yersinia pestis*
  (C) conclusively reported that the virus was derived from an early bacterium known as *Yersinia pestis*
  (D) in conclusion reported that the an early bacterium known as *Yersinia pestis* created the virus
  (E) conclusive reports that the virus was derived from an early bacterium known as Yersinia pestis

11.   <u>At nine years old, my parents gave me my first piano</u>.

  (A) At nine years old, my parents gave me my first piano
  (B) When I was nine years old, my parents gave me my first piano
  (C) My parents first gave me my first piano when I was nine years old
  (D) Upon my ninth birthday my parents gave me my first piano
  (E) My piano was at first given to me by my parents when I was nine years old

12.   <u>Being as I had confirmed the hotel</u> reservation through the Web site, I expected to have a room ready upon my arrival.

  (A) Being as I had confirmed the hotel
  (B) Being as I confirmed the hotel
  (C) Since I confirmed the hotel
  (D) Because I had confirmed the hotel
  (E) Because I confirmed the hotel

13. The celebrity chef always had enthusiastic fans <u>and they adored him</u>.

   (A) and they adored him
   (B) who adored him
   (C) and they adoring him
   (D) which adored him
   (E) whom adored him

14. That car alarm <u>has been ringing</u> for two hours; I wonder if someone will call the owner.

   (A) has been ringing
   (B) has rung
   (C) rang
   (D) will have been ringing
   (E) be rung

15. The groundbreaking paper introduced a new hypothesis on DNA coding, <u>discussing the science behind the discovery, explaining the process of scientists</u>.

   (A) discussing the science behind the discovery, explaining the process of scientists
   (B) discussed the science behind the discovery, and explained the process of the scientists
   (C) discussed the science behind the discovery, explaining the process of scientists
   (D) discussing the science behind the discovering, and also explaining the process of scientists
   (E) will discuss the science behind the discovery while explaining the process of the scientists

16. Both Dr. Rosenthal and Dr. Clare being well known for having authored many articles in their field.

 (A) Both Dr. Rosenthal and Dr. Clare being well known for having authored many articles in their field
 (B) Both Dr. Rosenthal and Dr. Clare are well known in their field for having authored many articles
 (C) Both Dr. Rosenthal and Dr. Clare are well known for having authored many articles in their field
 (D) They both authored many articles in their field, Dr. Rosenthal and Dr. Clare are well known
 (E) Having authored many articles both Dr. Rosenthal and Dr. Clare are well known in their field

17. The affects of the snowstorm could be seen everywhere.

 (A) affects of the snowstorm could be seen
 (B) affects of the snowstorm were
 (C) effects of the snowstorm could be seen
 (D) snowstorm affect could be seen
 (E) affect of the snowstorm could be

18. Grandparents, who were the first generation to attend college, taught their children to understand the importance of higher education.

 (A) Grandparents, who were the first generation to attend college, taught their children to
 (B) Grandparents, being the first generation to attend college, taught their children to
 (C) Having been the first generation to attend college, grandparents taught their children to
 (D) The children were taught by their grandparents, who were the first generation to attend college, to
 (E) The first grandparents generation to attend college, they taught their children to

19. Martin arrived at 8:32 A.M. <u>but Ms. Kravits had closed</u> the classroom doors.

    (A) but Ms. Kravits had closed
    (B) and Ms. Kravits had closed
    (C) but Ms. Kravits has had closed
    (D) but Ms. Kravits already closed
    (E) but, Ms. Kravits had closed

20. Susan <u>likes to listen to music and reading the latest novels</u>.

    (A) likes to listen to music and reading the latest novels
    (B) likes listening to music and to read the latest novels
    (C) likes listening to music and reading the latest novels
    (D) likes listens to music and reads the latest novels
    (E) like to listen to music and read the latest novels

21. J. K. Rowling visited our <u>school and she would sign</u> copies of the latest *Harry Potter* novel.

    (A) school and she would sign
    (B) school; where she would sign
    (C) school; in order to sign
    (D) school and then she could sign
    (E) school to sign

22. <u>A born musician who learned to play many instruments, Bobby's magnificent performances brought him</u> great renown.

    (A) A born musician who learned to play many instruments, Bobby's magnificent performances brought him
    (B) A born musician, who learned to play many instruments, Bobby's magnificent performances brought him
    (C) Bobby was a born musician and learned to play many instruments, his magnificent performances brought him
    (D) Born a musician and performer, Bobby learned to play many instruments which brought him
    (E) Bobby was born a musician, after learning to play many instruments, he performed magnificently and this brought him

23. <u>Between you and me, I would</u> rather spend my time at the pool.

    (A) Between you and me, I would
    (B) Between you and I, I would
    (C) Between you and I I would
    (D) Between us I would
    (E) Between you and I, I had

24. Sam will represent JFK High School in the speech <u>contest, his work in this having been excellent this year</u>.

    (A) contest, his work in this having been excellent this year
    (B) contest because his work in this having been excellent this year
    (C) contest, for he has done an excellent job this year
    (D) contest, for his work as an orator has been excellent this year
    (E) contest; this year his work as an orator having been excellent

25. <u>Reaching for the book on the shelf, the stepstool slipped out from under Ben</u>.

    (A) Reaching for the book on the shelf, the stepstool slipped out from under Ben
    (B) Reaching for the book on the shelf; the stepstool slipped out from under Ben
    (C) The stepstool slipped out from under Ben, as he reached for the book on the shelf
    (D) The stepstool slipped, as Ben reached for the book on the shelf, from under him
    (E) When Ben reached for the book on the shelf, the stepstool slipped from under him

chapter **8**

Improving Paragraphs

What's Being Tested?

The improving paragraphs section combines grammar and reading comprehension questions. Paragraph improvement sets are tests within a test. Think of each paragraph as a test and the sentences within the paragraph as the actual questions. The paragraph is composed of numbered sentences. The actual questions refer to these numbered sentences.

What to Do?

Let's look at the steps we should take to tackle these sets:

> ### *Improving Paragraph Steps*
> **Step 1:** Read the passage
> **Step 2:** Understand the question
> **Step 3:** Self-correct the error
> **Step 4:** Find the match

Step 1: Read the passage

Skim the paragraph to get a general idea of the passage. Don't get stuck on funny-sounding sentences as these paragraphs are chock-full of errors. Your job in the first read-through is just to get a basic summary of the passage.

Step 2: Understand the question

Carefully read the questions. What is the test asking you to do? Make sure that you understand what the question is asking before attempting to find the answer. The trickiest part about these questions is answering the question and not just fixing an error.

Step 3: Self-correct the error

Now that you understand what the question is asking you can figure out the answer. Keep the answer choices covered and answer. By correcting the error and finding a choice that matches your correction, you will be less likely to fall for the "trap" answer choice.

Step 4: Find the match

Now that you have self-corrected, find the answer choice correction that is closest to your self-correction. Plug in the answer you've selected to make sure your choice works in the sentence.

Let's take a look:

> **Directions:** the following passage is taken from a first draft of an essay. Some parts of the draft need to be rewritten.
>
> Read the passage and select the best answers to the questions that follow the passage.

(1) Boston was founded in 1630 by the Puritans and is one of the oldest cities in the United States. (2) It was built on Puritan ideals and beliefs. (3) Boston is sometimes called "The City on a Hill." (4) After the first governor, John Winthrop gave a sermon about the City's special covenant with God. (5) Today it is the largest city in New England and an important business and cultural center. (6) Boston played an important role during the American Revolution. (7) Several battles and great historical moments took place in or around the City. (8) Although not as prominent as New York, Boston plays an important

role in America's economy. (9) The City is home to many financial institutions. (10) There are also many universities which comprise an important section of the economy of the country. (11) Of course, tourism is important as it contributes to Boston's economy. (12) Millions of people come to Boston every year. (13) Whether to work, study, or simply take in the character of one of America's greatest cities.

> **Step 1:** Read the passage
> **Step 2:** Understand the question
> **Step 3:** Self-correct the error
> **Step 4:** Find the match

1. What should be done with sentence 5 (reproduced below)?

   Today it is the largest city in New England and an important business and cultural center.

   (A) (as is now)
   (B) insert it before sentence 1
   (C) insert it before sentence 2
   (D) delete it
   (E) insert it after sentence 7

> **Step 2:** Understand the question
>
>   *What is question 1 asking?*
>
>   _____
>   _____
>   _____
>
> **Step 3:** Self-correct the error
>
>   _____
>   _____
>   _____
>
> **Step 4:** Find the match

The answer best choice is E.

2. In context, which of the following is the best way to revise sentences 3 and 4 in order to combine the sentences?

(A) "The City on a Hill" as Boston is sometimes is called is known this way because of a sermon that John Winthrop gave about the City's covenant with God

(B) The name "The City on a Hill," as Boston is sometimes called, is derived from the first governor Winthrop's sermon on the City's covenant with God

(C) Based on governor John Winthrop's "The City on a Hill" sermon Boston is sometimes called by that name because of the City's covenant with God

(D) As a result of governor John Winthrop's sermon Boston is sometimes called "The City on a Hill" and that name is derived from the City's covenant with God

(E) Boston is sometimes called "The City on a Hill"; this moniker was given to the City after John Winthrop's "City on a Hill" sermon which suggested that Boston had a covenant with God

---

Step 2: Understand the question

What is question 2 asking?

_____

_____

_____

Step 3: Self-correct the error

_____

_____

_____

Step 4: Find the match

The answer best choice is B.

3. Where is the best place to have a paragraph break?

(A) no paragraph break is necessary
(B) before sentence 5
(C) before sentence 8
(D) after sentence 8
(E) after sentence 10

```
┌─────────────────────────────────────────────────────┐
│  Step 2:  Understand the question                    │
│                                                      │
│           What is question 3 asking?                 │
│           _____          │
│           _____          │
│           _____          │
│                                                      │
│  Step 3:  Self-correct the error                     │
│           _____          │
│           _____          │
│           _____          │
│                                                      │
│  Step 4:  Find the match                             │
└─────────────────────────────────────────────────────┘
```

The answer best choice is C.

4. In context, a statement supporting sentence 7 (reproduced below) would be on which topic?

    Although not as prominent as New York, Boston plays an important role in America's economy.

    (A) reasons why Boston is important to America's economy
    (B) explanation for the diverse nature of Boston's population
    (C) descriptions of financial institutions in America
    (D) suggested reading on economics principles
    (E) introduction to important American economies

```
┌─────────────────────────────────────────────────────┐
│  Step 2:  Understand the question                    │
│                                                      │
│           What is question 4 asking?                 │
│           _____          │
│           _____          │
│           _____          │
│                                                      │
│  Step 3:  Self-correct the error                     │
│           _____          │
│           _____          │
│           _____          │
│                                                      │
│  Step 4:  Find the match                             │
└─────────────────────────────────────────────────────┘
```

The answer best choice is A.

5. In context, which of the following is the best way to revise sentences 12 and 13 in order to combine the sentences?

(A) Millions of people come to Boston every year: for work, study, or simply take in the character of one of America's greatest cities

(B) Millions of people come to Boston every year whether for work, or study, or simply take in the character of one of America's greatest cities

(C) Millions of people come to Boston every year for work, study, or to simply take in the character of one of America's greatest cities

(D) Whether to work; study, or simply take in the character of one of America's greatest cities millions of people come to Boston every year

(E) Whether to work, study, or simply take in the character of one of America's greatest cities: millions of people come to Boston every year

---

Step 2: Understand the question

What is question 5 asking?

_____

_____

_____

Step 3: Self-correct the error

_____

_____

_____

Step 4: Find the match

The answer best choice is C.

Improving Paragraphs Drills

> **Directions:** The following passage is an early draft of an essay. Some parts of the passage need to be rewritten.
>
> Read the passage carefully and select the best answers for the questions that follow. Some questions are about particular sentences or parts of sentences and ask you to improve sentence structure or word choice. Other questions ask you to consider organization and development. In choosing answers, follow the requirements of standard written English.

1.   What are the steps for improving paragraphs?

> **Step 1:**
> **Step 2:**
> **Step 3:**
> **Step 4:**

(1) The people in ancient Egypt depended on the Nile for fertile land so that they could have an agricultural lifestyle. (2) Agriculture is farming or raising animals for food. (3) Agriculture depends on fertile land. (4) In Egypt the ancient Egyptians were able to cultivate crops because of fertile land caused by inundation. (5) Inundation is any flood that deposits a thick layer of silt which creates fertile soil good for farming.

(6) Another geographical feature that affected how they lived is the Red Lands. (7) The Red Lands were desert where no civilization existed. (8) It served as a barrier and protected the Egyptians. (9) The Red Lands were natural defenses because the land was so hot. (10) Therefore, it influenced how they lived. (11) You can see how the geography of a land shapes the land's civilization.

2. What sentence is best inserted as an introduction before sentence 1?

    (A) There are many reasons why the Nile was important for ancient Egyptians
    (B) The Nile is one of the world's longest rivers
    (C) The lifestyle of ancient peoples was often influenced by geographical features of the land
    (D) Without a doubt, the most important geographical feature of Egypt is the Nile
    (E) The ancient Egyptians were not Nomads because of the fertile land that they lived on

3. What should be done with sentence 2 (reproduced below)?

    Agriculture is farming or raising animals for food.

    (A) (as is now)
    (B) it should be combined with sentence 3
    (C) it should be deleted
    (D) it should be moved after sentence 3
    (E) it should be prefaced with, "As understood by ancient Egyptians…"

4. In context, which is the best way to revise sentence 4 (reproduced below)?

    In Egypt the ancient Egyptians were able to cultivate crops because of fertile land caused by inundation

    (A) Inundation caused fertile lands which were integral to the Egyptian system of agriculture
    (B) Fertile lands, caused by inundation, allowed the Egyptians to cultivate crops
    (C) The cultivation of crops was a result of the inundation that caused fertile lands
    (D) In Egypt, inundation occurred, creating fertile land for crop cultivation
    (E) The ancient Egyptians relied on inundation for their fertile land and crops

5. In context, which is the best revision of the underlined portion of sentence 6 (reproduced below)?

   Another geographical feature that affected how they lived is the Red Lands.

   (A) (as is now)
   (B) that influenced how they lived is
   (C) that affected how the Egyptians lived is
   (D) which affected how they lived is
   (E) which effected how they lived is

6. In context, which is the best revision of sentence 8 (reproduced below)?

   It served as a barrier and protected the Egyptians.

   (A) The geographical feature served as a barrier and protected the Egyptians
   (B) It, the Red Lands, served as a barrier and protected the Egyptians
   (C) The Red Lands served as a barrier and protected the Egyptians
   (D) The Egyptians were protected by the Red Lands and served as a barrier
   (E) Serving as a barrier and protecting the Egyptians was it

7. In context, which is the best revision of sentence 11 (reproduced below)?

   You can see how the geography of a land shapes the land's civilization.

   (A) (as is now)
   (B) One can see how the geography of a land shapes the land's civilization
   (C) It is amazing; the geography really does shape the land's civilization
   (D) The civilization is often shaped by the geography of the lands
   (E) Clearly, geographical aspects must shape the civilization of the land

(1) One of my fondest memories from childhood is our family Thanksgiving. (2) The entire immediate family would gather into the car and drive to the local farm. (3) We would select our turkey. (4) Inspecting all the options carefully. (5) Although our parents had the final say, my siblings and I made sure to cast the vote for the largest turkey. (6) After the selection process my mom and sisters would pile into the car and drive to the vegetable farm while dad and I stayed behind and waited for the turkey. (7) With a car full of produce, my mom and sisters would arrive. (8) It was back home for the family where everyone had a hand in cooking our meal. (9) Dad and I usually mastered the turkey: we brined it overnight and then carefully roasted it in the mom. (10) My mom prepared the side dishes. (11) My sisters were responsible for the dessert and usually made either apple or pumpkin pie. (12) By 5:00 P.M. on Thursday all the food was ready and the exhausted, but exhilarated, family would greet our visitors. (13) From far away came friends and relatives to join in our feast. (14) Us kids were usually relegated to the kitchen table while the adults sat at the grand dining room table. (15) But no complaints from us, we were closest to the food for extra helpings!

8. In context, which of the following is the best way to revise sentences 3 and 4 in order to combine the sentences?

(A) Following a careful inspection, we would select our turkey
(B) Inspecting the turkeys carefully, a selection would be made
(C) Inspecting our options carefully we would then select our turkey
(D) Our turkey would be selected; following a careful inspection
(E) We would begin with a careful inspection, thus a selection would occur

9. In context, which is the best revision for sentence 6 (reproduced below)?

After the selection process my mom and sisters would pile into the car and drive to the vegetable farm while dad and I stayed behind and waited for the turkey.

(A) (as is now)
(B) comma after "process"
(C) comma between "car" and "and"
(D) comma between "behind" and "and"
(E) exclamation point after "turkey"

10. In context, which of the following is the best way to revise sentences 7 and 8 in order to combine the sentences?

    (A) After shopping, with a car full of produce, my mom and sisters would arrive to drive everyone back home where everyone would have a hand in cooking our meal

    (B) We would drive back home with a car full of produce, and when we arrived, everyone would have a hand in cooking our meal

    (C) With a car full of produce, my mom and sisters would arrive, to drive everyone back home where everyone would have a hand in cooking our meal

    (D) Produce laden car we would drive home, and upon arriving, everyone would have a hand in cooking our meal

    (E) Together, everyone would drive back home, with a car full of produce, and have a hand in cooking our meal

11. Which of the following is the best way to revise sentence 13 (reproduced below)?

    From far away came friends and relatives to join in our feast.

    (A) Friends and relatives came from far away to enjoy our feast

    (B) Our friends and relatives from far away would join our feast

    (C) At the feast were our friends and relatives from far away

    (D) The feast had friends and relatives from far away

    (E) Friends and relatives would come from far away to join in our feast

12. In context, where in the passage would sentence 13 (reproduced below) best fit?

    From far away came friends and relatives to join in our feast.

    (A) (as is now)

    (B) the sentence should be deleted

    (C) before sentence 9

    (D) before sentence 12

    (E) at the end of the passage

13. In context, which of the following is the best way to revise sentences 14 and 15 in order to combine the sentences?

(A) The kids were relegated to the kitchen table because we didn't fit at the grand dining room table, but that was ok and we didn't complain because we were closest to the food for extra helpings!

(B) While the adults sat at the grand dining room table, we kids were relegated to the kitchen table; but no complaints could be heard from us as we were closest to the food for extra helpings!

(C) Us kids felt lucky to sit in the kitchen, with the adults at the grand dining room table, because we were closest to the food for extra helpings.

(D) No complaints could be heard from us kids who sat in the kitchen while the adults were at the grand dining room table: we were closest to the food for extra helpings!

(E) We kids were usually relegated to the kitchen table while the adults sat at the grand dining room table, however we didn't complain: we were closest to the food for extra helpings!

(1) J.D. Salinger is considered to be one of the greatest authors of our time. (2) He wrote many works of fiction and also short stories. (3) Perhaps his most well-known novel is *The Catcher in the Rye*. (4) *Catcher in the Rye* is a coming of age novel about an adolescent boy who is not satisfied with his life and leaves his boarding school because he is about to be kicked out to seek out adventure in New York City. (5) The boy's name is Holden Caulfield and Holden wanders the city during the late fall, right before the Christmas holiday. (6) While in the city, he checks into a hotel and meets some interesting people along the way. (7) Holden is very fond of his sister and thinks of her often. (8) For the majority of the novel Holden spends his time wandering about the city streets. (9) We see him in Central Park near the skating rink, in Times Square. (10) Also in Greenwich Village.

(11) Some believed that Salinger was overwhelmed by the fame *Catcher* received. (12) Since the book became a notorious American classic, Salinger managed to live a reclusive life, until he died in 2010. (13) Salinger has been an inspiration to many young writers.

(14) Holden Caulfield is somewhat of an American icon as an angst-ridden teenager who cannot seem to find a comfortable place in his world. (15) *Catcher in the Rye* is a novel that many people can identify with. (16) It has mystery, conflict, and the theme of indecision is an undercurrent throughout the scenes.

14. What is the purpose of this passage?

    (A) to describe an iconic character created by a great American writer
    (B) to explain a great American author's path to seclusion
    (C) to acquaint the reader with New York City
    (D) to compare fictional characters
    (E) to inspire young writers

15. In context, which of the following is the best way to revise sentences 2 and 3 in order to combine the sentences?

    (A) He wrote many works of fiction, including his most well-known novel, *The Catcher in the Rye*, and he also wrote short stories
    (B) An author of short stories and fiction, he is most well known for the novel *Catcher in the Rye*
    (C) A prolific writer; he is best known for his novel *Catcher in the Rye*, although he wrote many novels and short stories
    (D) Although best known for *Catcher in the Rye*, he wrote many works of fiction and short stories as well
    (E) Having written many works of fiction and short stories, he is best known for *Catcher in the Rye*

16. What should be done with sentence 4 (reproduced below)?

    Catcher in the Rye is a coming of age novel about an adolescent boy who is not satisfied with his life and leaves his boarding school because he is about to be kicked out to seek out adventure in New York City.

    (A) (as is now)
    (B) delete the entire sentence
    (C) break it into two sentences
    (D) insert a comma between "life" and "and"
    (E) delete "because he is about to be kicked out"

17. In context, which of the following is the best way to revise sentences 9 and 10 in order to combine the sentences?

   (A) We see him in Central Park near the skating rink, in Times Square, in Greenwich Village

   (B) We see him in Central Park near the skating rink, in Times Square, and also in Greenwich Village

   (C) In Greenwich Village, Central Park near the skating rink, in Times Square: we see him

   (D) He is seen in many places: in Central Park near the skating rink, in Times Square, in Greenwich Village

   (E) He is seen in many places such as Central Park near the skating rink, in Times Square, and in Greenwich Village

18. Which sentence does not fit with the rest of the passage and should be omitted?

   (A) sentence 5
   (B) sentence 7
   (C) sentence 10
   (D) sentence 12
   (E) sentence 14

19. What be a good transitional phrase to insert at the beginning of sentence 15 (reproduced below)?

   Catcher in the Rye is a novel that many people can identify with.

   (A) Without a doubt,
   (B) Certainly,
   (C) Because of the characters and plot
   (D) Despite the fact that it took place nearly sixty years ago,
   (E) Readers and writers alike find that

   (1) For some people jewelry, trinkets, or photographs bring back memories. (2) For me, it is setting foot into a particular location that instantly triggers remembrances of times past. (3) The most powerful association I have is with the beach and my mom. (4) Every time I visit a beach I instantly think back to spending long summer days

there with my mom as a teenager. (5) We're wearing bathing suits, we have our beach towels, the sun is shining, and our cooler is packed—that's for certain. (6) After settling down in the perfect spot my mom and I would go for a long walk along the water. (7) We'd talk about everything: my high school crush, the upcoming school year, or whatever is on my mind. (8) Then we would come back to our blankets and dig in to a great lunch. (9) Afterwards, we'd read or chat some more. (10) When the day is over we would drive home and greet dad with a barbeque dinner. (11) I remember those days vividly and when I'm on the beach I am almost transported to those days with my mom. (12) It is a comforting feeling knowing that I can visit the beach any time and take a trip down memory lane.

20. What is the primary purpose of this passage?

    (A) to explain how the narrator spent a day at the beach
    (B) to illustrate the importance of family vacations
    (C) to show how childhood memories bring joy later in life
    (D) to explain how memory works through association with places and things
    (E) to showcase the importance of sustaining marine ecology

21. In context, what can be added after sentence 2 (reproduced below) to create a transition?

    For me, it is setting foot into a particular location that instantly triggers remembrances of times past.

    (A) A walk on the beach instantly makes me think of my mother
    (B) If I want to remember something, I must go to the place where the memory was formed
    (C) My memory works by remembering memories when I am in a specific location
    (D) I have very strong associations with certain places
    (E) It is truly amazing how the memory works

22. What is the best way to revise sentence 4 (reproduced below)?

    Every time I visit a beach I instantly think back to spending long summer days there with my mom as a teenager.

    (A) (as is now)
    (B) A visit to the beach means that I'll instantly think back to spending long summer days there with my mom as a teenager
    (C) Every time I visit the beach, I instantly think back to being a teenager and spending long summer days with my mom at the beach
    (D) Now, every time I visit a beach I instantly think back to my teenage years and spending long summer days at the beach with my mom
    (E) Every time I visit a beach as a teenager, I think back to spending long summer days at the beach with my mom

23. What is the best way to revise the underlined portion of sentence 5 (reproduced below)?

    We're wearing bathing suits, we have our beach towels, the sun is shining, and our cooler is packed—that's for certain.

    (A) move "that's for certain" it to the front of the sentence
    (B) delete it
    (C) change to "those things were for certain"
    (D) add "As always" to the beginning of the sentence
    (E) change the dash after "packed" to a semicolon

24. In context, which of the following is the best way to revise sentences 8 and 9 in order to combine the sentences?

    (A) After our walk we would return to our blankets and dig into a great lunch, then we'd read or chat some more
    (B) After our walk and having eaten lunch, we would read or chat some more
    (C) Afterwards, we'd come back to our blankets and dig in to a great lunch, after that, we'd read or chat some more
    (D) Post walk and lunch we'd read or chat some more
    (E) After a great lunch, we'd read or chat some more

25. In context, which is the best revision of the underlined portion of sentence 11 (reproduced below)?

I remember those <u>days vividly and when I'm on the beach I am almost transported to those days with my mom</u>.

(A) (as is now)
(B) remove "and" and add a semicolon
(C) delete "I remember those days vividly and"
(D) add "this" after "and"
(E) add a colon after "vividly"

chapter **9**

Essay

General Info

Writing the SAT essay is nothing like writing in-school or take-home essays. During the SAT, there is little time for brainstorming, developing ideas, or proofreading. That's why you need to be prepared to write any essay on any prompt before ever even seeing the exam. You have 25 minutes. Ready. Set. Write!

What Kind of Essays Does the SAT Look For?

The SAT essay readers are looking for primarily three features in essays: organization, evidence, and grade-appropriate writing skills. So a good SAT essay is:

- Well-organized
- Well-supported
- Well-written

How Is the Essay Scored?

This is where we English people get mathematical. The essay score is a subscore of the Writing score. The essay is graded on a scale of 1 to 6 by two separate readers. Once your essay is graded, the score is multiplied by a secret constant number (K) and that score is added to the raw score from the multiple-choice section. Mathematically speaking:

Total raw score = multiple-choice score + (essay raw score × K)

To put it in perspective, the SAT essay counts for about 40 percent of your Writing score and a rather small portion of the entire exam. That means that while you shouldn't ignore it altogether, you definitely don't need to panic from now until the test. You should learn how to write the SAT essay but realize that more weight is placed on the multiple-choice sections.

Write Like You've Never Written Before

You are probably used to writing in the relaxed comfort of your home or classroom, with time and dictionary on your side. The SAT is different because you will have only a short period of time to write a cohesive and comprehensive essay.

Dealing With the Essay: A Five-Step Method

> ### Essay Steps
> **Step 1:** Read the prompt and reword it
> **Step 2:** Brainstorm
> **Step 3:** Outline
> **Step 4:** Write
> **Step 5:** Edit

Step 1: Read the prompt and reword it

Spend about 1 minute reading the prompt. Mentally reword the prompt to make sure that you understand what you need to write about. You will turn the reworded prompt into a topic sentence.

Step 2: Brainstorm

Brainstorming is an essential step. Jumping right into writing can leave you confused and unfocused. Spend 3 to 4 minutes pondering the prompt at hand and deciding which position you'd like to take. Remember that sometimes writing on a position you don't really believe is easier than writing on a position you are emotionally invested in. Jot down supporting examples while brainstorming.

Step 3: Outline

You are probably tempted to skip this step all together…don't! Trust us—it is as important as writing the actual essay. Spend 2 to 3 minutes outlining and you are guaranteed to add coherence to your essay that will otherwise be missing. Don't waste time making the outline neat—just make it work for you!

Your outline should look something like this:

I. *Intro*
  a. *Topic sentence—your position on the question; written as a statement*
  b. *Support for thesis and introduction of examples*

II. *Example One*
  a. *Example/evidence in support*
  b. *Example/evidence in support*

III. *Example Two (include a second example only if you have adequate time to fully introduce and support the example)*
  a. *Example/evidence in support*
  b. *Example/evidence in support*

V. *Conclusion*
  a. *Restate thesis in different words*
  b. *Make a general statement/clincher*

Step 4: Write

Now comes the hard part. You have about 15 minutes to write everything you have thought about and outlined. You already have your ideas and arguments so here is your chance to focus on grammar, punctuation, and sentence structure. Watch out for transitions, vocabulary, and clarity. When you are done make sure that your essay addresses the prompt.

Step 5: Edit

Almost done—but don't forget to proofread your essay. Think of your nagging English teacher who made you do rewrites. Although you only have about 2 minutes to edit, go through the essay and look for writing errors, skipped words, and lost commas.

Essay Structure

The structure of your essay should correspond to your outline. Let's review a rudimentary essay structure that can be applied to the SAT essay.

The Hourglass Essay

Introduction
(Topic/Response)

Body
(Why my response and
why is it important?)

Conclusion

Think of the essay as an hourglass. The content, if drawn as a picture, should look like an hourglass. We'll review a general essay here, but remember that the SAT essay will be shorter in length.

Introduction: Two to Four Sentences

Think of your introduction as funnel-shape that draws the reader into your piece.

By the end of the introduction, the reader should have a clear idea of the point you are trying to prove, and, best of all, a hint of the main ideas you plan to use to prove it.

- The first sentence should get the reader's attention. It should be on the general subject, not something specific.
- The next few sentences should lead the reader step by step through a chain of connected ideas that leads to the most important sentence of the introduction.
- That most important sentence is your thesis. It is the topic, idea, and main point of the essay in one sentence.

Body: Five to Ten Sentences (There Could be a Few Body Paragraphs)

The body paragraphs should explore and back up the thesis. These paragraphs should consist of one or more well-developed examples that prove your point. Make each argument or example into a separate paragraph. Stay on topic and make sure to address the topic of the thesis.

- Begin with a topic sentence that suggests the scope and reminds the reader why the paragraph is relevant to the thesis.
- Follow the topic sentence with supporting evidence.
- Explain how the evidence relates to the thesis.
- Show with examples—don't just tell.

Conclusion: Two to Three Sentences

Finally, wrap up your essay with a conclusion. Usually, an essay should have several sentences that restate the thesis, remind the reader of the essay's points, and lead the reader out of the essay with some general observations about the topic. Due to the time constraints, the SAT essay's clincher can be limited to one or two sentences.

Keep in Mind

- Vary your sentence structure.
- Use correct punctuation.
- Employ level-appropriate vocabulary.
- Support with examples—these can be personal, historical, or literary.
- Show, don't tell!
- Always leave a few minutes to proofread.
- Ask yourself … did I answer:
  - the correct question
  - the why
  - the why important

Let's Practice

Work through this practice topic as though it were the real thing. Use the spaces to practice the steps.

Think carefully about the issue presented in the following excerpt and the assignment below:

> A man who was completely innocent, offered himself as a sacrifice for the good of others, including his enemies, and became the ransom of the world. It was a perfect act.
>
> *Mohandas Karamchand Gandhi*

Assignment: Is altruism a necessary trait for peaceful coexistence in the world? Plan and write an essay in which you develop your point of view on this issue. Support your position with reasoning and examples from your reading, studies, experience, or observation.

Step 1: Read the prompt and reword it

_____

_____

_____

_____

Step 2: Brainstorm

_____

_____

_____

_____

Step 3: Outline

Intro _____

_____

Body _____

_____

Conclusion _____

_____

Step 4: Write

_____

_____

_____

_____

_____

_____

_____

_____

_____

_____

_____

_____

_____

_____

_____

_____

_____

_____

_____

_____

_____

_____

_____

_____

_____

_____

_____

_____

_____

_____

_____

_____

Step 5: Edit

Essay Topics

Sometimes coming up with supporting details on the spot is difficult. Brainstorm for supporting examples that you can use for different types of essays.

Historical Moment	
Main Players	
Important Dates	
The Gist of What Happened	
Why Did It Matter?	

Literary Work	
Author	
Main Characters	
The Gist of What Happened	
Themes	

SAT Essay Drills

You're ready to practice the SAT essay. Remember to use a timer and follow the directions. Consider having a peer or teacher "grade" your finished product.

Essay One

We want you to practice responding to all sides of an argument. For Essay One, practice writing responses for both sides of the argument.

Think carefully about the issue presented in the following excerpt and the assignment below:

> What counts is not necessarily the size of the dog in the fight—it's the size of the fight in the dog.
>
> *Dwight D. Eisenhower, in a speech on January 31, 1958*

Assignment: Is resolve more important than ability in determining a person's success? Plan and write an essay in which you develop your point of view on this issue. Support your position with reasoning and examples from your reading, studies, experience, or observation.

Drill 1: Argue "yes, resolve is more important than ability in determining a person's success."

Drill 2: Argue "no, resolve is not more important than ability in determining a person's success."

Essay Two

Think carefully about the issue presented in the following excerpt and the assignment below:

> Education's purpose is to replace an empty mind with an open one.
>
> *Malcolm Forbes*

Assignment: Is knowledge of those around us necessary for the elimination of intolerance? Plan and write an essay in which you develop your point of view on this issue. Support your position with reasoning and examples from your reading, studies, experience, or observation.

Writing Section Answer Key

Identifying Sentence Errors

1. Step 1: Read the sentence, Step 2: Look for common errors, Step 3: Eliminate no-error choices, Step 4: If everything looks good, select choice E
2. C
3. E
4. C
5. E
6. E
7. E
8. A
9. D
10. B
11. D
12. C
13. D
14. D
15. C
16. E
17. D
18. B
19. D
20. B
21. E
22. B
23. C
24. C
25. D

Improving Sentence Errors Drills

1. Step 1: Read the sentence, Step 2: Look for common errors, Step 3: Self-correct the error, Step 4: Plug it in
2. B
3. C
4. A
5. C
6. B
7. A
8. B
9. C
10. A
11. B
12. D
13. B
14. A
15. B
16. C
17. C
18. A
19. A
20. C
21. E
22. A
23. A
24. D
25. E

Improving Paragraph Drills

1. Step 1: Read the passage, Step 2: Understand the question, Step 3: Self-correct the error, Step 4: Find the match
2. C
3. B
4. B
5. C
6. A
7. B
8. A
9. B
10. B
11. A
12. D
13. E
14. A
15. A
16. C
17. B
18. B
19. D
20. C
21. D
22. D
23. B
24. E
25. B

Part IV

Math Section

Math Section Introduction

General Information

The Math section of the SAT is composed of three separate units of multiple-choice and grid-in questions. To beat the Math section, we will ask you to dig into the back of your brain where you keep information from grades 7 to 10. In case that information is buried too far down, we will review the math and go over the strategies (oh, and did we mention cool calculator tricks?).

Math Section Strategy

The questions in the Math section appear in order of difficulty. That means that the difficulty of the questions in each section increases from beginning to end. We will discuss how this will influence your strategy later, but do keep this in mind. In the meantime, let's take a look at some general strategy for the multiple-choice and grid-in questions.

Solving Multiple-Choice Problems

In general, you should solve the problems before looking at the answers. Follow the four-step process.

> ### Math Steps
> **Step 1:** Read the question
> **Step 2:** Solve the problem
> **Step 3:** Process of elimination
> **Step 4:** When in doubt, try it out

Step 1: Read the question

Paraphrase the question in your head to make sure you understand it and plan to solve it. Do not look at the answer choices.

Step 2: Solve the problem

Once you have solved the problem look at the answer choices. Pick the answer that matches yours.

Step 3: Process of elimination

The correct answer is hidden among four trick wrong answers. Eliminate answers that are too easy or too outrageous to get to the correct answer.

Step 4: When in doubt, try it out

Sometimes you may not know how to approach a problem. Before giving up, and only if you are doing well on time, try plugging the answer choices into the equations. Working backwards may help you find the answer.

Grid-Ins

The grid-in section is a free-for-all. You either know the answer or you don't. Aside from actually answering the questions, let's consider a few other things:

- Only the bubbles are graded. The numbers you write at the top don't really matter.
- There is no bubble for four decimals or for negative signs. If your answer has either, then it's wrong.
- Mixed numbers must be transformed into fraction form.

Formula Sheet and Common Errors

At the end of *each* chapter, you will find two charts titled Formulas You're Not Given That You Ought to Know and Common Mistakes You Need to Avoid. The titles speak for themselves. These charts appear more often than you might like, but *do not* skip over them. Keep going over them so that you really know the formulas and totally stay away from common mistakes. (Remember that all the choices are designed with the common mistakes the test-makers know students might make. Beat the test-makers at their own game!)

Keep in Mind

- **Ballpark It**—Estimate numerical values to solve problems and check your answers. Is the answer you came up with reasonable?
- **Diagrams**—Unless a picture is labeled "drawn to scale," don't trust your eyes.
- **Timing**—You don't have too much time to work out the problems and all the problems are worth the same number of points. As you solve the problems, don't get stuck trying to solve them in order. Work on the problems that you know, skip those you don't know, and then come back to the questions that are more difficult for you.
- **Fill It in**—If there are questions that you just don't know how to solve, grid in a reasonable solution such as 0 or 5. There is no penalty for wrong answers so guessing is better than not answering a question at all.

chapter 10

Numbers

In this chapter, we will learn techniques for solving a variety of numbers problems on the SAT. We will cover general number problems, exponents, radicals, charts and tables, unions and intersections, absolute values, and symbolic rules.

General Problems

There are several types of general number problems that come up on the SAT. Primarily, you'll need to know about odd and even numbers, as well as prime and composite numbers.

Integers are all the positive and negative whole numbers, including 0. For example, {...–3, –2, –1, 0, 1, 2, 3...} represents the set of integers. Odd and even numbers only apply to integers. An odd number is a number that cannot be evenly divided by 2 (e.g., 1, 3, 5, 7, 9, ...), whereas an even number is one that can be evenly divided by 2 (e.g., 2, 4, 6, 8, 10, ...). The last digit of an odd number is always 1, 3, 5, 7, or 9. The last digit of an even number is always 2, 4, 6, 8, or 0. For example, 17, 21, 93, and 169 are odd numbers, whereas 28, 42, 76, and 180 are even numbers.

Here are some rules for adding odd and even numbers:

Rule	Example
Even + Even = Even	10 + 12 = 22
Odd + Odd = Even	13 + 17 = 30
Even + Odd = Odd	98 + 7 = 105

A prime number is a whole number that only has two factors—itself and one. In case you need a refresher, a factor is a number that divides evenly into another. For example, 4 is a factor of 12 because 4 goes into 12 evenly. A composite number has factors in addition to one and itself. The numbers 0 and 1 are neither prime nor composite because neither has two or more factors. All even numbers are divisible by two, so all even numbers greater than two are composite numbers. All numbers that end in five are divisible by five, which implies that all numbers that end with five and are greater than five are also composite numbers.

There is usually a question or two on prime numbers. The last thing you want to do on the SAT is waste time thinking about which numbers are prime. Good test-takers commit the prime numbers between 2 and 101 to memory. They are {2, 3, 5, 7, 11, 13, 17, 19, 23, 29, 31, 37, 41, 43, 47, 53, 59, 61, 67, 71, 73, 79, 83, 89, 97, 101}.

There is a difference between odd and even numbers, and prime and composite numbers. Many students think that 51 is prime just because it is odd, but both 17 and 3 divide evenly into 51, so it's actually composite.

Let's take a look at some typical applications.

Examples

1. What is the product of the smallest prime number that is greater than 71 and the greatest prime number that is less than 71?

This is an easy problem if you've memorized the list of prime numbers! The greatest prime number less than 71 is 67, and the smallest prime number greater than 71 is 73. When you multiply 67×73 you get 4,891. That's it!

2.

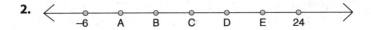

On the number line above, the point marks are equally spaced and their coordinates are shown. Of these coordinates, which is the least whose tens digit is equal to 1?

(A) A
(B) B
(C) C
(D) D
(E) E

Since the points on the number line are equally spaced, you know that each interval represents the same numerical quantity. There are six intervals between –6 and 24. The total distance between –6 and 24 is 30. If you divide 30 by 6, you get 5. That means that each time you move from one point to the next on the number line, from left to right, you are adding 5. For example, A = –1, B = 4, C = 9, and D = 14. We can stop there since we've found the first number that has a tens digit equal to 1. The correct answer is choice D.

3. The number *m* is a three-digit number. When *m* is divided by 6, the remainder is 4, and when *m* is divided by 5, the remainder is 1. What is the least possible value of *m*?

I like to think of these types of problems as "builder problems" because we build up from what we know. First, we are looking for a three-digit number, so every integer from 100 to 999 comes to mind. That the remainder is 4 when divided by 6 doesn't give much useful information, so we move on to the next bit that says the remainder is 1 when divided by 5. We know that all numbers that are divisible by 5 end in a 0 or a 5. If the remainder is 1, then the number we are looking for should end in a 1 or a 6 (just add 1 to 0 and 5). Then the question asks us to find the *least* possible value of *m*. The closest number to 100 that ends in a 1 or a 6 is 101. When we divide 101 by 6, we get a remainder of 5—not 4! So we move on to the next possible number ending in a 1 or a 6. That number is 106. When we divide 106 by 6, we get the requested remainder of 4. With practice, that's doable in 40 seconds or less. The correct answer is 106.

Exponents

Getting the exponent problems right on the SAT is as simple as knowing the basic rules for how exponents work.

I. Multiplying with the same base: $x^a x^b = x^{a+b}$

II. Multiplying with different bases: $x^a y^a = (xy)^a$

III. Raising a power to a power: $(x^a)^b = x^{ab}$

IV. Dividing with the same base: $\dfrac{x^a}{x^b} = x^{a-b}$

V. Dividing with different bases: $\dfrac{x^a}{y^a} = \left(\dfrac{x}{y}\right)^a$

VI. Raising to a negative power: $x^{-a} = \dfrac{1}{x^a}$ or $\left(\dfrac{x}{y}\right)^{-a} = \left(\dfrac{y}{x}\right)^a$

Any number raised to a power of 0 is equal to 1. Any number raised to a power of 1 is equal to itself.

You can apply any combination of these rules to a problem. Luckily, most of the problems involving exponents on the SAT use the same few strategies. Let's take a look at a few typical examples.

Examples

1. If j and k are positive integers and $2^{3j} = 16^k$, what is the value of $\dfrac{k}{j}$?

(A) $\dfrac{3}{4}$

(B) $\dfrac{1}{3}$

(C) 4

(D) $\dfrac{4}{3}$

(E) $\dfrac{3}{5}$

First, read the entire problem. Then identify what you're looking for. We want to know the value of $\dfrac{k}{j}$. That means we need to solve for k and j, and then divide. We are told that $2^{3j} = 16^k$. In the given form, we know very little about the values of k and j, so we have to transform each side of the equation so that the bases are the same. The numbers on the SAT are generally simple ones. We know that $2 \times 2 \times 2 \times 2 = 16$, so $2^4 = 16$. We can replace the 16 with 2^4 to get $2^{3j} = (2^4)^k$. If we apply exponent rule III to the right side of the equation, we get $2^{3j} = 2^{4k}$. Now that both sides have the same base, it's apparent that $3j = 4k$. Divide both sides by j, and then by 4 to get $\dfrac{k}{j} = \dfrac{3}{4}$. The correct choice is A.

2. If x and y are positive integers and $(x^{\frac{1}{4}}y^{\frac{1}{6}})^{12} = 1372$, what is the value of $x + y$?

(A) 28
(B) 18
(C) 9
(D) 5
(E) 2

This is a typical SAT problem. Since there are two variables, x and y, but only one equation, we cannot use a system of equations to solve directly for the values of x and y. The best method is almost always to use a factor tree. First, use exponent rules II and III to simplify the given expression. If we distribute the power of 12 to each of the exponents on x and y, we get $x^3 y^2 = 1372$. So we're really looking for two integers, one of which will be cubed and the other squared, which are then multiplied to get 1372. Create a factor tree for 1372. It's always best to factor by 2 so that you can see all the possible products. For example, $1372 = 686 \times 2 = 343 \times 2 \times 2$.

After only two factors, we can see the solution. The number 2 appears twice, so $y = 2$ because y is supposed to be squared. The value of x must be some number cubed that will equal 343. Again, the numbers are usually easy on the SAT, so you can just try a few on the calculator. Try $5 \times 5 \times 5 = 125$—nope, too small. Try $6 \times 6 \times 6 = 216$—nope, too small again, but closer! Try $7 \times 7 \times 7 = 343$—yes, it's a perfect match. So $x = 7$. Finally, $x + y = 7 + 2 = 9$. The correct choice is C. This would be considered a difficult problem on the SAT. With practice, you could definitely solve it in about a minute.

3. Which of the following expressions is equivalent to $8x^6$?

    I. $(4x^4)^{\frac{3}{2}}$

    II. $\dfrac{8x^{-2}}{x^{-8}}$

    III. $\left(\dfrac{1}{2x^2}\right)^{-3}$

(A) I only
(B) II only
(C) II and III only
(D) I and II only
(E) I, II, and III

For this type of problem, we apply the exponent rules to each of the three choices and see if we get $8x^6$. For choice I, apply exponent rule III: $(4x^4)^{\frac{3}{2}} = 4^{\frac{3}{2}} \times x^6 = 8x^6$. Finding out what $4^{\frac{3}{2}}$ equals is as easy as plugging into the calculator and outputting 8. Choice I works. Automatically, we can cross out choices B and C because they do not contain I. The remaining choices are A, D, and E. Choices D and E both contain II, so trying II next isn't going to help us decide on the right answer. If we test choice III, and it works, the answer must be E. If we test choice III, and it doesn't work, then we need to test II to determine if A or D is the correct response.

For choice III, apply exponent rule VI: $\left(\dfrac{1}{2x^2}\right)^{-3} = (2x^2)^3 = 2^3 \times x^6 = 8x^6$. Choice III works. Since I and III both work, II must also work, based on the choices. The correct answer is E.

Radicals

A square root is a factor of a number that yields the number when it is squared. Hence, if $a^2 = b$, then a is a square root of b.

Let a number be n. The square roots of the number are written as $\pm\sqrt{n}$. For cube roots, there is only one possible real solution. For example, $\sqrt[3]{8} = 2$, and $\sqrt[3]{-8} = -2$.

Index

$\underset{\displaystyle\uparrow}{\text{Index}}$

$\sqrt[2]{n}$ ← Radical sign
← Radicand

or

$\sqrt{n}$ ← Radical sign
← Radicand

Square root radical expressions

The product property of square roots states that for any real numbers a and b where $a \ge 0$ and $b \ge 0$, $\sqrt{ab} = \sqrt{a} \times \sqrt{b}$.

The quotient property of square roots states that for any real numbers a and b, where $a \ge 0$ and $b > 0$, $\sqrt{\dfrac{a}{b}} = \dfrac{\sqrt{a}}{\sqrt{b}}$.

Take it from someone who's done a whole lot of math—the best way to make sense of the rules is to see them in practice!

Examples

1. If $3\sqrt[3]{25n} = 5$, then $n =$

This is a typical grid-in problem on the SAT involving radicals. The idea is to think of $\sqrt[3]{25n}$ as its own variable. For example, if we were asked to solve $3x = 5$, we would simply divide both sides by 3 to get x. Similarly, the first step here is to divide both sides of the given equation by 3. We get $\sqrt[3]{25n} = \dfrac{5}{3}$. To "release" the n from the radical, we perform the opposite operation of the root. Since we have a cube root here, we would cube both sides to release the radical. If we had a square root, we would square both sides.

So $(\sqrt[3]{25n})^3 = \left(\dfrac{5}{3}\right)^3 \Rightarrow 25n = \dfrac{125}{27}$. To solve for n, simply multiply both sides by $\dfrac{1}{25}$, and get $n = \dfrac{5}{27}$. That's all there is to it!

2.

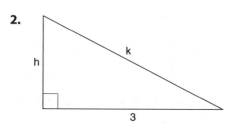

Note: Figure not drawn to scale.

In the right triangle above, if $h=5$, what is the value of k?

(A) $\sqrt{8}$

(B) $\sqrt{18}$

(C) 4

(D) $\sqrt{34}$

(E) 7

This is a simple application of the Pythagorean theorem. The Pythagorean theorem states that in a right triangle, the lengths of the three sides are related by the equation $a^2 + b^2 = c^2$, where c is the length of the hypotenuse. If $h=5$, then we have the lengths of both legs of the triangle. So $3^2 + 5^2 = k^2 \Rightarrow 9 + 25 = k^2 \Rightarrow 34 = k^2$. To solve for k, take the square root of both sides of the equation to get $k = \sqrt{34}$. The correct choice is D. Sometimes the SAT gives the choices in radical form, simplest radical form, or as a decimal approximation of the radical. If your answer doesn't look like one of the choices, just use the calculator to approximate the value of your radical, and then to approximate the values of the choices, and choose the one that matches.

This problem, by the way, is designed to trick you a bit. Many of us are used to seeing the {3, 4, 5} right triangle. Since two of the sides are 3 and 5, you can bet a lot people will choose choice C. However, 4 cannot be the length of the hypotenuse because a leg must always be shorter than the hypotenuse. Pythagorean triples are great, but be careful when and if you use them.

3.

2s

s

In the figure above, the perimeter of the triangle is $9+3\sqrt{3}$. What is the value of s?

(A) 3

(B) 6

(C) 9

(D) $\sqrt{3}$

(E) $3+\sqrt{3}$

This problem can be solved directly using the Pythagorean theorem, but it is much easier to check if the hypotenuse of a right triangle is twice as long as the shorter leg—then it's very likely that the special triangle theorem will apply.

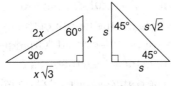

Special right triangles

There are two special right triangles: one for 30-60-90 right triangles, and the other for 45-45-90 right triangles. The triangle in this question is a 30-60-90 because the hypotenuse is two times as long as the shorter side. In a 45-45-90 triangle, the hypotenuse is always $\sqrt{2}$ times the length of a leg.

So we break it up. Based on the 30-60-90 rule, we know the missing side of our triangle will be $s\sqrt{3}$. The sum of the three sides (perimeter) is $s+2s+s\sqrt{3}$, which simplifies to $3s+s\sqrt{3}$. The perimeter of the triangle is supposed to be $9+3\sqrt{3}$. You can visually compare $3s+s\sqrt{3}$ and $9+3\sqrt{3}$. It's clear that $s=3$ makes the comparison work. So the correct choice is A. It might look tricky, but if you know the rules and the comparison trick, you can get it done rather quickly.

Charts and Tables

A lot of problems on the SAT can be solved quickly and accurately if you know the right tricks. When it comes to chart and table problems, the problems can be so different that there isn't a simple set of rules to follow. However, our recommendation is to carefully read and understand the chart or table, identify exactly what the question is asking, and then take a minute (or two in some cases) to make a thoughtful, justified decision. To understand a table or chart, identify what each row and column represent, and take a moment to understand how the chart or table is meant to be read. Some are read across, some vertically, and some both ways. The good thing is that these problems are very doable. Thinking about them carefully from the onset will actually save you more time than if you scramble to find a trick. Let's take a look at some common problems.

Examples

1.

Members of a movie watchers club			
	Teens	**Adults**	**Total**
Males	a	b	c
Females	d	e	f
Total	g	h	i

In the table above, each letter represents the number of members in a particular group of a movie club. Which of the following must be equal to *h*?

(A) *d + b*
(B) *g − i*
(C) *c + f − g*
(D) *a + e*
(E) *a + b + d + e*

First, take a moment to understand the chart. The row totals represent the total number of teens and adults for a particular gender in a movie club. The column totals represent the total number of males and females for a particular age group in a movie club. We want to know which of the choices is equal to *h*. The most obvious ways to express *h* is to sum *b + e* or to take the difference $i - g$. Since $b+e$ is not a choice, we need to either express b or e or both variables in terms of other variables. For example, b can be expressed as $c - a$, and e can be expressed as $f - d$. So $b+e$ is equally expressed as $c-a+e$, if we replace b, or $b+f-d$, if we replace e.

Since neither of those is a choice, we consider manipulating $i-g$. For example, g can be expressed $a+d$, and i can be expressed as $c+f$. If we replace i, we get $c+f-g$. That's choice C, so we're done! The trick is to think carefully and methodically, while taking the initial time to fully understand how the chart works. If you spend 30 seconds understanding the chart, you can very likely find the variation on h you need in another 30 seconds.

2.

Number of medical doctors		
	Male	**Female**
Prairieville	1600	3400
Thompsonville		648
Total		4048

The table above shows the number of medical doctors in the towns of Prairieville and Thompsonville, separated by gender. If the percentage of male medical doctors in Prairieville is half the percentage of male medical doctors in Thompsonville, what is the total number of male medical doctors in Prairieville and Thompsonville?

First, let's read the problem and try to understand the table. Reading the table across gives the number of male and female doctors in a particular town. Reading the table vertically gives the number of male or female doctors in each town, followed by a total by gender. We want to ultimately find the total number of male medical doctors in Prairieville and Thompsonville—so we're looking to fill in the bottom blank in the male column. To get the total, we need to find the number of male doctors in Thompsonville first. The problem states "the percentage of male medical doctors in Prairieville is half the percentage of male medical doctors in Thompsonville." The percentage of male medical doctors in Prairieville can be found by dividing the number of males by the total number of doctors in Prairieville: $\dfrac{1600}{1600+3400} = .32$, or 32%.

If the percentage of male doctors in Prairieville is half the percentage of male doctors in Thompsonville, then Thompsonville must have 64% male doctors and 36% female doctors. So 648 must represent 36% of the doctors in the town. Finding the number of male doctors in Thompsonville is as easy as making a proportion.

If I said 30 pencils represent 20% of the pencils in a box, and asked how many pencils 60% would represent, you would very easily say 90 pencils. That's because 20% divides into 60% exactly 3 times, so we just multiply 30 by 3 to get 90. The same idea applies here. Simply divide the percentage you want, 64%, by the percentage you know, 36%, and then multiply that number by 648 (just like in the pencil example). We get $\frac{.64}{.36} \times 648 = 1152$. So there are 1152 male medical doctors in Thompsonville. The final total is equal to the sum of the male doctors in both towns: 1600+1152=2752. The correct answer is 2752. Again, the trick is to understand the table well enough so that the solving process flows.

Unions and Intersections

A union of two or more sets represents the joining of the elements of one set with the elements of another. For example, if $A = \{-4, 2, 7, 9, 15\}$ and $B = \{-4, 7, 16, 20\}$, then the union of A and B, represented by $A \cup B$, is equal to $\{-4, 2, 7, 9, 15, 16, 20\}$. Notice that we simply wrote a new set that has all the elements of both sets, but we did not repeat the common elements in the new set.

An intersection of two or more sets represents the set that contains only the elements common to one or more sets. For example, if $A = \{-4, 2, 7, 9, 15\}$ and $B = \{-4, 7, 16, 20\}$, then the intersection of A and B, represented by $A \cap B$, is equal to $\{-4, 7\}$.

Union and intersection problems on the SAT tend to be similar from year to year. Let's take a look at a couple of practice problems.

Examples

1. If H is the set of odd integers, I is the set of multiples of 15, and J is the set of perfect square numbers, which of the following integers will be in all three sets?

(A) 4
(B) 45
(C) 75
(D) 81
(E) 225

First, identify if you're looking for an intersection or a union. The problem says to select a number that is in all three sets. Since all three sets must contain the number, we're looking for an intersection. If *H* is the set of odd integers, then we can automatically cross out choice A because 4 is an even number. If *I* is the set of multiples of 15, then we can automatically cross out choice D because 15 does not go into 81 evenly. If *J* is the set of perfect square numbers, then we can cross out choices B and C because they are not perfect square numbers (e.g., {1, 4, 9, 16, 25, 36, 49, 64, 81, 100…}) That leaves us with choice E as the final answer. The number 225 is the only one of the choices that would be in all three sets, and therefore be in the intersection of the three sets.

2. If there are 23 students in geometry, 19 students in history, and 14 students in both geometry and history, what is the total number of students who are in only geometry or only history?

(A)   14
(B)   19
(C)   23
(D)   28
(E)   42

This type of problem comes up all the time on the SAT. Such problems often come across as confusing, and they can take up a lot of time if you do not know how to solve them with a trick. We are looking for the total number of students in only geometry or only history. That means we need to find out the number of students who are in either course, but who are not enrolled in both courses. Of the 23 students taking geometry, some are also taking history. Of the 19 students taking history, some are also taking geometry. If we combine 23 + 19, we get a total of 42. The number 42 represents the total number of students in geometry, history, and both. The students taking both courses are counted twice in this model because they were already accounted for in the 23 *and* the 19. So we need to subtract 14 twice: 42 − 14 − 14 = 14! There are 14 students who are taking only geometry or only history. Choice A is the correct answer.

It's total coincidence, by the way, that 14 appeared so many times in the computation. In general, with this type of problem, it is useful to think of the following formula: $(A \cup B) = A + B - 2(A \cap B)$. Here, the *A* represents the number of students taking geometry, and the *B* represents the number of students taking history. So $A \cup B$ represents the quantity we are looking for. $(A \cup B) = 23 + 19 - 2(14) = 14$. Same answer!

Absolute Values

The absolute value of a number is equal to how far away the number is from zero. That's why the absolute value of a number is always positive. For example, $|10|=10$, and $|-10|=10$. Both 10 and -10 are 10 spaces away from zero on the number line. Absolute value problems that appear on the SAT are generally easy or medium in terms of difficulty. The trick to solving them is to think of all the possibilities for the variable. When we think of the equation $|x-5|=10$, we need to consider that $x=-5$ and $x=15$, because $|-5-5|=|-10|=10$ and $|15-5|=|10|=10$. Let's take a look at some typical problems.

Examples

1. If $3<|x|<8$ and $5<|y|<8$, which of the following must be true?

(A) $x<y$

(B) $y<x$

(C) $xy>0$

(D) $15<|xy|$

(E) $64<|xy|$

Whenever absolute value questions are posed this way, the first step is to consider the range of possible values of each variable. If $3<|x|<8$, then $3<x<8$ and $-8<x<-3$. If $5<|y|<8$, then $5<y<8$ and $-8<y<-5$. Now that we have the possible values for each variable, we can test the choices. Choice A is incorrect by counterexample; one possible value of x is 7 and a possible value of y is -7, so x is not always less than y. Choice B is incorrect because a possible value of y is 6 and a possible value of x is -5, so y is not always less than x. Choice C is incorrect because a possible value of y is 6 and a possible value of x is -5, and the product -30 is not greater than 0. Choice E is incorrect because when $x=-7.999$ (since it cannot actually equal -8 or 8) and $y=7.999$ (since it also cannot equal -8 or 8), the product $|xy|$ is just under 64. Choice D is the correct choice by default and also computationally. When $x=-3.001$ and $y=-5.001$, the lowest possible values of each variable, the product $|xy|$ is just over 15, making the inequality true.

2. $7<|3x-6|<15$, and x is a positive number, what is one possible value of x?

This is a direct solving problem. Since the problem asks for the positive value of x, which will always be the case for grid-in problems (you cannot grid in a negative number on the SAT, so you know your answers should always be positive), all we need to do is remove the absolute value and solve. For example: Remove the absolute value to get $7 < 3x - 6 < 15$. Add 6 to both sides to get $13 < 3x < 21$. Divide by 3 on both sides to get $\dfrac{13}{3} < x < 7$. You can pick any number that falls between $\dfrac{13}{3}$ and 7.

3. At Howard's Auto Company, machine *J* cuts a strip of steel that will be used to make a door for a car, and machine *K* accepts the strip of steel only if the weight (in pounds) is between $47\dfrac{5}{7}$ and $50\dfrac{2}{7}$. If machine *K* accepts a strip of steel weighing *x* pounds, which of the following describes all possible values of *x*?

(A) $|x + 49| < \dfrac{9}{7}$

(B) $|x + 49| < \dfrac{9}{7}$

(C) $|x - 49| > \dfrac{9}{7}$

(D) $|x - 49| = \dfrac{9}{7}$

(E) $|x - 49| < \dfrac{9}{7}$

This type of problem appears on most SAT exams. Unfortunately, most students get it wrong because building an inequality can be much more difficult than solving one. On a positive note, if you know the following formula, you can always get it right rather quickly. Whenever you are trying to find an inequality that represents a range of allowable values of a variable, like in the current problem, you'll be told the lower and higher end of the allowable values the variable can take on. First, take the average of the two numbers: $\dfrac{47\frac{5}{7} + 50\frac{2}{7}}{2} = 49$. Second, find the difference between the higher end and the average: $50\dfrac{2}{7} - 49 = \dfrac{9}{7}$. Third, fill in the formula: $|x - \text{average}| < \text{difference}$. In this example, we have $|x - 49| < \dfrac{9}{7}$. The correct answer choice is E.

Symbolic Rules

Symbolic rule problems can come as quite a surprise when you first encounter them because you're not sure what the symbol means. It turns out the symbol is completely arbitrary. The trick is to not give the symbol any thought. Instead, focus on the rule described in the problem.

Examples

1. For all positive integers x and y, let $x \odot y$ be defined as the whole number remainder when x is divided by y. If $x \odot 7 = 6$, what is the least possible value of x greater than 100?

First note that x and y can only be positive integers. We are told that $x \odot y$ is defined as the whole number remainder when x is divided by y. For example, $21 \odot 9 = 3$ because 9 goes into 21 two times evenly, with 3 as the remainder. The problem here asks us to find the least value of x greater than 100 such that $x \odot 7 = 6$. Simply find the most times 7 can go into 100 evenly. Since $7 \times 14 = 98$, we know that the least value greater than 100 that 7 divides into with a remainder of 6 must be equal to $98 + 6 = 104$. The correct answer is 104.

2. Let the operation Π be defined by $x \Pi y = \dfrac{2x - y}{y - 2x}$ for all numbers x and y, where $y \neq 2x$. If $2\Pi3 = 3\Pi y$, what is the value of y?

(A) -2
(B) -1
(C) 0
(D) 1
(E) There is more than one possible value of y

Normally, for this type of problem we would set up an equation: $2\Pi3 = 3\Pi y$. Plugging the numbers into the given rule, we get $\dfrac{2(2) - 3}{3 - 2(2)} = \dfrac{2(3) - y}{y - 2(3)}$. Simplifying, we get $\dfrac{1}{-1} = \dfrac{6 - y}{y - 6}$. Cross-multiply: $y - 6 = -1(6 - y)$. Distribute: $y - 6 = y - 6$. When we try to solve for y, both sides of the equation become 0. It's as if the y variable completely disappears. When something like this happens, it means there is no restriction on the value of the variable, or whatever value you can think of for y will work when you plug it in. For example, if we pick $y = 19, 19 - 6 = 19 - 6$. If we pick $y = -83$, we get $-83 - 6 = -83 - 6$. Whatever value we pick works. Therefore, the correct choice is E.

In this example, however, solving directly takes too much time. The best SAT test-taker would have simplified the original rule first: $x\Pi y = \dfrac{2x-y}{y-2x} \Rightarrow x\Pi y = \dfrac{2x-y}{-(2x-y)} \Rightarrow x\Pi y = \dfrac{1}{-1} \Rightarrow x\Pi y = -1$. It takes about 15 seconds to simplify the rule and see that any values of x and y, plugged into the rule in any combination or order, will always become -1. You can find choice E in about 20 seconds flat.

The Formulas You're Not Given That You Ought to Know

Arithmetic Operations

$$ab + ac = a(b + c)$$

$$a\left(\frac{b}{c}\right) = \frac{ab}{c}$$

$$\frac{\left(\frac{a}{b}\right)}{c} = \frac{a}{bc}$$

$$\frac{a}{\left(\frac{b}{c}\right)} = \frac{ac}{b}$$

$$\frac{a}{b} + \frac{c}{d} = \frac{ad + bc}{bd}$$

$$\frac{a}{b} - \frac{c}{d} = \frac{ad - bc}{bd}$$

$$\frac{a - b}{c - d} = \frac{b - a}{d - c}$$

$$\frac{a + b}{c} = \frac{a}{c} + \frac{b}{c}$$

$$\frac{ab + ac}{a} = b + c, \ a \neq 0$$

$$\frac{\left(\frac{a}{b}\right)}{\left(\frac{c}{d}\right)} = \frac{ad}{bc}$$

Exponent Rules

$$a^n a^m = a^{n+m}$$

$$\frac{a^n}{a^m} = a^{n-m} = \frac{1}{a^{m-n}}$$

$$(a^n)^m = a^{nm}$$

$$a^0 = 1, \ a \neq 0$$

$$(ab)^n = a^n b^n$$

$$\left(\frac{a}{b}\right)^n = \frac{a^n}{b^n}$$

$$a^{-n} = \frac{1}{a^n}$$

$$\frac{1}{a^{-n}} = a^n$$

$$\left(\frac{a}{b}\right)^{-n} = \left(\frac{b}{a}\right)^n = \frac{b^n}{a^n}$$

$$a^{\frac{n}{m}} = \left(a^{\frac{1}{m}}\right)^n = (a^n)^{\frac{1}{m}}$$

Linear Functions

$$y = mx + b \text{ or } f(x) = mx + b$$

Graph is a line with point $(0, b)$ and slope m.

Slope

Slope of the line containing the two points (x_1, y_1) and (x_2, y_2) is

$$m = \frac{y_2 - y_1}{x_2 - x_1} = \frac{\text{rise}}{\text{run}}$$

Slope–Intercept Form

The equation of the line with slope m and y-intercept $(0, b)$ is

$$y = mx + b$$

Point–Slope Form

The equation of the line with slope m and passing through the point (x_1, y_1) is

$$y - y_1 = m(x - x_1)$$

Distance Formula

If $P_1 = (x_1, y_1)$ and $P_2 = (x_2, y_2)$ are two points the distance between them is

$$d(P_1, P_2) = \sqrt{(x_2 - x_1)^2 + (y_2 - y_1)^2}$$

Constant Function

$$y = a \text{ or } f(x) = a$$

Graph is a horizontal line passing though the point $(0, a)$.

Factoring Formulas

$$x^2 - a^2 = (x + a)(x - a)$$

$$x^2 + 2ax + a^2 = (x + a)^2$$

$$x^2 - 2ax + a^2 = (x - a)^2$$

Common Mistakes You Need to Avoid

Error	Correction
$\dfrac{3}{0} \neq 0$ and $\dfrac{3}{0} \neq 3$	You can never divide by 0. Division by 0 is undefined.
$-4^2 \neq 16$	$-4^2 = -16$ and $(-4)^2 = 16$. Be careful how you use parentheses.
$(x^3)^4 \neq x^7$	$(x^3)^4 = x^{12}$. Raising a power to a power means you have to multiply, not add.
$\dfrac{x}{y+z} \neq \dfrac{x}{y} + \dfrac{x}{z}$	$\dfrac{3}{4} = \dfrac{3}{3+1} \neq \dfrac{3}{3} + \dfrac{3}{1} = 1+3 = 4$. You can only divide monomials (not binomials) into a numerator.
$\dfrac{x+cy}{x} \neq 1+cy$	$\dfrac{x+cy}{x} = 1 + \dfrac{cy}{x}$. If you divide a monomial into one piece of the numerator, you need to divide it into all the pieces.
$-b(y-1) \neq -by - b$	$-b(y-1) = -by + b$. Make sure you distribute to each piece inside the parentheses.
$(x+m)^2 \neq x^2 + m^2$	$(x+m)^2 = (x+m)(x+m) = x^2 + 2xm + m^2$. When raising a binomial to a power, make sure you FOIL! You may never "distribute" a power over a + or a − sign.

Chapter 10 Quiz—Numbers
25 Questions

Directions: For this quiz, solve each problem and decide which is the best of the choices given. For Student-Produced Response questions, solve each problem and record your solution.

Notes

1. The use of a calculator is permitted.
2. All numbers used are real numbers.
3. Figures that accompany problems in this test are intended to provide information useful in solving the problems. They are drawn as accurately as possible EXCEPT when it is stated in a specific problem that the figure is not drawn to scale. All figures lie in a plane unless otherwise indicated.
4. Unless otherwise specified, the domain of any function f is assumed to be the set of all real numbers x for which $f(x)$ is a real number.

Reference Information

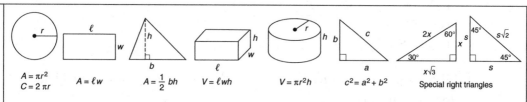

$A = \pi r^2$
$C = 2\pi r$

$A = \ell w$

$A = \frac{1}{2} bh$

$V = \ell wh$

$V = \pi r^2 h$

$c^2 = a^2 + b^2$

Special right triangles

The number of degrees of arc in a circle is 360.
The sum of the measures in degrees of the angles of a triangle is 180.

1. If $\dfrac{k}{4}$, $\dfrac{k}{6}$, and $\dfrac{k}{7}$ are all integers, then k must be divisible by

 (A) 24
 (B) 28
 (C) 35
 (D) 42
 (E) 84

2.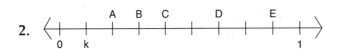

On the number line above, there are nine equally spaced intervals between 0 and 1. Which of the following represents the result of $\dfrac{k^{\frac{1}{6}}}{\left(k^{\frac{1}{6}}\right)^{-2}}$?

(A) A
(B) B
(C) C
(D) D
(E) E

3. If $a^9 = 629$ and $a^8 = 17b$, what is the value of $2ab$?

(A) 9
(B) 27
(C) 34
(D) 74
(E) 148

4. If p is a positive integer, then $(5 \times 10^{-2p}) + (1 \times 10^{-2p})$ must equal which of the following?

(A) $\dfrac{6}{10^{4p}}$

(B) $\dfrac{6}{10^{2p}}$

(C) $\dfrac{5}{10^{2p}}$

(D) $\dfrac{5}{10}$

(E) $\dfrac{5}{10^{4p}}$

5.

On the number line above, there are nine equal intervals between 0 and 1. What is the value of k?

6.

End of nth Month	Total Number of Jars Produced
End of 1st Month	410
End of 2nd Month	780
End of 3rd Month	870
End of 4th Month	1230
End of 5th Month	1400
End of 6th Month	1690

The table above shows the total number of jars of honey that were produced by the end of each of the first 6 months of honey-making season. How many jars of honey were produced during the 4th month of production?

7.

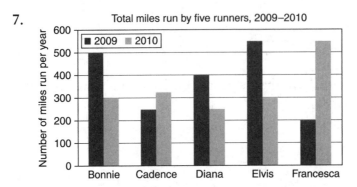

Total miles run by five runners, 2009–2010

According to the graph above, which runner had the greatest decrease in the number of miles run from 2009 to 2010?

(A) Bonnie
(B) Cadence
(C) Diana
(D) Elvis
(E) Francesca

8. There are 32 blouses on a rack at Henrietta's Department Store. Each blouse has a leopard print only, a zebra print only, or both a leopard print and a zebra print. If 17 of the blouses have a leopard print, and 27 of the blouses have a zebra print, how many blouses have both a leopard print and a zebra print?

9. Set $A = \{3, 5, 7, 11, 19, 31\}$

Set $B = \{4, 5, 9, 11, 31\}$

Set A and B are shown above. How many numbers in set A are also in set B?

(A) 0
(B) 2
(C) 3
(D) 5
(E) 11

10. If all cats in the Sheba Pet Club weigh less than 10 pounds, which of the following statements must be true?

   (A) No cat more than 10 pounds is a member of the Sheba Pet Club.
   (B) All cats over 10 pounds are members of the Sheba Pet Club.
   (C) All cats who are not members of the Sheba Pet Club are less than 10 pounds.
   (D) Every member of the Sheba Pet Club less than 10 pounds is a cat.
   (E) There is only one cat less than 10 pounds in the Sheba Pet Club.

11. In Iowa State, a law requires that blood donors weigh between 90 pounds and 210 pounds. If w represents a person's weight in pounds, which of the following inequalities can be used to determine whether a person in Iowa meets the regulations for donating blood?

   (A) $|w-150|<10$

   (B) $|w-60|<150$

   (C) $|w-10|<150$

   (D) $|w-150|<60$

   (E) $|w-10|<80$

12. If $|2x-15|=|x|$ and $x \neq 15$, then $x =$?

13. If $7<|2x-5|<9$ and x is negative, what is one possible value of $|x|$?

14. $|x+3|=10$

$|y-6|=7$

In the equations above, $x<0$ and $y<0$. What is the value of $x-y$?

(A) 0
(B) 6
(C) 8
(D) 20
(E) −14

15. Let $\overset{w}{\underset{y}{\cup}}x$ be defined as $\overset{w}{\underset{y}{\cup}}x = w^x + x^y$ for all positive integers w, x, and y. What is the value of $\overset{w}{\underset{y}{\cup}}5$?

16. Let the operations Φ and $\text{\textwhitehandle}$ be defined for all real numbers f and g as follows.

$f \Phi g = 2f - 3g$

$f \text{\textwhitehandle} g = 2f + g$

If $(3m)\Phi(2)=(4m)\,\text{\textwhitehandle}\,(-7)$, what is the value of m?

17. Let $\supseteq g$ be defined as $\dfrac{g^2}{4}+g$ for all negative integers, g. If $\supseteq g = h$, and h is a negative integer, which of the following is a possible value for h?

(A) −1
(B) −2
(C) −3
(D) −4
(E) −5

18. If a, b, c, and d are positive numbers satisfying $a^{\frac{1}{2}} = c^{-2}$ and $b^{-\frac{1}{2}} = d^2$, what is $(ab)^{\frac{1}{2}}$ in terms of c and d?

    (A) $\dfrac{1}{c^2 d^2}$

    (B) $\dfrac{c^2}{d^2}$

    (C) $\dfrac{d^2}{c^2}$

    (D) $c^2 d^2$

    (E) 1

19. If $b > 4$, the equation $\sqrt{b+16} = b - 4$ is equivalent to which of the following?

    (A) $b = b^2$
    (B) $b = b^2 + 32$
    (C) $b = b^2 - 8b + 16$
    (D) $b = b^2 - 8b$
    (E) $b = b^2 - 8b - 32$

20.

Bonnieville town driver registration data		
	Driving-Age Population	**Number of Registered Drivers**
Men	2,000	
Women	2,500	2,300

The table above gives the driver registration data for the town of Bonnieville at the time an insurance company is looking to revise its rates. According to its policy, the insurance company will raise its rates if the proportion of male drivers to the total driving-age population exceeds 40%. What is the least number of registered male drivers required for the insurance company to raise its rates?

21. If $\left|-5x+7\right|<3$, and x may not be an integer, what is one possible value of x?

22. How many integers between 30 and 40, exclusive, are each the product of exactly two different numbers, both of which are prime?

(A) Five
(B) Four
(C) Three
(D) Two
(E) One

23.

Georgina's Coat Store sales in December			
	Winter Coats	**Spring Coats**	**Total**
Cotton	3,200		7,000
Nylon	2,750		
Total			12,450

Georgina's Coat Store sells both winter and spring coats, each in two types of fabric, cotton and nylon. On the basis of the information in the table above, how many spring coats did Georgina's Coat Store sell in December?

24. Set E consists of all the positive integer multiples of 6 that are less than 50. Set F consists of all the positive integer multiples of 12 that are less than 80. Which of the following is $E \cup F$?

(A) $\{6, 12, 18, 24, 30, 36, 42, 48\}$

(B) $\{3, 6, 9, 12, 18, 36, 48\}$

(C) $\{6, 12, 24, 36, 48, 60)$

(D) $\{6, 12, 18, 24, 30, 36, 42, 48, 60, 72\}$

(E) $\{1, 6, 12, 18, 24, 30, 36, 42, 48, 60, 72\}$

25. For all positive integers j and k, let $j \cap k = \dfrac{jk}{j^2 + k^2}$. If h is a positive integer, what is $2h \cap 3h$?

(A) $\dfrac{5}{6}$

(B) $\dfrac{6}{13}$

(C) $\dfrac{1}{2}$

(D) $\dfrac{6}{5}$

(E) $\dfrac{5}{13}$

chapter 11

Algebra

In this chapter, we will learn techniques for solving a variety of algebra problems on the SAT. We will cover algebraic expressions, algebraic equalities, algebraic inequalities, and systems of equations.

Algebraic Expressions

Algebraic expression problems usually involve a given quantity or quantities that can be manipulated to produce a value for a desired quantity. The trick to solving these problems is usually to rely on your algebraic skills to transform the expressions rather than solve for the values of the particular variables. In many cases, you will not even be given enough information to solve for the variables directly! Let's take a look at 10 typical problems that make use of common transformations.

Examples

1. How old was a person exactly 7 years ago if exactly a years ago the person was b years old?

(A) $a+b+7$
(B) $a-b+7$
(C) $a+b-7$
(D) $a-b-7$
(E) $7-a-b$

The trick to thinking about this problem is understanding what you are being told. We want to know the person's age exactly 7 years ago. But we are being told the person's age exactly a years ago. So think of it like this: $Current\ Age - a = b$. The person's current age is therefore: $Current\ Age = a + b$. The person's age exactly 7 years ago was: $Current\ Age - 7 = a + b - 7$. The correct answer choice is C.

2.   Meredith just purchased a new cordless vacuum cleaner that requires 16 batteries. At the local electronics store, she finds that batteries only come in packs containing 3 batteries. What is the minimum number of packs of batteries Meredith must purchase to make the vacuum cleaner work?

(A)   2
(B)   3
(C)   4
(D)   5
(E)   6

This is a typical SAT problem. We know that batteries are only sold in packs of 3, and that Meredith needs 16 batteries. Since 3 does not go into 16 evenly, it is impossible for her to buy exactly 16 batteries, so Meredith must overbuy batteries in order to have at least 16. The least amount of packs she needs to purchase is equal to the smallest multiple of three that is greater than 16. That means she needs to buy $3\dfrac{batteries}{pack} \times 6\,packs = 18\ batteries$. The correct answer choice is E.

3.   If $a^3 b = 12$, what is the value of $3 \times \dfrac{a^5}{b} \times \dfrac{b^2}{a^2}$?

(A)   6
(B)   12
(C)   24
(D)   36
(E)   48

A poor test-taker is going to start out trying to solve for a or b. A good test-taker, however, will notice that it takes two different equations to solve for the exact values of two variables. In this problem, the trick to is to simplify the desired quantity first: $3 \times \dfrac{a^5}{b} \times \dfrac{b^2}{a^2} \Rightarrow 3 \times \dfrac{a^5}{a^2} \times \dfrac{b^2}{b} \Rightarrow 3 \times a^3 \times b \Rightarrow 3 \times a^3 b$. It's clear that we do not even need to know what a and b are equal to separately. We can simply substitute to get: $3 \times 12 = 36$. The correct answer choice is D.

4. A contracting company needs to clear 90 tons of rubble from a future building site. Workers have already cleared two-thirds of the rubble using a machine. If the machine can remove x tons of rubble every y minutes, and the machine costs z dollars per hour to run, then in terms of x, y, and z, how much will it cost to remove the rest of the rubble?

(A) $\dfrac{2z}{xy}$

(B) $\dfrac{yz}{2x}$

(C) $2xyz$

(D) $\dfrac{yx}{2z}$

(E) $\dfrac{2y}{xz}$

It's way too confusing to solve these types of problems in terms of the variables first. Instead, think of some simple numbers, and analyze what you would do with them intuitively. For example, think of the problem this way: There are 90 tons of rubbles to start. Two-thirds has been removed. That means there are 30 tons left to be removed. The machine removes 10 tons of rubble every 5 minutes, and the machine costs $80 per hour to run. We want to know how much it will cost to remove the remaining 30 tons of rubble. Intuitively, you would compute $\dfrac{30}{10} = 3$ to get the number of 5-minute intervals it will take to remove the rubble. It will take 15 minutes to remove the rubble. Then you would calculate $15 \times \dfrac{1}{60} = \dfrac{1}{4} \times 80 = \$20$ to get the cost of using the machine for 15 minutes. Now go back into the original variables. You would compute: $\dfrac{30}{x} \times y \times \dfrac{1}{60} \times z \Rightarrow \dfrac{30yz}{60x} \Rightarrow \dfrac{yz}{2x}$. The correct answer choice is B.

5. If $x + \dfrac{1}{x} = 10$, what is the value of $\dfrac{x^4 + 1}{x^2}$?

You have two options to solve this problem. It is possible to directly solve the given equation for x, and then plug that value into the desired algebraic expression. But on the SAT, that's a really bad idea. Solving the given equation would require you to first transform it into a quadratic equation, and then solve the quadratic via the quadratic equation. Way too much work for an SAT problem!

Instead, the trick is almost always the same. Square both sides of the given equation:

$$\left(x+\frac{1}{x}\right)^2=10^2 \Rightarrow \left(x+\frac{1}{x}\right)\left(x+\frac{1}{x}\right)=100 \xrightarrow{FOIL} x^2+1+1+\frac{1}{x^2}=100 \Rightarrow x^2+\frac{1}{x^2}=98.$$

The expression we are looking for, $\frac{x^4+1}{x^2}$, can be simplified to $x^2+\frac{1}{x^2}$ by dividing the denominator x^2 into each piece in the numerator. Once simplified, the expression is equivalent to what we got after we squared both sides of the equation and solved. The correct answer is 98.

6.   A particular gym gets members to join by offering the following pricing deal. The first year costs a dollars, and each year thereafter costs b dollars more than the first. For example, the second year costs $a + b$ dollars. How much can a customer expect to pay when purchasing a membership lasting w years?

(A) $a+(w-1)(a+b)$

(B) $a+w(a+b)$

(C) $(a-w)+w(a+b)$

(D) $\dfrac{a+(a+b)}{w}$

(E) $\dfrac{a}{w}+w(a+b)$

Most students are going to pick choice B because it appears to make immediate sense. The first year costs a dollars, and every year thereafter costs $a+b$ dollars. So the cost of w years should be $a+w(a+b)$. But this is incorrect. You need to take the cost of the first year into account. That means that the person will only be paying $a+b$ dollars for $w-1$ years, since the first year is set at a dollars. The cost over w years is therefore: $a+(w-1)(a+b)$. The correct choice is A.

7.   Which of the following is not equivalent to $9s^2+12s+4$?

(A) $9\left(s^2+\dfrac{4}{3}s+\dfrac{4}{9}\right)$

(B) $(3s+2)^2$

(C) $9\left(s+\dfrac{2}{3}\right)^2$

(D) $9(s+6)(s-2)$

(E) $36\left(\dfrac{1}{4}s^2+\dfrac{1}{3}s+\dfrac{1}{9}\right)$

You have two options here. The first is to distribute or multiply out each choice to see if you can reformulate it into the given expression. But that's time-consuming to do first. The easiest way is to eliminate as many choices as possible by plugging in an easy number. If we plug in $s = 0$ into $9s^2 + 12s + 4$, we get 4. Now plug $s = 0$ into each of the choices. Plugging into choice A, we get $9\left(\dfrac{4}{9}\right) = 4$, which is the same as the original. This means that for $s = 0$, the given expression and the expression in choice A are the same. It doesn't mean that they are always the same for all values of s. Plugging in an easy number can only show us which choices are not the same as the original if they yield an output other than 4. Plugging into B, we get $(2)^2 = 4$. In choice C, we get $9\left(\dfrac{2}{3}\right)^2 = 9\left(\dfrac{4}{9}\right) = 4$. In choice E, we get $36\left(\dfrac{1}{9}\right) = 4$. But in choice D, we get $9(6)(-2) = -108 \ne 4$. The only choice that does not output 4 is choice D. If two expressions are truly equivalent, then they give the same output for all possible inputs. The correct choice is D.

8. Both a and b are positive numbers. If $\dfrac{ab}{2} = \dfrac{x+a}{5-x}$, what is the value of x in terms of a and b?

(A) $5ab - 2a$

(B) $\dfrac{5ab - 2a}{2 + ab}$

(C) $\dfrac{2 - ab}{5ab + 2a}$

(D) $\dfrac{4ab - 2a}{2}$

(E) $\dfrac{5}{2}ab - a$

Plugging in is definitely a bad idea here because there are too many choices to consider. The best approach is to solve for x directly. Generally, when you need to solve for a variable that appears in both the numerator and denominator of a fraction, the only way to get the variable alone is to cross-multiply to remove the fractions, factor, and divide. For example: $\dfrac{ab}{2} = \dfrac{x+a}{5-x} \Rightarrow ab(5-x) = 2(x+a) \Rightarrow 5ab - abx = 2x + 2a \Rightarrow 2x + abx = 5ab - 2a \Rightarrow (2+ab)$. The correct answer choice is B.

9. As part of her final project for fashion class, Betsy has to make several dresses. The hem along the bottom of a dress requires three strips of fabric, each measuring 4 inches long. If Betsy had a 500-foot roll of fabric when she started and no fabric was wasted, which of the following represents the number of feet of fabric left on the roll after she made d dresses?

(A) $500 - 3d$

(B) $500 - 4d$

(C) $500 - 12d$

(D) $500 - d$

(E) $500 - \dfrac{1}{4}d$

First, let's identify the important parts of the problem. Betsy is making dresses. Each dress uses three 4-inch strips of fabric. She has 500 feet of fabric. We want to know how much fabric remains after making d dresses. The final solution must be in units of feet. Since 12 inches = 1 foot, and three 4-inch strips equal 12 inches, we know that each dress uses 1 foot of fabric. If she makes d dresses, then she uses $1 \times d = d$ feet of the 500-foot roll. The amount of fabric that remains must be equal to $500 - d$ feet. The correct choice is D.

10. If $a^2b = 25$ and $a + b^3 = 15$, then $a^3b + a^2b^4 = ?$

(A)   10

(B)   40

(C)   80

(D)   375

(E)   750

Just like in example problems 3 and 5 in this section, the trick is to *not* solve for the exact values of the variables. Instead, try to decipher the relationship between the given expressions and the desired quantity. We are given that $a^2b = 25$ and $a + b^3 = 15$ and we want to know what $a^3b + a^2b^4$ equals. The quantity we want looks "bigger," at least in terms of powers, than the two known quantities, which look "smaller." If we multiply the two known quantities, we can make their combined powers "bigger": $a^2b(a + b^3) = a^3b + a^2b^4$. The product happens to be exactly the quantity we are looking for, which will usually be the case on the SAT. To get the final answer, multiply 25×15 to get 375. The correct choice is D.

Algebraic Equalities

Algebraic equality problems usually involve an equation that needs to be solved or formulated. In word problems, you need to create the equality yourself by parsing the word forms into algebraic forms. Like most problems on the SAT, there are a few kinds that appear more often than others. Let's build some strategies as we go through the following problems together.

Examples

1. If $a \neq 2$ and $\dfrac{x}{5} = \dfrac{2-a}{3a-6}$, what is the value of x?

(A) -15

(B) -5

(C) $-\dfrac{5}{3}$

(D) $\dfrac{5}{3}$

(E) $\dfrac{10}{3}$

Our goal is to solve for x. The problem is that we have one equation containing two variables. It's not possible to solve for the value of x if we have more variables than we do equations. But if the question is asking for x, it must be possible. The first thing you should think in a case like this one is that the unwanted variable is going to somehow cancel out. Try factoring: $\dfrac{x}{5} = \dfrac{2-a}{3a-6} \Rightarrow \dfrac{x}{5} = \dfrac{2-a}{-3(2-a)}$. Once you factor the -3 out of the denominator, you can cancel the $2-a$ in the numerator with the $2-a$ in the denominator. We get: $\dfrac{x}{5} = \dfrac{1}{-3}$. Selectively cross-multiply the 5 up to the numerator on the right-hand side to solve for x: $\dfrac{x}{1} = \dfrac{5}{-3} \Rightarrow x = -\dfrac{5}{3}$. The correct answer choice is C.

2. If $3660 = 60(x + 1)$, then $x =$

(A) 10

(B) 36

(C) 60

(D) 61

(E) 360

The fastest way to solve for x here is to go with the algebra. No tricks! You could distribute the 60 to the $x+1$ first, but if we're looking for x, that will add two unnecessary algebraic steps. The best bet is to divide by the 60 on both sides first: $\dfrac{3660}{60}=x+1 \Rightarrow 61=x+1 \Rightarrow 60=x$. The correct choice is C.

3. "The sum of $4x$ and the square root of $9y$ is equal to the square root of the sum of $4x$ and $9y$." Which of the following is an expression for the statement in quotes?

(A) $\sqrt{4x+9y}=2x+3y$

(B) $4x+3\sqrt{y}=\sqrt{4x+9y}$

(C) $4x+3\sqrt{y}=2x+3y$

(D) $4x+\sqrt{9y}=(4x+9y)^2$

(E) $4x+\sqrt{9y}=2x+3y$

We need to translate the verbal expression into an algebraic expression. Take it one step at a time. First, deal with the part before the "is." "The sum of $4x$ and the square root of $9y$" means $4x+\sqrt{9y}$. We can simplify the $\sqrt{9y}$ to $3\sqrt{y}$ since 9 is a perfect square. The left-hand side is therefore $4x+3\sqrt{y}$. We cannot eliminate choices D and E yet because they happen to be equivalent to our simplified version. But choice A is out. "The square root of the sum of $4x$ and $9y$" translates to $\sqrt{4x+9y}$. We can *never* distribute a square root over an addition sign or a subtraction sign. You can bet that there is a choice with $2x+3y$ as the right-hand side. But that's the trick choice. The correct choice is B, $4x+3\sqrt{y}=\sqrt{4x+9y}$.

4. Shelby's washing machine is broken. The repair person says it will cost $400 to fix. The local appliance store is selling energy-efficient washing machines that reduce the owner's electric bill by $16 each month. If the new washing machine costs $1200, and Shelby elects to buy it, in how many months will her electric bill savings equal the difference between the price of the new washing machine and the cost of repairing the broken one?

(A) 20

(B) 25

(C) 50

(D) 75

(E) 100

The word problem is a lot to take in. It's always best to take a few extra seconds and give the problem a good read-through the first time. This way you give your brain the time it needs to identify important parts. We are looking for "how many months it will take for her electric bill savings to equal the difference between the price of the new washing machine and the cost of repairing the broken one." Let's start by finding that difference: $1200 − $400 = $800. We know that she will save $16 each month. So we divide $\frac{800}{16} = 50$. It will take 50 months for her to break even. The correct answer choice is C.

5. If $\frac{1}{8m} = \frac{s}{4m}$ and $m \neq 0$, what is the value of s?

(A)   4

(B)   2

(C)   1

(D) $\frac{1}{4}$

(E) $\frac{1}{2}$

Just like the first problem in this section, we have one equation containing two variables. If we want s, we need to find a way to eliminate m. Selectively cross-multiply the m in the denominator on the right-hand side to the numerator of the fraction on the left-hand side. We choose this route so that we can isolate s. For example, $\frac{1}{8m} = \frac{s}{4m} \Rightarrow \frac{4m}{8m} = \frac{s}{1} \Rightarrow \frac{4}{8} = s \Rightarrow \frac{1}{2} = s$. The correct answer choice is E.

Algebraic Inequalities

Algebraic inequalities are much like algebraic equalities. The only difference is that in an inequality, there is a range of possible values. In an equation, there is usually only one possible value. One of the most important skills you will need to solve inequalities on the SAT is to understand how to interpret them. The algebra skills do not change, but thinking in terms of a range of possibilities does. Let's go through a few typical examples together.

Examples

1. If $-4 \le h \le 2$ and $-3 \le k \le 5$, which of the following gives the set of all possible values of hk?

(A) $-4 \le hk \le 5$
(B) $-7 \le hk \le 7$
(C) $10 \le hk \le 12$
(D) $-20 \le hk \le 10$
(E) $-20 \le hk \le 12$

This is a typical SAT problem. Most students will simply multiply the two lower ends and the two higher ends to get the range of possible value for the product hk. But, especially when negatives are involved, the trick is always to multiply *all four* ways. For example: $-4 \times -3 = 12$, $-4 \times 5 = -20$, $2 \times -3 = -6$, and $2 \times 5 = 10$. Once you multiply all four ways, pick the lowest product and the highest product to make the new interval. The correct choice is E.

2.   Wanda is a door-to-door salesperson for a particular cosmetics company. In order to win a salesperson award, Wanda must sell at least $500 worth of cosmetics kits this week. If each kit costs $20 and she has already sold 12 kits, which of the following inequalities could be used to determine k, the number of remaining cosmetics kits Wanda must sell in order to reach her goal?

(A) $500 \ge (12) \cdot 20 - k$
(B) $500 \le (12) \cdot 20 + 20k$
(C) $500 \ge (12) \cdot 20 - 20k$
(D) $500 \le (12) \cdot 20 + k$
(E) $500 \ge (12) \cdot 20 + k$

Let's understand the quantity we're looking for first. The variable k represents the number of remaining kits she needs to sell. Each kit sells for $20. She has already sold 12 kits. That means she earns $(12) \cdot 20 + 20k$ dollars for however many more kits she sells. If she is to win the award, then she must earn at least $500. We can read that in two ways to get a win: 1) $500 is less than the amount she earns, or 2) the amount she earns is greater than $500. Both interpretations work, and way 1 happens to be a choice. The correct choice is B.

3. If $-1 < x < 0$, which of the following statements must be true?

 I. $x > x^3$

 II. $x^2 > x^3$

 III. $x > 8x$

(A)   I only

(B)   II only

(C)   I and II only

(D)   I and III only

(E)   II and III only

The only way to solve this type of problem is go through the choices and test for counterexamples. However, choosing your counterexamples wisely will save time, and it will also allow you to eliminate choices as you go along. For example, we know that $-1 < x < 0$. Pick a sample number like $-\frac{1}{2}$ to test out the choices. For choice I, $-\frac{1}{2} > \left(-\frac{1}{2}\right)^3 \Rightarrow -\frac{1}{2} > -\frac{1}{8}$. That's not true, since $-\frac{1}{2}$ is further from 0 than $-\frac{1}{8}$. So we know choice I doesn't work.

We can cross out choices A, C, and D. It's between B and E. Choice B says II only, and choice E says II and III only. Since both choices contain II, we automatically know that II must work! We don't even need to test it out. So we go right to considering III: $-\frac{1}{2} > 8\left(-\frac{1}{2}\right) \Rightarrow -\frac{1}{2} > -4$. That's definitely true, since $-\frac{1}{2}$ is closer to 0 than -4. Since III works, we know the correct choice must be E.

4. If a, b, c, and d are all positive integers, and $3a = 4b$, $\frac{b}{c} = \frac{6}{7}$, and $\frac{c}{d} = \frac{9}{10}$ are true, which of the following inequalities is true?

(A) $a < d < c < b$

(B) $a < b < c < d$

(C) $b < c < d < a$

(D) $b < d < c < a$

(E) $a < c < b < d$

The first thing we should do is get all the equations out of fraction form. Otherwise, we cannot "see" the relationship between the variables. Keeping the first equation as is, and cross-multiplying the latter two equations, we get: $3a = 4b$, $7b = 6c$, and $10c = 9d$. If you think intuitively, a smaller number needs to multiplied by a larger number to get a larger result.

For example, if you fill a cup with sugar versus with beans, there will be many more grains of sugar than beans because sugar grains are much smaller than beans. Using this logic, we can tell the order of the variables right away. The variable with the greatest coefficient must be smallest, and the variable with the smallest coefficient must be greatest. From $3a = 4b$, we know $b < a$; from $7b = 6c$, we know $b < c$; from $10c = 9d$, we know that $c < d$. Putting that together, we know that b must be the overall smallest, since it is less than a and c (and because $c < d$). We can cross out choices A, B, and E. Since $c < d$, we know choice D is out. The only choice left is C.

5. For which of the following values of x will the value of $2 - 5x$ be greater than 12?

(A) −3
(B) −2
(C) 1
(D) 2
(E) 3

You could set up an inequality to solve for x: $2 - 5x > 12 \Rightarrow -5x > 10 \Rightarrow x < -2$. (Remember to switch the direction of the inequality when you divide by a negative number!) This approach is easy, but it's way too costly timewise. Just plug in the choices, starting with the least value, since the coefficient of x is negative. For example, $2 - 5(-3) = 2 + 15 = 17$. That's greater than 12, so you're done. Stop testing. The correct choice is A.

6. If $|-x| < 5$ and $y^2 \geq 16$, what is the least possible value of $(x - y)^2$?

The trick for solving this type of problem is to think backwards. We are looking for the smallest possible value of a quantity squared. Whenever we square any number, we get a positive result, except when we square 0. The smallest possible number that can come from a square is 0. Since we have $(x - y)^2$, we could only get 0 if $x = y$. Now we go back and see if that's possible. We have $|-x| < 5$ and $y^2 \geq 16$. If $x = 4$, both inequalities work! So $(4 - 4)^2 = (0)^2 = 0$. The correct answer is 0. If we couldn't get x and y to be equal, we would slowly increment to smallest differences greater than 0 if x and y had to be integers, or greatest fractions less than 1 if x and y could be any kind of number. Though it will normally never be that tricky. The 0 trick is almost foolproof.

7. If $4x^2 < (4x)^2$, what value of x makes the statement false?

(A) $-\dfrac{1}{2}$

(B) 0

(C) 1

(D) 4

(E) No value of x makes the statement false

Plug in the choices for this problem. The inequality is too "easy" to solve for x. We're looking to see if one of the choices makes the inequality false. If A throug D work correctly, then E must be the answer. Try the easiest choice first, choice B. $4(0)^2 < (4 \times 0)^2 \implies 0 < 0$. That's false. The correct choice is B.

8. If $10a = 2b = 5c = 3d > 0$, which of the following is true?

(A) $a < b < c < d$

(B) $a < c < d < b$

(C) $b < d < c < a$

(D) $b < c < d < a$

(E) $d < b < c < a$

Just like in example problem 4 in this section, the greater the coefficient of the variable, the less the value of the variable. Always think of the sugar and beans example. Sugar is small, so it will take a lot of sugar grains to fill a cup. Beans are bigger, so it will take less of them to fill a cup. Since a has the greatest coefficient, 10, it must be the smallest, followed by c, d, and then b which is the largest. The correct answer choice is B.

9. If $w = 3$ and $-1 < y < 0$, which of the following has the greatest value?

(A) $5wy$

(B) $5wy^2$

(C) $5wy^6$

(D) $6wy^9$

(E) $6wy^{12}$

The value of w is always 3, and each of the choices is multiplied by the same w, so it doesn't matter what w equals. It will never make one of the choices proportionally larger or smaller than the others. It's a distracter, so we don't have to bother with it. The value of y, on the other hand, matters very much. It's a negative fraction, like $-\dfrac{1}{2}$. We can automatically eliminate choices A and D because the *y* in these choices has an odd power. When you raise a negative number to an odd power, you get a negative number. When you raise a negative number to an even power, you get a positive number. Choices B, C, and E are automatically larger than A and D because they will be positive for any value of *y*. When you raise a fraction that satisfies $-1 < x < 1$, excluding 0, to a power greater than 1, it will always get smaller. Therefore, choices C and E are out because they have higher powers than choice B. The correct choice is B.

10. Latoya is purchasing cans of tuna fish to make sandwiches for her children. Each sandwich requires one can of tuna fish, and cans of tuna are only sold in packages of four. If Latoya has three children, and each will receive one tuna fish sandwich on each of five days, what is the minimum number of packages of tuna fish Latoya must purchase to ensure she has enough tuna to make all of the sandwiches?

There's a lot of extraneous information about tuna fish and sandwiches. All we really need to understand is that 3 children times 1 sandwich each per day for 5 days equals 15 total sandwiches. If tuna fish is sold in packages of 4, the least number of packages Latoya needs to buy is 4, since 4 cans times 4 packages equals 16 total cans, which is at least enough to make the 15 required sandwiches. The correct answer is 4.

Systems of Equations

A system of equations is a set of equations that relates more than one variable. These can be quite difficult to solve when they come up in a math class, but they're usually easier on the SAT because they are designed to work themselves out. Of course, knowing a few tricks of the trade will help make the solving process much quicker. Off to the example problems!

Examples

1. Bonnie ordered $486 worth of soap to sell in Bonnie's Soap Shop. Brand A soap costs $2 per bar, and Brand B soap costs $3 per bar. If Bonnie ordered three times as many bars of Brand A soap as Brand B soap, how many bars of soap did Bonnie order altogether?

The best way to solve word problems involving systems of equations is to set up a "let" statement to organize the information. For example, "let" *a* = the number of Brand A bars and "let" *b* = the number of Brand B bars. Since Bonnie ordered a total of $486 worth of soap, the first equation we can make is: $2a+3b=486$. Since Bonnie ordered three times as many bars of Brand A soap as Brand B soap, the second equation we can make is: $a=3b$.

We want to know the total number of bars of soap Bonnie ordered. That means we need to know the values of a and b, and add them together. Since $a=3b$, we can substitute $3b$ easily into the first equation. We get: $2(3b)+3b=486 \Rightarrow 6b+3b=486 \Rightarrow 9b=486 \Rightarrow b=54$. To get the value of a, substitute $b=54$ into the second equation: $a=3(54) \Rightarrow a=162$. Now $a+b=162+54=216$. The correct answer is 216.

2. If $3x+2z=y$ and $3x+2y+2z=18$, what is the value of y?

(A) 3

(B) 6

(C) 9

(D) 18

(E) It cannot be determined from the information given

When a system of equations problem is not a word problem, we can usually solve it quickly using a special substitution. Here, we want the value of y. That means we need to eliminate x and z. We know that $3x+2z=y$ and $3x+2y+2z=18$. If we rearrange the second equation as $3x+2z+2y=18$, we can see that the first two terms match the first equation exactly. So we substitute: $3x+2z+2y=18 \Rightarrow y+2y=18 \Rightarrow 3y=18 \Rightarrow y=6$. The correct choice is B.

3. If $\dfrac{a}{3}=4b$ and $\dfrac{3}{5b}=4c$, then $ac=$

(A) $\dfrac{12}{5}$

(B) $\dfrac{4}{3}$

(C) $\dfrac{16}{5}$

(D) $\dfrac{9}{5}$

(E) $\dfrac{9}{16}$

This is a typical system of equations problem. The trick you should notice is that there are three variables, but only two equations. That means it is impossible to solve for the exact value of each variable. The number of variables must always equal the number of equations. When we cannot solve for the value of each variable, the trick is usually to multiply or divide the two equations. In other words, multiply or divide the right-hand sides and multiply or divide the left-hand sides. You can also multiply the left-hand side with the right-hand side of the other and vice versa. We want ac in this example, so we should multiply the opposite sides as follows: $\frac{a}{3} = 4b$ and $\frac{3}{5b} = 4c \Rightarrow \frac{a}{3} \times 4c = 4b \times \frac{3}{5b} \Rightarrow \frac{4ac}{3} = \frac{12b}{5b}$ $\xrightarrow{Cancel\ the\ b!} \frac{4ac}{3} = \frac{12}{5} \Rightarrow ac = \frac{12}{5} \times \frac{3}{4} \Rightarrow ac = \frac{9}{5}$. The correct choice is D.

4. At Luis's bookstore, the price of a new book is six times the price of a used book. The difference between the two prices is $11. What would be the total price of two new books and three used books?

(A) $26.40
(B) $28.60
(C) $30.80
(D) $33.00
(E) $44.00

Just like in the first problem in this section, we should make a let statement to organize the data. Let and. Since the price of a new book is 6 times the price of a used book, we know that $n = 6u$. Since the difference between the two prices is $11, we know that $n - u = 11$. We choose $n - u = 11$ over $u - n = 11$ because we know that new books are more expensive than used books, and we want to get a positive difference. We want to know the total price of two new books and three used books: $2n + 3u$. Solve for each variable by substitution. Since $n = 6u$, substitute $6u$ into the second equation to get $6u - u = 11 \Rightarrow 5u = 11 \Rightarrow u = 2.20$. To find the value of n, plug $u = 2.20$ into $n = 6u$ to get $n = 6(2.20) \Rightarrow n = 13.20$. Finally, $2n + 3u = 2(13.20) + 3(2.20) = 26.40 + 6.60 = 33.00$. The correct answer choice is D.

5. If $x^2 - y^2 = 45$ and $x + y = 9$, what is the value of x?

You can definitely expect to see a problem like this one on the SAT. It's difficult to solve if you do not know the trick. It's easy if you do. Step 1: Factor the difference of perfect squares equation to get $x^2 - y^2 = 45 \Rightarrow (x+y)(x-y) = 45$. Step 2: Substitute the known quantity, $x + y = 9$, into the factored equation from the first step and solve to $9(x - y) = 45 \Rightarrow x - y = 5$. Step 3: Add the two linear equations, $x + y = 9$ and $x - y = 5$, to get $x + y + x - y = 9 + 5 \Rightarrow 2x = 14 \Rightarrow x = 7$. The correct answer is 7. This process is foolproof.

The Formulas You're Not Given That You Ought to Know

Arithmetic Operations

$$ab + ac = a(b + c) \qquad a\left(\dfrac{b}{c}\right) = \dfrac{ab}{c}$$

$$\dfrac{\left(\dfrac{a}{b}\right)}{c} = \dfrac{a}{bc} \qquad \dfrac{a}{\left(\dfrac{b}{c}\right)} = \dfrac{ac}{b}$$

$$\dfrac{a}{b} + \dfrac{c}{d} = \dfrac{ad + bc}{bd} \qquad \dfrac{a}{b} - \dfrac{c}{d} = \dfrac{ad - bc}{bd}$$

$$\dfrac{a-b}{c-d} = \dfrac{b-a}{d-c} \qquad \dfrac{a+b}{c} = \dfrac{a}{c} + \dfrac{b}{c}$$

$$\dfrac{ab + ac}{a} = b + c,\ a \neq 0 \qquad \dfrac{\left(\dfrac{a}{b}\right)}{\left(\dfrac{c}{d}\right)} = \dfrac{ad}{bc}$$

Distance Formula

If $P_1 = (x_1, y_1)$ and $P_2 = (x_2, y_2)$ are two points the distance between them is

$$d(P_1, P_2) = \sqrt{(x_2 - x_1)^2 + (y_2 - y_1)^2}$$

Constant Function

$$y = a \text{ or } f(x) = a$$

Graph is a horizontal line passing though the point $(0, a)$.

Factoring Formulas

$$x^2 - a^2 = (x + a)(x - a)$$
$$x^2 + 2ax + a^2 = (x + a)^2$$
$$x^2 - 2ax + a^2 = (x - a)^2$$

Exponent Rules

$$a^n a^m = a^{n+m} \qquad \dfrac{a^n}{a^m} = a^{n-m} = \dfrac{1}{a^{m-n}}$$

$$(a^n)^m = a^{nm} \qquad a^0 = 1,\ a \neq 0$$

$$(ab)^n = a^n b^n \qquad \left(\dfrac{a}{b}\right)^n = \dfrac{a^n}{b^n}$$

$$a^{-n} = \dfrac{1}{a^n} \qquad \dfrac{1}{a^{-n}} = a^n$$

$$\left(\dfrac{a}{b}\right)^{-n} = \left(\dfrac{b}{a}\right)^n = \dfrac{b^n}{a^n} \qquad a^{\frac{n}{m}} = \left(a^{\frac{1}{m}}\right)^n = (a^n)^{\frac{1}{m}}$$

Linear Functions

$$y = mx + b \text{ or } f(x) = mx + b$$

Graph is a line with point $(0, b)$ and slope m.

Slope

Slope of the line containing the two points (x_1, y_1) and (x_2, y_2) is

$$m = \dfrac{y_2 - y_1}{x_2 - x_1} = \dfrac{\text{rise}}{\text{run}}$$

Slope–Intercept Form

The equation of the line with slope m and y-intercept $(0, b)$ is

$$y = mx + b$$

Point–Slope Form

The equation of the line with slope m and passing through the point (x_1, y_1) is

$$y - y_1 = m(x - x_1)$$

Common Mistakes You Need to Avoid

Error	Correction
$\dfrac{3}{0} \neq 0$ and $\dfrac{3}{0} \neq 3$	You can never divide by 0. Division by 0 is undefined.
$-4^2 \neq 16$	$-4^2 = -16$ and $(-4)^2 = 16$. Be careful how you use parentheses.
$(x^3)^4 \neq x^7$	$(x^3)^4 = x^{12}$. Raising a power to a power means you have to multiply, not add.
$\dfrac{x}{y+z} \neq \dfrac{x}{y} + \dfrac{x}{z}$	$\dfrac{3}{4} = \dfrac{3}{3+1} \neq \dfrac{3}{3} + \dfrac{3}{1} = 1 + 3 = 4$. You can only divide monomials (not binomials) into a numerator.
$\dfrac{x+cy}{x} \neq 1 + cy$	$\dfrac{x+cy}{x} = 1 + \dfrac{cy}{x}$. If you divide a monomial into one piece of the numerator, you need to divide it into all the pieces.
$-b(y-1) \neq -by - b$	$-b(y-1) = -by + b$. Make sure you distribute to each piece inside the parentheses.
$(x+m)^2 \neq x^2 + m^2$	$(x+m)^2 = (x+m)(x+m) = x^2 + 2xm + m^2$. When raising a binomial to a power, make sure you FOIL! You may never "distribute" a power over a + or a − sign.

Chapter 11 Quiz—Algebra
25 Questions

Directions: For this quiz, solve each problem and decide which is the best of the choices given. For Student-Produced Response questions, solve each problem and record your solution.

<table>
<tr><td rowspan="4">Notes</td><td>

1. The use of a calculator is permitted.
2. All numbers used are real numbers.
3. Figures that accompany problems in this test are intended to provide information useful in solving the problems. They are drawn as accurately as possible EXCEPT when it is stated in a specific problem that the figure is not drawn to scale. All figures lie in a plane unless otherwise indicated.
4. Unless otherwise specified, the domain of any function f is assumed to be the set of all real numbers x for which $f(x)$ is a real number.

</td></tr>
</table>

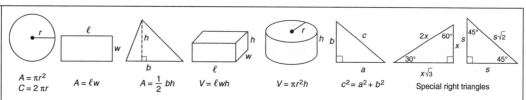

$A = \pi r^2$
$C = 2\pi r$ $A = \ell w$ $A = \frac{1}{2} bh$ $V = \ell w h$ $V = \pi r^2 h$ $c^2 = a^2 + b^2$ Special right triangles

The number of degrees of arc in a circle is 360.
The sum of the measures in degrees of the angles of a triangle is 180.

1. When Bonnie walked into Henrietta's Floral Shop, she decided to purchase several flower delivery subscriptions so that her home would always be decorated with the best floral arrangements. She purchased three subscriptions that deliver flowers once each month, three subscriptions that deliver flowers once every 6 months, and one subscription that delivers flowers once each day. Excluding leap years, how many flowers should Bonnie expect to receive in one full year?

2. To purchase a wedding gift that costs v dollars for one of the teachers at a school, x coworkers agreed to split the cost equally. On the day some of the teachers were collecting the money for the gift, w coworkers were not present. The teachers that were present each contributed equal, additional funds to cover the total cost of the gift. What is the additional amount, in terms of v, w, and x that each of the present teachers had to contribute to pay for the wedding gift?

   (A) $\dfrac{v}{x-w}$

   (B) $\dfrac{v}{x}$

   (C) $\dfrac{vw}{x(x-w)}$

   (D) $\dfrac{v-w}{x}$

   (E) $\dfrac{x-w}{vw}$

3. If $2y+3z=b$, then $6y+9z=$

   (A) $b-6$
   (B) $b+3$
   (C) $3b-3$
   (D) $3b$
   (E) $3b+3$

4. The sum of two consecutive even integers is y. In terms of y, what is the value of the greater of the two numbers?

   (A) $\dfrac{y}{2}+1$

   (B) $\dfrac{y}{2}$

   (C) $\dfrac{y}{2}-1$

   (D) $\dfrac{y}{2}-2$

   (E) $\dfrac{y}{2}+2$

5. If $4x + 16 = 28$, then $x + 4 =$

    (A) 2
    (B) 3
    (C) 4
    (D) 7
    (E) 14

6. If candy bars cost \$2 each and lollipops cost \$4 each, which of the following represents the cost, in dollars, of x candy bars and y lollipops?

    (A) $6(x+y)$
    (B) $2(x+2y)$
    (C) $6xy$
    (D) $2x+2y$
    (E) $3(x+y)$

7. At a local restaurant, the deluxe chicken nuggets meal contains 12 more nuggets than a regular chicken nuggets meal. If a regular chicken nuggets meal contains n nuggets, how many nuggets do 7 deluxe meals contain?

    (A) $7n+84$
    (B) $7n+12$
    (C) $7(n+84)$
    (D) $12(n+7)$
    (E) $12n+84$

8. Sheba works at a pet store, and she gets paid d dollars per day. Sheba must spend a total of $\dfrac{d}{6}$ dollars each day on travel to and from the pet store. If she saves the rest of her earnings, in terms of d, how long will it take Sheba to save \$2500?

    (A) $\dfrac{3000}{d}$

    (B) $\dfrac{2500}{d}$

    (C) $\dfrac{d}{3000}$

    (D) $3000d$

    (E) $\dfrac{d}{2500}$

9. If $ab = 72$ and $b = \dfrac{3}{4}$, what is the value of $\dfrac{5}{6}a$?

10. Six less than three times a number is equal to 12. What is the number?

11. If $(5x)y = 45$, then $xy =$

(A) 3
(B) 5
(C) 7
(D) 9
(E) 15

12. If $\dfrac{6}{x} = \dfrac{y}{12}$, what is the value of $(xy)^{-1}$?

13. "The sum of $2w$ and w^2 is equal to the product of w and $\dfrac{4}{9}$." Which of the following expressions gives the relationship written in quotes?

(A) $2w^3 = w + \dfrac{4}{9}$

(B) $3w^3 = \dfrac{4}{9}w$

(C) $2w^3 = \dfrac{4}{9}w$

(D) $2w + w^2 = w + \dfrac{4}{9}$

(E) $w(2 + w) = \dfrac{4}{9}w$

14. If $\dfrac{5 + \odot}{3} = 2\dfrac{2}{3}$, what number, when used in place of $\odot$, makes the statement true?

(A) -1
(B) 1
(C) 3
(D) 5
(E) 8

15. Sheba is younger than Bonnie but older than Clyde. If s, b, and c represent the ages of Sheba, Bonnie, and Clyde, respectively, which of the following is true?

(A) $s < b < c$
(B) $s < c < b$
(C) $c < b < s$
(D) $c < s < b$
(E) $b < s < c$

16. If $5x < 2y < 0$, which of the following is greatest?

(A) $-5x$
(B) $-2y$
(C) $-5x - 2y$
(D) 0
(E) $2y$

17. If $a+b=25$ and $b>5$, then which of the following must be true?

   (A) $a>20$
   (B) $a=20$
   (C) $a<20$
   (D) $a>0$
   (E) $b>20$

18. If $x>x^3>x^2$, then which of the following must be true?

   (A) $x<0$
   (B) $x>0$
   (C) $-1<x<0$
   (D) $0<x<1$
   (E) x is not a real number

19. The month of June has 30 days. In that month, Sheba had 5 days on which she had chores for every 1 day on which she did not have chores. For the month of June, the number of days on which Sheba had chores was how much greater than the number of days on which she did not have chores?

20. There are 24 floors in an apartment building. If each floor has at least 6 apartments but no more than 12 apartments, which of the following could not be the number of apartments in this building?

   (A) 144
   (B) 145
   (C) 216
   (D) 288
   (E) 289

21. If $ab = c$, $db = c$, and $bc \neq c$, which of the following is equal to d?

    (A) a
    (B) 1
    (C) $\dfrac{1}{a}$
    (D) $a - 1$
    (E) $1 - a$

22. If $3x - 6y = 12$ and $x + 3y = 15$, what is the value of $2x - 9y$?

    (A) 27
    (B) 3
    (C) $\dfrac{4}{5}$
    (D) -3
    (E) -6

23. A scale at a local grocery store only registers weights that are greater than 7 ounces. Sheba wanted to know the weights, in ounces, of three types of fruit. She weighed the fruits in pairs and got the following results.

    The banana and the apple weighed 9 ounces.
    The cantaloupe and the apple weighed 11 ounces.
    The banana and the cantaloupe weighed 10 ounces.

    What was the weight of the apple?

    (A) 4 ounces
    (B) 5 ounces
    (C) 6 ounces
    (D) 7 ounces
    (E) 8 ounces

24. ABC
      $+ \underline{CAB}$
      769

In the correctly solved addition problem above, the letters A, B, and C represent different digits. What is the value of $A+B+C$?

25. If x is $\dfrac{7}{2}$ of y, y is $\dfrac{3}{14}$ of z, and $z>0$, then x is what fraction of z?

12

Central Tendency, Sequences, and Probability

In this chapter, we will learn techniques for solving a variety of problems on the SAT. We will cover central tendency concepts such as mean, mode, median, and range, basic probability, and rules for solving sequences.

Mean

The mean (arithmetic mean or average) is the sum of the data in a frequency distribution divided by the number of data elements.

$$\text{mean} = \frac{\text{sum of data}}{\text{number of data elements}} = \frac{d_1 + d_2 + \ldots + d_n}{n}$$

The mode is the most frequently occurring value in a frequency distribution.

The range is the difference between the highest and the lowest values in a frequency distribution.

The best way to get better at solving central tendency problems is through practice. Let's work through a few example problems together.

Examples

1. Juanita purchased x donuts on Friday, 5 times as many donuts on Saturday as on Friday, and 6 less than 3 times as many donuts on Sunday as on Friday. What is the average (arithmetic mean) number of donuts Juanita purchased per day over the 3 days?

(A) $3x - 1$
(B) $3x - 2$
(C) $3x - 6$
(D) $3x + 2$
(E) $9x - 2$

As in any word problem, the first step is to organize the data. We know that Friday = x donuts, Saturday = $5x$ donuts, and Sunday = $3x - 6$ donuts. We want the mean number of donuts, so we add $x + 5x + 3x - 6 \Rightarrow 9x - 6$ and divide by 3 (three days) to get $\dfrac{9x - 6}{3} \Rightarrow 3x - 2$. Make sure you divide each term in the numerator by the 3 in the denominator. The correct answer choice is B.

2. If the average of m, $3m$, and $2m$ is 24, what is the value of m?

(A) 2
(B) 4
(C) 4.8
(D) 12
(E) 24

This problem can be solved directly by using the formula for arithmetic mean. For example, $\dfrac{m + 3m + 2m}{3} = 24 \Rightarrow \dfrac{6m}{3} = 24 \Rightarrow 2m = 24 \Rightarrow m = 12$. The correct answer choice is D.

3. The area of a square and an isosceles triangle are equal. The height of the isosceles triangle is equal to the length of a side of the square. If the sum of the areas of the square and the isosceles triangle is 15, what is the average (arithmetic mean) of the areas of the two figures?

(A) 0
(B) $\dfrac{15}{2}$
(C) $\dfrac{15}{4}$

(D) 15

(E) 30

This is a trick question! They want you to start setting up formulas for the area of a square and the area of a triangle, and then solve for the individual area of each figure, sum the areas, and finally find the average area. But you're smarter than that. To find an average, in general, all you do is find the sum of the data, and then divide by the number of data. In this problem, you already know the sum of the areas is equal to 15. All you need to do is divide $\frac{15}{2}$ because you have two shapes. The correct answer is B. This is a typical distracter problem. If you're careful, you can beat the trick and get your answer in about 5 seconds.

4. If 65% of the worms in a particular compost pile had an average (arithmetic mean) length of 5 inches, and 35% of the worms in the same compost pile had an average (arithmetic mean) length of 8 inches, what was the average (arithmetic mean) length, in inches, of all of the worms in the compost pile?

(A) 5.60

(B) 5.70

(C) 6.05

(D) 6.40

(E) 6.50

This is called a weighted average problem because we are not told how many worms of each length are in the compost pile. Instead we are told the percentage of worms of each length. Solving a weighted average problem is even easier than solving a regular average problem. Simply convert all percentages into decimal form, multiply them by their respective lengths, and add the results: $.65(5) + .35(8) = 3.25 + 2.8 = 6.05$. The correct answer choice is C.

Median

The median is the value of the middle element when the sample size is odd (or the average value of the two middle elements when the sample size is even) in a frequency distribution. To find the median, the data elements must be in order.

1. The median of a set of 47 consecutive even integers is 104. What is the greatest of these integers?

The last thing you want to do for this problem is write a list of all the integers until you find the greatest among them. Instead, imagine the problem this way. You have 47 integers. They are consecutive and even, like 2, 4, 6, 8, etc. In this case, we know that the median number is 104. Since there are 47 numbers all together, we know that there are 23 numbers less than the median, and 23 numbers greater than the median (23 + 23 + "the median itself" = 47). The greatest number in the list is therefore 23 consecutive even integers above 47. Since even numbers always advance by units of two, simply compute: 104 + 23(2) = 150. The correct answer is 150.

2. The median of a set of five positive integers is 11. If the greatest of these integers is four times the least integer, what is the greatest possible sum of all the numbers in this set?

This problem is only a couple of sentences long, but a lot of information is presented. We need to organize all the data. We know that there are five positive integers, and that the median is 11. The image that should come to mind is: ___, ___, 11, ___, ___. Now we know the greatest of these integers is four times the least integer, so we can add to the first image: x, ___, 11, ___, 4x. We are looking for the greatest possible sum of the five integers. We are not told that the integers need to be different. If we want the greatest sum, then we need to consider the largest possible values for any of the numbers without affecting 11 as the median.

There is no reason that the first two numbers cannot be 11: .11, 11, 11, ___, 4x. If the smallest number is 11, then the greatest number is $4 \times 11 = 44$. There is also no reason that the second largest number cannot also be 44: 11, 11, 11, 44, 44. The sum is 11 + 11 + 11 + 44 + 44 = 121. The correct answer is 121.

3.

Town	Average Springtime Temperature (°F)
Allentown	51°
Bonnietown	21°
Candytown	51°
Dyllantown	50°
Ellentown	33°
Francistown	$t°$
Georginatown	65°

The table above shows the average temperatures for seven towns during the springtime. If the median springtime temperature of the seven towns is 51°F, then the average springtime temperature of Francistown could be any of the following except.

(A)   50°F
(B)   51°F
(C)   55°F
(D)   65°F
(E)   78°F

For this type of problem, go back to the definition of median. A median is simply the middle number in a list of numbers arranges from least to greatest. To determine which of the choices may affect the median, list the temperatures you know first: 21, 33, 50, 51, 51, 65. We want the median to be 51. Go through the choices for *t* to see how the median is affected. For example, if we try choice E, 51 will be the median: 21, 33, 50, 51, 51, 65, 78. If we try choice D, 51 will still be the median: 21, 33, 50, 51, 51, 65, 65. If we try choice C, 51 will again be the median: 21, 33, 50, 51, 51, 55, 65. The only choice that does not produce 51 as the median is choice A: 21, 33, 50, 50, 51, 51, 65. We went through the wrong choices for demonstrative purposes, but you could have known that choice A would work over the other choices because it is the only choice less than the desired median. Choice A is the correct answer.

4. Helga noted that she is both the 14th oldest and 14th youngest applicant in a room of prospective drivers. If everyone in the room is a different age, how many applicants are in the room?

(A)   19
(B)   27
(C)   28
(D)   30
(E)   36

If we imagine all the prospective drivers standing in a line, we picture Helga exactly in the middle, with 13 people behind her (younger), and 13 people ahead of her (older). The total number of applicants is 13 + Helga herself + 13 = 27. The correct answer choice is B.

Sequences

The *n*th or general term of an arithmetic sequence is given by the formula:

$$a_n = a_1 + (n-1)d$$

where a_1 is the first term of the sequence, and *d* is the common difference.

For an arithmetic series, the sum of the first n terms of an arithmetic sequence is given by the formula:

$$S_n = \frac{n}{2}(a_1 + a_n)$$

where a_1 is the first term of the sequence and a_n is the nth term of the sequence.

A geometric sequence, on the other hand, moves from one term to the next by multiplying each progressive term by a common ratio.

More problems on the SAT are geometric than they are arithmetic. Let's take a look at a few typical examples.

1. 72, 12, 2, ...

In the sequence above, each term after the first term is $\frac{1}{6}$ of the term preceding it. What is the fifth term of this sequence?

This is a pretty straightforward problem. Since we are multiplying by a common ratio, $\frac{1}{6}$, to get each progressive term, the sequence is geometric. The first term is 72; the second term is $72 \times \frac{1}{6} = 12$; the third term is $12 \times \frac{1}{6} = 2$; the fourth term is $2 \times \frac{1}{6} = \frac{1}{3}$; and finally the fifth term is $\frac{1}{3} \times \frac{1}{6} = \frac{1}{18}$. The correct answer is $\frac{1}{18}$.

2. Each term in a sequence, except for the first, is equal to the previous term times a positive constant, x. If the fourth term of this sequence is 15 and the seventh term of this sequence is 405, what is the first term?

Once again, the problem suggests that we are dealing with a geometric sequence because we get progressive terms by multiplying by a common ratio, x. All we know is that the fourth term is 15 and that the seventh term is 405. But we want the first term. Set it up this way to get a visual: ?, __, __, 15, __, __, 405. To get the fifth term, we multiply the fourth term, 15, by x: $15x$. The sixth term would be $15x \cdot x = 15x^2$. The seventh term would be $15x^2 \cdot x = 15x^3$. But we know the seventh term is also equal to 405. This is an opportunity to solve for x, the common ratio: $15x^3 = 405 \Rightarrow x^3 = 27 \Rightarrow x = \sqrt[3]{27} \Rightarrow x = 3$. To get future terms, we would multiply by 3, so to get prior terms we divide by 3. If the fourth term is 15, then the third term is $\frac{15}{3} = 5$.

If the third term is 5, then the second term is $\frac{5}{3}$. If the second term is $\frac{5}{3}$, then the first term is $\frac{\frac{5}{3}}{3} = \frac{5}{9}$. The correct answer is $\frac{5}{9}$.

3.   1, –5, –5, ...

In the sequence above, each term after the second can be found by multiplying the two preceding terms together. For example, the third term is 1 × –5 = –5. How many of the first 149 terms of this sequence are negative?

(A)   49
(B)   98
(C)   99
(D)   100
(E)   148

This kind of sequence is neither arithmetic, because we are not adding, nor geometric, because we are not multiplying by a common ratio. The best way to solve this type of "no category" problem is to find a pattern. Each progressive term is found by multiplying the previous two terms. We can easily fill in the next few terms: 1, –5, –5, 25, –125, –3125 .... It's easy to see that the numbers are always going to get bigger, but the sign pattern starts to repeat. The signs are always going to be: +, –, –, +, –, –, +, –, – ···.

For every three terms, we get exactly two negatives. We want to know how many of the first 149 terms are negative, so see how many times three goes into 149 evenly: $\frac{149}{3} = 49\,R2$. That means we have 49 full repeats of +, –, –, which means we have 49 × 2 = 98 negatives. Then we have two terms left over, which follow the same rule: +, –. So we tack on one more negative to get 98 + 1 = 99 negatives. The correct answer is C. This is a very typical SAT problem.

4.   A sequence of numbers is obtained by adding 9 to each number before the next. The first term in the sequence is 4. What is the value of the 21st term?

This is a simple arithmetic sequence problem. It can be cumbersome if you do not know the formula. Otherwise, it's plug and chug. The first term is 4. We are always adding 9, so the common difference is 9. Since we want the 21st term, plug into the formula as follows: $a_{21} = 4 + (21 - 1)9 = 4 + (20)9 = 4 + 180 = 184$. The correct answer is 184.

Probability

Counting principles describe the total number of possibilities or choices for certain selections. The two fundamental counting principles are listed here.

Counting Principle I says: If the number of events is n, and the number of outcomes for each event in an experiment is t_i (such that $i = 1$ for the first event, 2 for the second event, ..., and n for the nth event), then the total number of outcomes for all event is $t_1 \times t_2 \times ... \times t_n$.

Counting Principle II says: If the number of mutually exclusive (no common elements) experiments is m, and the total number of outcomes for all events in each experiment is x_j (such that $j = 1$ for the first experiment, 2 for the second experiment, ..., and m for the mth experiment), then the total number of outcomes for all experiments is $x_1 + x_2 + ... + x_m$.

A permutation is the selection of subsets from a set of elements when the order of the selected elements is a factor, whereas a combination is the selection of subsets from a set of elements when the order of the selected elements is not a factor.

For example, for the three-letter set {R, S, T}, find the two-letter permutations by finding the following subsets:

$$\{R, S\}, \{R, T\}, \{S, R\}, \{S, T\}, \{T, R\}, \text{ and } \{T, S\}$$

Note that {R, S} and {S, R} are distinctive because the order of the elements R and S does matter in permutations.

In addition, for the three-letter set {R, S, T}, find the two-letter combinations by finding all the subsets:

$$\{R, S\}, \{R, T\}, \text{ and } \{S, T\}$$

Note the {R, S} and {S, R} are identical because the order of the elements R and S does not matter in combinations.

Probability problems on the SAT are usually very simple, as you will see in the examples. The trickier ones are really counting principle and combination problems, but once you have the basic drills down, you will do great. The information above may be a little overwhelming. If it is, don't get hung up on it. Just know the tricks explained in the examples below.

Examples

1. There are six roads from Sheldon to Arden and five roads from Arden to Woodrow. If Moesha drives from Sheldon to Woodrow and back, passes through Arden in both directions, and does not travel any road twice, how many different routes are possible for the round trip?

(A) 20
(B) 40
(C) 270
(D) 600
(E) 660

This is a counting principle problem. Once you know the drill, every problem like it will be straightforward. To get the number of routes she can take going from Sheldon to Woodrow, while passing through Arden, organize the possibilities this way: Sheldon $\xrightarrow{6}$ Arden $\xrightarrow{5}$ Woodrow. Going there, she has $6 \times 5 = 30$ possible routes. On the way back, she is not allowed to travel the same road again, so her possible routes looks like: Sheldon $\xleftarrow{5}$ Arden $\xleftarrow{4}$ Woodrow. Coming back, she can travel $5 \times 4 = 20$ possible routes. The total number of possible routes going both ways is therefore $30 \times 20 = 600$. The correct answer choice is D.

2. A jar contains g green marbles and r red marbles. If a marble is picked at random from this jar, the probability that the marble is green is $\frac{5}{6}$. What is the value of $\frac{r}{g}$?

(A) $\frac{1}{11}$

(B) $\frac{1}{5}$

(C) $\frac{3}{5}$

(D) $\frac{6}{5}$

(E) 5

We know that there are g green marbles and r red marbles in the jar. The probability of picking a green marble is $\frac{5}{6}$. The probability of picking a green marble is equal to the total number of green marbles divided by the total number of marbles in the jar: $\frac{g}{r+g}$. Therefore, the number of green marbles must be

$g = 5$ and the total number of marbles must be $r + g = 6$. That leaves one marble left over ($5 + 1 = 6$). Since there are only green and red marbles, the 1 remaining marble must be red. The value of $\dfrac{r}{g}$ is $\dfrac{1}{5}$. The correct answer choice is B.

3. Sheba's Hair Salon will send a team of 4 stylists to work on a bride's hair. The salon has 5 experienced stylists and 6 trainees. If a team consists of 1 experienced stylist and 3 trainees, how many different such teams are possible?

This is a combinations problem. You need to know how to access the combination function on your calculator. It's usually under MATH → PRB → nCr. To find the number of possible teams, you need to find the number of ways Sheba can choose 1 experienced stylist out of 5 experienced stylists, as well as the number of ways she can choose 3 trainees out of 6 trainees. Use the calculator to compute: 5 nCr 1 × 6 nCr 3 ⇒ 5 × 20 = 100. The correct answer is 100.

The Formulas You're Not Given That You Ought to Know

Arithmetic Operations

$$ab + ac = a(b+c)$$

$$a\left(\frac{b}{c}\right) = \frac{ab}{c}$$

$$\frac{\left(\dfrac{a}{b}\right)}{c} = \frac{a}{bc}$$

$$\frac{a}{\left(\dfrac{b}{c}\right)} = \frac{ac}{b}$$

$$\frac{a}{b} + \frac{c}{d} = \frac{ad+bc}{bd}$$

$$\frac{a}{b} - \frac{c}{d} = \frac{ad-bc}{bd}$$

$$\frac{a-b}{c-d} = \frac{b-a}{d-c}$$

$$\frac{a+b}{c} = \frac{a}{c} + \frac{b}{c}$$

$$\frac{ab+ac}{a} = b+c, \; a \neq 0$$

$$\frac{\left(\dfrac{a}{b}\right)}{\left(\dfrac{c}{d}\right)} = \frac{ad}{bc}$$

Exponent Rules

$$a^n a^m = a^{n+m}$$

$$\frac{a^n}{a^m} = a^{n-m} = \frac{1}{a^{m-n}}$$

$$(a^n)^m = a^{nm}$$

$$a^0 = 1, \; a \neq 0$$

$$(ab)^n = a^n b^n$$

$$\left(\frac{a}{b}\right)^n = \frac{a^n}{b^n}$$

$$a^{-n} = \frac{1}{a^n}$$

$$\frac{1}{a^{-n}} = a^n$$

$$\left(\frac{a}{b}\right)^{-n} = \left(\frac{b}{a}\right)^n = \frac{b^n}{a^n}$$

$$a^{\frac{n}{m}} = \left(a^{\frac{1}{m}}\right)^n = (a^n)^{\frac{1}{m}}$$

Distance Formula

If $P_1 = (x_1, y_1)$ and $P_2 = (x_2, y_2)$ are two points the distance between them is

$$d(P_1, P_2) = \sqrt{(x_2 - x_1)^2 + (y_2 - y_1)^2}$$

Constant Function

$$y = a \text{ or } f(x) = a$$

Graph is a horizontal line passing though the point $(0, a)$.

Factoring Formulas

$$x^2 - a^2 = (x+a)(x-a)$$

$$x^2 + 2ax + a^2 = (x+a)^2$$

$$x^2 - 2ax + a^2 = (x-a)^2$$

Linear Functions

$$y = mx + b \text{ or } f(x) = mx + b$$

Graph is a line with point $(0, b)$ and slope m.

Slope

Slope of the line containing the two points (x_1, y_1) and (x_2, y_2) is

$$m = \frac{y_2 - y_1}{x_2 - x_1} = \frac{\text{rise}}{\text{run}}$$

Slope–Intercept Form

The equation of the line with slope m and y-intercept $(0, b)$ is

$$y = mx + b$$

Point–Slope Form

The equation of the line with slope m and passing through the point (x_1, y_1) is

$$y - y_1 = m(x - x_1)$$

Common Mistakes You Need to Avoid

Error	Correction
$\dfrac{3}{0} \neq 0$ and $\dfrac{3}{0} \neq 3$	You can never divide by 0. Division by 0 is undefined.
$-4^2 \neq 16$	$-4^2 = -16$ and $(-4)^2 = 16$. Be careful how you use parentheses.
$(x^3)^4 \neq x^7$	$(x^3)^4 = x^{12}$. Raising a power to a power means you have to multiply, not add.
$\dfrac{x}{y+z} \neq \dfrac{x}{y} + \dfrac{x}{z}$	$\dfrac{3}{4} = \dfrac{3}{3+1} \neq \dfrac{3}{3} + \dfrac{3}{1} = 1 + 3 = 4$. You can only divide monomials (not binomials) into a numerator.
$\dfrac{x+cy}{x} \neq 1 + cy$	$\dfrac{x+cy}{x} = 1 + \dfrac{cy}{x}$. If you divide a monomial into one piece of the numerator, you need to divide it into all the pieces.
$-b(y-1) \neq -by - b$	$-b(y-1) = -by + b$. Make sure you distribute to each piece inside the parentheses.
$(x+m)^2 \neq x^2 + m^2$	$(x+m)^2 = (x+m)(x+m) = x^2 + 2xm + m^2$. When raising a binomial to a power, make sure you FOIL! You may never "distribute" a power over a $+$ or a $-$ sign.

Chapter 12 Quiz—Central Tendency, Sequences, and Probability
25 Questions

Directions: For this quiz, solve each problem and decide which is the best of the choices given. For Student-Produced Response questions, solve each problem and record your solution.

Notes

1. The use of a calculator is permitted.
2. All numbers used are real numbers.
3. Figures that accompany problems in this test are intended to provide information useful in solving the problems. They are drawn as accurately as possible EXCEPT when it is stated in a specific problem that the figure is not drawn to scale. All figures lie in a plane unless otherwise indicated.
4. Unless otherwise specified, the domain of any function f is assumed to be the set of all real numbers x for which $f(x)$ is a real number.

Reference Information

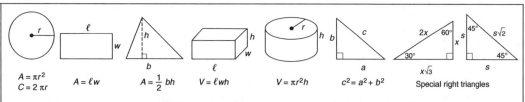

$A = \pi r^2$
$C = 2\pi r$
$A = \ell w$
$A = \frac{1}{2}bh$
$V = \ell wh$
$V = \pi r^2 h$
$c^2 = a^2 + b^2$
Special right triangles

The number of degrees of arc in a circle is 360.
The sum of the measures in degrees of the angles of a triangle is 180.

1. When the sum of the scores on a mathematics test is divided by the average (arithmetic mean) of the scores, the result is z. What does z represent?

   (A) The sum of the scores
   (B) The median of the scores
   (C) Half the average of the scores
   (D) The average score of each test-taker
   (E) The number of tests

2. The first term of a sequence is 16 and the second term is 4. The third term and each term thereafter is the average (arithmetic mean) of the two terms immediately preceding it. What is the value of the first term in the sequence that is not an integer?

3. The average (arithmetic mean) of a and b is $3c$, where $c \neq 0$. What is the average (arithmetic mean) of a, b, and $4c$?

    (A) $\dfrac{4c}{3}$

    (B) $\dfrac{7c}{3}$

    (C) $\dfrac{10c}{3}$

    (D) $4c$

    (E) $6c$

4. The median of a set of seven consecutive even integers is 24. What is the difference between the greatest of these seven integers and the least of these seven integers?

5.

Number of cars owned per driver in the driving club	
Number of Drivers	**Number of Cars Owned**
6	1
3	3
4	5
9	7

The table above shows the current number of drivers in a driving club that own a particular number of cars. Later, a new driver joined the club, and the average (arithmetic mean) number of cars per driver became equal to the median number of cars per driver. How many cars did the new driver own?

(A) 3
(B) 5
(C) 7
(D) 11
(E) 17

6.

Age of Clients at Sheba's Hair Salon	
Age of Clients	Number of Clients
25	23
35	36
45	40
55	40
60	49
65	12

At Sheba's Hair Salon, the clientele consists of 200 men and women of varying ages, as shown in the table above. What is the median age, in years, of the clients at Sheba's Hair Salon?

7. If $3x-8$, $x+2$, and $4x+1$ are all integers and $x+2$ is the median of these integers, which of the following could be a value for x?

(A) 5
(B) 6
(C) 7
(D) 9
(E) 11

8. Let a_n represent the nth term of a particular sequence. If $a_2 = 81$ and each term except the first is equal to the previous term divided by 9, then what is the first term that is not an integer?

   (A) a_4
   (B) a_5
   (C) a_6
   (D) a_7
   (E) a_8

9. 5, 10, 25, 70, 205

   The first number in the list above is 5. Which of the following gives a rule for finding each successive number in the list?

   (A) Add 5 to the preceding number.
   (B) Double the preceding number.
   (C) Double the preceding number and then add half the result.
   (D) Triple the preceding number and then subtract 5 from that result.
   (E) Subtract 5 from the preceding number, multiply the result by 2, and then add 15 to that result.

10. The nth term in a geometric sequence can be expressed as 2.5×4^n. What is the smallest term larger than 640?

11. A bag contains only green marbles, orange marbles, and purple marbles. The probability of randomly selecting a green marble from this bag is $\frac{1}{9}$, and the probability of randomly selecting an orange marble is $\frac{1}{3}$. Which of the following could be the total number of marbles in the bag?

    (A) 3
    (B) 6
    (C) 9
    (D) 12
    (E) 30

12. Exactly four candidates compete for the four student government positions in a school. If each candidate can assume any one role and no one will assume more than one role, how many different assignments of candidates are possible?

13. How many positive three-digit integers have the hundreds digit equal to 7 and the units digit (ones digit) equal to 5?

    (A) 10
    (B) 19
    (C) 35
    (D) 470
    (E) 480

14. Bridgette has 5 pairs of shoes, 7 skirts, and 4 blouses. If an outfit consists of exactly 1 pair of shoes, 1 skirt, and 1 blouse, how many different outfits could she wear?

    (A) 16
    (B) 48
    (C) 80
    (D) 135
    (E) 140

15. How many different ordered pairs (x, y) are there such that x is an odd integer, where $3 \leq x < 9$, and y is an integer, where $2 < y \leq 6$?

    (A) 9
    (B) 10
    (C) 12
    (D) 22
    (E) 24

16.   3, 5, 7, 3, 5, 7, 3, 5, ...

If the sequence above continues according to the pattern shown, what is the sum of the first 31 terms of the sequence?

(A)   143
(B)   150
(C)   153
(D)   158
(E)   165

17.   If the nth term of a sequence is $\frac{1}{4}(n^3 - n)$, then how much greater is the 14th term than the 6th term?

(A)   74
(B)   304
(C)   630
(D)   632
(E)   732

18.   The least and greatest numbers in a list of 9 real numbers are 4 and 21, respectively. The median of the list is 11, the list contains the numbers 10 and 12, and the number 14 appears most often in the list. Which of the following could be the average (arithmetic mean) of the numbers in the list?

       I.   10
       II. 11
       III. 11.5

(A)   II only
(B)   I and II only
(C)   I and III only
(D)   II and III only
(E)   I, II, and III

19. In a certain parking lot, there are 2 silver cars, 3 blue cars, 4 red cars, and 3 white cars. There are no other cars in the parking lot. What is the probability that a car randomly chosen from the parking lot is not blue?

    (A) $\dfrac{1}{6}$

    (B) $\dfrac{1}{4}$

    (C) $\dfrac{1}{3}$

    (D) $\dfrac{3}{4}$

    (E) $\dfrac{5}{6}$

20. If the average of four numbers is 22, and three of the numbers are 7, 11, and 18, then what is the fourth number?

21. The average of a set of seven numbers is 54. The average of three of those seven numbers is 38. What is the average of the other four numbers?

22. The mean age of the 14 members of a scuba diving club is 34. When a new member joins, the mean age increased to 37. How old is the new member?

23. Joe has 3 green marbles, 2 red marbles, and 5 blue marbles, and if all the marbles are dropped into a dark bag, what is the probability that Joe will pick out a green marble?

24. All of the students in a history class are junior or seniors. There are twice as many girls as boys in the class, and there are three times as many senior girls as junior girls. If a student is selected at random, what is the probability that the student is a junior girl?

25. If the 11th term of a geometric sequence is 11, and the 14th term of this sequence is 297, what is the 16th term of this sequence?

    (A) 22
    (B) 88
    (C) 187
    (D) 891
    (E) 2673

Coordinate Geometry

In this chapter, we will learn techniques for solving a variety of coordinate geometry problems on the SAT. We will cover coordinates, the distance and midpoint formulas, slope, basic linear equations, and the properties of parallel and perpendicular lines.

Coordinates

There are always a few simple reflection or coordinate problems on the SAT that are difficult to classify. As long as you know the basic rules for coordinates and are able to perform simple, manual transformations like shifts and reflections, you should be fine. Remember that when plotting coordinates on a grid, you move in the x direction first, and then in the y direction to form the point (x, y).

Let's go through a few common types together.

Examples

1.

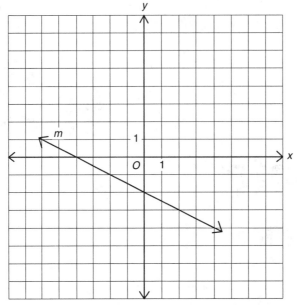

In the figure above, which of the following coordinates would lie on line *m* after it had been reflected across both the *y*-axis and the *x*-axis?

(A)   (4,3)
(B)   (−4,0)
(C)   (0,−2)
(D)   (−2,3)
(E)   (−4,2)

There are lots of special rules you could memorize for reflecting over the *y*-axis and the *x*-axis, but it almost always takes more time on SAT problems to recall and apply coordinate rules than to simply perform the transformations directly. One of the coordinates in the choices will lie on the image of the line after it has been reflected over the *y*-axis and the *x*-axis, in that order! Simply reflect a portion of the line manually, like so. The reflection over the *y*-axis is dashed, and the following reflection over the *x*-axis is bolded.

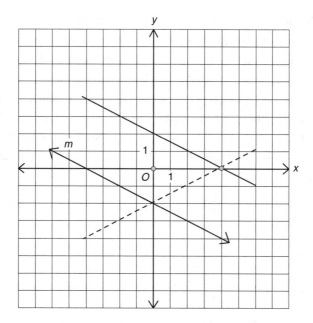

Now it's easy to see that the only coordinate in the choices that lies on the bold line is (−2, 3). The correct choice is D.

2.

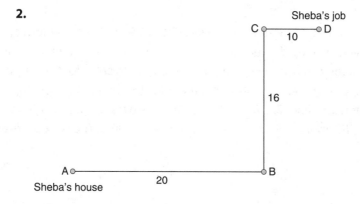

The figure above shows the route of Sheba's trip from her house to her job. Sheba travels 20 miles from A to B, 16 miles from B to C, and 10 miles from C to D. If she were able to travel from A to D directly, how much shorter, in miles, would the trip be?

(A) 8
(B) 10
(C) 12
(D) 13
(E) 15

There's a lot going on in this problem. First thing we need to do is break it down. We want to find out how much shorter her trip would be if she could travel directly from A to D. That means we need to find out the direct distance, and subtract the distance of her regular route. The distance she normally travels is easy to find: $20 + 16 + 10 = 46$ miles. Finding the direct distance is a little more difficult—but not if you know the trick. Redraw the diagram like below to create an encompassing right triangle. The new sides are either equal to lengths of the original sides or they are sums of the original sides.

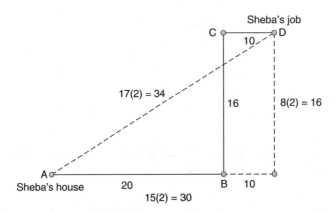

You get a new right triangle with side lengths of 16 and 30. The length of the hypotenuse is exactly the length you are looking for—the direct distance from A to D. You can use the Pythagorean theorem to solve for the length of the hypotenuse, or you can notice that the sides 16 and 30 form a multiple of the Pythagorean triple {8, 15, 17} − {16, 30, **34**}. Now subtract the direct distance from the original distance to get $46 - 34 = 12$ miles. The correct answer choice is C.

3.

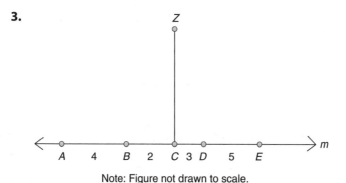

Note: Figure not drawn to scale.

In the figure above, $\overline{ZC}$ is perpendicular to m. Which of the following line segments (not shown) has the greatest length?

(A) $\overline{ZA}$
(B) $\overline{ZB}$
(C) $\overline{ZC}$
(D) $\overline{ZD}$
(E) $\overline{ZE}$

First, you need to be extra careful in this type of problem because the diagram is not drawn to scale. Second, if $\overline{ZC}$ is perpendicular to m, then any segment you connect from Z to either A, B, D, or E will form a right triangle. The hypotenuse of a right triangle increases in length as the lengths of the sides of the right triangle increase. The length of $\overline{ZC}$ is always the same, so the length from C to A, B, D, or E will determine the length of the hypotenuse. The longest distance from C to A, B, D, or E happens when you draw the segment connecting Z to E, which makes the length from C to E equal to 8. All the other possibilities will be less than 8. Therefore, the line segment $\overline{ZE}$ will have the greatest length because it is the hypotenuse of the triangle with the longest sides you can draw in the given diagram. The correct answer choice is E.

Distance

The formula for the distance between two points $P(x_1, y_1)$ and $Q(x_2, y_2)$ is as follows:

$$PQ = \sqrt{(x_2 - x_1)^2 + (y_2 - y_1)^2}$$

The midpoint formula for the coordinates of the midpoint $M(x, y)$ between two points $P(x_1, y_1)$ and $Q(x_2, y_2)$ is as follows:

$$M(x,y) = M\left(\frac{x_1 + x_2}{2}, \frac{y_1 + y_2}{2}\right)$$

These formulas look complicated, but they can be easy to apply once you've seen how they work in practice.

Examples

1. Five points, *A, B, C, D,* and *E,* lie on a line, not necessarily in that order. $\overline{AB}$ has a length of 32. Point *C* is the midpoint of $\overline{AB}$, and point *D* is the midpoint of $\overline{AC}$. If the distance between *D* and *E* is 6, what is one possible distance between *A* and *E*?

This is a typical starter problem in the grid-in section. A good diagram is essential to answer the problem quickly and accurately. We know that $\overline{AB}$ has a length of 32, so draw a long line segment and mark it with length 32. Point *C* is the midpoint of $\overline{AB}$, and point *D* is the midpoint of $\overline{AC}$. You can mark the locations of *C* and *D*, and calculate their lengths, as follows.

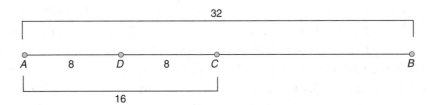

This part of the problem/diagram is fixed. Now we know that the distance between *D* and *E* is 6, and we are looking for one possible distance between *A* and *E*. From *D*, we can either go 6 units to the right or left, as follows.

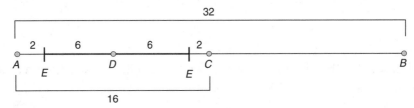

The possible locations of *E* are marked. The distance from *A* to *E* can be either 2 or 14.

2. What is the x-coordinate of the midpoint of the segment with endpoints of $(-3, 15)$ and $(10, -7)$?

Plug and chug! According to the midpoint formula, the x-coordinate of the midpoint of the segment with endpoints of $(-3, 15)$ and $(10, -7)$ is given by $M_x = \dfrac{-3+10}{2} = \dfrac{7}{2}$ or 3.5. That's all there is to it! If the problem asked for the y-coordinate of the midpoint, you would use the same formula, but substitute the two y endpoints instead of the x endpoints.

3. The following are coordinates of points in the xy-plane. Which of these points is nearest the origin?

(A) $\left(-\dfrac{1}{2}, 0\right)$

(B) $\left(\dfrac{1}{4}, 0\right)$

(C) $\left(-\dfrac{1}{4}, \dfrac{1}{4}\right)$

(D) $\left(\dfrac{1}{4}, \dfrac{1}{4}\right)$

(E) $\left(-\dfrac{1}{2}, -\dfrac{1}{2}\right)$

The point that is nearest the origin is the point that that is the smallest distance away from the origin. In other words, the problem is asking us to find the distance between each of the coordinates in the choices and the origin, $(0, 0)$. The distance formula $d = \sqrt{(x_2 - x_1)^2 + (y_2 - y_1)^2}$ requires that you find the difference between the x-coordinates of the two points and the difference between the y-coordinates of the two points. Since $(0, 0)$ is always one of the points, the difference between the x- and y-coordinates of the two points is equal to the x- and y-coordinates of the coordinates in the choices. In this example, it is easy to compute all five distances:

$$\left(-\dfrac{1}{2}, 0\right) \Rightarrow \sqrt{\left(-\dfrac{1}{2}\right)^2 + (0)^2} = \dfrac{1}{2} \quad \text{or} \quad .5$$

$$\left(\dfrac{1}{4}, 0\right) \Rightarrow \sqrt{\left(\dfrac{1}{4}\right)^2 + (0)^2} = \dfrac{1}{4} \quad \text{or} \quad .25$$

$$\left(-\frac{1}{4},\frac{1}{4}\right) \Rightarrow \sqrt{\left(-\frac{1}{4}\right)^2 + \left(\frac{1}{4}\right)^2} \approx .35$$

$$\left(\frac{1}{4},\frac{1}{4}\right) \Rightarrow \sqrt{\left(-\frac{1}{4}\right)^2 + \left(\frac{1}{4}\right)^2} \approx .35$$

$$\left(-\frac{1}{2},-\frac{1}{2}\right) \Rightarrow \sqrt{\left(-\frac{1}{2}\right)^2 + \left(\frac{1}{2}\right)^2} \approx .71$$

Choice B is obviously closest to the origin. We also could have thought about this problem visually to eliminate some of the choices. If we plotted $\left(-\frac{1}{2}, 0\right)$ on the coordinate plane, you could easily see that the distance from the origin is $\frac{1}{2}$ because the coordinate is exactly on the x-axis. The same reasoning applies for $\left(\frac{1}{4}, 0\right)$. It's easy to just see that the distance is $\frac{1}{4}$. We could know without computing their distances that choices C and D cannot be the answers because both points are reflections of each other over the y-axis, meaning they are visually the same distance from the origin. That leaves us with $\left(-\frac{1}{2}, -\frac{1}{2}\right)$, for which we must compute the distance to be sure of how it compares to choice B.

Slope

The slope of a line is the quotient of the difference between the y-coordinates and the difference between x-coordinates. Algebraically,

$$slope = \frac{y_2 - y_1}{x_2 - x_1}$$

where (x_1, y_1) and (x_2, y_2) are any two points on the line, and $x_1 \neq x_2$.

The x-intercept of a line is the x-coordinate of a point where the line crosses the x-axis $(y = 0)$. This implies that the x-intercept takes the form $(x, 0)$.

The y-intercept, on the other hand, of a line is the y-coordinate of a point where the line crosses the y-axis $(x = 0)$. This implies that the y-intercept takes the form $(0, y)$.

Problems involving slope are not too challenging on the SAT. Let's work through some common problem types together.

Examples

1.

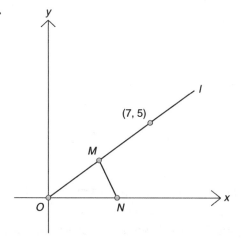

Line *m* (not shown) passes through *O* and intersects $\overline{MN}$ between *M* and *N*. What is one possible value of the slope of line *m*?

We're looking for a range of possible slopes that will pass through *O* and intersect $\overline{MN}$ between *M* and *N*. On the lower end, the slope of $\overline{ON} = 0$ because the slope of all horizontal lines is 0. On the higher end, the slope of $\overline{OM} = \dfrac{5-0}{7-0} = \dfrac{5}{7}$.

Therefore, the slope of a line that will pass through *O* and intersect $\overline{MN}$ between *M* and *N* can take on any value between: $0 < slope < \dfrac{5}{7}$.

2. In the *xy*-coordinate plane, the graph of $x = y^2 - 9$ intersects line *l* at $(0, w)$ and $(7, z)$. What is the greatest possible value of the slope of *l*?

This is a challenging problem because while it is possible to graph $x = y^2 - 9$, it is counterintuitive to do so. The easiest way is to solve the problem algebraically. We are told that the graph of $x = y^2 - 9$ intersects line *l* at $(0, w)$. That means that $(0, w)$ is a point on the graph of $x = y^2 - 9$. To solve for *w*, we can plug in the coordinates: $0 = w^2 - 9 \Rightarrow w^2 = 9 \Rightarrow w = 3$ or -3.

Since we know that $(7, z)$ is also a point on $x = y^2 - 9$, we can plug in to solve for $z: 7 = z^2 - 9 \Rightarrow z^2 = 16 \Rightarrow z = 4$ or -4. The line *l* can therefore pass through the points: $(0, 3)$ and $(7, 4)$, $(0, -3)$ and $(7, 4)$, $(0, 3)$ and $(7, -4)$, or $(0, 3)$ and $(7, -4)$. Since we are looking for the greatest possible slope, we calculate the slopes for the pairs. In order, the slopes are: $\dfrac{1}{7}$, 1, -1, and $-\dfrac{1}{7}$. The greatest among the possible slopes is 1. The correct response is 1.

3. In the *xy* plane, the equation of line *l* is $y = -3x + 2$. If line *m* is the reflection of line *l* in the *x*-axis, what is the equation of line *m*?

(A) $y = \dfrac{1}{3}x - 2$

(B) $y = -\dfrac{1}{3}x + 2$

(C) $y = \dfrac{1}{3}x + 2$

(D) $y = 3x - 2$

(E) $y = 3x + 2$

The best way to solve reflection problems is to draw a diagram. We know the equation of line *l* is $y = -3x + 2$. That means the *y*-intercept is at (0, 2), and the slope moves 1 to the right and 3 units down. The thick line in the diagram below represents the reflection of the original line over the *x*-axis.

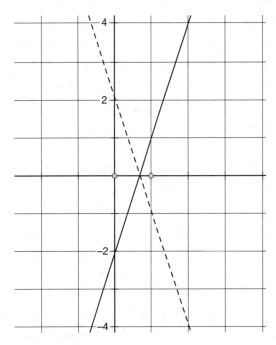

We can see that the reflected line hits the *y*-axis at (0, −2) and the slope of the line is the same, except it is moving in the positive direction. That means the sign of the slope changed, not the value. The new equation is $y = 3x - 2$.

The correct choice is D. Another way of analyzing the problem is computationally. A reflection over the *x*-axis simply negates the entire original equation. For example, the original equation $y = -3x + 2$ becomes $y = -(-3x + 2) \Rightarrow 3x - 2$. Either method works just as quickly, depending on how YOU learn and solve best.

Linear Equations

The equations of lines can be written in several forms. Each form implies the same information, but it can be very helpful to be able to move from one form to the next on the SAT. Certain situations call for different forms to make answering the question easier.

The linear equation in the standard form is written as $ax + by = c$ (where a, b, and c are constants, and x and y are variables).

The linear equation in the slope–intercept form is written as $y = mx + b$ (where m and b are constants, and x and y are variables) in which m is the slope and b is the *y*-intercept.

The linear equation written in point–slope form is written as $y - y_1 = m(x - x_1)$ (where m is the slope and (x_1, y_1) is any point on the line).

The equation in slope–intercept form is certainly the most popular, but knowing which form to use takes both practice and strategy!

Examples

1.

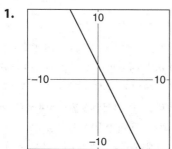

The figure above shows the graph of a line $y = ax + b$, where a and b are constants. Which of the following best represents the graph of the line $y = 3ax + b$?

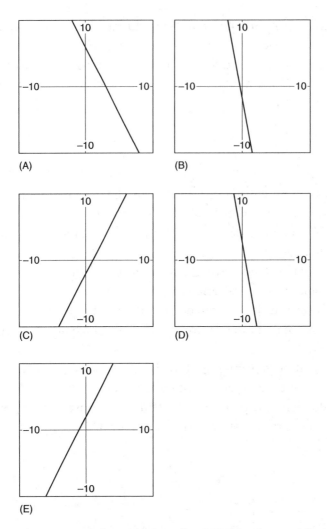

(A)   (B)   (C)   (D)   (E)

This is a typical problem on the SAT. What's so confusing is that there really isn't anything to compute. We're given a graph of a line and told its equation is $y = ax + b$, which doesn't say much. Then we need to determine which of the choices best represents $y = 3ax + b$. Here's the strategy you should follow: A slope that is between 0 and 1 is not steep. A slope that is bigger than 1 is steep, and slopes like 3, 4, 5, etc. are really steep, like a cliff! The original equation is $y = ax + b$, and the new equation is $y = 3ax + b$.

In the new equation, the y-intercept, b, stays the same. That means we can cross off choices A, B, and C because their y-intercepts are not the same as the y-intercept in the original graph. Then consider the slope. Multiplying the original slope, a, by 3 is not going to change the sign of the slope, but it is going to increase it. No change in the sign of the slope means that the line will move in the same direction, and an increase in the value of the slope means the line will get much steeper—think dangerous cliff! Of the remaining choices, D and E, D is clearly the correct one.

2.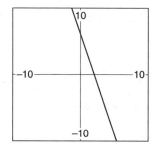

Which of the following could be the equation of the line represented in the graph above?

(A) $y = 3x + 6$
(B) $y = 3x - 6$
(C) $y = -3x - 4$
(D) $y = -3x - 6$
(E) $y = -3x + 6$

We want to figure out which one of the choices best represents the graph of the line in the picture. Let's go through what we know from the picture. First, the slope is negative. That means choices A and B are out. Next, we know the y-intercept is positive. That means choices C and D are out. The answer must be E.

3.

x	−6	−3	0	3
$f(x)$	−2	0	2	4

The table above gives values of the linear function f for selected values of x. Which of the following functions defines f?

(A) $f(x) = \dfrac{1}{2}x$

(B) $f(x) = 2x - 2$

(C) $f(x) = \dfrac{2}{3}x + 2$

(D) $f(x) = -x + 3$

(E) $f(x) = -2x + 6$

This type of problem will inevitably appear on your SAT exam. You are given a set of points that lie on one of the equations in the choices. To determine which equation is a perfect fit, simply plug the points into each of the equations. The SAT always anticipates that you will plug in easy points like $(-3, 0)$ and $(0, 2)$ first, so they purposely design the choices so that those points will work in many of them. You'll actually save a lot of time by testing a "weird" point first, such as $(-6, -2)$ or $(3, 4)$. Let's try $(3, 4)$ first:

$f(x) = \frac{1}{2}x \Rightarrow 4 = \frac{1}{2} \cdot 3 \Rightarrow 4 = 1.5$. Not true. A is out.

$f(x) = 2x - 2 \Rightarrow 4 = 2(3) - 2 \Rightarrow 4 = 4$. True. Maybe B is right.

$f(x) = \frac{2}{3}x + 2 \Rightarrow 4 = \frac{2}{3}(3) + 2 \Rightarrow 4 = 4$. True. Maybe C is right.

$f(x) = -x + 3 \Rightarrow 4 = -3 + 3 \Rightarrow 4 = 0$. Not true. D is out.

$f(x) = -2x + 6 \Rightarrow 4 = -2(3) + 6 \Rightarrow 4 = 0$. Not true. E is out.

We've narrowed it down to two choices. To find out which one is correct, simply plug in the other "weird" point, $(-6, -2)$.

$f(x) = 2x - 2 \Rightarrow -2 = 2(-6) - 2 \Rightarrow -2 = -14$. False. B is out.

$f(x) = \frac{2}{3}x + 2 \Rightarrow -2 = \frac{2}{3}(-6) + 2 \Rightarrow -2 = -2$. True. C is right.

It's as easy as plug, two, three!

Parallel and Perpendicular Lines

Parallel lines are lines in the same plane that never meet or touch. In the diagram below, lines l and m are parallel. We call line n a transversal because it is a line that cuts through two parallel lines. When a pair of parallel lines is cut by a transversal, special angle relationships are formed. The "why" doesn't really matter; you can just use your eyes to see that: $\angle 1 = \angle 5 = \angle 3 = \angle 7$, and that $\angle 2 = \angle 6 = \angle 4 = \angle 8$. These relationships only happen when the lines are parallel.

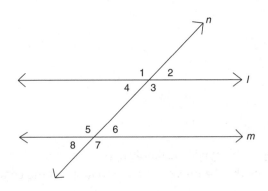

When we are dealing with equations of lines instead of a diagram, two lines are parallel if their slopes are equal.

Perpendicular lines are lines in the same plane that intersect at a right angle.

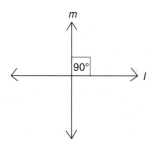

In computation, perpendicular lines have negative reciprocal slopes.

These rules are best learned through example. Let's work through some typical SAT problems together.

Examples

1.

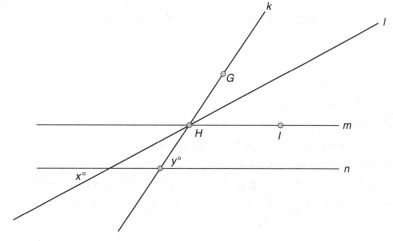

In the figure above (not drawn to scale), $m \parallel n$ and l bisects $\angle GHI$. If $65 < y < 75$, what is one possible value for x?

We are told that $m \parallel n$ Automatically, we know the special angle relationships described above are present. We also know that $65 < y < 75$. The easiest approach is to pick a value for y, like 70, and go from there. If $y = 70$, then $\angle GHI = 70$. If l bisects $\angle GHI$, then each half of the angle equals 35. Line l is a transversal cutting through lines m and n, which means special angle relationships are also formed.

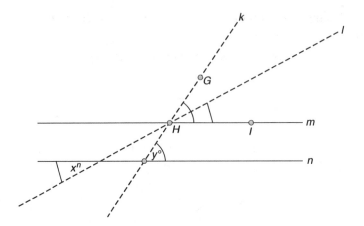

Using your eyes, you can see that the lower half of $\angle GHI$ matches perfectly with x. One possible value of x is 35, though any value satisfying $32.5 < x < 37.5$ is technically correct.

2. Line l passes through the origin and is perpendicular to the line given by the equation $3x + y = 9$. Which of the following points is not on line l?

(A) $(3, 1)$
(B) $(-3, -1)$
(C) $(-9, -3)$
(D) $(12, 4)$
(E) $(1, 3)$

We know that line l passes through the origin. That tells us $(0, 0)$ is a point on the line. Next, we are told that l is perpendicular to the line given by the equation $3x + y = 9$. That means the slope of line l is the negative reciprocal of the slope of the given line. Put the given equation into slope–intercept form (solve it for y) to find the slope: $y = -3x + 9$. The slope of the given line is -3. Therefore, the slope of line l is $\frac{1}{3}$.

Now we have enough information to find the equation of line l. The origin, $(0, 0)$, happens to be the y-intercept of line l, which means that $b = 0$. Therefore, line l takes the form $y = \frac{1}{3}x + 0$, or simply $y = \frac{1}{3}x$. Finally, test each of the points to see which one is not on the line. The only point that doesn't satisfy the equation is choice E, $(1, 3)$: $3 = \frac{1}{3}(1) \Rightarrow 3 = \frac{1}{3}$, which is not true. Choice E is the correct answer.

3. In the *xy*-plane, line *l* passes through the origin and is perpendicular to the line $-3x+2y=c$, where *c* is a constant. If the two lines intersect at the point $(p+1, p)$, what is the value of *c*?

(A) $-\dfrac{13}{5}$

(B) -1

(C) $-\dfrac{2}{5}$

(D) $\dfrac{2}{5}$

(E) 1

First, we know that $(0, 0)$ is a point on line *l* because line *l* passes through the origin. If we solve $-3x + 2y = c$ for *y*, we can see the slope: $-3x + 2y = c \Rightarrow 2y = 3x + c \Rightarrow y = \dfrac{3}{2}x + \dfrac{c}{2}$. Since the lines are perpendicular, the slope of line *l* is the negative reciprocal of $\dfrac{3}{2}$. The slope of line *l* is therefore $-\dfrac{2}{3}$. By the same reasoning in the previous example, the equation of line *l* is $y = -\dfrac{2}{3}x$. If the two lines intersect at the point $(p+1, p)$, then the point $(p+1, p)$ must satisfy the equation of line *l*. We can plug in $(p+1, p)$ to find the value of p: $p = -\dfrac{2}{3}(p+1) \Rightarrow p = -\dfrac{2}{3}p - \dfrac{2}{3} \Rightarrow \dfrac{5}{3}p = -\dfrac{2}{3} \Rightarrow p = -\dfrac{2}{3}\left(\dfrac{3}{5}\right) \Rightarrow p = -\dfrac{2}{5}$. Now that we know the value of *p*, the point $(p + 1, p)$ becomes $\left(\dfrac{3}{5}, -\dfrac{2}{5}\right)$.

We can plug this point into $-3x+2y=c$ to solve for the value of *c*: $-3\left(\dfrac{3}{5}\right) + 2\left(-\dfrac{2}{5}\right) = c \Rightarrow -\dfrac{9}{5} - \dfrac{4}{5} = c \Rightarrow -\dfrac{13}{5} = c$. That was a very difficult problem! But you'll be fine now that you've seen the method. The correct answer is A.

The Formulas You're Not Given That You Ought to Know

Arithmetic Operations

$$ab + ac = a(b + c)$$

$$a\left(\frac{b}{c}\right) = \frac{ab}{c}$$

$$\frac{\left(\dfrac{a}{b}\right)}{c} = \frac{a}{bc}$$

$$\frac{a}{\left(\dfrac{b}{c}\right)} = \frac{ac}{b}$$

$$\frac{a}{b} + \frac{c}{d} = \frac{ad + bc}{bd}$$

$$\frac{a}{b} - \frac{c}{d} = \frac{ad - bc}{bd}$$

$$\frac{a - b}{c - d} = \frac{b - a}{d - c}$$

$$\frac{a + b}{c} = \frac{a}{c} + \frac{b}{c}$$

$$\frac{ab + ac}{a} = b + c, \; a \neq 0$$

$$\frac{\left(\dfrac{a}{b}\right)}{\left(\dfrac{c}{d}\right)} = \frac{ad}{bc}$$

Exponent Rules

$$a^n a^m = a^{n+m}$$

$$\frac{a^n}{a^m} = a^{n-m} = \frac{1}{a^{m-n}}$$

$$(a^n)^m = a^{nm}$$

$$a^0 = 1, \; a \neq 0$$

$$(ab)^n = a^n b^n$$

$$\left(\frac{a}{b}\right)^n = \frac{a^n}{b^n}$$

$$a^{-n} = \frac{1}{a^n}$$

$$\frac{1}{a^{-n}} = a^n$$

$$\left(\frac{a}{b}\right)^{-n} = \left(\frac{b}{a}\right)^n = \frac{b^n}{a^n}$$

$$a^{\frac{n}{m}} = \left(a^{\frac{1}{m}}\right)^n = (a^n)^{\frac{1}{m}}$$

Linear Functions

$$y = mx + b \text{ or } f(x) = mx + b$$

Graph is a line with point $(0, b)$ and slope m.

Slope

Slope of the line containing the two points (x_1, y_1) and (x_2, y_2) is

$$m = \frac{y_2 - y_1}{x_2 - x_1} = \frac{\text{rise}}{\text{run}}$$

Distance Formula

If $P_1 = (x_1, y_1)$ and $P_2 = (x_2, y_2)$ are two points the distance between them is

$$d(P_1, P_2) = \sqrt{(x_2 - x_1)^2 + (y_2 - y_1)^2}$$

Constant Function

$$y = a \text{ or } f(x) = a$$

Graph is a horizontal line passing though the point $(0, a)$.

Slope–Intercept Form

The equation of the line with slope m and y-intercept $(0, b)$ is

$$y = mx + b$$

Point–Slope Form

The equation of the line with slope m and passing through the point (x_1, y_1) is

$$y - y_1 = m(x - x_1)$$

Factoring Formulas

$$x^2 - a^2 = (x + a)(x - a)$$

$$x^2 + 2ax + a^2 = (x + a)^2$$

$$x^2 - 2ax + a^2 = (x - a)^2$$

Common Mistakes You Need to Avoid

Error	Correction
$\dfrac{3}{0} \neq 0$ and $\dfrac{3}{0} \neq 3$	You can never divide by 0. Division by 0 is undefined.
$-4^2 \neq 16$	$-4^2 = -16$ and $(-4)^2 = 16$. Be careful how you use parentheses.
$(x^3)^4 \neq x^7$	$(x^3)^4 = x^{12}$. Raising a power to a power means you have to multiply, not add.
$\dfrac{x}{y+z} \neq \dfrac{x}{y} + \dfrac{x}{z}$	$\dfrac{3}{4} = \dfrac{3}{3+1} \neq \dfrac{3}{3} + \dfrac{3}{1} = 1 + 3 = 4$. You can only divide monomials (not binomials) into a numerator.
$\dfrac{x+cy}{x} \neq 1 + cy$	$\dfrac{x+cy}{x} = 1 + \dfrac{cy}{x}$. If you divide a monomial into one piece of the numerator, you need to divide it into all the pieces.
$-b(y-1) \neq -by - b$	$-b(y-1) = -by + b$. Make sure you distribute to each piece inside the parentheses.
$(x+m)^2 \neq x^2 + m^2$	$(x+m)^2 = (x+m)(x+m) = x^2 + 2xm + m^2$. When raising a binomial to a power, make sure you FOIL! You may never "distribute" a power over a $+$ or a $-$ sign.

Chapter 13 Quiz—Coordinate Geometry
25 Questions

Directions: For this quiz, solve each problem and decide which is the best of the choices given. For Student-Produced Response questions, solve each problem and record your solution.

Notes

1. The use of a calculator is permitted.
2. All numbers used are real numbers.
3. Figures that accompany problems in this test are intended to provide information useful in solving the problems. They are drawn as accurately as possible EXCEPT when it is stated in a specific problem that the figure is not drawn to scale. All figures lie in a plane unless otherwise indicated.
4. Unless otherwise specified, the domain of any function f is assumed to be the set of all real numbers x for which $f(x)$ is a real number.

Reference Information

$A = \pi r^2$
$C = 2\pi r$

$A = \ell w$

$A = \frac{1}{2} bh$

$V = \ell wh$

$V = \pi r^2 h$

$c^2 = a^2 + b^2$

Special right triangles

The number of degrees of arc in a circle is 360.
The sum of the measures in degrees of the angles of a triangle is 180.

1.

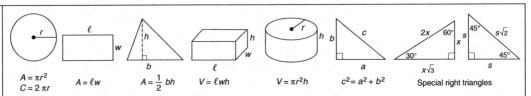

Which of the lettered points on the number line above could represent when the coordinate of point P is multiplied by the coordinate of point Q?

(A) A
(B) B
(C) C
(D) D
(E) E

2.

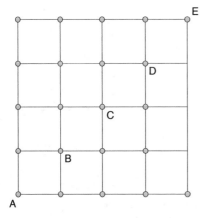

In the figure above, a path from point *A* to point *E* is determined by moving upward or to the right along the grid lines. How many different paths can be drawn from *A* to *E* that do not include either B, C, or D?

(A) 5
(B) 6
(C) 10
(D) 12
(E) 18

3.

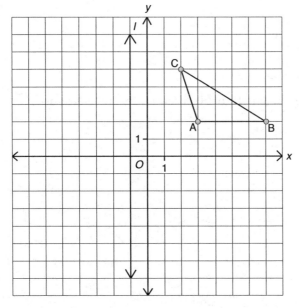

If the triangle in the figure above is reflected over the line *l*, what will be the coordinates of the reflection of point *A*?

(A) (−4, 2)
(B) (−6, 2)
(C) (−5, 2)
(D) (4, 2)
(E) (5, 2)

4.

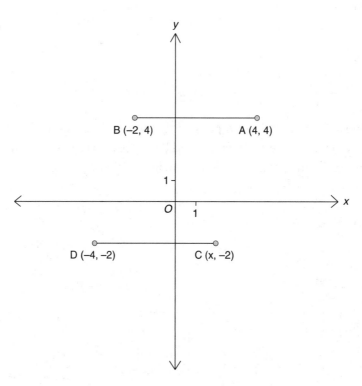

In the figure above, the length of *AB* is equal to the length of *CD*. What is the value of *x*?

(A) −4
(B) −2
(C) 2
(D) 4
(E) 6

5.

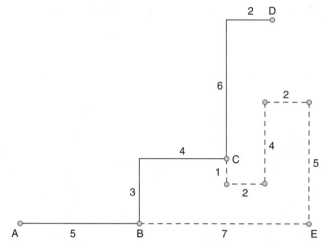

In the figure above, the usual route from Town A to Town D is indicated by the solid line. The broken line indicates a detour route from B to C through E. Each line segment is labeled with its length in miles. How many more miles is the trip from Town A to Town D via the detour than via the usual route?

(A) 8
(B) 10
(C) 12
(D) 14
(E) 15

6. For how many ordered pairs of integers (x, y) is $3x + 4y < 15$?

(A) 1
(B) 2
(C) 3
(D) 4
(E) 5

Questions 7 through 9 refer to the following figure and information.

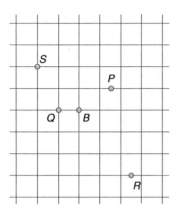

The grid above represents equally spaced streets in a town that has no one-way streets. *B* marks the corner where Bridgette's dog-walking company is located. Points *P*, *Q*, *R*, and *S* represent the locations of some of Bridgette's clients' houses. The dog-walking company defines a house's *d*-distance as the minimum number of blocks that a dog walker must travel from the company to reach the client's house. For example, the house at *P* is a *d*-distance of $2\frac{1}{2}$, and the house at *Q* is a *d*-distance of 1 from the company.

7. What is the *d*-distance of the house at *R* from the dog-walking company?

    (A) $4\frac{1}{2}$

    (B) 5

    (C) $5\frac{1}{2}$

    (D) 6

    (E) $6\frac{1}{2}$

8. What is the total number of different routes that a dog-walker can travel the *d*-distance from *B* to *S*?

    (A) 2
    (B) 4
    (C) 5
    (D) 6
    (E) 7

9. All of the houses in the town that are a *d*-distance of 4 from the Bridgette's
    dog-walking company must lie on a

    (A) circle
    (B) kite
    (C) right isosceles triangle
    (D) pair of parallel lines
    (E) square

10.

    In the figure above, $XZ = 28$ and $XY = YZ$. Point W (not shown) is on the
    line between X and Y such that $XW = WY$. What does WZ equal?

    (A) 7
    (B) 14
    (C) 17
    (D) 20
    (E) 21

11. Points A, B, C, and D lie on a line, in that order. If $CD > BC > AB$ and the
    length of CD is 8, which of the following could be the length of AD?

    (A) 23
    (B) 24
    (C) 25
    (D) 26
    (E) 27

12.

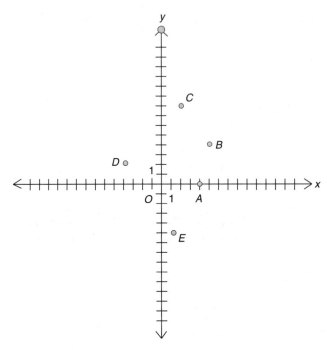

In the figure above, which of the following line segments (not shown) has a slope of 4?

(A) $\overline{AD}$
(B) $\overline{AC}$
(C) $\overline{AB}$
(D) $\overline{EC}$
(E) $\overline{DB}$

13.

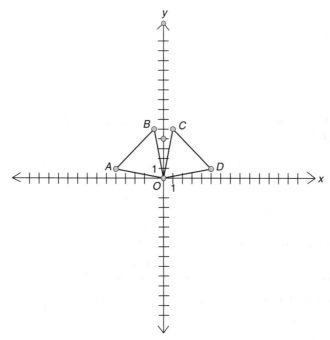

In the *xy*-coordinate system above, which of the following line segments has a slope of –1?

(A) $\overline{OA}$
(B) $\overline{OB}$
(C) $\overline{OC}$
(D) $\overline{DC}$
(E) $\overline{AB}$

14.

x	f(x)
0	m
1	18
2	n

The table above shows the values for a function f. If f is a linear function, what is the value of $m + n$?

(A) 18
(B) 27
(C) 36
(D) 54
(E) It cannot be determined from the information given

15. In the xy-coordinate plane, line m is the reflection of l about the x-axis. If the slope of line m is $\frac{2}{7}$, what is the slope of line l?

(A) $\dfrac{7}{2}$

(B) $\dfrac{2}{7}$

(C) $\dfrac{1}{7}$

(D) $-\dfrac{2}{7}$

(E) $-\dfrac{7}{2}$

16. Bridgette's morning routine consists of walking from her home to Happy Subway Station, going four stops on the rail, and walking from Joy Subway Station to her office, in that order. Bridgette always walks at the same pace. The distance from her home to Happy Subway Station is less than the distance from Joy Subway Station to her office. The subway moves more quickly than Bridgette can walk. If she does not rest between each of the activities in her morning routine, which of the following could be the graph of the distance she covers during the entire time of her morning routine?

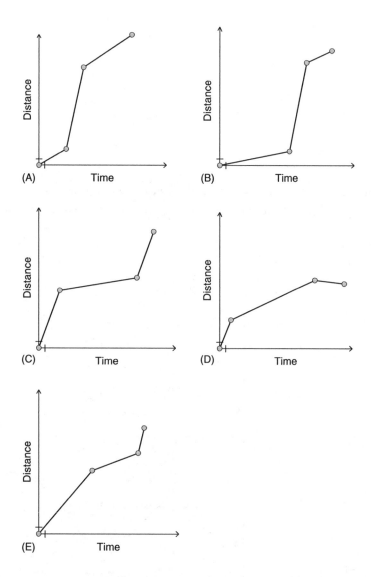

17. In the *xy*-plane, the line with equation $y = 4x + 12$ crosses the *x*-axis at the point with the coordinates (a, b). What is the value of *a*?

(A) −12
(B) −3
(C) 0
(D) 3
(E) 4

18.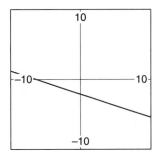

The figure above shows the graph of the line $y = mx + b$, where m and b are constants. Which of the following best represents the graph of the line $y = -3mx - b$?

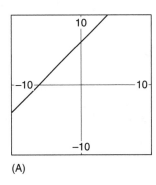

(A)

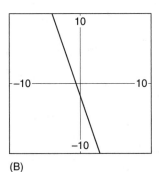

(B)

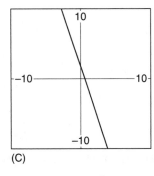

(C)

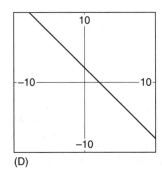

(D)

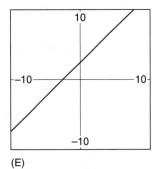

(E)

19.

t	−1	0	1	2
g(t)	9	6	3	0

The table above gives values of the linear function g for selected values of t. Which of the following defines g?

(A) $g(t) = t + 10$
(B) $g(t) = 3t + 6$
(C) $g(t) = 3t + 12$
(D) $g(t) = -3t + 6$
(E) $g(t) = -4t + 5$

20.

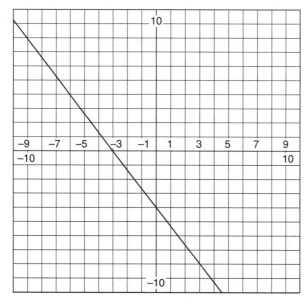

In the figure above, line l intersects the x-axis at $x = -3$ and the y-axis at $y = -4$. If line m (not shown) passes through the origin and is perpendicular to line l, what is the slope of line m?

21. Line *l* has a negative slope and passes through the origin. If line *k* is perpendicular to line *l*, which of the following must be true?

    (A) Line *k* passes through the origin
    (B) Line *k* has a negative slope
    (C) Line *k* has a positive slope
    (D) Line *k* has a positive *x*-intercept
    (E) Line *k* has a negative *y*-intercept

22. In the *xy*-coordinate plane, line *l* is perpendicular to the *x*-axis and passes through the point $(-3, -4)$. Which of the following is an equation of line *l*?

    (A) $y = 0$
    (B) $x = -3$
    (C) $x = -4$
    (D) $y + 4 = x + 3$
    (E) $y - 3 = x - 4$

23.

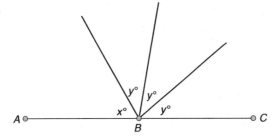

In the figure above, point *B* lies on $\overline{AC}$. If *x* and *y* are integers, which of the following is a possible value of *x*?

    (A) 20
    (B) 24
    (C) 28
    (D) 32
    (E) 35

24.

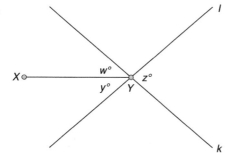

In the figure above, lines l and k intersect at point Y. If $z = 60$ and $w = 28$, what is the value of y?

(A) 28
(B) 30
(C) 32
(D) 44
(E) 88

25. Shelby and Bridgette leave their high school at the same time and walk for 5 hours. Shelby walks due west at the average rate of 8 miles per hour, and Bridgette walks due south at the average rate of 15 miles per hour. What is the straight line distance between them, in miles, at the end of the 5 hours?

(A) 23
(B) 35
(C) 65
(D) 85
(E) 115

Geometry

In this chapter, we will learn techniques for solving a variety of geometry problems on the SAT. We will cover basic polygons like triangles and quadrilaterals, circles, special shapes such as inscribed and circumscribed polygons, locus, area, and volume.

Triangles

Triangles can be categorized by the number of congruent sides they have. For example, a triangle with no congruent sides is a scalene triangle; a triangle with two congruent sides is an isosceles triangle; and a triangle with three congruent sides is an equilateral triangle.

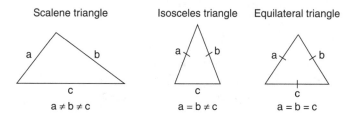

Triangles can also be categorized by their angles. For example, a triangle with three acute interior angles is an acute triangle; a triangle with one obtuse interior angle is an obtuse triangle; a triangle with one right interior angle is a right triangle; and a triangle with three congruent interior angles is an equiangular triangle. An equiangular triangle is also an equilateral triangle.

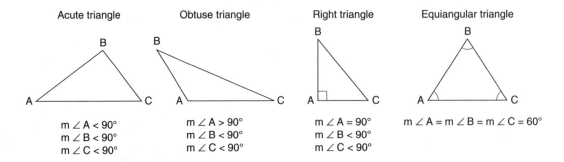

In addition to being able to classify triangles based on sides and angles, you need to know three main properties. The first is that the sum of the measures of the three interior angles is always 180 degrees. The second property is that the sum of the lengths of any two sides must be greater than the length of the third side.

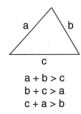

$$a + b > c$$
$$b + c > a$$
$$c + a > b$$

The third property is that the exterior angle of a triangle is equal to the sum of the measures of the two remote interior angles. The last property is the most important one to know.

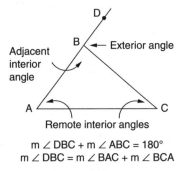

$$m \angle DBC + m \angle ABC = 180°$$
$$m \angle DBC = m \angle BAC + m \angle BCA$$

The area of a triangle is equal to one half the product of its base and height.

Area $= \dfrac{1}{2} \times b \times h$

Finally, there are two special right triangles you should know, one for 30-60-90 right triangles, and the other for 45-45-90 right triangles. In a 30-60-90 right triangle, the hypotenuse is two times as long as the shorter side (opposite the 30 degree angle), and the side opposite the 60 degree angle is $\sqrt{3}$ times as long as the shorter side. In a 45-45-90 triangle, the hypotenuse is always $\sqrt{2}$ times the length of a leg. The following diagrams help make sense of the written explanation.

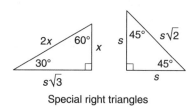

Special right triangles

Even though some of these rules sound complicated, you have been working with them for so many years that they will begin to flow naturally—with a little practice!

Examples

1.

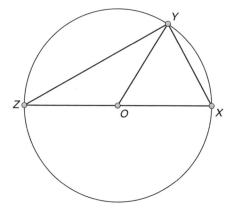

In the figure above, triangle XYZ is inscribed in the circle with center O and diameter $\overline{XZ}$. If $XY = YO$, what is the degree measure of $\angle XYO$?

(A)   15°

(B)   30°

(C)   45°

(D)   60°

(E)   It cannot be determined from the information given

Most geometry problems on the SAT are straightforward problems with a lot of distracter information in the problem itself and in the accompanying diagram. Here, we want to know the degree measure of ∠XYO. We are told that XY = YO. Since O is the center of the circle, YO happens to be radius of the circle. Because all the radii in a circle are equal in length, we also know that YO = XO. In this way, all three sides of triangle XYO are equal in length, XY = YO = XO, making the triangle equilateral and equiangular. Therefore, the degree measure of < XYO is 60. This was an easy problem with a lot of extra information, especially in the diagram. Know your content and your tricks well enough to be able to see past the distracters. The correct answer is D.

2.

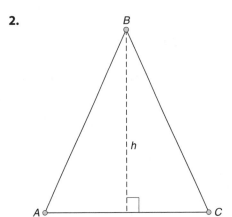

In triangle *ABC* above, *AC* is $\dfrac{4}{9}$ of *h*, the length of the altitude. What is the area of triangle *ABC* in terms of *h*?

(A) $\dfrac{h^2}{9}$

(B) $\dfrac{2h^2}{9}$

(C) $\dfrac{2h}{9}$

(D) $\dfrac{4h^2}{9}$

(E) $\dfrac{8h^2}{9}$

We want to know area of triangle *ABC* in terms of *h*. According to the formula for the area of a triangle, $\dfrac{1}{2}bh$, we need to know the length of the base and the height. From the diagram, it's clear that the height of the triangle is *h*.

From the problem, it's clear that the base, AC, is $\dfrac{4}{9}h$. Plugging into the formula, we get: $Area = \dfrac{1}{2} \times \dfrac{4}{9}h \times h = \dfrac{2}{9}h^2$. The correct answer choice is B.

3.

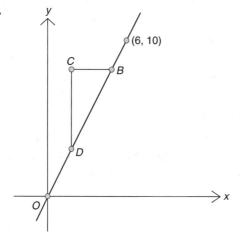

In the figure above (not drawn to scale), if the legs of triangle BCD are parallel to the axes, which of the following could be the lengths of the sides of triangle BCD?

(A) $3, 4, 5$

(B) $3, 5, \sqrt{34}$

(C) $4, 5, 4\sqrt{17}$

(D) $3, 3, 3\sqrt{2}$

(E) $6, 8, 10$

The most important piece of information here is that the legs of triangle BCD are parallel to the axes. Because the axes are always perpendicular, this information tells us triangle BCD is a right triangle. There is a second, not-so-obvious right triangle in the diagram, which is drawn in the next figure.

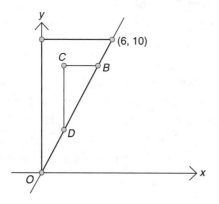

The bolded triangle and the small triangle BCD must be similar. In simple terms, that just means triangle BCD is a shrunken version of the big triangle in bold. If we find the lengths of the side of the bold triangle, then the lengths of the sides of the small triangle BCD must be a smaller multiple of those sides. We know the point (6, 10) is a vertex of the triangle. Following the coordinate, we know the horizontal leg is 6, and the vertical leg is 10. The sides of the big triangle must be {6, 10, "number bigger than 10"}. We don't really care about the length of the hypotenuse because we are just scanning the choices to see which one is a scale multiple of the big set. Choice B, {3, 5, $\sqrt{34}$}, is exactly half the size of {6, 10, "number bigger than 10"}. Choice B is the correct answer. Notice that the order of the numbers in the set means everything. If we are not consistent with ordering from least to greatest, we might have mistakenly thought choice A was the answer simply because it contains a 6 and a 10.

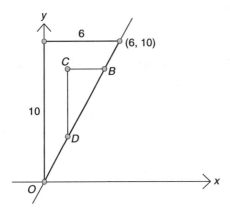

Quadrilaterals

All quadrilaterals have two things in common. The sum of the measures of the interior angles is 360°, and there are exactly four sides.

In general, the sum of the interior angles of a polygon with n sides is given by the formula $180(n-2)$. In the case of a quadrilateral, the value of n is 4, so it follows that $180(4-2)=180(2)=360$, as expected.

Like all polygons, the sum of the exterior angles of a quadrilateral is 360°. A quadrilateral is the only polygon that happens to have the same sum of interior angles as it does exterior angles. A pentagon, for example, has $180(5-2) = 180(3) = 540°$ on the inside but only 360° on the outside. The sum of the interior angles changes from polygon to polygon, but the sum of the exterior angles is the same for all polygons.

You need to know the basic properties of some special quadrilaterals, such as parallelograms, rectangles, rhombuses, and squares. As you read through the properties below, try to understand the written explanations, as well as the accompanying diagrams.

A parallelogram is a quadrilateral with two pairs of parallel sides. Altitude (or height) is the segment perpendicular to the base. Special parallelograms are rectangles, squares, and rhombuses.

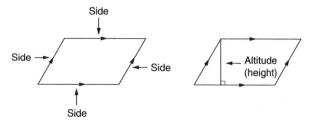

A rectangle is a parallelogram with four right angles, two pairs of congruent opposite sides, and two congruent diagonals.

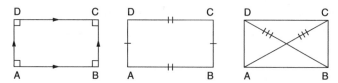

A rhombus is a parallelogram with two pairs of congruent opposite angles, four congruent sides, and two perpendicular diagonals that bisect the angles of a rhombus.

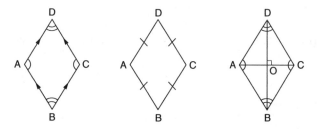

A square is a parallelogram with four right angles, four congruent sides, and two congruent diagonals.

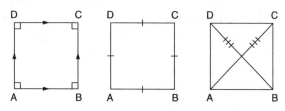

You also need to know certain formulas for the perimeter and area of the special quadrilaterals. The perimeter formula is always the same: add the lengths of the sides. But the area formulas differ a little from shape to shape.

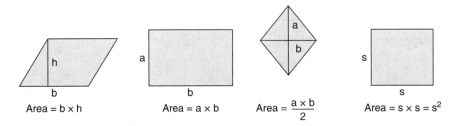

Area = b × h   Area = a × b   Area = $\dfrac{a \times b}{2}$ Area = s × s = s²

Let's work through a few practice problems together.

Examples

1.

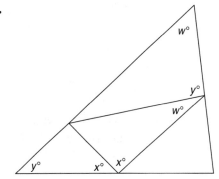

In the figure above, what is the value of *w* in terms of *x* and *y*?

(A) $180 + x - y$
(B) $180 - 2x + 2y$
(C) $180 + x + y$
(D) $180 - x - y$
(E) $180 - 2x - 2y$

This is a typical example on the SAT that presents itself as a triangle problem because the main diagram looks like a triangle, when it is in fact a quadrilateral problem. See the highlighted quadrilateral in the diagram below.

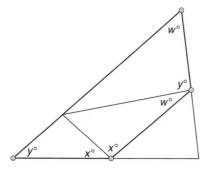

Now it's easy to tell that the sum of all the *x*, *y*, and *w* measures is equal to 360°, since the sum of the interior angles of any quadrilateral is exactly 360°. For example, $w+y+w+x+x+y=360 \Rightarrow 2w+2x+2y=360 \Rightarrow w+x+y=180 \Rightarrow w=180-x-y$. That's all there is to it! The correct answer choice is D.

2.

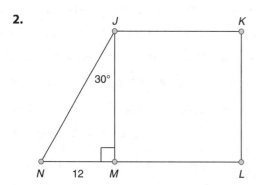

In the figure above, *JKLM* is a square and *NM* = 12. What is the area of *JKLM*?

Many polygon problems on the SAT combine triangles and quadrilaterals, so it's extra important to know the properties of both. Here we want to know the area of *JKLM*. Visually, *JKLM* is a square, which means we need to know the length of one side to find the area. Square *JKLM* and triangle *JMN* are attached at *JM*. We need to focus on finding *JM* using triangle properties. From the diagram, triangle *JMN* is a right triangle with a 30° angle. That means it is a 30-60-90 triangle. According to the 30-60-90 triangle relationship, side *JM* is exactly $12\sqrt{3}$. Since *JM* is also a side of the square, the area of the square is simply $(12\sqrt{3})^2 = 432$ (computed using the calculator).

3.

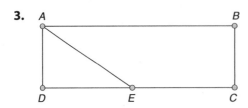

In the figure above, *ABCD* is a rectangle. The area of triangle *ADE* is 9 and $EC = \frac{4}{7}DC$. What is the area of *ABCD*?

This type of triangle-quadrilateral-area problem always comes up on the SAT, usually as an upper-level medium problem or possibly a hard-level problem. The trick to solving them is generally the same—be as formulaic as possible. We know the area of the triangle, but we want the area of the rectangle. In this type of problem, the formula for the area of what we know will almost always produce the area of the shape we want. You'll see what this means in a moment.

First, write the formula for the area of what you know, and substitute the given area: *Area of Triangle* $= \frac{1}{2}(AD)(DE) \Rightarrow 9 = \frac{1}{2}(AD)(DE)$. We are told that $EC = \frac{4}{7}DC$. The length of *DE*, the remaining piece of *DC*, must be $\frac{3}{7}DC$ since *ED* and *EC* need to make a whole. Now replace *DE* with $\frac{3}{7}DC$ in our area formula, and simplify: $9 = \frac{1}{2}(AD)\left(\frac{3}{7}DC\right) \Rightarrow 9 = \frac{1}{2}\cdot\frac{3}{7}(AD)(DC) \Rightarrow 9 = \frac{3}{14}(AD)(DC) \Rightarrow \frac{14}{3}\cdot 9 = (AD)(DC) \Rightarrow 42$. Now think about what the quantity $(AD)(DC)$ really represents. It's exactly the formula we would use to find the area of the rectangle, if we actually knew the side lengths. These problems almost always work this way, so know the process we did here. The correct answer is 42.

Circles

A circle is the set of points that are equidistant from a point in the plane, called the center. The center of a circle is also the intersection of any two distinct diameters. A diameter is a chord inside of a circle that spans the maximum distance from one point on a circle to another. A radius is a segment that spans the distance from the center to any point on a circle. Therefore, the length of the radius is equal to half the length of the diameter: $d = 2r$.

The segment that joins any two distinct points on a circle is a chord. The diameter is also a chord, but it's special because it passes through the center, and it is the longest chord in a circle.

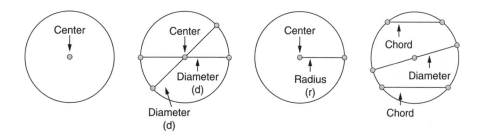

Most important is that a circle has exactly 360°. We always think of the famous basketball move "doing a 360" to remember that a circle has 360°.

The circumference of a circle is the product of pi and the diameter (or twice the radius), and the area of a circle is the product of π and the square of the radius.

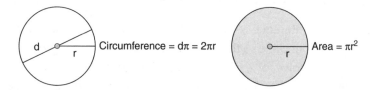

Let's apply these special circle properties as we go through a few typical SAT problems.

Examples

1.

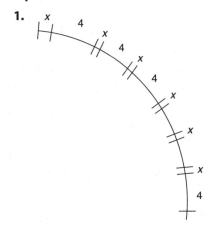

The figure above (not drawn to scale) shows part of a circle whose circumference is 120. If arcs of length 4 and length x continue around the entire circle so that there are 16 arcs of each length, what is the degree measure of each of the arcs of length x?

(A) 9.0°

(B) 9.5°

(C) 10.0°

(D) 10.5°

(E) 11.0°

First, we need to really understand what we are solving for. Think about it this way. If we were cutting a pizza into four slices, each slice would be 90° from the center. If we cut the pizza into eight slices, each piece would be 45° from the center. In these simple examples, we just "know" that the degree measures of the slices are 90 and 45. But what we are actually doing is 360 divided by the number of slices we want. For example, $\frac{360}{8} = 45°$. We will use this concept to solve the current problem.

The total circumference is 120, and arcs of length 4 and length x continue around the entire circle so that there are 16 arcs of each length. We can make an equation to solve for x, since the sum of the arcs must equal the circumference: $16(4)+16(x)=120 \Rightarrow 64+16x=120 \Rightarrow 16x=56 \Rightarrow x=3.5$. To find out the degree measure of each slice measuring 3.5, you need to use the concept we discussed. Divide 360 by the number of slices measuring 3.5: $360 \div \left(\frac{120}{3.5}\right)=10.5°$. That was a tough problem! But, luckily, the process is always the same. The correct answer choice is D.

2.   Currently, a unicyclist has a red marking at the exact top of the wheel of his unicycle. The red marking will disappear after the marking touches the ground 40 times, which is after the unicyclist travels 908.5π inches. What is the current number of inches between the red marking and the ground?

The tricky part of this problem is visualizing what is happening to the red marking as the wheel turns, as well as understanding what we are looking for. We want to know the current number of inches between the red marking and the ground. In other words, the red marking is currently at the top of the wheel and the ground is directly below it. That means the "current" number of inches is exactly the diameter of the wheel.

If the red marking is at the top of the wheel now, then it only has to make one-half of a turn to exactly touch the ground. Then it needs to make 39 full turns. The first half-turn produces 1 touch, and the next 39 full turns produce 39 touches to make 40 touches in all, which is the number of touches required to make the marking disappear. If the wheel traveled a total of 908.5π inches, then we can find the circumference of the wheel by dividing the total distance by the number of turns: $\dfrac{908.5\pi}{39.5} = 23\pi$ inches. Since the circumference of a circle is equal to the diameter times pi, it's clear that the diameter is exactly 23 inches.

3.

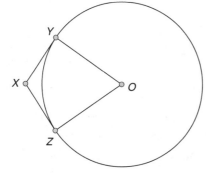

In the figure above (not drawn to scale), $\overline{XY}$ and $\overline{XZ}$ are tangent at points Y and Z, respectively, to the circle with center at point O. If a is the average of the degree measures of $\angle OYX$ and $\angle YXZ$, what is the largest possible integer value of a?

We want to know the largest possible integer value of a, given that a is the average of the degree measures of $\angle OYX$ and $\angle YXZ$. Since $\overline{XY}$ and $\overline{XZ}$ are tangent at points Y and Z, we know that the measures of $\angle OYX$ and $\angle OZX$ must each be 90°. Since $XYOZ$ is a quadrilateral, and two angles are already each 90°, angles $\angle O$ and $\angle X$ must be supplementary, or sum to 180°, to make up the required sum of 360° for a quadrilateral.

If we want the largest possible integer value of a, given that a is the average of the degree measures of $\angle OYX$ and $\angle YXZ$, then we want to the two angles to be as large as possible. No matter what, the measure of $\angle OYX$ is stuck at 90°. But the measure of $\angle YXZ$ can be as much as 178°, with the understanding that $\angle YXZ$ and $\angle O$ are supplementary and the average must be an integer. At first, you might think that $\angle YXZ$ should equal 180°, but it can't because then $\angle O$ would disappear! Also the measure of $\angle YXZ$ can't equal 179° because then the average, a, would not be an integer. We can calculate the average as follows: $a = \dfrac{90 + 178}{2} = 134.$

4.

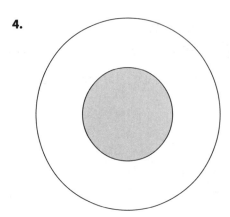

The figure above (not drawn to scale) consists of two circles that have the same center. If the unshaded area is 144π square inches and the smaller circle has a radius of 5 inches, what is the radius, in inches, of the larger circle?

We are looking for the radius of the larger circle. We know for sure that the radius of the small circle is 5 inches, so the area of the small circle is equal to $5^2\pi \Rightarrow 25\pi$ square inches. We know that the area of the unshaded part of the circle is 144π square inches. Adding $25\pi+144\pi$, we get a total area of 169π square inches. The radius of the larger circle must be 13, since $13^2\pi \Rightarrow 169\pi$. The correct answer is 13.

Inscribed and Circumscribed Polygons

A polygon is inscribed in another polygon when it is drawn inside the other polygon. On the other hand, a polygon is circumscribed when it is drawn around another polygon so that it touches all that polygon's vertices. Put simply, problems involving inscribed and circumscribed polygons require you to think about the properties of multiple shapes at once. There are lots of fancy theorems and formulas for special inscribed and circumscribed polygons, but they are often more difficult to remember and more complex to use than just thinking about the problem directly.

Let's work on this intuitive approach together in the next few examples.

Examples

1.

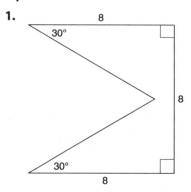

What is the perimeter of the figure above?

(A)   32
(B)   34
(C)   40
(D)   48
(E)   52

The perimeter of the figure is the sum of the lengths of each of the five sides. We know three out of the five sides measure 8. However, finding the other two takes some creativity. Imagine connecting the two leftmost endpoints to form a triangle inside the square. Since the whole angles must be 90° each, the missing angles must measure 90−30=60° each. The vertex angle inside the square must also equal 60°, since the sum of the three angles inside the triangle must equal 180°.

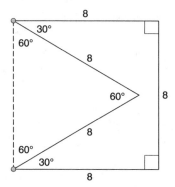

The triangle inside is equilateral. Since one side is 8, the other two sides must also be 8. The perimeter of the original polygon is 8 + 8 + 8 + 8 + 8 = 40. The correct answer choice is C.

2.

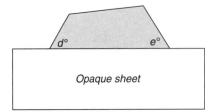

In the figure above, a shaded polygon that has equal sides and angles is partially covered with an opaque sheet of paper. If $d+e=60$, how many sides does the polygon have?

(A)   15
(B)   12
(C)   10
(D)   9
(E)   6

This seems like a tricky problem because so many shapes and rules are involved. Let's break it down. The exposed part of the shaded polygon is a quadrilateral, though the whole polygon has some other number of sides. The sum of the interior angles of a quadrilateral is 360°. Since the shaded polygon has equal sides and angles, the two unknown angles on top must each equal: $\dfrac{360-(d+e)}{2} \Rightarrow \dfrac{360-60}{2} \Rightarrow \dfrac{300}{2} \Rightarrow 150°$. If the interior angle is equal to 150°, then the exterior angle must equal 30° because the interior angle and exterior angle are always supplementary. According to polygon law, the sum of the exterior angles of every polygon is 360°. The number of sides in the shaded polygon is therefore: $\dfrac{360°}{30°}=12$. The correct answer is B.

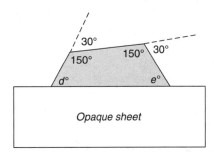

3.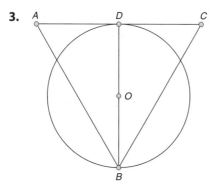

In the figure above, triangle *ABC* is equilateral, with side length of 8. If $\overline{BD}$ is a diameter of the circle with center *O*, then the area of the circle is

(A) 48π

(B) 12π

(C) $2\sqrt{3}\pi$

(D) $2\sqrt{3}\pi$

(E) $4\sqrt{3}\pi$

Especially with inscribed or circumscribed polygon problems, it's easiest to work backwards. We want to know the area of the circle. In order to find the area of a circle, we need to know the radius. In the diagram, the diameter of the circle doubles as the height of the triangle. Of course, if we can find the length of the diameter, then we can halve it to get the radius. Since the triangle *ABC* is equilateral, angles *A* and *C* are both 60°. The height cuts angle *B* exactly in half, producing two 30° angles, and consequently two 30-60-90 triangles. According to the 30-60-90 rule, the length of *DB* is exactly $\sqrt{3}$ times the length of *DC*. Since the whole side *AC* = 8, both *AD* and *DC* must each equal 4. That means the length of *DB*, which is both the the height of the triangle *and* the diameter of the circle, is $4\sqrt{3}$. The radius is equal to half the diameter, or $2\sqrt{3}$. Finally, the area of the circle is: $r^2\pi \Rightarrow (2\sqrt{3})^2\pi \Rightarrow 12\pi$. The correct answer is B.

4. A sphere of radius *m* inside a cube touches each one of the six sides of the cube. What is the volume of the cube, in terms of *m*?

(A) m^3

(B) $2m^3$

(C) $\dfrac{\sqrt{3}}{4}m^3$

(D) $\dfrac{4}{3}m^3$

(E) $8m^3$

A good diagram is key to getting through this problem. We are told that the sphere is inscribed in the cube, and that its radius is *m*.

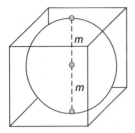

If we draw the two radii from the center of the sphere to the exact top and bottom of the cube, we create a diameter that is exactly as long as an edge of the cube. The edge of the cube is equal to *2m*. Since the volume of a cube is determined by the formula, $V = edge^3$, we have that $V = (2m)^3 = 8m^3$. The correct response is choice E.

Locus

A locus is, simply put, the set of points that satisfies a given condition. You need to know a few basic locus conditions to be able to solve locus problems on the SAT.

All points on a circle are equidistant from the center of the circle. (The distance of any point from the center of the circle is the radius.)

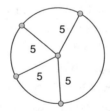

Two lines are equidistant if and only if they are parallel lines.

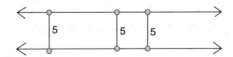

The locus of all points equidistant from a given line is a parallel line. (The distance is measured along a perpendicular.)

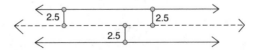

All points on a sphere are equidistant from the center of the sphere.

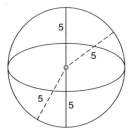

Some of these conditions seem complicated, but luckily they are not too difficult to apply. Let's work through some typical SAT problems.

Examples

1. In the *xy*-plane, how many points are a distance of 6 units from the origin?

(A) 1
(B) 2
(C) 4
(D) 8
(E) More than 8

Here, you need to image the origin as a single point. The locus condition for a point is a circle of a particular radius, in this case, 6 units. Every point on the circle is 6 units from the origin. There are infinitely many points on the circle. The correct answer choice is E.

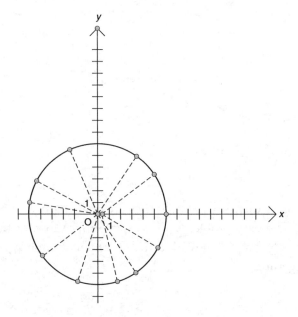

2. Bobby and Meredith are standing on flat ground, and they are a distance of 80 feet apart. A secret treasure is buried 60 feet away from Bobby and 40 feet away from Meredith. What is the maximum number of locations where the treasure could be buried?

(A)   0
(B)   1
(C)   2
(D)   3
(E)   Cannot be determined from the information given

The key to solving this problem is a good diagram. Start by drawing each condition separately, and then see where the loci intersect. The correct answer choice is C.

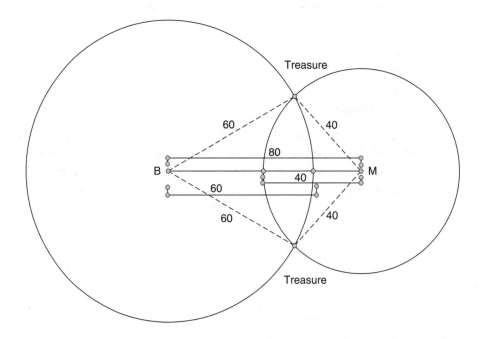

Area

Area problems on the SAT are either really easy, or they are really hard. There's usually no middle ground. The easy problems are simple applications of the area formulas for different polygons. We'll work through some common types of harder area problems together.

Examples

1.

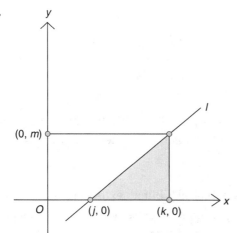

In the figure above (not drawn to scale), $3k = 5m$ and the area of the shaded triangle is $\frac{1}{3}$ the area of the rectangle. What is the slope of line l?

This type of problem comes up frequently. If you can get the drill down here, then doing it on the SAT should be quite easy. First, we know that the area of the shaded triangle is $\frac{1}{3}$ the area of the rectangle. We can tell that the upper-right corner of the rectangle has coordinates (k, m). The base of the triangle measures $k - j$, and the height is m. The base of the rectangle is k, and the height is also m. That means we can write an equation that compares the two areas: $\frac{1}{2}(k-j)(m) = \frac{1}{3}(k)(m) \Rightarrow k - j = \frac{2}{3}k$. Next, we are told that $3k = 5m$. Solving for m, we get: $m = \frac{3}{5}k$.

Now that we have two quantities in terms of k and j, we have enough information to determine the slope of line l. In general, the slope of line l equals $\frac{m - 0}{k - j} \Rightarrow \frac{m}{k - j}$. We can substitute the values we found in the first part:

$\frac{\frac{3}{5}k}{\frac{2}{3}k} \Rightarrow \frac{\frac{3}{5}}{\frac{2}{3}} \Rightarrow \frac{3}{5} \times \frac{3}{2} = \frac{9}{10}$. The slope of line l is $\frac{9}{10}$. Is it tricky? Yes. But now you know the drill!

2.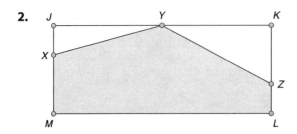

In the rectangle above, the ratio of JX to XM is 2:3, the ratio of LZ to ZK is 2:3, and Y is the midpoint of $\overline{JK}$. What fraction of the area of the rectangle is shaded?

This problem can be solved algebraically, but it's extremely difficult and time-consuming to do so. Instead, you want to take advantage of the fact that the diagram is drawn to scale. If the ratio of JX to XM is 2:3 and the ratio of LZ to ZK is 2:3, then we can effectively split the whole rectangle horizontally into five rectangles (2+3=5). Since Y is the midpoint of $\overline{JK}$, we can continue to split the whole rectangle into two smaller rectangles vertically through Y, as follows:

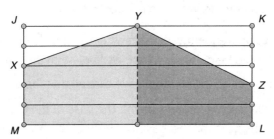

All you are interested in is the fraction of the rectangle that is shaded. Now that the diagram is split up horizontally and vertically, you can see that the whole rectangle is divided into 10 equally sized smaller rectangles, 5 within each vertical half. Simply imagine the partially shaded parts of the top two rectangles in the first row filling in the partially unshaded parts of the rectangles in the second and third rows, as follows:

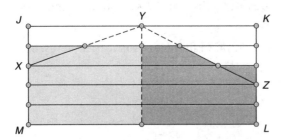

Now you can simply count that there are exactly 7.5 shaded rectangles. Since there are 10 rectangles all together, the fraction of the rectangle that is shaded is $\frac{7.5}{10} \Rightarrow \frac{3}{4}$. The correct response is $\frac{3}{4}$.

3.

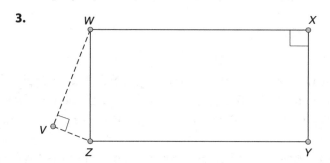

If the area of rectangle *WXYZ* is 64, and the ratio of *WX* to *XY* to *ZV* is 8:2:1, then what is the measure of ∠*YZV* in degrees?

This problem is nearly impossible to solve if you are not thinking of the special 30-60-90 right triangle. First, fill out the ratio lengths 8:2:1, as follows:

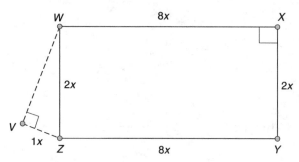

Then consider triangle *VWZ*. The hypotenuse is 2*x*, one side is 1*x*, and the other side must be $\sqrt{3}x$, according to the Pythagorean theorem, or the 30-60-90 rule. The measure of ∠*VZW*, is 60°, since it is the angle opposite the side with length $\sqrt{3}x$.

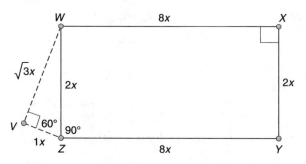

The measure of $\angle WZY$ is 90° simply because of the properties of a rectangle. The sum of $\angle VZW$ and $\angle WXY$ is exactly the angle measure we are looking for. The measure of $\angle YZV$ is 150°.

The area being 64 has nothing to do with anything! It's a distracter.

Volume

Volume questions on the SAT are usually straightforward. The formulas for volume are always given to you at the beginning of each math section, though you should be familiar with how to reference them and, more importantly, how to use them.

Most volume questions are of the comparison type, meaning the SAT will ask you to compare the volumes of two figures, or the SAT might give you the volume, and you'll need to figure out other information by working the formula backwards. Here are the basic shapes you should know:

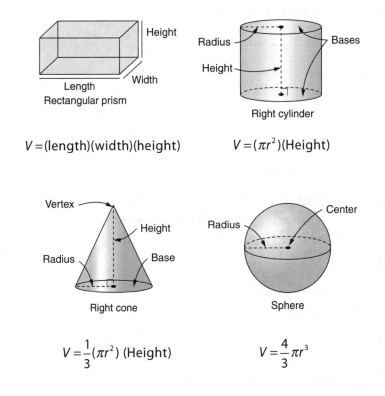

Rectangular prism

$V = $(length)(width)(height)

Right cylinder

$V = (\pi r^2)$(Height)

Right cone

$$V = \frac{1}{3}(\pi r^2)\ (\text{Height})$$

Sphere

$$V = \frac{4}{3}\pi r^3$$

Let's work through a couple of practice problems together.

Examples

1. A right circular cylinder with radius 6 and height 3 has volume x. In terms of x, what is the volume of a right circular cylinder with radius 6 and height 9?

(A) $x+6$

(B) x

(C) $3x$

(D) $6x$

(E) $9x$

We are told that a right circular cylinder with radius 6 and height 3 has volume x. So we turn to the formula: $V = (\pi r^2)(Height) \Rightarrow x = \pi(6)^2(3) \Rightarrow x = 108\pi$. Now we want to know, in terms of x, the volume of a right circular cylinder with radius 6 and height 9. We can find the volume of the new cylinder first: $V = (\pi r^2)(Height) \Rightarrow V = \pi(6)^2(9) \Rightarrow V = 324\pi$. Since $3 \times 108\pi = 324\pi$, we know that the volume, in terms of x, is $3 \times x$, or simply $3x$. The correct response is C.

2. What is the maximum number of rectangular blocks measuring 4 inches by 2 inches by 1 inch that can be packed into a cube-shaped box whose interior measures 8 inches on an edge?

(A) 32

(B) 54

(C) 64

(D) 128

(E) 256

This type of problem inevitably shows up on real SAT exams. You need to figure out how many smaller blocks can fit into the larger box. The trick is to find the volume of each, and then divide the smaller into the larger. This tells you exactly how many small bricks fit into the larger space. For example, $V_{small} = 4 \times 2 \times 1 = 8$ and $V_{big} = 8 \times 8 \times 8 = 512$. Now we can divide: $\dfrac{V_{big}}{V_{small}} = \dfrac{512}{8} = 64$. Exactly 64 bricks fit into the cube. The correct response is C.

The Formulas You're Not Given That You Ought to Know

Arithmetic Operations

$ab + ac = a(b + c)$ $\quad a\left(\dfrac{b}{c}\right) = \dfrac{ab}{c}$

$\dfrac{\left(\dfrac{a}{b}\right)}{c} = \dfrac{a}{bc}$ $\qquad \dfrac{a}{\left(\dfrac{b}{c}\right)} = \dfrac{ac}{b}$

$\dfrac{a}{b} + \dfrac{c}{d} = \dfrac{ad + bc}{bd}$ $\qquad \dfrac{a}{b} - \dfrac{c}{d} = \dfrac{ad - bc}{bd}$

$\dfrac{a - b}{c - d} = \dfrac{b - a}{d - c}$ $\qquad \dfrac{a + b}{c} = \dfrac{a}{c} + \dfrac{b}{c}$

$\dfrac{ab + ac}{a} = b + c,\ a \neq 0$ $\quad \dfrac{\left(\dfrac{a}{b}\right)}{\left(\dfrac{c}{d}\right)} = \dfrac{ad}{bc}$

Exponent Rules

$a^n a^m = a^{n+m}$ $\qquad \dfrac{a^n}{a^m} = a^{n-m} = \dfrac{1}{a^{m-n}}$

$(a^n)^m = a^{nm}$ $\qquad a^0 = 1,\ a \neq 0$

$(ab)^n = a^n b^n$ $\qquad \left(\dfrac{a}{b}\right)^n = \dfrac{a^n}{b^n}$

$a^{-n} = \dfrac{1}{a^n}$ $\qquad \dfrac{1}{a^{-n}} = a^n$

$\left(\dfrac{a}{b}\right)^{-n} = \left(\dfrac{b}{a}\right)^n = \dfrac{b^n}{a^n}$ $\quad a^{\frac{n}{m}} = \left(a^{\frac{1}{m}}\right)^n = (a^n)^{\frac{1}{m}}$

Distance Formula

If $P_1 = (x_1, y_1)$ and $P_2 = (x_2, y_2)$ are two points the distance between them is

$$d(P_1, P_2) = \sqrt{(x_2 - x_1)^2 + (y_2 - y_1)^2}$$

Constant Function

$y = a$ or $f(x) = a$

Graph is a horizontal line passing though the point $(0, a)$.

Factoring Formulas

$x^2 - a^2 = (x + a)(x - a)$

$x^2 + 2ax + a^2 = (x + a)^2$

$x^2 - 2ax + a^2 = (x - a)^2$

Linear Functions

$y = mx + b$ or $f(x) = mx + b$

Graph is a line with point $(0, b)$ and slope m.

Slope

Slope of the line containing the two points (x_1, y_1) and (x_2, y_2) is

$$m = \frac{y_2 - y_1}{x_2 - x_1} = \frac{\text{rise}}{\text{run}}$$

Slope–Intercept Form

The equation of the line with slope m and y-intercept $(0, b)$ is

$$y = mx + b$$

Point–Slope Form

The equation of the line with slope m and passing through the point (x_1, y_1) is

$$y - y_1 = m(x - x_1)$$

Common Mistakes You Need to Avoid

Error	Correction
$\dfrac{3}{0} \neq 0$ and $\dfrac{3}{0} \neq 3$	You can never divide by 0. Division by 0 is undefined.
$-4^2 \neq 16$	$-4^2 = -16$ and $(-4)^2 = 16$. Be careful how you use parentheses.
$(x^3)^4 \neq x^7$	$(x^3)^4 = x^{12}$. Raising a power to a power means you have to multiply, not add.
$\dfrac{x}{y+z} \neq \dfrac{x}{y} + \dfrac{x}{z}$	$\dfrac{3}{4} = \dfrac{3}{3+1} \neq \dfrac{3}{3} + \dfrac{3}{1} = 1 + 3 = 4$. You can only divide monomials (not binomials) into a numerator.
$\dfrac{x + cy}{x} \neq 1 + cy$	$\dfrac{x+cy}{x} = 1 + \dfrac{cy}{x}$. If you divide a monomial into one piece of the numerator, you need to divide it into all the pieces.
$-b(y-1) \neq -by - b$	$-b(y-1) = -by + b$. Make sure you distribute to each piece inside the parentheses.
$(x + m)^2 \neq x^2 + m^2$	$(x+m)^2 = (x+m)(x+m) = x^2 + 2xm + m^2$. When raising a binomial to a power, make sure you FOIL! You may never "distribute" a power over a + or a – sign.

Chapter 14 Quiz—Geometry
25 Questions

Directions: For this quiz, solve each problem and decide which is the best of the choices given. For Student-Produced Response questions, solve each problem and record your solution.

Notes

1. The use of a calculator is permitted.
2. All numbers used are real numbers.
3. Figures that accompany problems in this test are intended to provide information useful in solving the problems. They are drawn as accurately as possible EXCEPT when it is stated in a specific problem that the figure is not drawn to scale. All figures lie in a plane unless otherwise indicated.
4. Unless otherwise specified, the domain of any function f is assumed to be the set of all real numbers x for which $f(x)$ is a real number.

Reference Information

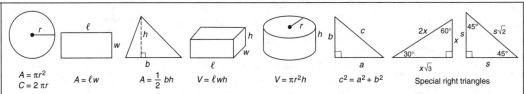

$A = \pi r^2$
$C = 2\pi r$ $A = \ell w$ $A = \frac{1}{2} bh$ $V = \ell wh$ $V = \pi r^2 h$ $c^2 = a^2 + b^2$ Special right triangles

The number of degrees of arc in a circle is 360.
The sum of the measures in degrees of the angles of a triangle is 180.

1.

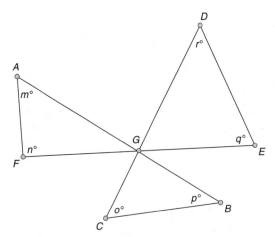

In the figure above (not drawn to scale), $\overline{AB}$, $\overline{CD}$, and $\overline{EF}$ intersect at G. If $m = 35$, $n = 95$, $o = 60$, $p = 65$, and $q = 80$, what is the value of r?

(A) 20
(B) 25
(C) 40
(D) 45
(E) It cannot be determined from the information given

2.

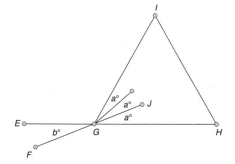

In the figure above, ΔGHI is equilateral and $\overline{EH}$ and $\overline{FJ}$ intersect at point P. What is the value of b?

3.

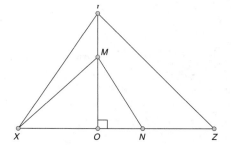

In ΔXYZ above (not drawn to scale), $\dfrac{YM}{MO} = \dfrac{2}{3}$ and $\dfrac{XN}{XZ} = \dfrac{3}{5}$. What is the value of the fraction $\dfrac{area\ \Delta XMN}{area\ \Delta XYZ}$?

4.

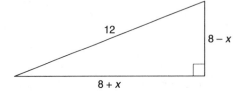

The figure above is a right triangle (not drawn to scale). What is the value of $64 + x^2$?

(A) 8
(B) 72
(C) 73
(D) 128
(E) 144

5.

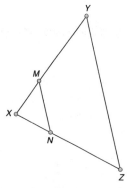

Note: Figure not drawn to scale.

In ΔXYZ above, $XY = XZ$, M is the midpoint of $\overline{XY}$, and N is the midpoint of $\overline{XZ}$. If $XM = a$ and $MN = 6$, what is the length of YZ?

(A) 8
(B) 12
(C) $2a$
(D) $6a$
(E) $6a^2$

6.

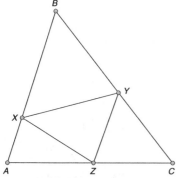

Note: Figure not drawn to scale.

In the figure above, $AB = BC$ and $XY = YZ = XZ$. If the measure of $\angle ABC = 46°$ and the measure of $\angle BXY = 32°$, what is the measure of $\angle XZA$?

(A) 20°
(B) 25°
(C) 30°
(D) 35°
(E) 40°

7.

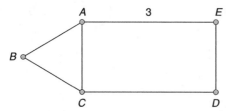

In the figure above, ABC is an equilateral triangle and $CDEA$ is a rectangle with an area of 6. What is the perimeter of polygon $ABCDE$?

(A) 6
(B) 8
(C) 10
(D) 12
(E) 14

8.

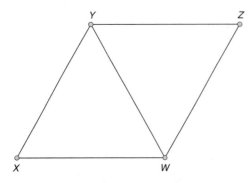

In the figure above, triangle XYW and triangle ZWY are equilateral. What is the ratio of the length of $\overline{XZ}$ (not shown) to the length of $\overline{WY}$?

(A) $\sqrt{2}$ to 1
(B) $\sqrt{3}$ to 3
(C) $\sqrt{3}$ to 2
(D) $\sqrt{3}$ to 1
(E) $\sqrt{3}$ to $\sqrt{2}$

9. When each side of a square is shortened by 6 inches, the area of the square is decreased by 132 square inches. What is the length, in inches, of one side of the original square?

(A) 14
(B) 15
(C) 16
(D) 17
(E) 18

10.

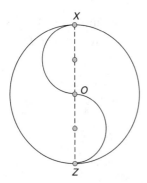

The circle above has center O and diameter XZ. The two semicircles have diameters OX and OZ. If the circumference of the circle is 64π, what is the length of the curved path from X to Z through O?

(A) 8π
(B) 16π
(C) 32π
(D) 48π
(E) 64π

11.

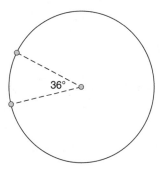

Roxana makes metal dishes. For one style of dish, she cuts wedges from a metal disk, as shown in the diagram above. Each wedge makes a 36° angle at the center of the disk. If the weight of each uncut disk is a uniformly distributed 44.6 grams, how many grams does each wedge weigh?

12. One circle has a radius of $\frac{1}{4}$ and another circle has a radius of 1. What is the ratio of the area of the larger circle to the area of the smaller circle?

(A) 32:1
(B) 16:1
(C) 8:1
(D) 4:1
(E) 2:1

13.

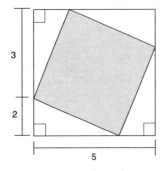

In the figure above, what is the area of the shaded region?

14.

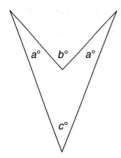

If $a = 35$ and $c = 50$ in the figure above (not drawn to scale), what is the value of b?

(A) 85
(B) 90
(C) 100
(D) 110
(E) 120

15.

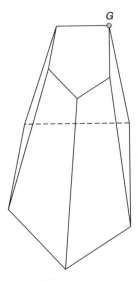

The three-dimensional figure above has 2 parallel bases and 15 edges. Line segments are to be drawn connecting vertex G with each of the other 9 vertices in the figure. How many of these segments will not lie on an edge of the figure?

16.   Points *A, B, C,* and *D* lie in a plane. How many squares, having *A, B, C,* and *D* as vertices, and an area of 24 square inches, can be drawn in the plane?

(A) 0

(B) 1

(C) 3

(D) 4

(E) more than 4

17.

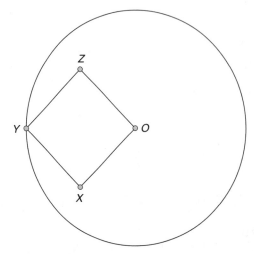

In the figure above, O is the center of the circle. If the area of square OXYZ is 72, and vertex Y is on the circle, what is the area of the circle?

(A) 144π
(B) 72π
(C) 36π
(D) $12\sqrt{2}\pi$
(E) $6\sqrt{2}\pi$

18.

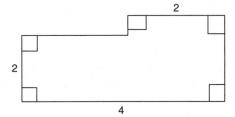

The area of the figure above is $\dfrac{28}{3}$. What is the perimeter of the figure?

19.

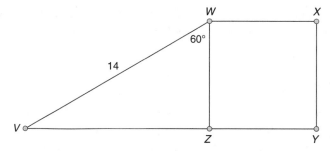

In the figure above, *WXYZ* is a square and *VW* = 14. What is the area of square *WXYZ?*

20.

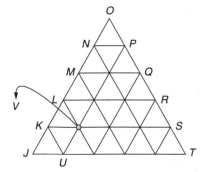

The figure above is composed of 25 small triangles that are congruent and equilateral. If the area of rhombus *JKVU* is 15, what is the area of △*JOT?*

(A) 62.5
(B) 93.75
(C) 96.25
(D) 187.5
(E) 190

21. A right circular cylinder with a radius of 2 units and height of 2 units has a volume that is closest in value to the volume of a rectangular solid with dimensions, in units,

    (A) 1 by 2 by 1
    (B) 2 by 2 by 3
    (C) 2 by 3 by 3
    (D) 2 by 2 by 4
    (E) 3 by 2 by 4

22. How many cubical blocks, each with edges of length 3 centimeters, are needed to fill a rectangular box that has inside dimensions 18 centimeters by 27 centimeters by 39 centimeters?

    (A) 54
    (B) 216
    (C) 351
    (D) 702
    (E) 936

23.

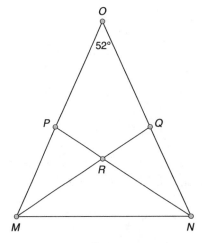

In triangle MNO above, $\overline{MQ}$ and $\overline{NP}$ are the angle bisectors of angle OMN and angle ONM. What is the measure of angle PRQ?

    (A) 108°
    (B) 112°
    (C) 116°
    (D) 120°
    (E) 124°

24. $\overline{AC}$ is the diagonal of square $ABCD$ and has length $8\sqrt{2}$. What is the perimeter of square $ABCD$?

25. In rectangle $WXYZ$, point Q is the midpoint of $\overline{WX}$. If the area of quadrilateral $YZQX$ is $\dfrac{3}{4}$, what is the area of rectangle $WXYZ$?

(A) $\dfrac{1}{3}$

(B) $\dfrac{9}{16}$

(C) 1

(D) $\dfrac{16}{9}$

(E) $\dfrac{9}{2}$

chapter 15

Proportions

In this chapter, we will learn techniques for solving a variety of problems on the SAT. We will cover simple ratios, percents, inverse and direct proportions, and harmonic mean.

Simple Ratios

A *ratio* is a quotient of one number (or variable) a to another number (or variable) b. It can be expressed in three ways: 1) $a{:}b$; 2) $\frac{a}{b}$, and 3) $a \div b$. The ratio $a{:}b$ is read as a to b.

For example, to write the ratio of 2 hours:30 minutes in simplest form, do the following:

$$2 \text{ hours:}30 \text{ minutes} = 120 \text{ minutes:}30 \text{ minutes} = 4{:}1$$

A *proportion* is an equation of two ratios. It can be expressed in two ways: 1) $a{:}b = c{:}d$; and 2) $\frac{a}{b} = \frac{c}{d}$. The proportion $a{:}b = c{:}d$ is read as a is to b as c is to d in which a and d are the extremes, and b and c are the means. Hence, the proportion $a{:}b = c{:}d$ can also be written as $ad = bc$ (this is basically an example of cross-multiplication).

Let's develop some strategies for ratios together!

Examples

1. In a mixture of cashews and walnuts, the ratio by weight of cashews to walnuts is 5 to 7. How many pounds of cashews will there be in 15 pounds of this mixture?

(A)   6.00
(B)   6.25
(C)   7.50
(D)   8.75
(E)   9.00

This is a typical ratio problem on the SAT. All we know is that the ratio by weight of cashews to walnuts is 5 to 7. That doesn't tell us anything about how many pounds of each nut are present. So we need to think of the ratio like this: You have a big bowl. In it, you have cashews and walnuts. 5 parts are cashews and 7 parts are walnuts. That means you have 12 parts all together. So the ratio of cashews to the whole bowl of nuts is 5 to 12, or $\frac{5}{12}$.

Since we are looking for how many pounds of cashews there will be in 15 pounds of the mixture, we just need to multiply the ratio $\frac{5}{12}$ by 15: $\frac{5}{12} \times 15 = 6.25$. The correct answer is B.

2. In a recent contest, a total of 140,000 votes were cast for two opposing performers—Sheba and Claire—to win an award. If Sheba won by a ratio of 9 to 7, how many votes were cast for Claire?

(A)   52,500
(B)   61,250
(C)   70,000
(D)   78,750
(E)   87,500

This problem is very similar to the previous one, except a little trickier. This time, we know that there were a total of 140,000 votes, and that Sheba won the contest by a ratio of 9 to 7. Once again: We have a big bowl full of 140,000 votes that are either for Sheba or Claire. 9 parts of the votes are for Sheba (since Sheba won, she needs to have the bigger chunk), and 7 parts are for Claire. That means we have 16 parts all together. The ratio of Claire's votes to total votes is $\frac{7}{16}$. Since we are looking for the number of votes Claire received, we just need to multiply that ratio $\frac{7}{16}$ by 140,000: $\frac{7}{16} \times 140,000 = 61,250$. The correct answer is B.

3. In a bag of marbles, $\frac{1}{6}$ of the marbles are red, $\frac{5}{12}$ of the marbles are orange, and $\frac{1}{4}$ of the marbles are yellow. If the remaining 8 marbles are green, how many marbles are in the bag?

(A)   16

(B)   24

(C)   32

(D)   40

(E)   48

This type of problem looks and sounds like a probability problem, but it is a ratio problem. I like to think of it as "know some parts, want to find the missing part" problem. We know that $\frac{1}{6}$ of the marbles are red, $\frac{5}{12}$ of the marbles are orange, and $\frac{1}{4}$ of the marbles are yellow, and some fraction, call it x, has to represent the remaining green marbles. The first step is to solve for x. If we had all the ratios for the different-colored marbles and added them up, the sum should be exactly 1, in order to make a "whole." Use the calculator to add: $\frac{1}{6} + \frac{5}{12} + \frac{1}{4}$. If you enter the fractions carefully, you'll get a sum of .83333.... You can turn this number into a fraction by hitting: MATH, ENTER, ENTER. You'll get $\frac{5}{6}$. That means there is exactly $\frac{1}{6}$ left (since $1 - \frac{5}{6} = \frac{1}{6}$), which must represent x, the ratio of green marbles. Now think about it. We know there are exactly 8 green marbles. So $\frac{1}{6}$ times the total number of marbles should equal 8. In equation form, $\frac{1}{6} \times Total = 8 \implies Total = 48$. The total number of marbles is 48, and the correct response is E.

Percents

Percent literally means "out of 100." That's why if you get 8 out of 10 questions right on an exam, you score an 80%. For percent and decimal questions, there are two basic strategies—one for each of the common ways these types of questions are asked. Look at the following examples.

Type	Translation	Example and Answer
x is y percent of n	$x = y\% \times n$	24 is 15% of what number? $24 = 15\% \times n$ $n = 24 \div 15\% = 160$
x percent of y is n	$x\% \times y = n$	11% of 50 is what number? $11\% \times 50 = n$ $n = 5.5$

These strategies are much easier to understand through example. Let's work through some conceptual and computational problems together.

Examples

1. A canister of juice from concentrate contains 80 milliliters of a juice and water solution that is 20% juice. If j more milliliters of juice are added to the solution, which of the following expresses the percentage of juice in the new solution?

(A) $\dfrac{16 \times 100}{80 + j}\%$

(B) $\dfrac{(16 + j) \times 100}{80 + j}\%$

(C) $\dfrac{16 \times (j + 100)}{80 + j}\%$

(D) $\dfrac{16}{80 + j}\%$

(E) $\dfrac{16 + j}{80 + j}\%$

We know that there are 80 milliliters of liquid in the canister. The liquid is made up of juice and water, and 20% of the total liquid is juice. Essentially, 20% of 80 milliliters is $.20 \times 80 = 16$ milliliters of juice. So 16 milliliters of the total 80 milliliters is juice, and the rest is water. Now we want to add j more milliliters of juice to the solution. Once we add the juice, the total milliliters of juice will be the 16 milliliters we already had, plus the j added milliliters, or $16 + j$ milliliters of juice. Adding juice without taking away water also increases the total liquid in the canister by j milliliters, meaning the total liquid becomes $80 + j$ milliters.

To find out the percentage of juice in the new solution, we need to divide the total juice by the total liquid, *and* times the quotient by 100%. Therefore, the percentage of juice in the new solution is $\dfrac{(16 + j) \times 100}{80 + j}\%$. Most students forget to multiply the final quotient by 100%, which is why most students incorrectly choose choice E. But you're smarter than that! The correct answer is B.

2. A 1200-square-meter parcel of land is bought for $400,000 and then divided into six equally sized plots. The first five plots are then sold at a price of $380 per square meter. If the overall profit is to be at least 30%, what is the minimum selling price of the sixth plot?

(A) $42,000
(B) $98,800
(C) $109,200
(D) $140,000
(E) $152,000

We know that a 1200-square-meter parcel of land is bought and then divided into six equally sized plots. That means each plot is $\dfrac{1200}{6}=200$ square meters. If the selling price is $380 per square meter, then each plot sells for $200 \times \$380 = \$76,000$. Therefore, the first five plots sell for $\$76,000 \times 5 = \$380,000$. That's the first part of the problem.

We also know that the land was bought for $400,000. If we must make a 30% profit, then our total sales have to be 30% more than the purchasing price. So we calculate $.30 \times \$400,000 = \$120,000$. Now add that amount to the purchase price, $\$400,000 + \$120,000 = \$520,000$, to get the total amount we need to earn from the sales in order to make a 30% profit.

Finally, to get the selling price of the sixth plot, simply find the difference between how much we need to make and how much we already sold. For example, $\$520,000 - \$380,000 = \$140,000$. The correct response is D.

3.   Beth and Simon are both art dealers. Beth's weekly compensation consists of $800 plus 25% of her sales. Simon's weekly compensation consists of $600 plus 30% of his sales. If both dealers had the same amount of sales and the same compensation for a particular week, what was that compensation, in dollars?

This is a system of equations problem involving percents. Set up the equations: *Beth's Compensation* $= 800 + .25x$ and *Simon's Compensation* $= 600 + .30x$, where x is the dollar amount of their respective sales. Since they have equal compensations, we can set the equations equal to each other to solve for x: $800 + .25x = 600 + .30x \Rightarrow .05x = 200 \Rightarrow x = 4000$. Remember that we want to know their compensation, *not* their sales, so we have one last step to plug 4000 back in for x in either one of the equations. For example, $800 + .25(4000) = \$1800$. We would get the same amount if we plugged into the other equation. The correct response is 1800.

Inverse and Direct Proportion

Two quantities, y and x, are said to be directly proportional, proportional, or "in direct proportion" if y is given by a constant multiple of x, i.e., $y = cx$ for c, a constant.

In simple terms, a relationship that is directly proportional means that the two variables "move" in the same direction. For example, if you increase your studying, then your grades should also increase. Or if you eat less, then your weight should also go down.

On the other hand, two quantities y and x are said to be inversely proportional or "in inverse proportion" if y is given by a constant multiple of $\frac{1}{x}$, i.e., $y = \frac{c}{x}$ for c, a constant.

In simple terms, a relationship that is indirectly proportional means that the two variables "move" in opposite directions. For example, as your age increases, your energy decreases. Or, as you decrease your driving speed, the time taken for your journey increases.

Let's work through a few examples together to see how these principles are applied in practice. These problems almost always come up on real SATs. They can be tricky, but once you know the drills, you can apply them exactly.

Examples

1. If y varies inversely as x, and if $y = 12$ when $x = b$, and $y = 16$ when $x = b + 6$, what is the value of b?

(A) −288

(B) −24

(C) 6

(D) 32

(E) 288

Inversely and directly proportional problems should be very mechanical. First, we are told that y varies inversely as x. That means our data are going to fit the form $y = \frac{c}{x}$. If $y = 12$ when $x = b$, then we substitute for x and y: $12 = \frac{c}{b}$. Now solve the equation for c: $c = 12b$. Rewrite the new equation by replacing c: $y = \frac{12b}{x}$. Once you solve for c, and write the new equation, simply substitute the values for the condition that $y = 16$ when $x = b + 6$: $16 = \frac{12b}{b+6}$. Finally, solve for the value of b: $16(b + 6) = 12b \Rightarrow 16b + 96 = 12b \Rightarrow 4b = -96 \Rightarrow b = -24$. The correct answer choice is B.

x	y
4	$\dfrac{1}{8}$
6	$\dfrac{1}{18}$
8	$\dfrac{1}{32}$

2. Which of the following could be true about the relationship between x and y shown in the table above?

(A) y is inversely proportional to the square of x
(B) y is inversely proportional to the square root of x
(C) y is directly proportional to the square of x
(D) y is inversely proportional to x
(E) y is directly proportional to x

The first thing you need to do in this type of question is examine the data. Notice that as x increases, y decreases. That means the relationship is inversely proportional. So we can eliminate C and E from the possible choices. Next examine the remaining choices and see how they relate to the data. Choice D says y is inversely proportional to x—if this were the case, then the values of y would be the reciprocal of all the values of x. That's not the case, so D is out. Choice B says y is inversely proportional to the square root of x—if that were the case, then all the values of y would take the form of $\dfrac{1}{\sqrt{x}}$. For the second data point, there is no way that the square root of 6 could be 18. So B is out.

Now we examine choice A, which says y is inversely proportional to the square of x. If we look at the data, $4 \Rightarrow \dfrac{1}{8}$, or seen differently, $4 \Rightarrow \dfrac{1}{.5(4)^2}$. Next, $6 \Rightarrow \dfrac{1}{18}$, or seen differently, $6 \Rightarrow \dfrac{1}{.5(6)^2}$. Finally, $8 \Rightarrow \dfrac{1}{32}$, or seen differently, $8 \Rightarrow \dfrac{1}{.5(8)^2}$. Choice A fits the data perfectly. The values of y are consistently in the form of 1 over .5 times x^2. The correct answer choice is A. On the real SAT, you don't need to go through all the detail we went through here. You can just test a point or two and "see" the relationship.

3. If y is directly proportional to x^2 and $y = \dfrac{1}{18}$ when $x = \dfrac{1}{3}$, what is the positive value of x when $y = \dfrac{8}{25}$?

(A) $\dfrac{1}{9}$

(B) $\dfrac{2\sqrt{2}}{5}$

(C) $\dfrac{4}{5}$

(D) $\dfrac{5}{4}$

(E) $\dfrac{72}{25}$

The steps you need to know to solve this problem are nearly identical to those in the first problem in this section. Let's go through the drill again. If y is directly proportional to x^2, then we can write the initial equation $y = cx^2$. Next we can solve for c by plugging in the initial condition that $y = \dfrac{1}{18}$ when $x = \dfrac{1}{3}$. For example, $\dfrac{1}{18} = c\left(\dfrac{1}{3}\right)^2 \Rightarrow c \times \dfrac{1}{9} = \dfrac{1}{18} \Rightarrow c = \dfrac{9}{18} \Rightarrow c = \dfrac{1}{2}$. The new equation can now be written by replacing c: $y = \dfrac{1}{2}x^2$. Finally, to find the positive value of x when $y = \dfrac{8}{25}$, we plug in: $\dfrac{8}{25} = \dfrac{1}{2}x^2 \Rightarrow x^2 = \dfrac{8}{25} \times \dfrac{2}{1} \Rightarrow x^2 = \dfrac{16}{25} \Rightarrow x = \sqrt{\dfrac{16}{25}} \Rightarrow x = \dfrac{4}{5}$. The correct answer choice is C. Notice that in computational inversely and directly proportional problems, the drill is always the same, with the single exception of which initial form of the proportional equation you use.

Harmonic Mean

The harmonic mean is useful for measures of central tendency problems in data that consist of rates or frequencies. All SAT problems that can be solved using the harmonic mean formula can also be solved without the harmonic mean formula. But knowing how to use the harmonic mean can turn a 3-minute solution into a 30-second solution! Note that problems involving the harmonic mean have historically been posed as hard-level problems only. They only come up once in a while, but you should be prepared. Let's look at a couple of examples.

Examples

1. Suppose Sheba and Dylan go on a road trip. They drive from Alabama to Mississippi at a constant speed of 80 miles per hour. On the way back from Mississippi to Alabama, they drive at a constant speed of 60 miles per hour. What is the average speed for the round trip?

At first, it seems like an easy problem. The solution should simply be $\frac{60 + 80}{2} = 70$ mph. The problem with that approach is that taking an arithmetic average would imply that the time for the return trip was the same as the time for the trip going. That cannot be the case because the return trip was the same distance, but it was traveled at a lesser speed.

So we have to reconsider the problem at hand. If x is the distance between Alabama and Mississippi, then the time going is equal to $\frac{x}{80}$. (That's just the distance going over the speed going.) The time it took to return is equal to $\frac{x}{60}$ because only the speed changed while the distance remained the same. The total round-trip distance traveled is $2x$. The average speed for the round trip is equal to the total distance traveled over the total time traveled:

$$\frac{2x}{\frac{x}{80} + \frac{x}{60}} \quad \Rightarrow \quad \frac{2}{\frac{1}{80} + \frac{1}{60}} = 68.57 \text{ mph}$$

The general formula to find the harmonic mean when two rates are being considered is therefore:

$$\text{Avg. rate} = \frac{2}{\frac{1}{r_1} + \frac{1}{r_2}}$$

Let's take a look at how to apply it in a typical SAT problem.

2. Helga drives to work at an average speed of 30 miles per hour and returns home along the same route at an average speed of 50 miles per hour. If her total travel time is 4 hours, what is the total number of miles in the round trip to and from work?

(A)   60

(B)   75

(C)   120

(D)   150

(E)   160

The correct choice is D. According to the formula, Helga's average rate equals $\frac{2}{\frac{1}{30} + \frac{1}{50}} = 37.5$ miles per hour. Since she travels for 4 hours, we multiply $4 \times 37.5 = 150$ total miles traveled.

The Formulas You're Not Given That You Ought to Know

Arithmetic Operations

$$ab + ac = a(b + c)$$

$$a\left(\dfrac{b}{c}\right) = \dfrac{ab}{c}$$

$$\dfrac{\left(\dfrac{a}{b}\right)}{c} = \dfrac{a}{bc}$$

$$\dfrac{a}{\left(\dfrac{b}{c}\right)} = \dfrac{ac}{b}$$

$$\dfrac{a}{b} + \dfrac{c}{d} = \dfrac{ad + bc}{bd}$$

$$\dfrac{a}{b} - \dfrac{c}{d} = \dfrac{ad - bc}{bd}$$

$$\dfrac{a - b}{c - d} = \dfrac{b - a}{d - c}$$

$$\dfrac{a + b}{c} = \dfrac{a}{c} + \dfrac{b}{c}$$

$$\dfrac{ab + ac}{a} = b + c, \, a \neq 0$$

$$\dfrac{\left(\dfrac{a}{b}\right)}{\left(\dfrac{c}{d}\right)} = \dfrac{ad}{bc}$$

Exponent Rules

$$a^n a^m = a^{n+m}$$

$$\dfrac{a^n}{a^m} = a^{n-m} = \dfrac{1}{a^{m-n}}$$

$$(a^n)^m = a^{nm}$$

$$a^0 = 1, \, a \neq 0$$

$$(ab)^n = a^n b^n$$

$$\left(\dfrac{a}{b}\right)^n = \dfrac{a^n}{b^n}$$

$$a^{-n} = \dfrac{1}{a^n}$$

$$\dfrac{1}{a^{-n}} = a^n$$

$$\left(\dfrac{a}{b}\right)^{-n} = \left(\dfrac{b}{a}\right)^n = \dfrac{b^n}{a^n}$$

$$a^{\frac{n}{m}} = \left(a^{\frac{1}{m}}\right)^n = (a^n)^{\frac{1}{m}}$$

Linear Functions

$$y = mx + b \text{ or } f(x) = mx + b$$

Graph is a line with point $(0, b)$ and slope m.

Distance Formula

If $P_1 = (x_1, y_1)$ and $P_2 = (x_2, y_2)$ are two points the distance between them is

$$d(P_1, P_2) = \sqrt{(x_2 - x_1)^2 + (y_2 - y_1)^2}$$

Slope

Slope of the line containing the two points (x_1, y_1) and (x_2, y_2) is

$$m = \dfrac{y_2 - y_1}{x_2 - x_1} = \dfrac{\text{rise}}{\text{run}}$$

Constant Function

$$y = a \text{ or } f(x) = a$$

Graph is a horizontal line passing though the point $(0, a)$.

Slope–Intercept Form

The equation of the line with slope m and y-intercept $(0, b)$ is

$$y = mx + b$$

Point–Slope Form

The equation of the line with slope m and passing through the point (x_1, y_1) is

$$y - y_1 = m(x - x_1)$$

Factoring Formulas

$$x^2 - a^2 = (x + a)(x - a)$$

$$x^2 + 2ax + a^2 = (x + a)^2$$

$$x^2 - 2ax + a^2 = (x - a)^2$$

Common Mistakes You Need to Avoid

Error	Correction
$\dfrac{3}{0} \neq 0$ and $\dfrac{3}{0} \neq 3$	You can never divide by 0. Division by 0 is undefined.
$-4^2 \neq 16$	$-4^2 = -16$ and $(-4)^2 = 16$. Be careful how you use parentheses.
$(x^3)^4 \neq x^7$	$(x^3)^4 = x^{12}$. Raising a power to a power means you have to multiply, not add.
$\dfrac{x}{y+z} \neq \dfrac{x}{y} + \dfrac{x}{z}$	$\dfrac{3}{4} = \dfrac{3}{3+1} \neq \dfrac{3}{3} + \dfrac{3}{1} = 1 + 3 = 4$. You can only divide monomials (not binomials) into a numerator.
$\dfrac{x+cy}{x} \neq 1 + cy$	$\dfrac{x+cy}{x} = 1 + \dfrac{cy}{x}$. If you divide a monomial into one piece of the numerator, you need to divide it into all the pieces.
$-b(y-1) \neq -by - b$	$-b(y-1) = -by + b$. Make sure you distribute to each piece inside the parentheses.
$(x+m)^2 \neq x^2 + m^2$	$(x+m)^2 = (x+m)(x+m) = x^2 + 2xm + m^2$. When raising a binomial to a power, make sure you FOIL! You may never "distribute" a power over a + or a − sign.

Chapter 15 Quiz—Proportions
25 Questions

Directions: For this quiz, solve each problem and decide which is the best of the choices given. For Student-Produced Response questions, solve each problem and record your solution.

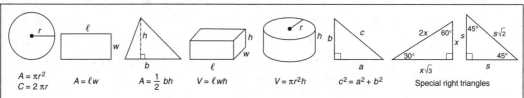
1. On Michael's birthday, he and his friends decided to share a cake. Michael cut the cake in half, took his piece, and then passed the remaining half to another friend, who then cut the piece in half, took her piece, and then passed the remaining half to the next friend. If this process continued until everyone had a piece of cake, which of the following could be the fraction of the original cake that one of Michael's friends had?

   (A) $\dfrac{1}{28}$

   (B) $\dfrac{1}{30}$

   (C) $\dfrac{1}{32}$

(D) $\dfrac{1}{34}$

(E) $\dfrac{1}{36}$

2. In a race, Bonnie can run 4 miles in 24 minutes. If she runs for $1\dfrac{1}{5}$ hours at this rate, how far will she run?

(A) 4 miles
(B) 8 miles
(C) 10 miles
(D) 12 miles
(E) 16 miles

3. If a and b are integers, $6 < b < 20$, and $\dfrac{a}{b} = \dfrac{3}{4}$, how many possible values are there for a?

(A) One
(B) Two
(C) Three
(D) Four
(E) Five

4. Bridgette mowed $\dfrac{1}{5}$ of her lawn. If she mowed 14 acres of lawn, how many acres of unmowed lawn remain?

(A) 28
(B) 35
(C) 42
(D) 56
(E) 70

5. If the ratio of x to y is 3 to 4, and the ratio of y to z is 5 to 6, what is the ratio of x to z?

(A) 3:5
(B) 5:12
(C) 2:9
(D) 5:8
(E) 5:4

6. In a mixture of popcorn and potato chips, the ratio by weight of popcorn to potato chips is 4 to 3. How many ounces of potato chips will there be in 3 ounces of this mixture?

(B) 80

7. A refrigerator manufacturing company produced 400 refrigerators in the first week of the month. Because its owners installed a new piece of machinery, its production increased 65% from the first week to the second week. How many refrigerators did the company produce the second week?

8. A clothing vendor charges $39 for a certain type of jacket. This price is 30% more than the amount it costs the vendor to buy one of these jackets. During a sale, the vendor's employees may purchase any item at 40% off the vendor's cost. How much would it cost an employee to purchase a jacket of this type during a sale?

(A) $16.38
(B) $18.00
(C) $23.40
(D) $24.18
(E) $27.30

9. If x and y are positive numbers, which of the following is equivalent to $x\%$ of $4y$?

    (A) $4xy$

    (B) $\dfrac{xy}{4}$

    (C) $\dfrac{y}{25x}$

    (D) $\dfrac{x}{25y}$

    (E) $\dfrac{xy}{25}$

10. There are 35 more men than women enrolled in Haverton College. If there are x women enrolled, then, in terms of x, what percent of those enrolled are women?

    (A) $\dfrac{x}{100(2x+35)}\%$

    (B) $\dfrac{100x}{x+35}\%$

    (C) $\dfrac{x}{2x+35}\%$

    (D) $\dfrac{100x}{2x+35}\%$

    (E) $\dfrac{x}{x+35}\%$

11. The force required to stretch a spring beyond its natural length is proportional to how far the spring is being stretched. If a force of 20 pounds stretches a spring 6 centimeters beyond its natural length, what force, in pounds, is needed to stretch this spring 25 centimeters beyond its natural length?

    (A) $76.\overline{6}$
    (B) 80
    (C) $83.\overline{3}$
    (D) $86.\overline{6}$
    (E) 90

12. Which of the following tables shows a relationship in which c is directly proportional to d?

(A)

c	d
1	5
2	6
3	7

(B)

c	d
3	12
4	20
5	30

(C)

c	d
5	15
6	24
7	35

(D)

c	d
7	28
8	32
9	36

(E)

c	d
3	9
6	12
9	15

13.

Speed of travel of a particle at varying densities	
Density	**Speed**
8	Twice as fast as a density of 16
16	Twice as fast as a density of 24
24	Twice as fast as a density of 32

According to the table above, a particle moving through a substance with a density of 24 would travel how many times as fast as a particle moving through a substance with a density of 40?

(A) 2
(B) 4
(C) 8
(D) 16
(E) 32

14. For a certain piece of computer equipment, the increase in equipment cost is directly proportional to the increase in the amount of computer memory the equipment provides. If the equipment cost increases $72 when the amount of memory is increased by 20 megabytes, by how much will equipment cost increase when the amount of memory is increased by 25 megabytes?

(A) $18
(B) $64
(C) $77
(D) $90
(E) $108

15. For every 40 games a baseball team plays, it loses 12 games. What is the ratio of the team's losses to wins?

(A) 3:10
(B) 7:10
(C) 3:7
(D) 7:3
(E) 10:3

16. Egbert has red, blue, and green marbles in the ratio of 5:4:3, and he has a total of 36 marbles. How many blue marbles does Egbert have?

17. Given that $y = \dfrac{x^3}{2z}$, if z triples while x doubles, what is the effect on y?

18. A farm has geese that lay only gold eggs and regular eggs. On a certain day, the geese lay a total of 750 eggs, in which the ratio of gold to regular eggs is 7:3. If the ratio of gold eggs to regular eggs is to be changed to 3:4 by adding only regular eggs, how many regular eggs must be added?

19. During a rainstorm, z ounces of rain collect in a bucket every y minutes. How many ounces of rain are collected in x minutes?

    (A) $\dfrac{z}{xy}$

    (B) $\dfrac{y}{xy}$

    (C) $\dfrac{xz}{y}$

    (D) $\dfrac{xy}{z}$

    (E) $\dfrac{yz}{x}$

20. A cake is made from milk, beaten eggs, and flour mixed in the ratios 3 to 4 to 7, respectively, by weight. What fraction of the mixture by weight is beaten eggs?

    (A) $\dfrac{1}{7}$

    (B) $\dfrac{4}{3}$

    (C) $\dfrac{4}{7}$

    (D) $\dfrac{2}{7}$

    (E) $\dfrac{2}{3}$

21. When the positive even integer x is increased by 40% of itself, the result is between 20 and 30. What is one possible value of x?

22. Mary ate $\dfrac{3}{4}$ of her cake on Monday. If she ate half of the remaining cake on Tuesday, and left the rest for Wednesday, what fraction of the original cake remained on Wednesday?

23. If the ratio of x to y is 4 to 5, and the ratio of z to y is 3 to 2, what is the ratio of x to z?

    (A) 2:5
    (B) 5:15
    (C) 8:15
    (D) 6:5
    (E) 12:5

24. In a mixture of tuna fish and mayonnaise, the ratio by weight of tuna fish to mayonnaise is 7 to 3. How many ounces of tuna fish will there be in 10 ounces of this mixture?

25. Corey drives to work at an average speed of 27 miles per hour and returns home along the same route at an average speed of 33 miles per hour. If his total travel time is 3 hours, what is the total number of miles in the return trip from work?

(A) 44.55
(B) 45.00
(C) 59.40
(D) 89.10
(E) 90.00

Functions

In this chapter, we will learn techniques for solving a variety of functions problems on the SAT. We will cover quadratic graphs and equations, exponential growth, intersections, rules for evaluating, and transformations of functions on the plane.

Quadratics

A quadratic function takes the form $y = ax^2 + bx + c$, where a, b, and c are constants (regular numbers) and x is the input and y is the output.

When quadratic functions are graphed, they can go up or down, as follows:

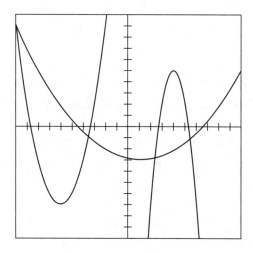

Most quadratic questions on the SAT are either computational or factoring problems. You're not going to need to know too much about the properties of quadratics, except for the ones we will discuss in this section. Let's take a look.

Examples

1.

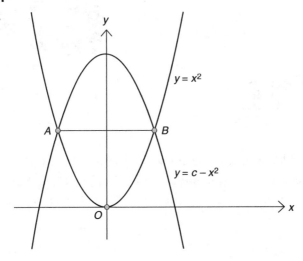

The figure above shows the graphs of $y = x^2$ and $y = c - x^2$ for some constant c. If the length of $\overline{AB}$ is equal to 8, what is the value of c?

(A) −16
(B) 0
(C) 12
(D) 16
(E) 32

This type of problem always comes up on the SAT. To solve for the value of c, you need find a complete coordinate to plug in for x and y. We're told that the length of AB is 8. Since the parabola $y = x^2$ has symmetry over the y-axis, we know that AB measures 4 on both sides. That means, for example, that B is exactly 4 units to the right of the origin O, or that the x-coordinate of B is 4.

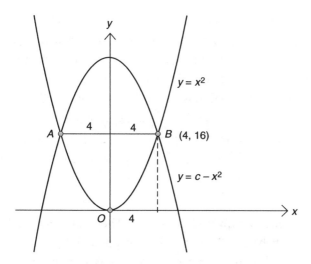

To find the corresponding y-coordinate of B, simply plug $y = 4$ into the equation that does not contain c, in this case $y = x^2$: $y = 4^2 \implies y = 16$. Now we have a complete coordinate for B, $(4, 16)$. The point B also happens to lie on the graph of $y = c - x^2$. Now solving for c is as easy as plugging in $(4, 16)$. For example, $16 = c - 4^2 \implies 16 = c - 16 \implies c = 32$. The correct response is E. These problems generally work the same way, so know the drill—and show no fear!

2.

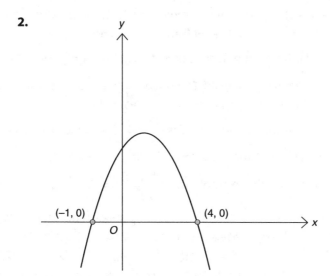

The figure above shows the graph of a quadratic function in the xy-plane. Of all the points (x, y) on the graph, for what value of x is the value of y greatest?

One of the most special properties of parabolas, the graphs of quadratic functions, is that they have perfect symmetry. If a parabola is going upward, then it has a minimum point. If a parabola is going upside down, then it has a maximum point, or a "highest" point. The minimum or maximum of a parabola always happens at the x-coordinate that is exactly in the middle of the points where the parabola hits the x-axis. In this case, the parabola hits the x-axis at –1 and at 4. The x-value in the middle of –1 and 4 is $\dfrac{-1+4}{2}=\dfrac{3}{2}$ or 1.5. It's that easy! The correct response is 1.5.

3. $h(x)=k-(h-3x)^2$

At time $x = 0$, a ball was thrown upward from an initial height of 16 feet. Until the ball hit the ground, its height, in feet, after x seconds was given by the function h(x) above, in which k and h are positive constants. If the ball reached its maximum height of 80 feet at time $x = \dfrac{8}{3}$ seconds, what was the height, in feet, of the ball at time $x = 2$?

There are several ways to solve this type of problem, which is considered quite difficult on the SAT. While it's usually easier to avoid "special" formulas that don't generally apply, this is one case when knowing a formula makes things super easy. According to quadratic rules, the vertex form of a downward parabola is $y=k-(h-x)^2$. Essentially, the point at which the parabola turns (the maximum) determines the values of h and k. In this problem, we are told that the ball reached its maximum height of 80 feet at time $x = \dfrac{8}{3}$ seconds.

Try to imagine the situation in your head: Throw a ball into the air, and it starts to go up and up, until it "turns" and starts to come down and down, mimicking the shape of a parabola. Here, the "turning point" is $\left(\dfrac{8}{3}, 80\right)$. The value of k is always the height of the ball when it turns, so $k = 80$. To find h, set up the equation $h - 3x = 0$, and plug in $x = \dfrac{8}{3}$. For example, $h-3\left(\dfrac{8}{3}\right)=0 \Rightarrow h-8=0 \Rightarrow h=8$.

Now that we know the values of h and k, the new equation becomes $h(x) = 80-(8-3x)^2$. To find the height, in feet, of the ball at time $x = 2$, simply plug in $x = 2$: $h(2) = 80-(8-3(2))^2 \Rightarrow h(2)=80-(8-6)^2 \Rightarrow h(2)=80-(2)^2 \Rightarrow h(2)=80-4$. The height at $x = 2$ is exactly 76 feet. The correct response is 76. Just as a note, the fact that "at time $x = 0$, a ball was thrown upward from an initial height of 16 feet" is a distracter. It doesn't mean anything in terms of finding the solution, at least when you use the method we did.

Exponential Growth

In the real world, things can grow or decay at different rates. In other words, things grow or decay at nonconstant rates. For example, bacteria starts off with a small population, and then "boom"—within hours there are billions of bacteria. Or think of a balloon deflating—at first, the air goes out slowly, then all of a sudden it comes out at a faster rate. These types of changes in rate of growth or decay are called exponential.

To solve exponential problems, use the formula: $A(t) = P(1 \pm r)^t$, where $A(t) =$ the final amount, $P =$ the original amount, $r =$ the rate of growth/decay, and $t =$ the number of changes/time.

These problems tend to be easy or medium level on the SAT. Let's work through a few examples together.

Examples

1. If a population of 100 grows by 5% per year, how large will the population be in 50 years?

This is a grid-in problem on the SAT. To solve it, identify that we are dealing with a growing population, and set up the special formula. For example, $A(t) = P(1 + r)^t \Rightarrow A(50) = 100(1 + .05)^{50} \Rightarrow A(50) = 100(1.05)^{50} \Rightarrow A(50) = 1147$. The correct response is 1147. Notice that we used a "+" in the formula as opposed to a "–" because in this example we are "growing." Also, notice that we changed the percent to its decimal form before plugging it into the formula.

2. The cost of maintenance on a home increases each year by 15 percent, and Harriet paid $4000 this year for maintenance on her house. If the cost a for maintenance on Harriet's home t years from now is given by the function $a(t) = 4000x^t$, what is the value of x?

(A)   0.15
(B)   0.60
(C)   1.15
(D)   1.60
(E)   600

This problem has a lot of distracter information. The given formula, $a(t) = 4000x^t$, is just a fancy way of setting up the equation for growth that we would normally do ourselves. It doesn't really matter how much Harriet paid for maintenance! All we want to know is the value of x. In the given formula, x is a different way of saying $1 + r$. Here, the rate of increase is 15%, so $r = .15$. That means $x = 1 + .15 = 1.15$. The correct response is C.

Intersections

Intersections are exactly what you might think they are. They're simply questions that ask you to identify the intervals on which a graph of a function is negative, positive, or zero. To solve these problems, you just need to use your eyes. No complicated math involved! Let's take a look at a typical example together.

Examples

1.

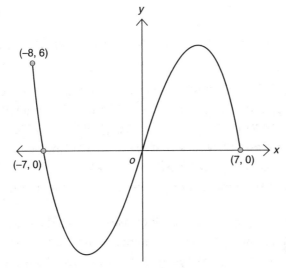

Based on the graph of the function f above, what are the values of x for which $f(x)$ is negative?

(A) $-8 < x < 0$
(B) $-7 < x < 0$
(C) $-8 < x < -7$
(D) $-7 < x < 7$
(E) $-8 < x < -7$ and $0 < x < 7$

The question is asking us to identify the interval on which the graph is negative. The graph is negative when it is below the x-axis. It's positive when the graph is above the x-axis. And the graph is neither positive nor negative when it exactly crosses the x-axis—it's exactly zero! Using just your eyes, you can see that the graph is below the x-axis from $-7 < x < 0$ only. The correct response is B.

Factoring and Zeros

Factoring and zeros are highly related concepts. Factoring is a process that reveals zeros. Zeros are the points at which a graph of a function hits the x-axis, or the values of x that, when plugged in, make the function equal zero. Zeros are also called roots or solutions. Factoring problems on the SAT tend to be simpler than some of the factoring problems you encounter in school. The skill of factoring is best understood through practice. Let's work through a few common problem types together.

Examples

1. If $f(x) = \dfrac{x^2 - 1}{x^2 - 8x + 7}$, what is one number not in the domain of $f(x)$?

    The form of this function is just like a fraction. The domain of a function refers to the specific values that x is allowed to be. Just like in a regular fraction without variables, it's not possible to divide by zero. In this example, we need to find the particular values of x that, when plugged in, make the denominator equal zero. The numerator can be whatever it wants to be! So we use factoring to reveal the zeros of the denominator: $x^2 - 8x + 7 \implies (x - 7)(x - 1) \implies x \neq 1$ and 7.

    Notice that we were only concerned with the denominator. To factor $x^2 - 8x + 7$, we needed to find two numbers that multiply to give 7 and that combine to give -8. So we thought of -7 and -1, because $-7 + -1 = -8$, and $(-7)(-1) = 7$. Next, the values that are *not* in the domain are the opposite value of the factors, specifically, 7 and 1. We choose the opposite values because, when plugged in, they make the factor equal 0. For example, $(7 - 7)(1 - 1) = (0)(0)$. You can grid-in either 7 or 1.

2. What root do $x^2 - 4x - 32$ and $x^2 + 2x - 8$ have in common?

    (A) -8
    (B) -4
    (C) 0
    (D) 2
    (E) 4

Roots are the same thing as zeros. To find the zeros, simply factor both quadratic equations. For example, $x^2 - 4x - 32 \Rightarrow (x-8)(x+4) \Rightarrow x=8$ and -4 and $x^2 + 2x - 8 = 0 \Rightarrow (x+4)(x-2) \Rightarrow x=-4$ and 2. The common root is -4. The correct response is B.

3. If $a(3x-2)(x+1)=0$ and $x<-1$, what is the value of a?

(A) -2
(B) -1
(C) 0
(D) $\dfrac{2}{3}$
(E) 1

This is actually a very difficult factoring problem because we need to analyze the equation rather than solve it. We want to solve for the value of a. We are told that $a(3x-2)(x+1)=0$. Normally, we would want to solve for the zeros. If we do, we get $3x-2=0 \Rightarrow 3x=2 \Rightarrow x=\dfrac{2}{3}$ and $x+1=0 \Rightarrow x=-1$. However, we are also told that $x<-1$. Since both of our zeros, $\dfrac{2}{3}$ and -1, are greater than or equal to -1, we know that even though they are zeros, we cannot use them! Here's the trick—if x cannot be $\dfrac{2}{3}$ and -1, then both of our factors can *never* equal zero.

However, $a(3x-2)(x+1)=0$. Since $(3x-2)$ and $(x+1)$ cannot be zero, a must be equal to 0. That's because we are multiplying the three pieces of the equation together. In order for the product to equal 0, at least one of the pieces must equal 0. That leaves us with no choice—a equals 0. The correct choice is C.

4. $(y+5)(y-h)=y^2+3y+k$

In the equation above, h and k are constants. If the equation is true for all values of y, what is the value of k?

(A) -15
(B) -10
(C) -2
(D) 2
(E) 10

If you look at the right-hand side of the equation, it is in unfactored form. The left-hand side is in factored form. Think about the problem as if you were factoring the right-hand side into the left-hand side. You would need two numbers that combine to make +3 and two numbers that multiply to make k. On the left-hand side, the "two numbers" are 5 and $-h$, so we can solve backward. We know that when we combine 5 and $-h$, we need to get +3: $5 + -h = 3 \Rightarrow -h = -2 \Rightarrow h = 2$. Now that $h = 2$, we know that k is the product of the two special numbers. Therefore, $k = 5 \times -2 = -10$. The correct response is B.

5. If x and y are positive integers and $x^2 - y^2 = 11$, what is the value of x?

(A) 5
(B) 6
(C) 7
(D) 9
(E) 11

This kind of problem pops up all the time on the SAT. The trick is to factor "both" sides. For example, $x^2 - y^2 = 11 \Rightarrow (x + y)(x - y) = 11$. Really, we are looking for two numbers that multiply to make 11. The only way to multiply two numbers to get 11 is to multiply 11 by 1. Therefore, $x + y$ must equal 11, and $x - y$ must equal 1. That's a system of equations. For example, $x + y = 11$ and $x - y = 1$. If we add the equations together by combining the left-hand side and the right-hand side, we get $x + y + x - y = 11 + 1 \Rightarrow 2x = 12 \Rightarrow x = 6$. We can stop right there because the problem only asks us to calculate the value of x. The correct response is B. If you want to check it, though, $x = 6$ and $y = 5$. It works!

Evaluating

Evaluating means "plugging in" in the sense that you are strategically plugging in coordinates, special values, or expressions to solve an equation. When you evaluate, you need be careful to follow all necessary algebraic rules and, most importantly, to plug in with a plan. Let's work through three of the most common types of evaluating problems on the SAT and try to generalize strategies for them.

Examples

1. If x is an integer greater than 1 and if $y = x^2 + \dfrac{x+1}{x-1}$, which of the following must be true?

    I. $y \neq x$

    II. y is not an integer

    III. $y > 0$

(A) I only

(B) III only

(C) I and II only

(D) I and III only

(E) I, II, and III

These problems can be tricky. Realistically, the only way to solve them is to test the choices, and use elimination techniques to hone in on the right answer. We are told that x is an integer greater than 1 and that $y = x^2 + \dfrac{x+1}{x-1}$. That x is an integer greater than 1 means that y is always defined, since only a value of x equal to 1 could make the denominator on the right-hand side equal to 0. Also, we can only plug in numbers greater than 1.

Choice I says $y \neq x$: If we were to plug in any number for x, the value of y could never be equal to the evaluated expression on the right-hand side because the right-hand side is a number squared, which is always positive, plus some other fractional piece, which is always positive, since any value of x greater than 1 will make $\dfrac{x+1}{x-1}$ positive. Choice I must be true—the value of y is always greater than the inputted value of x! All we can cross out now is choice B, but choices A, C, D, and E remain because each contains I.

Choice II says y is not an integer: If we choose $x = 2$, we get $y = (2)^2 + \dfrac{2+1}{2-1} = 4 + \dfrac{3}{1} = 4 + 3 = 7$. The value of y can certainly be an integer, so II is false. Now we can cross out C and E, since they contain II. The only possible answers are A and D. Even if we cannot figure out choice III, we've narrowed our choices down to 50%.

Luckily, choice III is easy to determine. Choice III says $y > 0$: As described in the analysis of choice I, we know that y is always positive for any value of x we are allowed to plug in, namely, all $x > 1$. We also know that $\dfrac{x+1}{x-1}$ is always positive for all $x > 1$. The sum of two positive numbers is always positive.

That means that *y* must also be positive, or $y > 0$. Choice III is true. That means D must be the correct answer. Phew! That was certainly a hard one!

2.   In the *xy*-coordinate system, $(\sqrt{10},\ a)$ is one of the points of intersection of the graphs $y = 2x^2 - 19$ and $y = -2x^2 + b$, where *b* is a constant. What is the value of *b*?

(A)   24
(B)   23
(C)   22
(D)   21
(E)   20

We want to know the value of *b*. In order to solve for the value of a variable, we can only have that variable in an equation. For example, $y = -2x^2 + b$ has a *y*, an *x*, and a *b*. Before we can solve for *b*, we need to know *y* and *x*. The given point $(\sqrt{10},\ a)$ is missing the *y* value. We need to use the other equation, $y = 2x^2 - 19$, to solve for the missing *y* value in the point, and then plug the point into $y = -2x^2 + b$ to solve for *b*.

First, plug $(\sqrt{10},\ a)$ into $y = 2x^2 - 19$: $a = 2(\sqrt{10})^2 - 19 \Rightarrow a = 2(10) - 19 \Rightarrow a = 20 - 19 \Rightarrow a = 1$. The complete coordinate is therefore $(\sqrt{10},\ 1)$. We can plug into $y = -2x^2 + b$ to solve for *b*: $1 = -2(\sqrt{10})^2 + b \Rightarrow 1 = -2(10) + b \Rightarrow 1 = -20 + b \Rightarrow b = 21$. That's all there is to it! Just lots of plugging in. The correct response is D.

3.   Let the function *g* be defined by $g(x) = 12 + \dfrac{x^2}{9}$. If $g(3k) = 7k$, what is one possible value of *k*?

These "strange"-looking problems come up all the time, usually as hard problems, on the SAT. If you substitute carefully, they can be quite easy. We are looking for one possible value of *k*, given that $g(3k) = 7k$. The expression "$g(3k)$" just means to substitute 3*k* for every *x* you see in the function $g(x)$. For example,

$$g(3k) = 7k \Rightarrow 12 + \frac{(3k)^2}{9} = 7k \Rightarrow 12 + \frac{9k^2}{9} = 7k \Rightarrow 12 + k^2 = 7k$$

$$\Rightarrow k^2 - 7k + 12 = 0 \Rightarrow (k-4)(k-3) = 0 \Rightarrow k = 4 \text{ and } 3$$

That's all there is to it. If you plug in carefully, and solve it out, you'll get the solution! Just remember how to plug in for expressions like "$g(3k)$." You can grid-in either 3 or 4 as your answer.

Transformations

In this section, we are going to see how knowledge of some fairly simple graphs can help us graph more complicated graphs. Collectively, the methods we're going to be looking at are called transformations.

Vertical shifts are transformations that shift a graph either up or down. Given the graph of $f(x)$, the graph of $g(x) = f(x) + c$ will be the graph of $f(x)$ shifted up or down by c units, depending on the sign of c. If c is positive, then the graph goes up. If c is negative, then the graph goes down. For example, $g(x) = x^2 + 4$ is the graph of x^2 shifted upward by 4 units. The graph of $g(x) = x^2 - 4$ is the graph of x^2 shifted downward by 4 units.

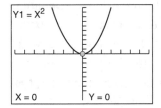 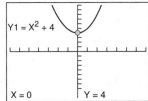 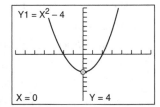

Horizontal shifts are fairly simple as well, although there is one bit where we need to be careful. In this case, if we've got the graph of $f(x)$ the graph of $g(x) = f(x + c)$ will be the graph of $f(x)$ shifted left by c units if c is positive, or right by c units if c is negative. Be careful with horizontal shifts. The graph moves in the opposite direction that you think it would!

For example, $g(x) = (x - 4)^2$ is the graph of x^2 shifted to the right by 4 units. The graph of $g(x) = (x + 4)^2$ is the graph of x^2 shifted to the left by 4 units.

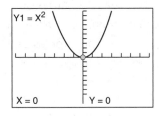 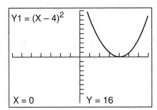 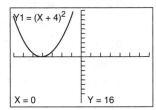

Vertical and horizontal transformations can happen alone or simultaneously. Let's work through a few typical SAT problems together.

Examples

1.

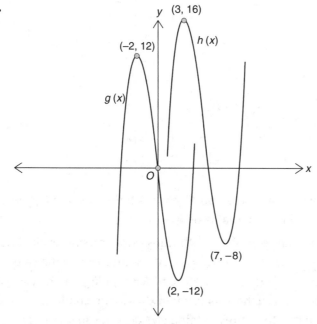

The figure above shows the graphs of the functions g and h. The function g is defined by $g(x) = \frac{1}{2}x^3 - 8x$. The function h is defined by $h(x) = g(x + b) + c$, where b and c are constants. What is the value of bc?

(A) −20
(B) −5
(C) −4
(D) 4
(E) 20

We want to solve for the value of bc. In that case, we need find both b and c. Since $h(x) = g(x + b) + c$, we know that b represents the horizontal shift, and c represents the vertical shift. It means nothing that $g(x) = \frac{1}{2}x^3 - 8x$—since we are solving for b and c, all we need to do is analyze two corresponding points on the graphs. Using your eyes, you can see that the point $(-2, 12)$ becomes the point $(3, 16)$. The point moves to the right (horizontally) by 5 units, which means the value of b is −5. The point moves up (vertically) by 4 units, which means the value of c is 4. Therefore, $bc = (-5)(4) = -20$. The correct response is A.

2.

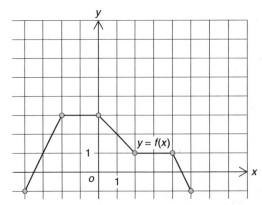

The figure above shows the graph of $y = f(x)$. If the function h is defined by $h(x) = 3f(2x) + 1$, what is the value of $h(2)$?

This type of problem combines both transformation and evaluating techniques. We are told that $h(x) = 3f(2x) + 1$. We want to know the value of $h(2)$. So we plug 2 in for x: $h(2) = 3f(4) + 1$. The trick is figuring out the value of $f(4)$. The value of $f(4)$ is really the y value when $x = 4$ in the graph above. If you go to $x = 4$, and look for the corresponding y value, you can see that the y value is exactly 1. That means $f(4) = 1$. So plug in: $h(2) = 3(1) + 1 = 3 + 1 = 4$. The correct response is 4.

3. The quadratic function g is given by $g(x) = ax^2 + bx + c$, where a and c are negative constants. Which of the following could be the graph of g?

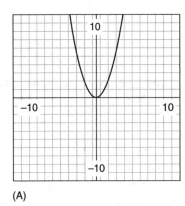

(A)

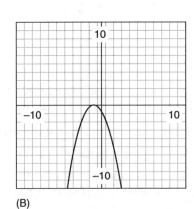

(B)

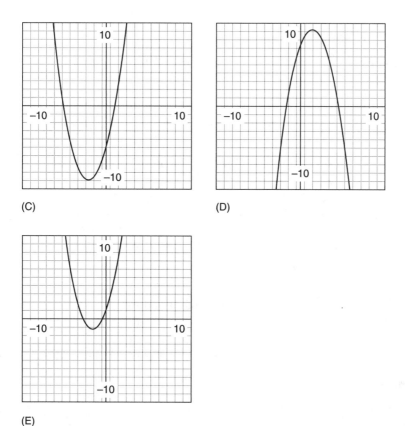

(C)

(D)

(E)

We are given $g(x) = ax^2 + bx + c$, where a and c are negative constants, and we want to pick the graph that best represents the information. In a quadratic function, the sign of a determines whether the parabola opens upward or downward. A negative value of a means the parabola opens downward. Now we can cross out A, C, and E because they do not open downward. The value of c determines the y-intercept of the parabola. A negative value of c shifts the parabola downward, and it means that the y-intercept must be negative. Conversely, a positive value of c means the parabola shifts upward, and that the y-intercept must be positive. In this case, only choice B satisfies the condition that c is negative because the parabola hits the y-axis below the x-axis. Choice B is the correct answer.

The Formulas You're Not Given That You Ought to Know

Arithmetic Operations

$ab + ac = a(b + c)$ $a\left(\dfrac{b}{c}\right) = \dfrac{ab}{c}$

$\dfrac{\left(\dfrac{a}{b}\right)}{c} = \dfrac{a}{bc}$ $\dfrac{a}{\left(\dfrac{b}{c}\right)} = \dfrac{ac}{b}$

$\dfrac{a}{b} + \dfrac{c}{d} = \dfrac{ad+bc}{bd}$ $\dfrac{a}{b} - \dfrac{c}{d} = \dfrac{ad-bc}{bd}$

$\dfrac{a-b}{c-d} = \dfrac{b-a}{d-c}$ $\dfrac{a+b}{c} = \dfrac{a}{c} + \dfrac{b}{c}$

$\dfrac{ab + ac}{a} = b + c, \, a \neq 0$ $\dfrac{\left(\dfrac{a}{b}\right)}{\left(\dfrac{c}{d}\right)} = \dfrac{ad}{bc}$

Distance Formula

If $P_1 = (x_1, y_1)$ and $P_2 = (x_2, y_2)$ are two points the distance between them is

$$d(P_1, P_2) = \sqrt{(x_2 - x_1)^2 + (y_2 - y_1)^2}$$

Constant Function

$y = a$ or $f(x) = a$

Graph is a horizontal line passing though the point $(0, a)$.

Factoring Formulas

$x^2 - a^2 = (x+a)(x-a)$
$x^2 + 2ax + a^2 = (x+a)^2$
$x^2 - 2ax + a^2 = (x-a)^2$

Exponent Rules

$a^n a^m = a^{n+m}$ $\dfrac{a^n}{a^m} = a^{n-m} = \dfrac{1}{a^{m-n}}$

$(a^n)^m = a^{nm}$ $a^0 = 1, \, a \neq 0$

$(ab)^n = a^n b^n$ $\left(\dfrac{a}{b}\right)^n = \dfrac{a^n}{b^n}$

$a^{-n} = \dfrac{1}{a^n}$ $\dfrac{1}{a^{-n}} = a^n$

$\left(\dfrac{a}{b}\right)^{-n} = \left(\dfrac{b}{a}\right)^n = \dfrac{b^n}{a^n}$ $a^{\frac{n}{m}} = \left(a^{\frac{1}{m}}\right)^n = (a^n)^{\frac{1}{m}}$

Linear Functions

$y = mx + b$ or $f(x) = mx + b$

Graph is a line with point $(0, b)$ and slope m.

Slope

Slope of the line containing the two points (x_1, y_1) and (x_2, y_2) is

$$m = \dfrac{y_2 - y_1}{x_2 - x_1} = \dfrac{\text{rise}}{\text{run}}$$

Slope–Intercept Form

The equation of the line with slope m and y-intercept $(0, b)$ is

$$y = mx + b$$

Point–Slope Form

The equation of the line with slope m and passing through the point (x_1, y_1) is

$$y - y_1 = m(x - x_1)$$

Common Mistakes You Need to Avoid

Error	Correction
$\dfrac{3}{0} \neq 0$ and $\dfrac{3}{0} \neq 3$	You can never divide by 0. Division by 0 is undefined.
$-4^2 \neq 16$	$-4^2 = -16$ and $(-4)^2 = 16$. Be careful how you use parentheses.
$(x^3)^4 \neq x^7$	$(x^3)^4 = x^{12}$. Raising a power to a power means you have to multiply, not add.
$\dfrac{x}{y+z} \neq \dfrac{x}{y} + \dfrac{x}{z}$	$\dfrac{3}{4} = \dfrac{3}{3+1} \neq \dfrac{3}{3} + \dfrac{3}{1} = 1 + 3 = 4$. You can only divide monomials (not binomials) into a numerator.
$\dfrac{x+cy}{x} \neq 1 + cy$	$\dfrac{x+cy}{x} = 1 + \dfrac{cy}{x}$. If you divide a monomial into one piece of the numerator, you need to divide it into all the pieces.
$-b(y-1) \neq -by - b$	$-b(y-1) = -by + b$. Make sure you distribute to each piece inside the parentheses.
$(x+m)^2 \neq x^2 + m^2$	$(x+m)^2 = (x+m)(x+m) = x^2 + 2xm + m^2$. When raising a binomial to a power, make sure you FOIL! You may never "distribute" a power over a + or a − sign.

Chapter 16 Quiz—Functions
25 Questions

Directions: For this quiz, solve each problem and decide which is the best of the choices given. For Student-Produced Response questions, solve each problem and record your solution.

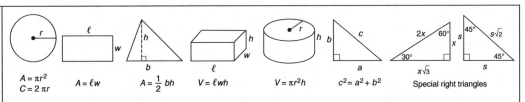
1. April purchased an automobile for $10,000, and the value of the automobile decreases by 25 percent each year. That value, in dollars, of the automobile t years from the date of purchase is given by the function A, where $A(t) = 10000\left(\dfrac{3}{4}\right)^t$. How many years from the date of purchase will the value of the automobile be closest to $2,375?

(A) 2
(B) 3
(C) 4
(D) 5
(E) 6

2. The graph in the xy-plane of a quadratic function f contains the points $(0, 0)$, $(-1, 3)$, and $(-3, 3)$. What is the maximum value of $f(x)$?

    (A) 9
    (B) 8
    (C) 6
    (D) 4
    (E) 3

3.

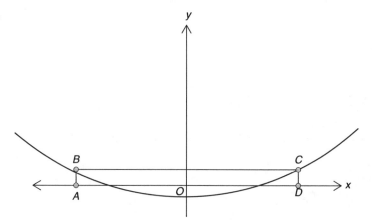

The figure above shows the graph of the function $y = x^2 - a$. Points B and C lie on the graph of the function and are the vertices of rectangle $ABCD$. If $BC = 8$ and the area of rectangle $ABCD$ is 22, what is the value of a?

(A) $\dfrac{19}{4}$

(B) $\dfrac{33}{4}$

(C) $\dfrac{53}{4}$

(D) $\dfrac{67}{4}$

(E) $\dfrac{75}{4}$

4. If $\dfrac{x^2+2x-15}{x^2-7x+12}=5$, what is the value of x?

5. If $x^2=5x-6$, which of the following must be true?

   (A) $x=4$
   (B) $x<3$
   (C) $x>2$
   (D) $x^2<x$
   (E) $x^2>x$

6. If $(4x+4)(4-x)=0$, what are all the possible values of x?

   (A) 0 only
   (B) −1 only
   (C) 4 only
   (D) −1 and 4 only
   (E) 0, −1, and 4

7. In the xy-coordinate system, $(d, 0)$ is one of the points of intersection of the graphs of $y=x^2-12$ and $y=-x^2+20$. If d is positive, what is the value of d?

   (A) 3
   (B) 4
   (C) 16
   (D) 32
   (E) 256

8. Questions 8 and 9 refer to the following functions f and g.

   $f(x)=4x-4$
   $g(x)=x^2$

   Evaluate: $f(6)-g(5)$

   (A) −20
   (B) −5

    (C) −1

    (D) 1

    (E) 45

9. Which of the following is equivalent to $g(k+2)$?

    (A) $g(k) + f(k)$

    (B) $g(k) - f(k)$

    (C) $g(k) - f(k) - 4$

    (D) $g(k) + f(k) + 8$

    (E) It is impossible to determine given the information provided

10. If k is a positive integer and $\dfrac{k+2}{k^2} = \dfrac{3}{8}$, then $k =$

    (A) 1

    (B) 2

    (C) 3

    (D) 4

    (E) 5

11.

x	y
1	0.5
2	4.0
3	7.5
4	11.0

Which of the following equations expresses y in terms of x for each of the four pairs of values show in the table above?

    (A) $y = 3x - 2.5$

    (B) $y = 3.5x - 3$

    (C) $y = 3.5x + 7.5$

    (D) $y = 0.5x$

    (E) $y = 0.5x - 1.5$

12. A company's profit, I, in dollars, for producing m refrigerators in one day is given by $I = 600x - 30x^2$. If the company produces 20 refrigerators in one day, then, according to this formula, what is the profit for that day?

    (A) $0

    (B) $1200

(C) $2400

(D) $3600

(E) $4800

13. Let the function f be defined by $f(x) = 3x - 4$. If $\frac{1}{4} f(\sqrt{s}) = 2$, what is the value of s?

(A) $\dfrac{4}{3}$

(B) $\dfrac{2}{\sqrt{3}}$

(C) 4

(D) $\dfrac{64}{9}$

(E) 16

14. The graph of $y = x^2$ is shifted to the right 6 units. What is the equation of the resulting graph?

(A) $y = x^2 - 6$

(B) $y = x^2 + 6$

(C) $y = 6x^2$

(D) $y = \dfrac{1}{6} x^2$

(E) $y = (x - 6)^2$

15. Of the following graphs, which has the property that no two points on the graph have equal y-coordinates?

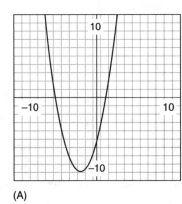

(A)

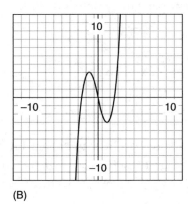

(B)

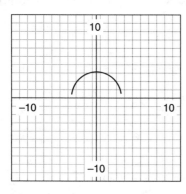

(C)

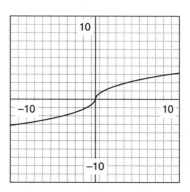

(D)

(E)

16. If the function g is defined by $g(x)=-2x+5$, then $-3g(x)+15=$

(A) $-5x+5$

(B) $-5x-15$

(C) $6x$

(D) $6x+5$

(E) $6x-40$

17.

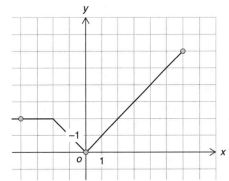

The graph of $y = g(x)$ is shown above. Which of the following could be the graph of $y = g(x - 3)$?

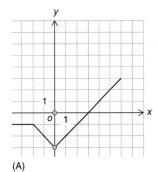

(A)

(B)

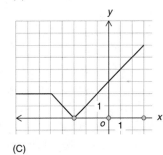

(C)

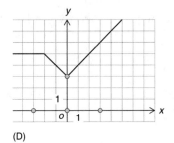

(D)

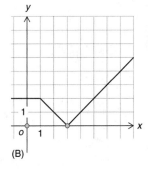

(E)

18.

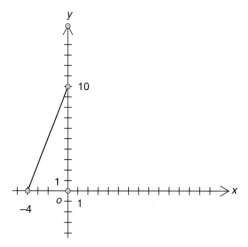

The figure above shows the graph of the function $f(x) = mx + b$, where m and b are constants. What is the slope of the graph of the function $g(x) = f(x+2)$?

(A) $-\dfrac{9}{2}$

(B) $-\dfrac{7}{2}$

(C) $-\dfrac{5}{2}$

(D) $\dfrac{7}{2}$

(E) $\dfrac{9}{2}$

19. If $f(x) = 2x - 3$, $g(x) = x + 1$, $h(x) = 3x$, and $g(f(3)) - h(x) = 1$, what is the value of x?

(A) 0
(B) 0.5
(C) 1
(D) 1.5
(E) 2

20. The graph of $y = f(x)$ is shown in the figure below. Which of the following could be $f(x)$?

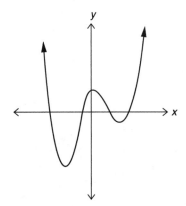

(A) $x^2 + cx$

(B) $x^3 + ax^2 + bx + c$

(C) $-x^4 + ax^3 + bx^2 + cx + d$

(D) $x^4 + ax^2 + b$

(E) $x^4 + b^2x^2 + c^2$

21. If $f(x) = \dfrac{3x}{4-x}$, what is $f(x+1)$?

(A) $\dfrac{3x}{x-3}$

(B) $\dfrac{3x+1}{5-x}$

(C) -1

(D) $\dfrac{3x+3}{3-x}$

(E) $\dfrac{3x+1}{4-x}$

22. Suppose $h(x) = x^2 + 2x$ and $j(x) = \left|\dfrac{x}{4} + 2\right|$. What is $j(h(4))$?

23. Which numbers are not in the domain $f(x) = \dfrac{x}{x^2 + 5x + 6}$?

   (A) 0 only
   (B) –2 only
   (C) –3 only
   (D) –3 and –2 only
   (E) –3, –2, and 0

24. If $f(x) = 2x^2 + 4$ for $-3 < x < 5$, then what is the range of values of $f(x)$?

   (A) $0 < f(x) < 54$
   (B) $4 < f(x) < 54$
   (C) $12 < f(x) < 54$
   (D) $22 < f(x) < 54$
   (E) $-4 < f(x) < 54$

25. If temperature is $f(x)$ and time is x, which of the following best describes a bucket of cold water left outside on a hot day?

(A)

(B)

(C)

(D)

(E)

Answer Key

Chapter 10	Chapter 11	Chapter 12	Chapter 13
1. E	1. 407	1. E	1. C
2. B	2. C	2. $\dfrac{17}{2}$	2. D
3. D	3. D	3. C	3. C
4. B	4. A	4. 12	4. C
5. $\dfrac{1}{9}$	5. D	5. E	5. D
6. 360	6. B	6. 55	6. E
7. D	7. A	7. A	7. C
8. 12	8. A	8. B	8. C
9. C	9. 80	9. D	9. E
10. A	10. 6	10. 2560	10. E
11. D	11. D	11. C	11. A
12. 5	12. $\dfrac{1}{72}$	12. 24	12. C
13. $-2 < x < -1$	13. E	13. A	13. D
14. C	14. C	14. E	14. C
15. 244	15. D	15. C	15. D
16. $\dfrac{1}{2}$	16. C	16. C	16. A
17. D	17. C	17. C	17. B
18. A	18. E	18. D	18. E
19. D	19. 20	19. D	19. D
20. 1801	20. E	20. 52	20. $\dfrac{3}{4}$
21. $\dfrac{4}{5} < x < 2,\ x \neq 1$	21. A	21. 66	21. C
22. A	22. D	22. 79	22. B
23. 6,500	23. B	23. $\dfrac{3}{10}$	23. B
24. D	24. 11	24. $\dfrac{1}{6}$	24. C
25. B	25. $\dfrac{3}{4}$	25. E	25. D

Chapter 14

1. B
2. 20°
3. $\dfrac{9}{25}$
4. B
5. B
6. B
7. D
8. D
9. A
10. C
11. 4.46
12. B
13. 13
14. E
15. 6
16. E
17. A
18. $\dfrac{40}{3}$
19. 49
20. D
21. E
22. D
23. C
24. 32
25. C

Chapter 15

1. C
2. D
3. C
4. D
5. D
6. $\dfrac{9}{7}$
7. 660
8. B
9. E
10. D
11. C
12. D
13. B
14. D
15. C
16. 12
17. $\dfrac{8}{3}$
18. 475
19. C
20. D
21. 16, 18, 20
22. $\dfrac{1}{8}$
23. C
24. 7
25. A

Chapter 16

1. D
2. D
3. C
4. $\dfrac{25}{4}$
5. E
6. D
7. B
8. B
9. D
10. D
11. B
12. A
13. E
14. E
15. D
16. C
17. B
18. C
19. C
20. E
21. D
22. 8
23. D
24. B
25. A

Part V

Practice Tests

In this chapter, you will apply the techniques and practices you have learned in the previous sections. Practice tests are designed to be just like the real SAT exam, so take them very seriously. Make sure to take these practice tests in a test environment and time yourself. Good luck!

TCT Compass Personal Strategy for the SAT

The Thinking Caps Tutoring Compass Personal Strategy for the SAT exam is to be taken after you have read each of the sections carefully and completed all of the chapter quizzes. Like we've discussed earlier in this book, a good prep will help raise your pre-prep score by refreshing and increasing your content knowledge, as well as by showing you tricks you can use to solve problems on the SAT more quickly and accurately. We want every student who uses the prep material in this book to have a fair chance at learning the content and the tricks before taking practice tests, which is why we do not do pre-prep diagnostic exams. Instead, we suggest that you take the following compass test to help you understand what kinds of questions you are able to answer, both in terms of content and in terms of level of difficulty. At the end of the exam, you should use the special scoring guide to compute your predicted score on the SAT and to receive some personalized strategies based on your testing patterns.

Before you take this exam, it is very important to remember the following:

- Take the test early in the morning, around eight or nine o'clock, preferably on a Saturday. If you are going to make the best of the time you spend preparing for the SAT, you want the conditions under which you practice to resemble the conditions of the actual exam as closely as possible!

- If at all possible, take this compass test and other practice tests at a local library or school. Your bedroom or dining room is likely to be full of distracters. It might sound silly, but you do not want to feel too comfortable when taking the test. A library or a school is most likely where you will be taking the real test, so taking your practice tests in these places will help you acclimate to the real testing environment.

- Get a good night's sleep before taking any practice test!

- Eat a nutritious breakfast.

- Bring a spare set of batteries along with your calculator. If your batteries should die, the testing location will not provide you with new ones.

- Make sure you take this compass test and all practice tests in real time. We know how tempting it will be to split up the sections over several days or to give yourself a few extra minutes to get through the problems—but don't! On the real test, you will not have a minute less or a minute more than the allowed time. The time limit is a very real thing you need to get used to now—not on test day.

- The grid-in section is the only place on the SAT where you are not penalized for answering problems incorrectly. Point is: Never leave a grid-in problem blank because any guess gives you a greater chance of getting a point than no guess at all.

Answer Sheet

Last Name:_____   First Name:_____

Date:_____   Testing Location:_____

Directions For Test

- Remove these answer sheets from the book and use them to record your answers to this test.
- This test will require 3 hours and 20 minutes to complete. Take this test in one sitting.
- The time allotment for each section is written clearly at the beginning of each section. This test contains
- Six 25-minute sections, two 20-minute sections, and one 10-minute section.
- This test is 25 minutes shorter than the actual sat, which will include a 25-minute "experimental" section that does not count toward your score. That section has been omitted from this test.
- You may take one short break during the test, of no more than 10 minutes in length.
- You may only work on one section at any given time.
- You must stop ALL work on a section when time is called.
- If you finish a section before the time has elapsed, check your work on that section. You may not work on any other section.
- Do not waste time on questions that seem too difficult for you.
- Use the test book for scratchwork, but you will receive credit only for answers that are marked on the answer sheets.
- You will receive one point for every correct answer.
- You will receive no points for an omitted question.
- For each wrong answer on any multiple-choice question, your score will be reduced by ¼ point.
- For each wrong answer on any "numerical grid-in" question, you will receive no deduction.

When you take the real SAT, you will be asked to fill in your personal information in grids as shown below.

Start with number 1 for each new section. If a section has fewer questions than answer spaces, leave the extra answer spaces blank. Be sure to erase any errors or stray marks completely.

SECTION 2

1 (A) (B) (C) (D) (E)	11 (A) (B) (C) (D) (E)	21 (A) (B) (C) (D) (E)	31 (A) (B) (C) (D) (E)
2 (A) (B) (C) (D) (E)	12 (A) (B) (C) (D) (E)	22 (A) (B) (C) (D) (E)	32 (A) (B) (C) (D) (E)
3 (A) (B) (C) (D) (E)	13 (A) (B) (C) (D) (E)	23 (A) (B) (C) (D) (E)	33 (A) (B) (C) (D) (E)
4 (A) (B) (C) (D) (E)	14 (A) (B) (C) (D) (E)	24 (A) (B) (C) (D) (E)	34 (A) (B) (C) (D) (E)
5 (A) (B) (C) (D) (E)	15 (A) (B) (C) (D) (E)	25 (A) (B) (C) (D) (E)	35 (A) (B) (C) (D) (E)
6 (A) (B) (C) (D) (E)	16 (A) (B) (C) (D) (E)	26 (A) (B) (C) (D) (E)	36 (A) (B) (C) (D) (E)
7 (A) (B) (C) (D) (E)	17 (A) (B) (C) (D) (E)	27 (A) (B) (C) (D) (E)	37 (A) (B) (C) (D) (E)
8 (A) (B) (C) (D) (E)	18 (A) (B) (C) (D) (E)	28 (A) (B) (C) (D) (E)	38 (A) (B) (C) (D) (E)
9 (A) (B) (C) (D) (E)	19 (A) (B) (C) (D) (E)	29 (A) (B) (C) (D) (E)	39 (A) (B) (C) (D) (E)
10 (A) (B) (C) (D) (E)	20 (A) (B) (C) (D) (E)	30 (A) (B) (C) (D) (E)	40 (A) (B) (C) (D) (E)

SECTION 3

1 (A) (B) (C) (D) (E)	11 (A) (B) (C) (D) (E)	21 (A) (B) (C) (D) (E)	31 (A) (B) (C) (D) (E)
2 (A) (B) (C) (D) (E)	12 (A) (B) (C) (D) (E)	22 (A) (B) (C) (D) (E)	32 (A) (B) (C) (D) (E)
3 (A) (B) (C) (D) (E)	13 (A) (B) (C) (D) (E)	23 (A) (B) (C) (D) (E)	33 (A) (B) (C) (D) (E)
4 (A) (B) (C) (D) (E)	14 (A) (B) (C) (D) (E)	24 (A) (B) (C) (D) (E)	34 (A) (B) (C) (D) (E)
5 (A) (B) (C) (D) (E)	15 (A) (B) (C) (D) (E)	25 (A) (B) (C) (D) (E)	35 (A) (B) (C) (D) (E)
6 (A) (B) (C) (D) (E)	16 (A) (B) (C) (D) (E)	26 (A) (B) (C) (D) (E)	36 (A) (B) (C) (D) (E)
7 (A) (B) (C) (D) (E)	17 (A) (B) (C) (D) (E)	27 (A) (B) (C) (D) (E)	37 (A) (B) (C) (D) (E)
8 (A) (B) (C) (D) (E)	18 (A) (B) (C) (D) (E)	28 (A) (B) (C) (D) (E)	38 (A) (B) (C) (D) (E)
9 (A) (B) (C) (D) (E)	19 (A) (B) (C) (D) (E)	29 (A) (B) (C) (D) (E)	39 (A) (B) (C) (D) (E)
10 (A) (B) (C) (D) (E)	20 (A) (B) (C) (D) (E)	30 (A) (B) (C) (D) (E)	40 (A) (B) (C) (D) (E)

SECTION 4

1 (A) (B) (C) (D) (E)	11 (A) (B) (C) (D) (E)	21 (A) (B) (C) (D) (E)	31 (A) (B) (C) (D) (E)
2 (A) (B) (C) (D) (E)	12 (A) (B) (C) (D) (E)	22 (A) (B) (C) (D) (E)	32 (A) (B) (C) (D) (E)
3 (A) (B) (C) (D) (E)	13 (A) (B) (C) (D) (E)	23 (A) (B) (C) (D) (E)	33 (A) (B) (C) (D) (E)
4 (A) (B) (C) (D) (E)	14 (A) (B) (C) (D) (E)	24 (A) (B) (C) (D) (E)	34 (A) (B) (C) (D) (E)
5 (A) (B) (C) (D) (E)	15 (A) (B) (C) (D) (E)	25 (A) (B) (C) (D) (E)	35 (A) (B) (C) (D) (E)
6 (A) (B) (C) (D) (E)	16 (A) (B) (C) (D) (E)	26 (A) (B) (C) (D) (E)	36 (A) (B) (C) (D) (E)
7 (A) (B) (C) (D) (E)	17 (A) (B) (C) (D) (E)	27 (A) (B) (C) (D) (E)	37 (A) (B) (C) (D) (E)
8 (A) (B) (C) (D) (E)	18 (A) (B) (C) (D) (E)	28 (A) (B) (C) (D) (E)	38 (A) (B) (C) (D) (E)
9 (A) (B) (C) (D) (E)	19 (A) (B) (C) (D) (E)	29 (A) (B) (C) (D) (E)	39 (A) (B) (C) (D) (E)
10 (A) (B) (C) (D) (E)	20 (A) (B) (C) (D) (E)	30 (A) (B) (C) (D) (E)	40 (A) (B) (C) (D) (E)

SECTION 6

1 (A) (B) (C) (D) (E)	11 (A) (B) (C) (D) (E)	21 (A) (B) (C) (D) (E)	31 (A) (B) (C) (D) (E)
2 (A) (B) (C) (D) (E)	12 (A) (B) (C) (D) (E)	22 (A) (B) (C) (D) (E)	32 (A) (B) (C) (D) (E)
3 (A) (B) (C) (D) (E)	13 (A) (B) (C) (D) (E)	23 (A) (B) (C) (D) (E)	33 (A) (B) (C) (D) (E)
4 (A) (B) (C) (D) (E)	14 (A) (B) (C) (D) (E)	24 (A) (B) (C) (D) (E)	34 (A) (B) (C) (D) (E)
5 (A) (B) (C) (D) (E)	15 (A) (B) (C) (D) (E)	25 (A) (B) (C) (D) (E)	35 (A) (B) (C) (D) (E)
6 (A) (B) (C) (D) (E)	16 (A) (B) (C) (D) (E)	26 (A) (B) (C) (D) (E)	36 (A) (B) (C) (D) (E)
7 (A) (B) (C) (D) (E)	17 (A) (B) (C) (D) (E)	27 (A) (B) (C) (D) (E)	37 (A) (B) (C) (D) (E)
8 (A) (B) (C) (D) (E)	18 (A) (B) (C) (D) (E)	28 (A) (B) (C) (D) (E)	38 (A) (B) (C) (D) (E)
9 (A) (B) (C) (D) (E)	19 (A) (B) (C) (D) (E)	29 (A) (B) (C) (D) (E)	39 (A) (B) (C) (D) (E)
10 (A) (B) (C) (D) (E)	20 (A) (B) (C) (D) (E)	30 (A) (B) (C) (D) (E)	40 (A) (B) (C) (D) (E)

Start with number 1 for each new section. If a section has fewer questions than answer spaces, leave the extra answer spaces blank. Be sure to erase any errors or stray marks completely.

SECTION 7

1 Ⓐ Ⓑ Ⓒ Ⓓ Ⓔ   11 Ⓐ Ⓑ Ⓒ Ⓓ Ⓔ   21 Ⓐ Ⓑ Ⓒ Ⓓ Ⓔ   31 Ⓐ Ⓑ Ⓒ Ⓓ Ⓔ
2 Ⓐ Ⓑ Ⓒ Ⓓ Ⓔ   12 Ⓐ Ⓑ Ⓒ Ⓓ Ⓔ   22 Ⓐ Ⓑ Ⓒ Ⓓ Ⓔ   32 Ⓐ Ⓑ Ⓒ Ⓓ Ⓔ
3 Ⓐ Ⓑ Ⓒ Ⓓ Ⓔ   13 Ⓐ Ⓑ Ⓒ Ⓓ Ⓔ   23 Ⓐ Ⓑ Ⓒ Ⓓ Ⓔ   33 Ⓐ Ⓑ Ⓒ Ⓓ Ⓔ
4 Ⓐ Ⓑ Ⓒ Ⓓ Ⓔ   14 Ⓐ Ⓑ Ⓒ Ⓓ Ⓔ   24 Ⓐ Ⓑ Ⓒ Ⓓ Ⓔ   34 Ⓐ Ⓑ Ⓒ Ⓓ Ⓔ
5 Ⓐ Ⓑ Ⓒ Ⓓ Ⓔ   15 Ⓐ Ⓑ Ⓒ Ⓓ Ⓔ   25 Ⓐ Ⓑ Ⓒ Ⓓ Ⓔ   35 Ⓐ Ⓑ Ⓒ Ⓓ Ⓔ
6 Ⓐ Ⓑ Ⓒ Ⓓ Ⓔ   16 Ⓐ Ⓑ Ⓒ Ⓓ Ⓔ   26 Ⓐ Ⓑ Ⓒ Ⓓ Ⓔ   36 Ⓐ Ⓑ Ⓒ Ⓓ Ⓔ
7 Ⓐ Ⓑ Ⓒ Ⓓ Ⓔ   17 Ⓐ Ⓑ Ⓒ Ⓓ Ⓔ   27 Ⓐ Ⓑ Ⓒ Ⓓ Ⓔ   37 Ⓐ Ⓑ Ⓒ Ⓓ Ⓔ
8 Ⓐ Ⓑ Ⓒ Ⓓ Ⓔ   18 Ⓐ Ⓑ Ⓒ Ⓓ Ⓔ   28 Ⓐ Ⓑ Ⓒ Ⓓ Ⓔ   38 Ⓐ Ⓑ Ⓒ Ⓓ Ⓔ
9 Ⓐ Ⓑ Ⓒ Ⓓ Ⓔ   19 Ⓐ Ⓑ Ⓒ Ⓓ Ⓔ   29 Ⓐ Ⓑ Ⓒ Ⓓ Ⓔ   39 Ⓐ Ⓑ Ⓒ Ⓓ Ⓔ
10 Ⓐ Ⓑ Ⓒ Ⓓ Ⓔ   20 Ⓐ Ⓑ Ⓒ Ⓓ Ⓔ   30 Ⓐ Ⓑ Ⓒ Ⓓ Ⓔ   40 Ⓐ Ⓑ Ⓒ Ⓓ Ⓔ

SECTION 8

1 Ⓐ Ⓑ Ⓒ Ⓓ Ⓔ   11 Ⓐ Ⓑ Ⓒ Ⓓ Ⓔ   21 Ⓐ Ⓑ Ⓒ Ⓓ Ⓔ   31 Ⓐ Ⓑ Ⓒ Ⓓ Ⓔ
2 Ⓐ Ⓑ Ⓒ Ⓓ Ⓔ   12 Ⓐ Ⓑ Ⓒ Ⓓ Ⓔ   22 Ⓐ Ⓑ Ⓒ Ⓓ Ⓔ   32 Ⓐ Ⓑ Ⓒ Ⓓ Ⓔ
3 Ⓐ Ⓑ Ⓒ Ⓓ Ⓔ   13 Ⓐ Ⓑ Ⓒ Ⓓ Ⓔ   23 Ⓐ Ⓑ Ⓒ Ⓓ Ⓔ   33 Ⓐ Ⓑ Ⓒ Ⓓ Ⓔ
4 Ⓐ Ⓑ Ⓒ Ⓓ Ⓔ   14 Ⓐ Ⓑ Ⓒ Ⓓ Ⓔ   24 Ⓐ Ⓑ Ⓒ Ⓓ Ⓔ   34 Ⓐ Ⓑ Ⓒ Ⓓ Ⓔ
5 Ⓐ Ⓑ Ⓒ Ⓓ Ⓔ   15 Ⓐ Ⓑ Ⓒ Ⓓ Ⓔ   25 Ⓐ Ⓑ Ⓒ Ⓓ Ⓔ   35 Ⓐ Ⓑ Ⓒ Ⓓ Ⓔ
6 Ⓐ Ⓑ Ⓒ Ⓓ Ⓔ   16 Ⓐ Ⓑ Ⓒ Ⓓ Ⓔ   26 Ⓐ Ⓑ Ⓒ Ⓓ Ⓔ   36 Ⓐ Ⓑ Ⓒ Ⓓ Ⓔ
7 Ⓐ Ⓑ Ⓒ Ⓓ Ⓔ   17 Ⓐ Ⓑ Ⓒ Ⓓ Ⓔ   27 Ⓐ Ⓑ Ⓒ Ⓓ Ⓔ   37 Ⓐ Ⓑ Ⓒ Ⓓ Ⓔ
8 Ⓐ Ⓑ Ⓒ Ⓓ Ⓔ   18 Ⓐ Ⓑ Ⓒ Ⓓ Ⓔ   28 Ⓐ Ⓑ Ⓒ Ⓓ Ⓔ   38 Ⓐ Ⓑ Ⓒ Ⓓ Ⓔ
9 Ⓐ Ⓑ Ⓒ Ⓓ Ⓔ   19 Ⓐ Ⓑ Ⓒ Ⓓ Ⓔ   29 Ⓐ Ⓑ Ⓒ Ⓓ Ⓔ   39 Ⓐ Ⓑ Ⓒ Ⓓ Ⓔ
10 Ⓐ Ⓑ Ⓒ Ⓓ Ⓔ   20 Ⓐ Ⓑ Ⓒ Ⓓ Ⓔ   30 Ⓐ Ⓑ Ⓒ Ⓓ Ⓔ   40 Ⓐ Ⓑ Ⓒ Ⓓ Ⓔ

SECTION 9

1 Ⓐ Ⓑ Ⓒ Ⓓ Ⓔ   11 Ⓐ Ⓑ Ⓒ Ⓓ Ⓔ   21 Ⓐ Ⓑ Ⓒ Ⓓ Ⓔ   31 Ⓐ Ⓑ Ⓒ Ⓓ Ⓔ
2 Ⓐ Ⓑ Ⓒ Ⓓ Ⓔ   12 Ⓐ Ⓑ Ⓒ Ⓓ Ⓔ   22 Ⓐ Ⓑ Ⓒ Ⓓ Ⓔ   32 Ⓐ Ⓑ Ⓒ Ⓓ Ⓔ
3 Ⓐ Ⓑ Ⓒ Ⓓ Ⓔ   13 Ⓐ Ⓑ Ⓒ Ⓓ Ⓔ   23 Ⓐ Ⓑ Ⓒ Ⓓ Ⓔ   33 Ⓐ Ⓑ Ⓒ Ⓓ Ⓔ
4 Ⓐ Ⓑ Ⓒ Ⓓ Ⓔ   14 Ⓐ Ⓑ Ⓒ Ⓓ Ⓔ   24 Ⓐ Ⓑ Ⓒ Ⓓ Ⓔ   34 Ⓐ Ⓑ Ⓒ Ⓓ Ⓔ
5 Ⓐ Ⓑ Ⓒ Ⓓ Ⓔ   15 Ⓐ Ⓑ Ⓒ Ⓓ Ⓔ   25 Ⓐ Ⓑ Ⓒ Ⓓ Ⓔ   35 Ⓐ Ⓑ Ⓒ Ⓓ Ⓔ
6 Ⓐ Ⓑ Ⓒ Ⓓ Ⓔ   16 Ⓐ Ⓑ Ⓒ Ⓓ Ⓔ   26 Ⓐ Ⓑ Ⓒ Ⓓ Ⓔ   36 Ⓐ Ⓑ Ⓒ Ⓓ Ⓔ
7 Ⓐ Ⓑ Ⓒ Ⓓ Ⓔ   17 Ⓐ Ⓑ Ⓒ Ⓓ Ⓔ   27 Ⓐ Ⓑ Ⓒ Ⓓ Ⓔ   37 Ⓐ Ⓑ Ⓒ Ⓓ Ⓔ
8 Ⓐ Ⓑ Ⓒ Ⓓ Ⓔ   18 Ⓐ Ⓑ Ⓒ Ⓓ Ⓔ   28 Ⓐ Ⓑ Ⓒ Ⓓ Ⓔ   38 Ⓐ Ⓑ Ⓒ Ⓓ Ⓔ
9 Ⓐ Ⓑ Ⓒ Ⓓ Ⓔ   19 Ⓐ Ⓑ Ⓒ Ⓓ Ⓔ   29 Ⓐ Ⓑ Ⓒ Ⓓ Ⓔ   39 Ⓐ Ⓑ Ⓒ Ⓓ Ⓔ
10 Ⓐ Ⓑ Ⓒ Ⓓ Ⓔ   20 Ⓐ Ⓑ Ⓒ Ⓓ Ⓔ   30 Ⓐ Ⓑ Ⓒ Ⓓ Ⓔ   40 Ⓐ Ⓑ Ⓒ Ⓓ Ⓔ

SECTION 10

1 Ⓐ Ⓑ Ⓒ Ⓓ Ⓔ   11 Ⓐ Ⓑ Ⓒ Ⓓ Ⓔ   21 Ⓐ Ⓑ Ⓒ Ⓓ Ⓔ   31 Ⓐ Ⓑ Ⓒ Ⓓ Ⓔ
2 Ⓐ Ⓑ Ⓒ Ⓓ Ⓔ   12 Ⓐ Ⓑ Ⓒ Ⓓ Ⓔ   22 Ⓐ Ⓑ Ⓒ Ⓓ Ⓔ   32 Ⓐ Ⓑ Ⓒ Ⓓ Ⓔ
3 Ⓐ Ⓑ Ⓒ Ⓓ Ⓔ   13 Ⓐ Ⓑ Ⓒ Ⓓ Ⓔ   23 Ⓐ Ⓑ Ⓒ Ⓓ Ⓔ   33 Ⓐ Ⓑ Ⓒ Ⓓ Ⓔ
4 Ⓐ Ⓑ Ⓒ Ⓓ Ⓔ   14 Ⓐ Ⓑ Ⓒ Ⓓ Ⓔ   24 Ⓐ Ⓑ Ⓒ Ⓓ Ⓔ   34 Ⓐ Ⓑ Ⓒ Ⓓ Ⓔ
5 Ⓐ Ⓑ Ⓒ Ⓓ Ⓔ   15 Ⓐ Ⓑ Ⓒ Ⓓ Ⓔ   25 Ⓐ Ⓑ Ⓒ Ⓓ Ⓔ   35 Ⓐ Ⓑ Ⓒ Ⓓ Ⓔ
6 Ⓐ Ⓑ Ⓒ Ⓓ Ⓔ   16 Ⓐ Ⓑ Ⓒ Ⓓ Ⓔ   26 Ⓐ Ⓑ Ⓒ Ⓓ Ⓔ   36 Ⓐ Ⓑ Ⓒ Ⓓ Ⓔ
7 Ⓐ Ⓑ Ⓒ Ⓓ Ⓔ   17 Ⓐ Ⓑ Ⓒ Ⓓ Ⓔ   27 Ⓐ Ⓑ Ⓒ Ⓓ Ⓔ   37 Ⓐ Ⓑ Ⓒ Ⓓ Ⓔ
8 Ⓐ Ⓑ Ⓒ Ⓓ Ⓔ   18 Ⓐ Ⓑ Ⓒ Ⓓ Ⓔ   28 Ⓐ Ⓑ Ⓒ Ⓓ Ⓔ   38 Ⓐ Ⓑ Ⓒ Ⓓ Ⓔ
9 Ⓐ Ⓑ Ⓒ Ⓓ Ⓔ   19 Ⓐ Ⓑ Ⓒ Ⓓ Ⓔ   29 Ⓐ Ⓑ Ⓒ Ⓓ Ⓔ   39 Ⓐ Ⓑ Ⓒ Ⓓ Ⓔ
10 Ⓐ Ⓑ Ⓒ Ⓓ Ⓔ   20 Ⓐ Ⓑ Ⓒ Ⓓ Ⓔ   30 Ⓐ Ⓑ Ⓒ Ⓓ Ⓔ   40 Ⓐ Ⓑ Ⓒ Ⓓ Ⓔ

Diagnostic Test

Essay
Time—25 minutes

Write your essay on separate sheets of standard lined paper.

The essay gives you an opportunity to show how effectively you can develop and express ideas. You should, therefore, take care to develop your point of view, present your ideas logically and clearly, and use language precisely.

Your essay should be written on the lines provided on your answer sheet—you will receive no other paper on which to write. You will have enough space if you write on every line, avoid wide margins, and keep your handwriting to a reasonable size. Remember that people who are not familiar with your handwriting will read what you write. Try to write or print so that what you are writing is legible to those readers.

Important reminders:

- **A pencil is required for the essay.** An essay written in ink will receive a score of zero.
- **Do not write your essay in your test book.** You will receive credit for what you write on your answer sheet.
- **An off-topic essay will receive a score of zero.**
- **If your essay does not reflect your original and individual work, your test scores may be cancelled.**

You have twenty-five minutes to write an essay on the topic assigned below.

Think carefully about the issue presented in the following excerpt and the assignment below.

Life must be a constant education; one must learn everything, from speaking to dying.

Gustave Flaubert

Assignment: Are people born with innate wisdom or does our knowledge come from experience? Plan and write an essay in which you develop your point of view on this issue. Support your position with reasoning and examples taking from your reading, studies, experiences, or observations.

Begin writing your essay on a separate sheet of paper.

If you finish before time is called, you may check your work on this section only.
Do not turn to any other section in the test.

Section 2
Time—25 Minutes
20 Questions

Directions: For this section, solve each problem and decide which is the best of the choices given. Fill in the corresponding circle on the answer sheet. You may use any available space for scratch work.

Notes

1. The use of a calculator is permitted.
2. All numbers used are real numbers.
3. Figures that accompany problems in this test are intended to provide information useful in solving the problems. They are drawn as accurately as possible EXCEPT when it is stated in a specific problem that the figure is not drawn to scale. All figures lie in a plane unless otherwise indicated.
4. Unless otherwise specified, the domain of any function f is assumed to be the set of all real numbers x for which $f(x)$ is a real number.

Reference Information

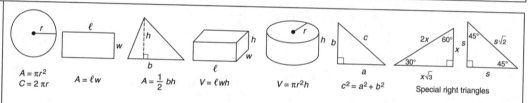

$A = \pi r^2$
$C = 2\pi r$

$A = \ell w$

$A = \frac{1}{2} bh$

$V = \ell wh$

$V = \pi r^2 h$

$c^2 = a^2 + b^2$

Special right triangles

The number of degrees of arc in a circle is 360.
The sum of the measures in degrees of the angles of a triangle is 180.

1. A "perfect number" is a positive integer that is equal to the sum of all of its divisors excluding itself. Which of the following is a perfect number?

(A) 8
(B) 12
(C) 28
(D) 33
(E) 37

2. If $96,000 = 9.6 \times 10^n$, what is the value of n?

    (A) 1
    (B) 2
    (C) 3
    (D) 4
    (E) 5

3. If $\sqrt[3]{x} \times \sqrt[3]{2}$ is an integer, which of the following could not be the value of x?

    (A) $\dfrac{1}{2}$
    (B) 3
    (C) 4
    (D) 32
    (E) 108

4.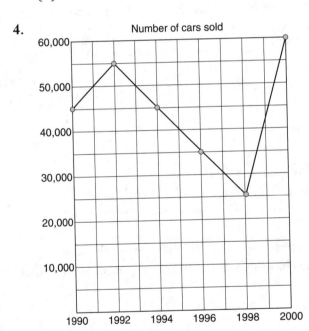

According to the graph above, which of the following is closest to the decrease per year in the number of cars sold between 1992 and 1998?

(A) 5,000
(B) 7,500
(C) 10,000
(D) 25,000
(E) 55,000

5. If X and Y are two sets of numbers, and every number in Y is exactly one-half the value of every number in X, which of the following must be true?

(A) X and Y contain the same number of elements
(B) X contains more numbers than Y
(C) X cannot contain fractions
(D) X and Y do not have any common numbers
(E) Y contains only numbers that are divisible by two

6.

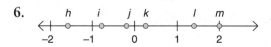

On the number line above, h, i, j, k, l, and m are coordinates of the indicated points. Which of the following is closest in value to $|i + 2k|$?

(A) i
(B) j
(C) k
(D) l
(E) m

7. For all numbers a and b, let the operation $*$ be defined by $a*b = a^2 - b^2$. If e and f are positive integers, which of the following can be equal to zero?

     I. $e*f$
     II. $e*(e-f)$
     III. $(e+f)* - (e+f)$

(A) I only
(B) II only
(C) III only
(D) I and II
(E) I and III

8. In an aquatic skills competition, Georgina held her breath for x seconds, Seth held his breath three times longer than Georgina, and Maybelline held her breath for 15 seconds less than twice as long as Georgina. In terms of x, what is the average number of seconds the three competitors can hold their breath?

(A) $2x - 15$
(B) $6x - 5$
(C) $2x - 5$
(D) $5x - 5$
(E) $3x - 8$

9. If x and y are integers such that $x > y > 0$ and $x^2 - y^2 = 15$, which of the following can be the value of $x + y$?

     I. 3
     II. 5
     III. 15

(A) I only
(B) II only
(C) I and II only
(D) II and III only
(E) I, II, and III

10. If $y = \frac{1}{3}x + 9$ and $x < 3$, which of the following represents all the possible values for y?

(A) $y < 10$

(B) $y > 10$

(C) $y > 9\frac{2}{3}$

(D) $y < 9\frac{2}{3}$

(E) $y\frac{2}{3} < y < 10$

11. $4x + 3y + 3z = 25$

$2x + y + z = 8$

If the equations above are true, which of the following is the value of $y + z$?

(A   −9

(B) −4.5

(C) 0

(D) 4.5

(E) 9

12. The average (arithmetic mean) of a and b is 25, and the average of c and d is 17. What is the average of a, b, c, and d?

(A) 4

(B) 8

(C) 14

(D) 21

(E) 42

13. In a set of seven different numbers, which of the following cannot affect the value of the median?

(A) Tripling each number

(B) Decreasing each number by 1

(C) Increasing the smallest number only

(D) Decreasing the fifth-largest number only

(E) Increasing the fifth-largest number only

14. Given a sequence of integers where every third term is a multiple of 4 and every second term is a multiple of 5, which of the following could be the value of the 156th term?

(A) 92
(B) 115
(C) 104
(D) 120
(E) 224

15.

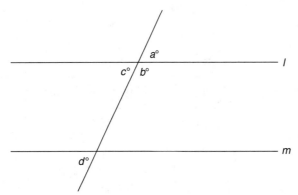

In the figure above, $l \| m$ and $d = 60$. What is the value of $a + b + c$?

(A) 230
(B) 240
(C) 250
(D) 260
(E) 300

16.

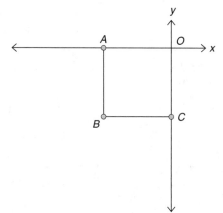

In the figure above, $AB = BC$ and the coordinates of B are $(k, -3)$. What is the value of k?

(A) 3
(B) $\sqrt{3}$
(C) 0
(D) $-\sqrt{3}$
(E) -3

17. When it is noon Eastern standard time (EST) in Newark, it is 9:00 AM Pacific standard time (PST) in Los Angeles. A jet took off from Newark at noon EST and arrived in Los Angeles at 6:00 PM PST on the same day. If a second jet left Los Angeles at noon PST and took exactly the same amount of time for the trip, what was the jet's arrival time (EST) in Newark?

(A) 10:00 PM EST
(B) 11:00 PM EST
(C) 12:00 PM EST
(D) 1:00 PM EST
(E) 2:00 PM EST

18.

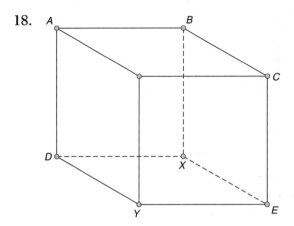

On the cube in the figure above, each of the following points is the same distance from *X* as it is to *Y* except:

(A) A
(B) B
(C) C
(D) D
(E) E

19.

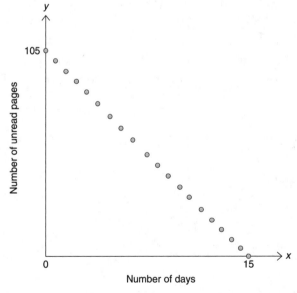

Number of days

The graph above shows the number of Priscilla's unread pages in a novel over a 15-day period. The points on the graph all lie on which of the following lines?

(A) $y = 15x - 105$
(B) $y = 15x + 105$
(C) $y = 7x - 105$
(D) $y = 105 - 7x$
(E) $y = 105 - 15x$

20. If a positive integer n is picked at random from the positive integers less than or equal to 10, what is the probability that $4n - 5 > 11$?

(A) $\dfrac{2}{5}$

(B) $\dfrac{1}{2}$

(C) $\dfrac{3}{5}$

(D) $\dfrac{7}{10}$

(E) $\dfrac{9}{10}$

Section 3
Time—25 minutes
24 questions

Turn to Section 3 (page 326) of your answer sheet to answer the questions in this section.

Directions: For each question in this section, select the best answer from among the answer choices given and fill in the corresponding circle on the answer sheet.

Each sentence below has one or two question blanks, each blank indicating that something has been omitted. Beneath the sentence are five words or sets of words labeled A through E. Choose the word or set of words that, when inserted in the sentence, *best* fits the meaning of the sentence as a whole.

Example:

Susan preferred to be ____, hoping to avoid confusion due to miscommunication.
(A) **direct**
(B) devious
(C) cunning
(D) austere
(E) terse

1. Because of the library's _____ late fees, many patrons ignored due dates and borrowed books for longer than the four-week lending period.

    (A) objective
    (B) nominal
    (C) unimportant
    (D) dispensable
    (E) lofty

2. During the late summer months, pea and cucumber plants grew _____ in our backyard yielding _____ volumes of vegetables.

    (A) rampant...enormous
    (B) gradually...abundant
    (C) pervasive...massive

(D) quickly...limited
(E) scrutinized...copious

3. The writer's prose lacked _____ and his readers often found his stories monotonous and _____.

(A) enthusiasm...entertaining
(B) sophistication...mundane
(C) practice...exhilarating
(D) purpose...overpowering
(E) complexity...inspiring

4. Mr. Bennet's professional goals and commitment to his students, driven by the desire to improve education, _____ personal interests and ambitions.

(A) superseded
(B) followed
(C) ensued
(D) rankled
(E) vindicated

5. Leonard was _____ to the insults of his competitors and simply ignored the unkind remarks.

(A) impervious
(B) amenable
(C) steadfast
(D) obdurate
(E) exposed

The passages below are followed by questions based on their content; questions that follow a pair of related passages may also be based on the relationship between the paired passages. Answer the questions on the basis of what is *stated* or *implied* in the passage in any introductory material that may be provided.

Questions 6 through 9 are based on the following passages.

Passage 1

The traveler will doubtless bring back with him such antiquities as he is permitted to export. A word of general advice on this matter
Line   may not be out of place here. The essential value of antiquities, apart from their purely artistic interest, lies in the circumstances
5   in which they are found. The inexperienced traveler is apt to pick up a number of objects haphazard, without accurately noting their find-spots, and even, getting tired of them, as a child of flowers that he has picked, to discard them a mile or two away. If the first act is a blunder, the second is a crime; it is better to leave them
10   lying in place. For the same reason, it is highly desirable that objects found together (e.g., the contents of a tomb) should as far as possible be kept together, or at least that accurate record of the whole group should be made, since the archaeological value of a find may depend on a single object, apparently of small importance.

6. The author's attitude toward travelers can best be described as

    (A) assertively hostile
    (B) condescendingly tolerant
    (C) carefully respectful
    (D) aggressively frustrated
    (E) ardently encouraging

7. The author compares the "inexperienced traveler" to a child with flowers (lines 5–8) in order to

    (A) demonstrate the curiosity of an amateur archeologist is similar to that of a inquisitive child
    (B) give an example of the non-erudite approach to archeology

    (C) suggest how unimportant a small object may be
    (D) explain how a flower can become as valuable as an antiquity
    (E) emphasize the capricious nature of the amateur archeologist

Passage 2

        The aim of the Boy Scouts is to supplement the various existing
educational agencies, and to promote the ability in boys to do things
Line for themselves and others. It is not the aim to set up a new
organization to parallel in its purposes others already established.
5 The opportunity is afforded these organizations, however, to introduce
into their programs unique features appealing to interests which are
universal among boys. The method is summed up in the term Scoutcraft,
and is a combination of observation, deduction, and handiness, or the
ability to do things. Scoutcraft includes instruction in First Aid,
10 Life Saving, Tracking, Signaling, Cycling, Nature Study, Seamanship,
Campcraft, Woodcraft, Chivalry, Patriotism, and other subjects. This
is accomplished in games and team play, and is pleasure, not work, for
the boy. All that is needed is the out-of-doors, a group of boys, and
a competent leader.

8. The above passage would most likely appear in a/an

    (A) historical document on the Boy Scouts
    (B) handbook for parents
    (C) advertisement in a school magazine
    (D) community proposal
    (E) appendix to a book on Scoutcraft

9. The author suggests that "instruction in First Aid, Life Saving..."
(lines 9–13)

    (A) are skills learned through practice
    (B) are the necessary foundations to a boy's education
    (C) are more important than traditional education
    (D) must be fostered in boys who are not able to do things for
themselves
    (E) require methodical introduction by an experienced leader

Questions 10 through 15 are based on the following passage.

The text is intended to familiarize the reader with the town of Chertsey in England.

The county of Surrey is rich to overflowing in memories, both of
persons and events, and the little quaint and quiet town of Chertsey
could tell of the gorgeous and gloomy past as much as many of its
ancient neighbors within a day's drive of the city. Had its old abbey
stones but tongues, how they could discourse of years when a visit
to Chertsey was an undertaking; though now the distance is but half
an hour.

Nowhere within 20 miles of London does the Thames appear more
queenly, or sweep with greater grace through its fertile dominions,
than it does at Chertsey. It is, indeed, delightful to stand on the bridge
in the glowing sunset of a summer evening, and turning from the
refreshing green of the Shepperton Range, look into the deep clear
blue of the flowing river, while the murmur of the waters rushing
through Laleham Lock give a sort of spirit music to the scene. On the
right, as you leave Chertsey, the river bends gracefully towards the
double bridge of Walton, and to the left, it undulates smoothly along,
having passed Runnymede and Staines, while the almost conical hill
of St. Anne's attracts attention by its abrupt and singular form when
viewed from the vale of the Thames.

About a mile, on the Walton side, from our favorite bridge (Old
Camden tells us so), is the spot where Cæsar crossed the Thames.
Were the peasantry as imaginative as their brethren of Killarney, what
legends would have grown out of this tradition; how often would the
"noblest Roman of them all" have been seen by the pale moonlight
leading his steed over the waters of the rapid river—how many would
have heard Cassivelaunus himself during the stillness of some
particular Midsummer night working at the rude defence which can
still be traced beneath the blue waters of the Thames. What hosts of
pale and ghastly spectres would have risen from those tranquil banks,
and from the deepest hollows of the rushing current, and—like the
Huns, who almost live on the inspired canvas of Kaulbach,—fought
their last earthly battle, again and again, in the spirit world, amid the
stars! But ours is no region of romance; even remnants of history,

Line

5

10

15

20

25

30

which go beyond the commonest capacity, are rejected as dreams, or
35 put aside as legends. But history has enough to tell to interest us all;
and we may be satisfied with the abundant enjoyment we have in
delicious rambles through the lanes and up the hills, along the fair
river's banks, and among the many traditional ruins of ancient and
beautiful Surrey.

10. This passage is most likely be found in a

(A) historical document
(B) high school textbook
(C) guidebook for visitors
(D) personal diary
(E) editorial article

11. The personification paragraph 1 primarily serves to

(A) demonstrate that the town is part of the community fabric
(B) place the town in the role of an inviting community leader
(C) suggest that the town holds secrets of its residents
(D) contrast varying hypotheses of Chertsey's history
(E) underline the narrator's relationship with Chertsey

12. In line 5 "discourse" most nearly means

(A) address
(B) chat
(C) recollect
(D) explain
(E) reminisce

13. The questions in paragraph 3 serve to

(A) solve unanswered mysteries
(B) explore common historical misconceptions
(C) consider the events of the past
(D) satisfy the curiosity of the reader
(E) ponder the origin of legends

14. The sentence beginning "But ours is no region..." (line 33) suggests that

    (A) historical evidence is preferred over legends
    (B) most visitors do not fully appreciate the romance of the region
    (C) stories about the region are rejected by historians
    (D) historical views are unpopular in the region
    (E) fables are not relevant to most people's daily lives

15. In line 37 "delicious" most nearly means

    (A) scrumptious
    (B) agreeable
    (C) appetizing
    (D) attractive
    (E) tranquil

Questions 16 through 24 are based on the following passage.

This passage is from a book on the history of mathematics.

Of the development of Hindoo mathematics we know but
little. A few manuscripts bear testimony that the Indians
Line   had climbed to a lofty height, but their path of ascent is
no longer traceable. It would seem that Greek mathematics
5   grew up under more favorable conditions than the Hindoo,
for in Greece it attained an independent existence, and was
studied for its own sake, while Hindoo mathematics always
remained merely a servant to astronomy. Furthermore, in
Greece mathematics was a science of the people, free to be
10   cultivated by all who had a liking for it; in India, as in Egypt, it
was in the hands chiefly of the priests. Again, the Indians were
in the habit of putting into verse all mathematical results they
obtained, and of clothing them in obscure and mystic language,
which, though well adapted to aid the memory of him who
15   already understood the subject, was often unintelligible to
the uninitiated. Although the great Hindoo mathematicians
doubtless reasoned out most or all of their discoveries, yet
they were not in the habit of preserving the proofs, so that the
naked theorems and processes of operation are all that have

20 come down to our time. Very different in these respects were
the Greeks. Obscurity of language was generally avoided,
and proofs belonged to the stock of knowledge quite as much
as the theorems themselves. Very striking was the difference
in the bent of mind of the Hindoo and Greek; for, while
25 the Greek mind was preeminently geometrical, the Indian
was first of all arithmetical. The Hindoo dealt with number,
the Greek with form. Numerical symbolism, the science of
numbers, and algebra attained in India far greater perfection
than they had previously reached in Greece. On the other
30 hand, we believe that there was little or no geometry in India
of which the source may not be traced back to Greece. Hindoo
trigonometry might possibly be mentioned as an exception,
but it rested on arithmetic more than on geometry.

…

An interesting but difficult task is the tracing of the
35 relation between Hindoo and Greek mathematics. It is
well known that more or less trade was carried on between
Greece and India from early times. After Egypt had become
a Roman province, a more lively commercial intercourse
sprang up between Rome and India, by way of Alexandria.
40 A priori, it does not seem improbable, that with the trace of
merchandise there should also be an interchange of ideas.

That communications of thought from the Hindoos to the
Alexandrians actually did take place, is evident from the
fact that certain philosophic and theological teachings of the
45 Manicheans, Neo-Platonists, Gnostics, show unmistakable
likeness to Indian tenets. Scientific facts passed also from
Alexandria to India. This is shown plainly by the Greek origin
of some of the technical terms used by the Hindoos. Hindoo
astronomy was influenced by Greek astronomy. Most of the
50 geometrical knowledge which they possessed is traceable to
Alexandria, and to the writings of Heron in particular. In
algebra there was, probably, a mutual giving and receiving.
We suspect that Diophantus got the first glimpses of algebraic
knowledge from India. On the other hand, evidences have
55 been found of Greek algebra among the Brahmins. The

earliest knowledge of algebra in India may possibly have
been of Babylonian origin. When we consider that Hindoo
scientists looked upon arithmetic and algebra merely as tools
useful in astronomical research, there appears deep irony in
60 the fact that these secondary branches were after all the only
ones in which they won real distinction, while in their pet
science of astronomy they displayed an inaptitude to observe,
to collect facts, and to make inductive investigations.

16. It can be reasonably inferred from this passage that

(A) while we can assume that Hindus made significant contributions to
     the field of mathematics no evidence remains of their work
(B) mathematical advancement relied on isolated schools of thought
(C) academic exploration is most effective when people in different
     places work together
(D) research carried out by modern mathematicians does not rely on
     foundations formed by ancient scholars
(E) ideas and knowledge were shared by peoples before the advent of
     modern technology

17. A primary reason that knowledge of Hindu mathematics is not wide-
     spread is that

(A) the study of the subject was limited to those with unique training
(B) the subject was used only by astronomers
(C) it was overshadowed by innovation in the Greek study of
     mathematics
(D) familiarity with a special language was needed to understand the
     subject
(E) mathematical proofs were developed in secrecy

18. In line 12, "habit" most nearly means

(A) practice
(B) tradition
(C) schedule
(D) pattern
(E) preference

19. The sentence beginning "Numerical symbolism, the science of numbers…" (line 27) is used to

    (A) demonstrate the beauty of Indian mathematics
    (B) explain the variation in different branches of mathematics
    (C) illustrate that Indian mathematicians were primarily interested in the studies of geometry and trigonometry
    (D) provide examples of the branch of thought favored by Indian mathematicians
    (E) rationalize why all mathematics relies on the study of arithmetic

20. According to the first paragraph, a primary difference between Grecian and Indian approaches to mathematics was that

    (A) Greeks encouraged the scrupulous annotation of mathematical processes while the Hindus used inscrutable note-taking methods
    (B) Greeks believed that mathematics should be used in daily life whereas Hindus contained the study to mathematical schools
    (C) Only Greek priests studied mathematics while the study of the subject was open to all Hindus
    (D) Greeks studied mathematics solely for the exploration of life science and Hindus studied mathematics for application to astronomy
    (E) Greek mathematicians desired to pass along their knowledge while Hindus destroyed all evidence of new discoveries

21. The purpose of the second paragraph (lines 34–41) in relation to the passage is to

    (A) provide a plausible hypothesis for the ways knowledge was exchanged
    (B) acquaint the reader with the long-established history of trade routes
    (C) question the originality of ideas formulated in Alexandria
    (D) introduce the idea that the study of mathematics originated from necessities of trade
    (E) lament the deplorable conditions of trade between Rome and India

22. The statement "We suspect that Diophantus..." (line 53) serves to

   (A) provide supporting evidence for a previously introduced idea
   (B) emphasize the disparate problem-solving approaches to compatible topics
   (C) illustrate a practical approach to a theoretical dilemma
   (D) argue that Diophantus was many years ahead of his time
   (E) suggest the limits of Greek mathematicians

23. It can be inferred from the third paragraph that

   (A) the foundation of Greek mathematics is rooted solely in Indian teachings
   (B) philosophers from Alexandria traveled to India
   (C) there was a shared exchange of ideas between India and Greece
   (D) mathematics would not exist without the contributions of the Greeks and Indians
   (E) astronomy served as the intersection of math and science

24. The phrase beginning "When we consider that Hindoo scientists..." (line 57), suggests that

   (A) Indians should have dedicated more energy to the study of mathematics than science
   (B) in retrospect, Indian contribution to math exceeds that of the contributions to science
   (C) the Indian role in the study of mathematics vindicated the errors made in scientific discovery
   (D) Indians preferred the sciences to math
   (E) Indian scientists did not place any importance on the study of mathematics

STOP
If you finish before time is called, you may check your work on this section only.
Do not turn to any other section in the test.

Section 4
Time—25 Minutes
18 Questions

Directions: This section contains two types of questions. You have 25 minutes to complete both types. For questions 1–8, solve each problem and decide which is the best of the choices given. Fill in the corresponding circle on the answer sheet. Questions 9–18 require that you solve the problem and record your answers on a grid. A problem may have more than one solution, but only one solution of your choosing may be recorded. No Student-Produced Response question may have a negative solution. You may use any available space for scratch work and for registering your answer.

Notes

1. The use of a calculator is permitted.
2. All numbers used are real numbers.
3. Figures that accompany problems in this test are intended to provide information useful in solving the problems. They are drawn as accurately as possible EXCEPT when it is stated in a specific problem that the figure is not drawn to scale. All figures lie in a plane unless otherwise indicated.
4. Unless otherwise specified, the domain of any function f is assumed to be the set of all real numbers x for which $f(x)$ is a real number.

Reference Information

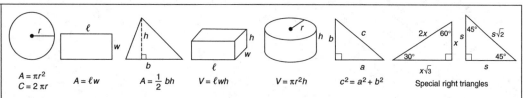

$A = \pi r^2$
$C = 2\pi r$
$A = \ell w$
$A = \frac{1}{2}bh$
$V = \ell wh$
$V = \pi r^2 h$
$c^2 = a^2 + b^2$
Special right triangles

The number of degrees of arc in a circle is 360.
The sum of the measures in degrees of the angles of a triangle is 180.

1. If $|7 - x| < 11$, which of the following is a possible value of x?

   (A) −3
   (B) −4
   (C) −5
   (D) −6
   (E) −7

2.

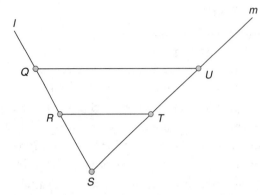

In the figure above (not drawn to scale), points Q, R, and S are equally spaced on line *l* and points S, T, and U are equally spaced on line *m*. If SQ = 8, SU = 12, and QU = 14, what is the perimeter of quadrilateral QRTU?

(A) 29
(B) 30
(C) 31
(D) 32
(E) 33

3.

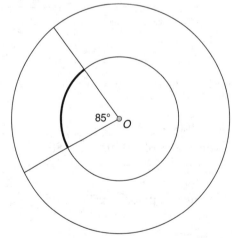

Point O is the center of both circles in the figure above. If the circumference of the large circle is 144 and the radius of the small circle is half of the radius of the large circle, what is the length of the darkened arc?

(A) 68
(B) 34

(C) 17
(D) 8
(E) 6

4. In order to make jewelry, Juanita buys silver. The price of silver is x dollars for 10 ounces, and each ounce makes y pieces of jewelry. In terms of x and y, what is the dollar cost of the silver required to make 2 pieces of jewelry?

(A) $\dfrac{x}{5y}$

(B) $\dfrac{5x}{y}$

(C) $5xy$

(D) $\dfrac{y}{5x}$

(E) $\dfrac{5y}{x}$

5. Two spherical beach balls, one with radius 8 and the other with diameter 14, are tangent to each other. If X is any point on one beach ball and Y is any point on the other beach ball, what is the maximum possible length of $\overline{XY}$?

(A) 8
(B) 15
(C) 22
(D) 30
(E) $30\sqrt{2}$

6.
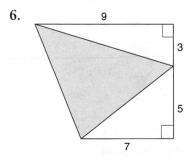

In the figure above, what is the area of the shaded triangle?

(A) 30
(B) 31
(C) 32
(D) 33
(E) 34

7.

Which of the following has the same volume as the cylinder shown above with radius x and height $3x$?

(A) A cylinder with radius $3x$ and height x
(B) A cylinder with radius $3\pi x$ and height $\dfrac{x}{3\pi}$
(C) A cube with edge $3x$
(D) A cube with edge $3\pi x$
(E) A rectangular solid with dimensions x, $3x$, and $3\pi^2 x$

8.

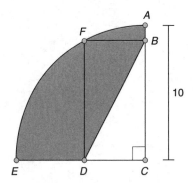

In the figure above, arc *AFE* is one quarter of a circle with C and radius 10. If the length plus the width of rectangle *BFDC* is 7, then the perimeter of the shaded region is

(A) $15 + 5\pi$

(B) $21 + 5\pi$

(C) $23 + 5\pi$

(D) $17 + 10\pi$

(E) $13 + 10\pi$

9. If x is $\dfrac{1}{6}$ of y, y is $\dfrac{3}{7}$ of z, and $z > 0$, then what is the value of $\dfrac{x}{z}$?

10.

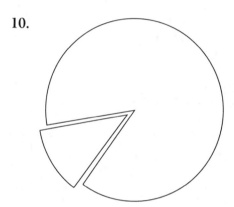

Sharkina cut a circular pita bread into wedge-shaped pieces, one of which is shown above. The tip of each piece is at the center of the pita bread and the angle at the tip is always greater than 24°, but less than 45°. What is one possible value for the number of pieces into which the pita bread is cut?

11. What is the greatest of five consecutive odd integers if the sum of these integers equals 4975?

12. $tx + 15y = -5$

The equation above is the equation of a line in the xy-plane, and t is a constant. If the slope of the line is -5, what is the value of t?

13.

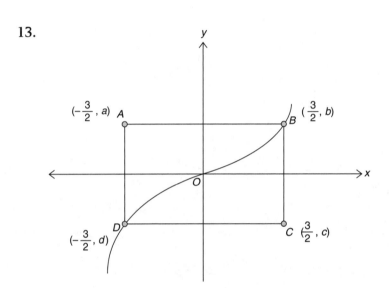

In the figure above (not drawn to scale), $ABCD$ is a rectangle. Points B and D lie on the graph of $y = cx^3$, where c is a constant. If the area of $ABCD$ is 12, what is the value of c?

14.

Month	Number of Hamburgers Purchased
January	3122
February	h
March	2459
April	1201
May	4662

The table above shows the number of hamburgers purchased at Sheba's Hamburger Shack from January through May. If the median number of hamburgers purchased for the 5 months was 2459, what is the greatest possible value for h?

15. $3x = 2y + 3x$
$4z = 6y + 5x$

In the system above, if $x > 0$, what is the value of $\frac{x}{z}$?

16.   If $\frac{4}{5}x$ is an integer and $4\frac{2}{3} < 7x < 11\frac{1}{3}$, what is the value of x?

17.   The value of a rare stamp always increases at a rate of $50 per year. If it was valued at $1000 in 1980, in what year will the value be $1850?

18.   A measuring cup contains $\frac{1}{6}$ of a cup of milk. It is then filled to the 1-cup mark with a mixture that contains equal amounts of oil, milk, and water. What fraction of the final mixture is milk?

Section 6
Time—25 minutes
35 questions

Turn to Section 6 (page 326) of your answer sheet to answer the questions in this section.

Directions: For each question in this section, select the best answer from among the answer choices given and fill in the corresponding circle on the answer sheet.

The following sentences test correctness and effectiveness of expression. Part of each sentence or the entire sentence is underlined; beneath each sentence are five ways of phrasing the underlined material. Choice A repeats the original phrasing; the other four choices are different. If you think the original phrasing produces a better sentence than any of the alternatives, select choice A; if not, select one of the other choices.

In making your selection, follow the requirements of standard written English; that is, pay attention to grammar, choice of words, sentence construction, and punctuation. Your selection should result in the most effective sentence—clear and precise, without awkwardness or ambiguity.

Example:

The numerous biographies published about Roosevelt's life <u>are testament to his great achievements</u>.

(A) are testament to his great achievements
(B) is testament to his great achievements
(C) **stand as a testament for his great achievement**
(D) full of achievement, the books are testament
(E) are testaments to his great achievements

1. <u>I heard that my parents were planning to get a puppy for my birthday while I was outside their bedroom door.</u>

(A) I heard that my parents were planning to get a puppy for my birthday while I was outside their bedroom door
(B) While I was outside my parents' bedroom door, I heard them planning to get a puppy for my birthday

    (C) While I was outside their bedroom door, I heard them planning to get a puppy for my birthday

    (D) Outside their bedroom door, I heard that my parents were planning to get a puppy for my birthday

    (E) I heard that my parents were planning to get a puppy for my birthday because I was outside the bedroom door

2.   The book Nancy <u>was looking</u> for is on the coffee table.

    (A) was looking
    (B) looked
    (C) has looked
    (D) been looking
    (E) has had a look

3.   The old algebra textbook <u>is easier to use than the new textbook</u>.

    (A) is easier to use than the new textbook
    (B) is easier to use then the new textbook
    (C) was easier to use than the new textbook
    (D) has been easier to use than the new textbook
    (E) is easier to be used then the new textbook

4.   When I uploaded the new software on the computer, <u>it crashed</u>.

    (A) it crashed
    (B) it had crashed
    (C) it crash
    (D) the machine crashed
    (E) the machine had crashed

5.   Before enrolling in AP Bio, <u>you should carefully consider what prerequisites are required</u>.

    (A) you should carefully consider what prerequisites are required
    (B) prerequisites that are required should be carefully considered
    (C) prerequisites should be carefully considered
    (D) you should consider carefully the required prerequisites
    (E) the required prerequisites should be carefully considered by you

6. <u>Although I spent three months training</u>, I did not feel ready for the marathon.

(A) Although I spent three months training
(B) Although I spent three months in training
(C) Although I trained for three months
(D) With training for three months
(E) Although three months were spent training

7. Wine-making has a <u>long and illustrious history, and it is especially popular</u> with the older generation.

(A) long and illustrious history, and it is especially popular
(B) long and illustrious history and it is especially popular
(C) long and illustrious history, and thus is especially popular
(D) long and illustrious history, and the activity is especially popular
(E) an especially popular, long, and illustration history

8. Ben's room was filled with crumpled papers, old soda cans, <u>and the garbage cans were overflowing</u>.

(A) and the garbage cans were overflowing
(B) and overflowing garbage cans
(C) and the garbage cans overflowed
(D) and had overflowing garbage cans
(E) and garbage cans that had overflowed

9. The nurse visited our <u>classrooms and she would give</u> all the students eye exams.

(A) classrooms and she would give
(B) classrooms to give
(C) classrooms, in order to give
(D) classrooms; where she would give
(E) classrooms, with her giving

10. Airport regulations require <u>not only presenting a photo ID but also to submit</u> to a metal detector test whenever we travel by air.

(A) not only presenting a photo ID but also to submit
(B) we not only present a photo ID but to also submit

(C) we not only present a photo ID but also submit

(D) not only the presentation of photo ID, but also submission

(E) not only to present a photo ID but also submitting

11. Every one of the girls in the dance class <u>is trying to do her best</u>.

(A) is trying to do her best

(B) tried to her best

(C) kept trying to do her best

(D) is trying to do their best

(E) tried to do their best

The following sentences test your ability to recognize grammar and usage errors. Each sentence contains either a single error or no error at all. No sentence contains more than one error. The error, if there is one, is underlined and lettered. If the sentence contains an error, select the one underlined part that must be changed to make the sentence correct. If the sentence is correct, select choice E. In choosing answers, follow the requirements of standard written English.

Example:

<u>The other boys</u> and <u>him quickly</u> agreed <u>to meet</u> at the nearby pizza parlor.
     A   B   C   D

<u>No error</u>.
  E

---

12. The paper <u>has</u> excellent ideas and <u>demonstrates</u> knowledge <u>of the topic</u>;
            A   B   C

however, the draft should be edited with <u>carefully</u>. <u>No error</u>.
                                   D   E

13. If a student <u>wants</u> to <u>do well</u> in school, <u>you</u> must work diligently,
               A   B   C

participate in class, and <u>complete all</u> homework. <u>No error</u>.
                      D   E

14. While I was listening to the radio, the sound suddenly gets fuzzy.
    A   B   C   D
    No error.
         E

15. Our professor said that our research papers will be due on Friday and
         A   B
    that we should be sure to Email everything by the end of the school day.
             C   D
    No error.
         E

16. Although nitrogen occurs naturally in the environment, man has
                    A   B
    drastically increased its concentration in the past century and a half.
         C   D
    No error.
         E

17. Myself and my friends went to the stationary store to purchase school
    A   B   C
    supplies. No error.
       D   E

18. The school bookstore was sold out of the text but I was able to find it
                          A   B   C   D
    at the local book shop. No error.
                              E

19. The new school computers, which are smaller and work faster, cost half
                              A   B
    as much as the computers we already had. No error.
        C   D   E

20. The trip was interesting, informative, and also relaxing. No error.
        A   B   C   D   E

21. I did not understand the material when the <u>teacher introduced</u> it in
                                                        A
   <u>class, but</u> I was <u>able to learn</u> the concepts <u>after I practiced</u> the homework
      B   C   D
   problems. <u>No error.</u>
                 E

22. There <u>seems</u> to <u>be</u> several classes <u>with</u> <u>demanding</u> expectations.
              A   B   C   D
   <u>No error.</u>
      E

23. Numbers <u>fascinate him so</u> he <u>wants to be</u> a mathematician. <u>No error.</u>
                 A   B   C   D   E

24. <u>A variety of</u> dishes <u>were displayed</u> at <u>the school</u> bake sale. <u>No error.</u>
         A   B   C   D   E

25. The experiment <u>we</u> performed <u>in class</u> <u>caused</u> an interesting <u>effect</u>.
                      A   B   C   D
   <u>No error.</u>
      E

26. <u>Everyone is entitled</u> to <u>their</u> opinion. <u>No error.</u>
       A   B   C   D   E

27. The principal <u>requested</u> a list of students <u>that</u> needed <u>additional review</u>
                      A   B   C
   <u>and tutorial</u>. <u>No error.</u>
       D   E

28. <u>The stack</u> of <u>books</u> <u>sitting on</u> the table. <u>No error.</u>
        A   B   C   D   E

29. Susan's assertion <u>that</u> the school <u>should not have</u> sports teams <u>differs</u>
                         A   B   C
   <u>dramatically</u> from <u>most students</u>. <u>No error.</u>
       D   E

Directions: The following passage is an early draft of an essay. Some parts of the passage need to be rewritten.

Read the passage carefully and select the best answers for the questions that follow. Some questions are about particular sentences or parts of sentences and ask you to improve sentence structure or word choice. Other questions ask you to consider organization and development. In choosing answers, follow the requirements of standard written English.

(1) Eleanor Roosevelt was born Anna Eleanor Roosevelt in New York City in November 1884. (2) She is best known as the wife of President Franklin Delano Roosevelt, Eleanor was an active civil servant in her own right. (3) Even after her husband's death Eleanor Roosevelt continued to be a prominent activist. (4) At a time when few women had careers, Eleanor maintained a busy travel schedule, held weekly press conferences, and wrote a newspaper column. (4) Eleanor was instrumental in FDRs politics and due to her husband's illness often made public appearances on his behalf. (5) She supported Roosevelt's New Deal policies, worked as a civil rights activist, and was appointed by Truman as a delegate to the United Nations. (6) She worked tirelessly to campaign for John. F. Kennedy. (7) She also was also an instrumental member of many of Kennedy's committees. (8) When JFK became the President, she was appointed to various positions including a committee of the Peace Corps. (9) As Eleanor had great interest in women's rights Kennedy also installed her on Presidential Commission on the Status of Women.

30. In context, which is the best revision for sentence 2 (reproduced below)?

    She is best known as the wife of President Franklin Delano Roosevelt, Eleanor was an active civil servant in her own right.

    (A) add "therefore" before "Eleanor"
    (B) insert "Although," at the beginning of the sentence
    (C) change the comma to a semicolon
    (D) capitalize "wife"
    (E) begin the sentence with "Eleanor was an active civil servant in her own right"

31. What should be done with sentence 3 (reproduced below)?

Even after her husband's death Eleanor Roosevelt continued to be a prominent activist.

(A) (as is now)
(B) delete it
(C) insert it after sentence 5
(D) change "prominent" to "leading"
(E) insert "Furthermore," at the beginning of the sentence

32. In context, which of the following is the best way to revise sentences 6 and 7?

(A) (as is now)
(B) Eleanor worked tirelessly to campaign for John F. Kennedy and was thusly instrumental member of many of his committees.
(C) Eleanor had many important roles during John F. Kennedy's candidacy and presidency: she tirelessly promoted his campaign and later served as a member on many committees.
(D) Eleanor was important for John F. Kennedy because she worked tirelessly to campaign for him and was an instrumental member of many of his committees.
(E) Kennedy owes much to Eleanor Roosevelt for she campaigned tirelessly on his behalf and served on many of his committees.

33. In context, which is the best version of the underlined portions of sentence 8 (reproduced below)?

When JFK became the President, <u>she was appointed</u> to various positions including a committee of the Peace Corps.

(A) Roosevelt was appointed
(B) she was given an appointment
(C) an appointment was given to Roosevelt
(D) he gave Roosevelt an appointment
(E) JFK appointed her, Roosevelt,

34. In context, which is the best revision for sentence 9 (reproduced below)?

As Eleanor had great interest in women's rights Kennedy also installed her on Presidential Commission on the Status of Women.

(A) (as is now)

(B) Wherein Eleanor had great interest in women's rights Kennedy, installed her on Presidential Commission on the Status of Women.

(C) Due to Eleanor's interest in women's rights, Kennedy installed Roosevelt to the Presidential Commission on the Status of Women.

(D) Kennedy appointed her a member of the Presidential Commission on the Status of Women because of her great interest in women's rights.

(E) As Eleanor had a great interest in women's rights, Kennedy appointed her to the Presidential Commission on the Status of Women.

35. Which of the following would make the most logical final sentence for the essay?

(A) Eleanor Roosevelt achieved a great deal in her life.

(B) Thus, she became an advisor and confidante to JFK.

(C) Roosevelt also received many honorary degrees for her work.

(D) For all of her great work and service, Roosevelt is one of the most admired women of the 20th century.

(E) Many books and movies have documented Eleanor Roosevelt's amazing life.

STOP
If you finish before time is called, you may check your work on this section only.
Do not turn to any other section in the test.

Section 7
Time—25 minutes
24 questions

Turn to Section 7 (page 327) of your answer sheet to answer the questions in this section.

Directions: For each question in this section, select the best answer from among the answer choices given and fill in the corresponding circle on the answer sheet.

Each sentence below has one or two question blanks, each blank indicating that something has been omitted. Beneath the sentence are five words or sets of words labeled A through E. Choose the word or set of words that, when inserted in the sentence, *best* fits the meaning of the sentence as a whole.

Example:

Susan preferred to be ____, hoping to avoid confusion due to miscommunication.
(A) **direct**
(B) devious
(C) cunning
(D) austere
(E) terse

1. Everyone in the family enjoyed the ____ computer program because it had many different uses.

    (A) versatile
    (B) helpful
    (C) informative
    (D) incompetent
    (E) entertaining

2. He was a ____ guest; staying just for a few days.

    (A) transient
    (B) enduring
    (C) provisional
    (D) vexing
    (E) undeviating

3. The museum is known for its ____ collection: an overwhelmingly hetero-geneous compilation of the founders' memorabilia.

   (A) callous
   (B) motley
   (C) enigmatic
   (D) somnolent
   (E) methodical

4. The range of colors that students could wear to school was ____ by the administration's stringent rules regarding dress.

   (A) circumscribed
   (B) reinforced
   (C) mitigated
   (D) insinuated
   (E) disciplined

5. The teachers commented on the child's ____ behavior: she quickly became irritated when not the center of attention.

   (A) meticulous
   (B) superfluous
   (C) incredulous
   (D) petulant
   (E) misfortunate

6. There was no ____ to him: Mr. Billings behaved ____ in professional and personal settings.

   (A) obscurity...comically
   (B) mischief...harmoniously
   (C) duality...consistently
   (D) mystery...erratically
   (E) anonymity...secretly

7. For a celebrity, even a trip to a playground does not insure safety; among the regular visitors, several attendees wore the listening devices, ____ clothing, and overly prepared looks of security personnel.

   (A) nondescript
   (B) arrogate

(C) variegated

(D) listless

(E) bravado

8. The North East was not the only ____ of the Democratic movement, but support there was particularly intense last summer after the party claimed victory in the disputed elections.

(A) aspersion

(B) trenchant

(C) locus

(D) plumb

(E) leviathan

The passages below are followed by questions based on their content; questions that follow a pair of related passages may also be based on the relationship between the paired passages. Answer the questions on the basis of what is <u>stated</u> or <u>implied</u> in the passage in any introductory material that may be provided.

Questions 9 through 12 are based on the following passages.

Passage 1

The interpretation of personal names has always had an attraction for the learned and others, but the first attempts to classify and explain
Line   our English surnames date, so far as my knowledge goes, from 1605. In that year Verstegan published his Restitution of Decayed
5   Intelligence, which contains chapters on both font-names and surnames, and about the same time appeared Camden's Remains Concerning Britain, in which the same subjects are treated much more fully. Both of these learned antiquaries make excellent reading, and much curious information may be gleaned from their
10   pages, especially those of Camden, whose position as Clarencieux King-at-Arms gave him exceptional opportunities for genealogical research. From the philological point of view they are of course untrustworthy, though less so than most modern writers on the same subject.

9. All of the following can be inferred from the passage about the study of names EXCEPT

(A) both scholars and amateurs engage in the study of names
(B) books on the study of names are dry and tedious reading
(C) understanding of family history informs the study of names
(D) modern study of names has not produced superior results
(E) the study of names is not an exact science

10. "Curious" in line 9 most nearly means

(A) peculiar
(B) inquisitive
(C) interesting
(D) listless
(E) bizarre

Passage 2

Line

5

Since the revival of the bath of antiquity, and its introduction into this country under the name of the Turkish bath, this method of bathing has become very generally adopted; and although onward progress is rendered less rapid than it might be, by the widespread popular ignorance that ascribes an element of danger to the bath, erroneous impressions are being gradually removed, and the continual building of new baths testifies to the manner in which the institution flourishes on British soil.

10

To what extent the delusion concerning the supposed danger connected with this form of bathing is to be ascribed to popular ignorance and prejudice, or to the fact that baths of unsuitable design and construction, and of faulty heating and ventilation, are put before the public, it would be hard to say. Certain it is that the latter cause has done much—very much—injury.

11. The author's attitude toward detractors of Turkish baths can be described as

(A) cavalier
(B) ambivalent

(C) annoyed

(D) wavering

(E) angry

12. The principal function of the second paragraph is to

(A) argue for the importance of building superiorly designed baths

(B) illustrate the trend toward revitalizing of an ancient tradition

(C) explore the causes of public bias toward baths

(D) provide an explanation of the bath's resurgent popularity

(E) contrast the functionality of old baths with lackadaisical design of modern baths

Questions 13 through 24 are based on the following passage.

The following two passages consider the experiences of women in society in the early 1900s. Passage 1 is written by a British activist and political figure; Passage 2 is from the introduction to a book on mobilizing woman power.

Passage 1

The spirit of women in this greatest of world struggles cannot, in its essence, be differentiated from the spirit of men. They are one.
Line The women of our countries in the mass feel about the issues of this struggle just as the men do; know, as they do, why we fight, and like
5   them, are going on to the end. The declarations of our Government as to conditions for peace are ours, too, and when we vote, we shall show the spirit of women is clearly and definitely on the side of freedom, justice and democracy.

Our actions speak louder than any words can ever do, and the record
10   of our women's sacrifices and work stand as great silent witnesses to our spirit. There is nothing we have been asked to do that we have not done and we have initiated great pieces of work ourselves. The hardest time was in the beginning when we waited for our tasks, feeling as if we beat stone walls, reading our casualty lists, receiving our wounded,
15   caring for the refugees, doing everything we could for the sailor and soldier and his dependents, helping the women out of work, but feeling there was so much more to do behind the men—so very much more—for which we had to wait. We did all the other things

faithfully and, so far as we could, prepared ourselves and when the
20   tasks came, we volunteered in tens of thousands, every kind of
woman, young, old, middle-aged, rich and poor, trained and untrained,
and today we have 1,250,000 women in industry directly replacing
men, 1,000,000 in munitions, 83,000 additional women in Government
Departments, 258,300 whole and part-time women workers on the
25   land. We are recruiting women for the Women's Army Auxiliary Corps
at the rate of 10,000 a month and we have initiated a Women's Royal
Naval Service. We have had the help of about 60,000 VAD's
(Voluntary Aid Detachment of Red Cross) in Hospitals in England
and France, and on our other fronts, in addition to our thousands of
30   trained nurses.

The women in our homes carry on—no easy task in these days of
shortages in food and coal and all the other difficulties, saving,
conserving, working, caring for the children, with so many babies
whose fathers have never seen them, though they are one to two
35   years old, and so many babies who will never see their fathers.

Some of our women have died on active service, doctors, nurses and
orderlies. Our most recent and greatest loss is in the death of
Dr. Elsie Inglis, the initiator of the Scottish Women's Hospitals, who
died on November 26th, three days after she had safely brought back
40   her Unit from South Russia, which had been nursing the Serbians
attached to the Russian army.

One who was with her at the end writes, "It was a great triumphant
going forth." There was no hesitation, no fear. As soon as she knew
she was going, that the call had come, with her wonted decision of
45   character, she just readjusted her whole outlook. "For a long time I
meant to live," she said, "but now I know I am going. It is so nice
to think of beginning a new job over there! But I would have liked to
have finished one or two jobs here first!"

Passage 2

No man who is not blind can fail to see that we have entered a new day
Line   in the great epic march of the ages. For good or for evil the old days
have passed; and it rests with us, the men and women now alive,

to decide whether in the new days the world is to be a better or a
5   worse place to live in, for our descendants.

In this new world women are to stand on an equal footing with men, in
ways and to an extent never hitherto dreamed of. In this country they
are on the eve of securing, and in much of the country have already
secured, their full political rights. It is imperative that they should
10   understand, exactly as it is imperative that men should understand, that
such rights are of worse than no avail, unless the will for the performance
of duty goes hand in hand with the acquirement of the privilege.

If the women in this country reinforce the elements that tend to a
softening of the moral fiber, to a weakening of the will, and unwillingness
15   to look ahead or to face hardship and labor and danger for a high ideal—
then all of us alike, men and women, will suffer. But if they show, under
the new conditions, the will to develop strength, and the high idealism
and the iron resolution which under less favorable circumstances were
shown by the women of the Revolution and of the Civil War, then our
20   nation has before it a career of greatness never hitherto equaled. ...
Equality of right does not mean identity of function; but it does
necessarily imply identity of purpose in the performance of duty.

Mrs. Blatch shows why every woman who inherits the womanly virtues
of the past, and who has grasped the ideal of the added womanly
25   virtues of the present and the future, should support this war with all
her strength and soul. She testifies from personal knowledge to the
hideous brutalities shown toward women and children by the Germany
of to-day; and she adds the fine sentence: "Women fight for a place in
the sun for those who hold right above might."

30   She shows why women must unstintedly give their labor in order to
win this war; and why the labor of the women must be used to back
up both the labor and the fighting work of the men, for the fighting
men leave gaps in the labor world which must be filled by the work
of women. She says in another sentence worth remembering, "The
35   man behind the counter should of course be moved to a muscular
employment; but we must not interpret his dalliance with tapes and
ribbons as a proof of a superfluity of men."

13. The primary purpose of Passage 1 is to

(A) challenge a traditional stance
(B) describe a complex process
(C) examine an irrational impulse
(D) urge a radical course of action
(E) demonstrate a specific reality

14. "This struggle" in lines 3–4 of Passage 1 refers to

(A) women's fight for equal voting rights
(B) the ongoing war
(C) the difference in the spirit of men and women
(D) women's right to serve in the military
(E) how differently women and men view freedom and justice

15. In line 19 of Passage 1, "faithfully" most nearly means

(A) thoroughly
(B) authentically
(C) confidentially
(D) accurately
(E) truthfully

16. The author of Passage 1 mentions the word "initiated" (line 26) to suggest that women

(A) carefully carried out the orders of their superiors
(B) applied their energy and dedication to all available outlets
(C) were most useful in starting volunteer organizations
(D) set off to the front without supervision
(E) were mainly interested in working on behalf of their own efforts

17. In Passage 1, the author's statement that "women in our homes carry on" suggests that

(A) some women were not able to leave home because of newborn children
(B) the work done at home was as difficult and important as that in the front lines
(C) keeping women at home allowed the country to conserve valuable resources

(D) women whose husbands were killed during the war were forced to stay home with children

(E) women working from home created additional shortages

18. In Passage 1, the author mentions Dr. Elsie Inglis (line 38) primarily to

(A) support an argument that women are equally capable to serving as doctors during war

(B) present an example of the kind of resolve women demonstrated during the war

(C) compare a female doctor's attitude to a male doctor's attitude

(D) discuss the wartime obligations of women

(E) illustrate how women were more willing than men to return to war

19. In Passage 2, the author's attitude toward Mrs. Blatch can best be described as

(A) genuinely respectful

(B) condescendingly tolerant

(C) entirely awestruck

(D) solemnly appreciative

(E) generally apathetic

20. The tone of lines 9–10 in Passage 2 ("It is imperative … understand") is best described as

(A) confiding

(B) defiant

(C) caution

(D) resigned

(E) admonishing

21. In Passage 2, the phrase "such rights…privilege" (lines 11–12) suggests that

(A) the desires of activists have changed over the years

(B) the success of women and men depends on performance in duty

(C) acquiring equality and rights is a privilege

(D) women have achieved equality to men

(E) with rights to power comes the responsibility to take action

22. The author of Passage 2 presents an argument in lines 13–20 ("If the women…hitherto equaled.") that can most accurately be called

(A) anecdotal
(B) political
(C) pragmatic
(D) impracticable
(E) facetious

23. Passage 1 and Passage 2 both suggest that

(A) all of humanity will suffer if women are not granted equal treatment to men
(B) the spirit and moral fiber are central to women's behavior
(C) women have proven themselves able through actions during times of war
(D) men's skills is superfluous with the addition of women workers
(E) women will resume working inside the home when soldiers return from war

24. It can be inferred that Passage 1 and Passage 2 would both support which of the following generalizations?

(A) Women embraced their chance to work outside the home
(B) Redistribution of power must occur from government programs to volunteer organizations
(C) Women were anxious about fulfilling new responsibilities
(D) Men's and women's wages should be completely equal
(E) Women's progress during the war caused the deterioration of men's status

STOP
If you finish before time is called, you may check your work on this section only.
Do not turn to any other section in the test.

Section 8
Time—20 Minutes
16 Questions

Directions: For this section, solve each problem and decide which is the best of the choices given. Fill in the corresponding circle on the answer sheet. You may use any available space for scratch work.

Notes

1. The use of a calculator is permitted.
2. All numbers used are real numbers.
3. Figures that accompany problems in this test are intended to provide information useful in solving the problems. They are drawn as accurately as possible EXCEPT when it is stated in a specific problem that the figure is not drawn to scale. All figures lie in a plane unless otherwise indicated.
4. Unless otherwise specified, the domain of any function f is assumed to be the set of all real numbers x for which $f(x)$ is a real number.

Reference Information

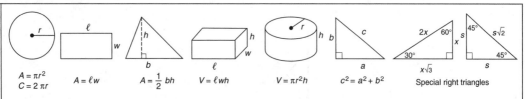

$A = \pi r^2$
$C = 2\pi r$

$A = \ell w$

$A = \frac{1}{2} bh$

$V = \ell wh$

$V = \pi r^2 h$

$c^2 = a^2 + b^2$

Special right triangles

The number of degrees of arc in a circle is 360.

The sum of the measures in degrees of the angles of a triangle is 180.

1. At a market, a shopper finds 8 baskets of onions. Each basket contains exactly 9 onions. If the shopper removes 1 onion from basket 1, 2 onions from basket 2, 3 onions from basket 3, and so on, until the shopper removes 8 onions from basket 8, what percent of the original onions remain?

   (A) 45%
   (B) 50%
   (C) 55%
   (D) 60%
   (E) 65%

2. If y is inversely proportional to x and $y = 20$ when $x = 6$, what is the value of y when $x = 80$?

    (A) $\dfrac{2}{3}$

    (B) $\dfrac{3}{2}$

    (C) $13\dfrac{1}{3}$

    (D) 24

    (E) $266\dfrac{2}{3}$

3.

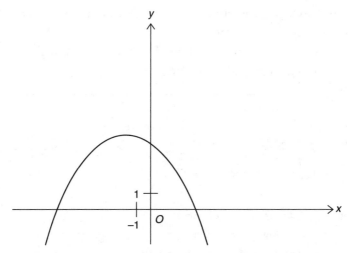

    The figure above shows the graph of a quadratic function f whose maximum is $f(-2)$. If $f(a) = 0$, which of the following could be the value of a?

    (A) -3
    (B) -2
    (C) -1
    (D) 0
    (E) 1

4. $b(t) = 400(1.08)^t$

    The function above can be used to model the population of a certain strain of bacteria. If $b(t)$ gives the number bacteria living in a culture dish *t* minutes after 12:00 PM on a given day, which of the following is true about the population of the bacteria from 12:00 PM to 2:00 PM on the same day?

(A) It increased by about 465
(B) It increased by about 865
(C) It increased by about 40,000
(D) It increased by about 4,100,000
(E) It decreased by about 465

5.

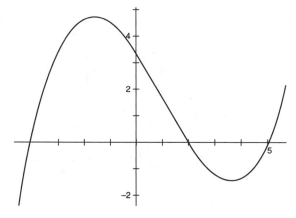

How many times does the graph of $y = -x^2 + 4$ intersect the above graph?

(A) None
(B) One
(C) Two
(D) Three
(E) Four

6. Which of the following is the graph of a function f such that $f(x) = 0$ for exactly three different values between -7 and 7?

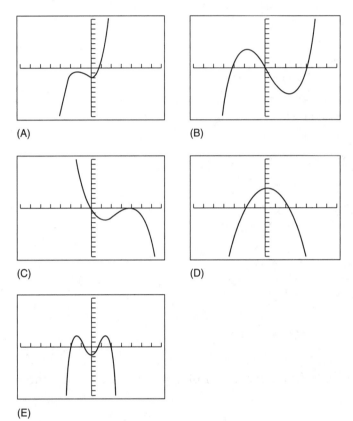

(A)   (B)

(C)   (D)

(E)

7.

x	y
-3	-15
-1	-7
0	-3
2	5
4	13

Which of the following equations is satisfied by the five pairs of numbers listed in the table above?

(A) $y = x^3 + 12$
(B) $y = 2x - 3$
(C) $y = x^2 - 8$
(D) $y = 4x - 3$
(E) $y = 2x + 5$

8.

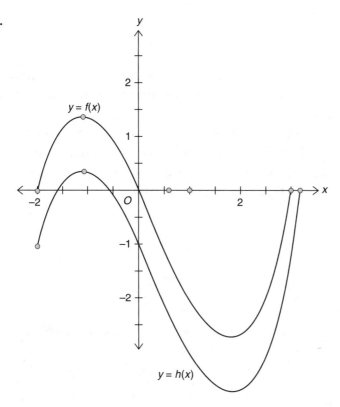

The graphs of the functions f and h in the interval from $x = -2$ to $x = 3$ are shown above. Which of the following could express h in terms of f?

(A) $h(x) = f(x - 1)$
(B) $h(x) = f(x) + 1$
(C) $h(x) = f(x - 1) + 1$
(D) $h(x) = f(x - 1)$
(E) $h(x) = f(x) - 1$

9. If *m* is negative and greater than −1, then which of the following is greatest?

(A) m^2

(B) m

(C) $100\,m$

(D) $\dfrac{100}{m}$

(E) $-\dfrac{100}{m}$

10. Georgina must test a set of 15 cakes from various bakeries to find out which one tastes best. Each cake has been assigned a number from 1 to 15. She always tastes the cakes in numerical order, and she must repeat the tasting process each time she finishes tasting all the cakes. If she tastes a cake she does not like, she always goes back to the beginning and starts over. If Georgina does not like cake 7, which of the following could represent the number of times she tested the cakes?

(A) 20

(B) 21

(C) 52

(D) 60

(E) 17

11. If $9\sqrt{27} = s\sqrt{t}$, where *s* and *t* are positive integers and *s* > *t*, which of the following could be the value of *st*?

(A) 9

(B) 27

(C) 81

(D) 162

(E) 243

12.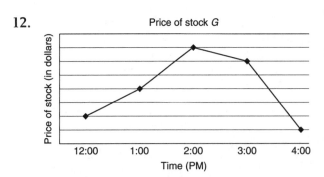

Price of stock G

On a particular day, Bonnie was analyzing the price of stock G. She recorded the change in price of the stock each hour, as indicated in the chart above. Each unit on the vertical axis represents $4. If the price of the stock increased 20% from 12:00 PM to 1:00 PM, what was the price of the stock at 2:00 PM?

(A) $40
(B) $48
(C) $60
(D) $72
(E) cannot be determined

13. At Jefferson Republic High School, some of the students on the fencing team are also on the math team and all the members of the math team are either sophomores or seniors. Which of the following must also be true?

(A) Every member of the math team is also on the fencing team
(B) All the members of the fencing team are sophomores or seniors
(C) A sophomore on the math team must also be on the fencing team
(D) A junior may not be on both the fencing team and the math team
(E) If only sophomores and seniors are on the fencing team, then all the members of the fencing team are also on the math team

14. If a, b, and c are integers, let $(a, c) \Delta b$ be defined to be true only if $c \le a < b$. If $(-4, c) \Delta 1$ is true, which of the following could be a possible value of c?

     I. −4
     II. −3
     III. 0

(A) I only
(B) II only
(C) III only
(D) I and III only
(E) II and III only

15. If $\dfrac{m^2-1}{m} \cdot \dfrac{1}{m-1} \cdot \dfrac{m+1}{m} = \dfrac{16}{k}$ for positive integers m and k, what is the value of k?

(A) 3
(B) 4
(C) 9
(D) 32
(E) 256

16. The town of Olive Branch is x miles from Brigitte's home in Little Rock. She drives an average rate of 51 miles per hour going from her home to Olive Branch. On the way back, she takes the same route, but due to poor weather conditions, she travels at an average rate of 17 miles per hour. What is Brigitte's average speed, in miles, for the time she is on the road?

(A) 12.75
(B) 17.00
(C) 25.50
(D) 34.00
(E) 68.00

Section 9
Time—20 minutes
19 questions

Turn to Section 9 (page 327) of your answer sheet to answer the questions in this section.

Directions: For each question in this section, select the best answer from among the answer choices given and fill in the corresponding circle on the answer sheet.

Each sentence below has one or two question blanks, each blank indicating that something has been omitted. Beneath the sentence are five words or sets of words labeled A through E. Choose the word or set of words that, when inserted in the sentence, *best* fits the meaning of the sentence as a whole.

Example:

Susan preferred to be ____, hoping to avoid confusion due to miscommunication.
(A) **direct**
(B) devious
(C) cunning
(D) austere
(E) terse

1. Although the teacher dedicated the first 15 minutes of class for quiet reflection, the students could usually be found laughing and talking ____ about non-school-related topics.

   (A) animatedly
   (B) lifelessly
   (C) swiftly
   (D) honestly
   (E) hurriedly

2. When the Rocky Mountains emerged millions of years ago, isolated deserts formed, leaving ____ opportunity for speciation and diversification to occur.

    (A) ample
    (B) placid
    (C) convivial
    (D) insufficient
    (E) astounding

3. It was a/an ____ afternoon, and the children had taken shelter from the heat indoors, where cool breeze ____ from the air conditioner.

    (A) prevalent...deployed
    (B) cloying...seethed
    (C) requisite...floated
    (D) exquisite...churned
    (E) parching...wafted

4. Abigail's dramatic voice and poetic songs made her a/an ____ figure in her high school jazz band.

    (A) established
    (B) unsettling
    (C) abysmal
    (D) anomalous
    (E) prominent

5. During the campaign, the candidate spoke out ____ for women's rights and ____ the opposition's statements questioning the importance of universal suffrage.

    (A) brazenly... denounced
    (B) vehemently...oppressed
    (C) brashly...supported
    (D) unperturbedly...doubted
    (E) intermittently...condemned

6. Because the writer often relied on ____ language, his prose frequently seemed ____ to critics and readers who failed to comprehend its meaning.

(A) accessible…abstruse
(B) arcane…unequivocal
(C) esoteric…impenetrable
(D) hackneyed…exotic
(E) lucid…grating

The passages below are followed by questions based on their content; questions that follow a pair of related passages may also be based on the relationship between the paired passages. Answer the questions on the basis of what is *stated* or *implied* in the passage in any introductory material that may be provided.

Questions 7 through 19 are based on the following passages.

This passage is from a book examining the early thinkers of biological science.

Widely different opinions have been held from time to time of the value of Aristotle's biological labours. This philosopher's reputation has,
Line   perhaps, suffered most from those who have praised him most. The praise has often been of such an exaggerated character as to have become
5   unmeaning, and to have carried with it the impression of insincerity on the part of the writer. Such are the laudations of Cuvier. To say as he does, "Alone, in fact, without predecessors, without having borrowed anything from the centuries which had gone before, since they had produced nothing enduring, the disciple of Plato discovered and
10   demonstrated more truths and executed more scientific labours in a life of sixty-two years than twenty centuries after him were able to do," is of course to talk nonsense, for the method which Aristotle applied was that which Hippocrates had used so well before him; and it is evident to any one that both his predecessors and contemporaries are frequently
15   laid under contribution by Aristotle, although the authority is rarely, if ever, stated by him unless he is about to refute the view put forward. Exaggerated praise of any author has a tendency to excite depreciation correspondingly unjust and untrue. It has been so in the case of this great man. In the endeavour to depose him from the
20   impossible position to which his panegyrists had exalted him, his detractors have gone to any length. The principal charges brought against his biological work have been inaccuracy and hasty

generalization. In support of the charge of inaccuracy, some of the extraordinary statements which are met with in his works are adduced.

25 "These," Professor Huxley says, "are not so much to be called errors as stupidities." Some, however, of the inaccuracies alleged against Aristotle are fancied rather than real. Thus he is charged with having represented that the arteries contained nothing but air; that the aorta arose from the right ventricle; that the heart did not beat in any other

30 animal but man; that reptiles had no blood, etc.; although in reality he made no one of these assertions. There remain, nevertheless, the gross misstatements referred to above, and which really do occur. Such, for instance, as that there is but a single bone in the neck of the lion; that there are more teeth in male than in female animals; that the mouth

35 of the dolphin is placed on the under surface of the body; that the back of the skull is empty, etc. Although these absurdities undoubtedly occur in Aristotle's works, it by no means follows that he is responsible for them. Bearing in mind the curious history of the manuscripts of his treatises, we shall find it far more reasonable to conclude that such

40 errors crept in during the process of correction and restoration, by men apparently ignorant of biology, than that (to take only one case) an observer who had distinguished the cetacea from fishes and had detected their hidden mammæ, discovered their lungs, and recognized the distinct character of their bones, should have been so blind as to fancy that the

45 mouth of these animals was on the under surface of the body.

That Aristotle made hasty generalizations is true; but it was unavoidable. Biology was in so early a stage that a theory had often of necessity to be founded on a very slight basis of facts. Yet, notwithstanding this drawback, so great was the sagacity of this philosopher, that many of his

50 generalizations, which he himself probably looked upon as temporary, have held their ground for twenty centuries, or, having been lost sight of, have been discovered and put forward as original by modern biologists. Thus "the advantage of physiological division of labour was first set forth," says Milne-Edwards, "by myself in 1827;" and yet Aristotle had

55 said that "whenever Nature is able to provide two separate instruments for two separate uses, without the one hampering the other, she does so, instead of acting like a coppersmith, who for cheapness makes a spit-and-a-candlestick in one. It is only when this is impossible that she uses one organ for several functions."

60 In conclusion, we may say that the great Stagirite expounded the true
principles of science, and that when he failed his failure was caused by
lack of materials. His desire for completeness, perhaps, tempted him at
times to fill in gaps with such makeshifts as came to his hand; but no
one knew better than he did that "theories must be abandoned unless
65 their teachings tally with the indisputable results of observation."

7. The passage can primarily be described as

(A) scientific evidence used to counter an established theory
(B) humorous anecdotes countered by profound insight
(C) skeptical explanation evolving into a unbiased analysis
(D) a case study followed by a scientific hypothesis
(E) an account leading to a general observation

8. The author's tone is one of

(A) astonishment
(B) reverence
(C) worship
(D) loathing
(E) indifference

9. In the first paragraph, the reference to Cuvier (line 6) primarily serves to
support the claim that

(A) Aristotle's reputation suffered from exaggerated praise
(B) no previous scientist produced the lasting influence of Aristotle
(C) Aristotle had as many critics as admirers
(D) many opinions existed on Aristotle's contribution to science
(E) Aristotle's scientific work was inimitable but unoriginal

10. It can be inferred from the statement "it is evident to any one..."
(lines 13–14) that Aristotle

(A) plagiarized the scientific hypotheses of his colleagues
(B) relied on work of other scientists
(C) countered his predecessors' theories
(D) completed the work Hippocrates started
(E) emulated the approaches of his contemporaries

11. "Charged" in line 27, most nearly means

   (A) accused of
   (B) credited with
   (C) responsible for
   (D) predisposed to
   (E) liable for

12. In lines 27–36, the author discusses misstatements attributed to Aristotle in order to

   (A) strengthen an argument with corroborating evidence
   (B) show that varying explanations may be logically related
   (C) illustrate the futility of exaggerated allegations
   (D) demonstrate how widely held beliefs lose credibility as new findings emerge
   (E) expand the discussion to include a different type of explanation

13. The author's parenthetical reference in line 41 [(to take only one case)] serves to

   (A) justify why Aristotle believed that the animal mouth was located under the surface of the body
   (B) highlight Aristotle's process of learning through experience
   (C) explain that Aristotle is merely an observer of the natural environment
   (D) rationalize the lack of scientific evidence for Aristotle's conclusions
   (E) illustrate a point about Aristotle's deep understanding of biology

14. According to the passage the actual inaccuracies in Aristotle's work are most likely a result of
       I. A dearth of resources
       II. Errors occurring during editing and transcription
       III. Aristotle's desire to produce a primary scientific work

   (A) I only
   (B) II only
   (C) I and II only
   (D) II and III only
   (E) I, II, and III

15. The sentence beginning "Biology was in so early..." (line 47) primarily serves to

(A) suggest that science was malleable its early stages
(B) contrast a previous assertion made by scientists
(C) show the variety of processes to approaching a problem
(D) emphasize the complexity of proving scientific theories
(E) indicate how science has changed since Aristotle's time

16. The statement "which he himself probably looked upon as temporary..." (line 50) suggests that Aristotle

(A) expected innovation to cause his work to be obsolete
(B) planned to re-examine his hypotheses with additional evidence
(C) generalized information with the anticipation that science is not permanent
(D) understood the limits of his knowledge
(E) considered his work unimportant and open for revision

17. The example of biologist's Milne-Edwards's theory regarding division of labor (line 53) primarily serves to

(A) emphasize the permanence of Aristotle's theories
(B) suggest the predictability in scientific discovery
(C) show the continuity in scientific theory
(D) demonstrate how modern biologists confirmed Aristotle's hypotheses
(E) illustrate variance of scientific opinion

18. The quotation "theories must be abandoned unless their teachings tally with the indisputable results of observation" in lines 64–65 is used in order to

(A) demonstrate Aristotle's conviction in his theories
(B) illustrate the significance of the scientific process
(C) exemplify the fallacy of abandoning hypotheses without observation
(D) underscore Aristotle's belief in the importance of scientific evidence
(E) repudiate theories proposed by earlier scientists

19. In line 60, "expounded" most nearly means

    (A) discovered
    (B) explained
    (C) justified
    (D) introduced
    (E) revealed

STOP
If you finish before time is called, you may check your work on this section only.
Do not turn to any other section in the test.

Section 10
Time—10 minutes
14 questions

Turn to Section 10 (page 327) of your answer sheet to answer the questions in this section.

Directions: For each question in this section, select the best answer from among the answer choices given and fill in the corresponding circle on the answer sheet.

The following sentences test correctness and effectiveness of expression. Part of each sentence or the entire sentence is underlined; beneath each sentence are five ways of phrasing the underlined material. Choice A repeats the original phrasing; the other four choices are different. If you thing the original phrasing produces a better sentence than any of the alternatives, select choice A; if not, select one of the other choices.

In making your selection, follow the requirements of standard written English; that is, pay attention to grammar, choice of words, sentence construction, and punctuation. Your selection should result in the most effective sentence—clear and precise, without awkwardness or ambiguity.

Example:

The numerous biographies published about Roosevelt's life <u>are testament to his great achievements</u>.
(A) are testament to his great achievements
(B) is testament to his great achievements
(C) **stand as a testament for his great achievement**
(D) full of achievement, the books are testament
(E) are testaments to his great achievements

1. <u>There is three students</u> in Mr. Horn's advanced math class.

    (A) There is three students
    (B) There are three students
    (C) Their are three student
    (D) They're three students
    (E) Three students is

2. Every one of the boys on the soccer team <u>is trying to do their best.</u>

    (A) is trying to do their best
    (B) are trying to do their best
    (C) tried to do their best
    (D) is trying to do his best
    (E) is trying doing his best

3. The <u>effects of the tropical rainstorm could be seen</u> everywhere.

    (A) effects of the tropical rainstorm could be seen
    (B) effects of the tropical rainstorm could have been seen
    (C) affects of the tropical rainstorm could be seen
    (D) affects of the tropical rainstorm were seen
    (E) tropical rainstorm left effects

4. Mary's painting <u>is brighter than Ken's</u>.

    (A) is brighter than Ken's
    (B) is brighter than Ken's painting
    (C) is more bright than Ken's
    (D) is brightened than Ken's painting
    (E) is brighter then Ken's

5. Larry cooked his sick sister homemade chicken <u>soup, yet she wouldn't eat anything</u>.

    (A) soup, yet she wouldn't eat anything
    (B) soup, yet she couldn't eat anything
    (C) soup; yet she wouldn't eat anything
    (D) soup; though she wouldn't eat anything
    (E) soup yet she wouldn't eat anything

6. The song's cheerful tune and its lyrical wit <u>give the listener pleasure</u>.

    (A) give the listener pleasure
    (B) please the listener
    (C) gives on pleasure who is listening
    (D) pleases the listener
    (E) give pleasures to the listener

7. Sonny's party <u>was so exhilarating, it lasted until</u> 4:00 AM.

    (A) was so exhilarating, it lasted until
    (B) was so exhilarating, that it lasted until
    (C) was so exhilarating; it lasted until
    (D) was so exhilarating; the party lasted until
    (E) was such an exhilaration that it lasted until

8. After the tropical rains <u>had passed, a rainbow sprang up</u> over the mountains.

    (A) had passed, a rainbow sprang up
    (B) had passed: a rainbow sprang up
    (C) passed a rainbow sprang up
    (D) pass, a rainbow sprang up
    (E) passes, a rainbow springs up

9. They <u>felt bad about losing</u> the game.

    (A) felt bad about losing
    (B) felt bad about loosing
    (C) felt badly about losing
    (D) felt badly in losing
    (E) felt bad to lose

10. <u>Since it is raining today, I need an umbrella</u>.

    (A) Since it is raining today, I need an umbrella
    (B) Since it is raining today; I need an umbrella
    (C) Since it is raining today, I will need an umbrella
    (D) It is raining today, thus I need an umbrella
    (E) I will need an umbrella since it is raining today

11. The <u>aviation pioneer Amelia Earhart, was the first</u> woman to receive the Distinguished Flying Cross.

    (A) aviation pioneer Amelia Earhart, was the first
    (B) aviation pioneer Amelia Earhart; was the first
    (C) aviation pioneer Amelia Earhart was the first
    (D) pioneer of aviation, Amelia Earhart, was the first
    (E) first aviation pioneer, Amelia Earhart, was the

12. The reason debut albums are often their writers' most extraordinary work <u>is that it draws upon</u> all of life's experiences.

    (A) is that it draws upon
    (B) is that these efforts draw upon
    (C) is their drawing upon
    (D) is because of them drawing upon
    (E) is due to works drawing upon

13. <u>Reaching for the apple, the ladder slipped out from under her</u>.

    (A) Reaching for the apple, the ladder slipped out from under her
    (B) When reaching for the apple, the ladder slipped out from under her
    (C) When she reached for the apple, the ladder slipped out from under her
    (D) By reaching for the apple, the ladder slipped out from under her
    (E) The ladder slipped our from under her, reaching for the apple

14. I like to study several days before the <u>test because you don't have to worry about cramming</u> at the last minute.

    (A) test because you don't have to worry about cramming
    (B) test because that way you don't have to worry about cramming
    (C) test so that you don't have to worry about cramming
    (D) test because I don't have to worry about cramming
    (E) test because I then don't have to worry about cramming

TCT Compass Personal Strategy for the SAT Scoring Guide

To score your compass test, fill out the following chart as carefully as possible. First, fill in your answers in the column "Your Answer." Then grade across. For example, if your answer and the correct answer match, then put a check in the "Right" column for that problem. If your answer and the correct answer do not match, then put a check in the "Wrong" column for that problem. If you left the problem blank, put a check in the "Blank" column.

Important note for when you are scoring Section 4, Problems 9 through18 *only*: If your answer and the correct answer match, then put a check in the "Right" column for that problem. If your answer and the correct answer do not match, then put a check in the "Blank" column for that problem. You are never to mark a check in the "Wrong" column for these problems.

The Level-of-Difficulty scale ranges from E = Easy, M = Medium, to H = Hard.

Section 2						
Problem	Your Answer	Correct Answer	Right	Wrong	Blank	Level of Difficulty
1		C				E
2		D				E
3		B				E
4		A				M
5		A				E
6		C				M
7		E				M
8		C				M
9		D				M
10		A				M
11		E				M
12		D				M
13		E				M
14		D				M
15		B				M
16		E				M
17		C				H
18		B				M
19		D				H
20		C				H

(Continued)

Section 4						
Problem	**Your Answer**	**Correct Answer**	**Right**	**Wrong**	**Blank**	**Level of Difficulty**
1		A				E
2		C				E
3		C				M
4		A				M
5		D				M
6		D				H
7		B				M
8		C				H
9		$\dfrac{1}{14}$				E
10		9, 10, 12				E
11		999				M
12		75				M
13		$\dfrac{8}{9}$				M
14		2459				M
15		$\dfrac{4}{5}$				H
16		$\dfrac{5}{4}$				M
17		1997				M
18		$\dfrac{4}{9}$				H
Section 8						
1		B				E
2		B				E
3		E				M
4		D				M
5		C				E
6		B				M
7		D				M
8		E				M
9		E				M
10		C				H
11		C				M
12		C				M
13		D				M

(Continued)

Section 8						
Problem	Your Answer	Correct Answer	Right	Wrong	Blank	Level of Difficulty
14		A				M
15		C				H
16		C				H

Now that the chart is completely filled out, compute the following quantities:

1. Total Number Right: _____

2. Total Number Wrong: _____

3. Total Number Wrong ÷ 4: _____

4. Round the number you computed in Step 3 to the nearest whole number: _____

5. Total Number Right – Number from Step 4 = _____ – _____ = _____

6. The number in Step 5 is your Raw Math Score. Use the table below to predict your SAT Math Section score. **Predicted SAT Math Section Score =** _____

Raw Score	Scaled Score	Raw Score	Scale Score	Raw Score	Scale Score
54	800	35	600	16	420
53	800	34	590	15	420
52	780	33	580	14	410
51	760	32	570	13	400
50	740	31	560	12	390
49	730	30	550	11	380
48	720	29	540	10	370
47	710	28	530	9	360
46	700	27	530	8	350
45	690	26	520	7	330
44	680	25	510	6	320
43	670	24	500	5	310
42	660	23	490	4	290
41	650	22	480	3	280
40	640	21	470	2	260
39	630	20	460	1	240
38	620	19	450	0	210
37	620	18	440	−1	200
36	610	17	430	−2 or below	200

7. Total Easy Problems Right: _____

8. Total Medium Problems Right: _____

9. Total Hard Problems Right: _____

10. (Total Easy Problems Right ÷ 11) * 100 = _____%

11. (Total Medium Problems Right ÷ 33) * 100 = _____%

12. (Total Hard Problems Right ÷ 10) * 100 = _____%

Great job! You've completed your TCT Compass Test, and you are ready for some specially tailored tips to "point" you in the right direction as you continue with the remaining practice exams.

Wrong Answers: If the total number of wrong answers (Step 2) is more than five, then you may want to reread the sections of this book to make sure you have the content and the tricks down. Or you may want to consider leaving more problems blank when you aren't completely sure which choice is the correct one. Remember that you lose points for answering a problem incorrectly, but you do not lose points for leaving a problem blank. In other words, it is usually in your favor to *not* guess. Minimizing the number of problems you get wrong is to your benefit.

Easy Problems: If the percent calculated in Step 10 is:

- 0 to 60%—Reread all the sections to make sure you understand the basic content and strategies. Also, carefully study the Common Mistakes and Special Rules list at the beginning of each chapter quiz.

- 60 to 80%—Reread the sections you have the most trouble with and retake the chapter quiz for each section you choose to review. Also, go back to the problems you answered incorrectly and make sure you didn't make any careless errors. If you did make careless errors, write them down and make a mental note not to make them in the future.

- 80 to 100%—Great work. It looks like you have the easy-level problems down pat.

Medium Problems: If the percent calculated in Step 11 is:

- 0 to 60%—Reread all the sections to make sure you understand the basic content and strategies. Also, carefully study the Common Mistakes and Special Rules list at the beginning of each chapter quiz.

- 60 to 80%—Reread the sections you have the most trouble with and retake the chapter quiz for each section you choose to review. Also, go back to the problems you answered incorrectly and make sure you didn't make any careless errors. If you did make careless errors, write them down and make a mental note not to make them in the future. Additionally, you know yourself better than anyone. If there is a particular topic that you "just don't get" and have made a real effort to understand, then you might consider skipping the one or two problems of this type. By skipping over them (leaving them blank), you might save yourself 2 to 5 minutes that could have been used to get some other problems right that you got wrong due to time. Just a suggestion to think about!

- 80 to 100%—Great work. It looks like you have the medium-level problems down pat.

Hard Problems: If the percent calculated in Step 12 is:

- 0 to 60%—While it is possible to learn the content well enough and to practice enough to improve greatly on the hard-level problems, it is extremely difficult to do so. For the most part, the students who get the hard problems right are the ones who are "math people" to boot. We think you should consider automatically leaving the last two or three problems blank in every section. This will save you several minutes on each section to focus on the easy- and medium-level problems, which you can get right, given a little more time. Remember, colleges never see which level problems you get right. They only see the final score. So it's more important to spend and shift your time wisely to maximize your final score than to worry about answering super-challenging problems. A thought to ponder.

- 60 to 80%—Reread the sections you have the most trouble with and retake the chapter quiz for each section you choose to review. Also, go back to the problems you answered incorrectly and make sure you didn't make any careless errors. If you did make careless errors, write them down and make a mental note not to make them in the future. Additionally, you should consider skimming the last two or three problems in every section. If the problem is of a type that you "get," then take the minute to solve it out. However, if you know that problem is of a type that you normally "don't get," then you should consider automatically leaving it blank. Remember, the best way to maximize your score is to answer problems correctly. Using your time wisely is the easiest way to make that happen.

- 80 to 100%—Wow and gee whiz! It looks like you have the hard-level problems down pat.

Verbal Section

Section 3

Sentence Completion						
Problem	Your Answer	Correct Answer	Right	Wrong	Blank	Level of Difficulty
1		B				E
2		A				E
3		B				M
4		A				H
5		A				M

Section 7

Sentence Completion						
Problem	Your Answer	Correct Answer	Right	Wrong	Blank	Level of Difficulty
1		A				E
2		A				M
3		B				M
4		A				M
5		D				M
6		C				M
7		A				H
8		C				H

Section 9

Sentence Completion						
Problem	Your Answer	Correct Answer	Right	Wrong	Blank	Level of Difficulty
1		A				E
2		A				E
3		E				H
4		E				M
5		A				H
6		C				H

Sentence Completion Compass

Compute the following quantities:

1. Total Easy Problems Right: _____
2. Total Medium Problems Right: _____
3. Total Hard Problems Right: _____
4. Total Problems Wrong: _____
   (Total Easy Problems Right ÷ 5) * 100 = _____
5. (Total Medium Problems Right ÷ 8) * 100 = _____
6. (Total Hard Problems Right ÷ 5) * 100 = _____

Compass Tips:

Wrong Answers: If the total number of wrong answers (Step 4) is more than three then you may want to reread the Sentence Completion Steps section of this book to make sure you have a good understanding of the process. You may also want to continue doing vocabulary flashcards and building your vocabulary.

Easy Problems: If you are getting any easy-level problems wrong:

• Reread the Sentence Completion Section to make sure you understand the basic content and strategies.

• Go back to the problems you answered incorrectly and make sure you didn't make any careless errors. If you did make careless errors, write them down and make a mental note not to make them in the future.

• Determine whether you are having trouble with the vocabulary (you do not recognize the words) or you are missing the "definition" part of the sentence.

• Continue reviewing your vocabulary flashcards.

• Use the drills section to practice finding the "definition" of the sentence.

Medium Problems: If the percent calculated in Step 5 is:

• 0 to 60%—Reread the Sentence Completion Section to make sure you understand the basic content and strategies. Repeat all drills and complete extra practice of Sentence Completion steps.

• 60 to 80%—Determine whether you are getting stuck on the vocabulary or the "definition" part of the sentence. If you are finding that you do not know the words, consider omitting the question. For medium questions, we suggest that if you are able to narrow down the choices to two (or eliminate three choices) then it is a good idea to guess. However, if you're not able to eliminate one or two choices then you're best off omitting the question. If you're recognizing the vocabulary, but having trouble with the sentence then go back to the drills section and practice the steps. Leaving problems blank when you aren't completely sure which choice is the correct one is an important strategy. Remember that you lose points for answering a problem incorrectly, but you do not lose points for leaving a problem blank. In other words, it is usually in your favor to *not* guess if you are just randomly guessing. Minimizing the number of problems you get wrong is to your benefit.

- 80 to 100%—Great work. It looks like you have the medium-level problems down pat.

Hard Problems: If the percent calculated in Step 6 is:

- 0 to 60%—While it is possible to know the vocabulary well enough and to practice enough to improve greatly on the hard-level problems, it is extremely difficult to do so. The hard-level questions present the most difficult vocabulary and introduce dense sentences. If you are consistently making errors in the hard questions then we suggest you should consider automatically leaving the last two or three problems blank in every sentence completion section. This will save you several minutes on each section to focus on the easy- and medium-level problems, which you can get right, given a little more time. Remember, colleges never see which level problems you get right. They only see the final score. So it's more important to spend and shift your time wisely to maximize your final score than to worry about answering super challenging problems.

- 60 to 80%—Determine whether you are getting stuck on the vocabulary or the "definition" part of the sentence. If you are finding that you do not know the words, consider omitting the question. For hard questions, we suggest that if you are able to narrow down the choices to two (or eliminate three choices) then it is a good idea to guess. However, if you're not able to eliminate one or two choices then you're best off omitting the question. If you're recognizing the vocabulary, but having trouble with the sentences then go back to the drills section and practice the steps. Remember, omitting questions that you have "no clue" about is okay. Rather than struggling with a hard question that doesn't make sense, spend the time confirming your accuracy on the medium and easy questions.

- 80 to 100%—Wow and gee whiz! It looks like you have the hard-level problems down pat.

Section 3

Reading Comprehension						
Problem	Your Answer	Correct Answer	Right	Wrong	Blank	Type of Question
6		B				Short passage General question
7		E				Short passage Specific question
8		B				Short passage General question
9		A				Short passage Specific question
10		C				Long passage General question
11		A				Long passage General question
12		E				Long passage Specific question
13		C				Long passage Specific question
14		A				Long passage Specific question
15		D				Long passage Specific question
16		E				Long passage General question
17		A				Long passage General question
18		A				Long passage Specific question
19		D				Long passage Specific question
20		A				Long passage Specific question
21		A				Long passage General question
22		A				Long passage Specific question
23		C				Long passage General question
24		B				Long passage Specific question

Section 7

Reading Comprehension						
Problem	Your Answer	Correct Answer	Right	Wrong	Blank	Type of Question
9		B				Short passage General question
10		C				Short passage Specific question
11		C				Short passage General question
12		C				Short passage General question
13		E				Double passage General question
14		B				Double passage Specific question
15		A				Double passage Specific question
16		B				Double passage Specific question
17		B				Double passage Specific question
18		B				Double passage Specific question
19		A				Double passage General question
20		C				Double passage Specific question
21		E				Double passage Specific question
22		C				Double passage Specific question
23		C				Double passage General question
24		A				Double passage General question

Section 9

Reading Comprehension						
Problem	Your Answer	Correct Answer	Right	Wrong	Blank	Type of Question
7		E				Very long passage General question
8		B				Very long passage General question
9		A				Very long passage Specific question
10		B				Very long passage Specific question
11		A				Very long passage Specific question
12		C				Very long passage Specific question
13		E				Very long passage Specific question
14		C				Very long passage Specific question
15		E				Very long passage Specific question
16		D				Very long passage Specific question
17		A				Very long passage Specific question
18		D				Very long passage Specific question
19		B				Very long passage Specific question

Reading Comprehension Compass

Compute the following quantities:

1. Total Problems Wrong: _____

Types of Passages

2. Total Short Passage Problems Right: _____
3. Total Short Passage Problems Wrong/Blank: _____
4. Total Long Passage Problems Right: _____
5. Total Long Passage Problems Wrong/Blank: _____

6. Total Double Passage Problems Right: _____

7. Total Double Passage Problems Wrong/Blank: _____

8. Total Very Long Passage Problems Right: _____

9. Total Very Long Passage Problems Wrong/Blank: _____

Types of Questions

10. Total General Problems Right: _____

11. Total General Problems Right: _____

12. Total Specific Problems Right: _____

13. Total Specific Problems Right: _____

Compass Tips:

Wrong Answers: If the total number of wrong answers is more than three, then you may want to reread the section pertinent to the types of errors you are making to make sure you have a good understanding of the process.

Passage Problems: If the errors you are making are clustered in a passage type then you will want to focus your review of passage-specific strategies.

Short Passage Problems: If you are getting one or more questions with short passages wrong:

- Reread the Short Passage Section to make sure you understand the basic content and strategies.
- Go back to the questions you answered incorrectly and make sure you didn't make any careless errors. If you did make careless errors, write them down and make a mental note not to make them in the future.
- Practice reading the questions and paraphrasing the question in your own words.
- Make sure that you are reading the passages slowly and carefully. Pay attention to how much time you are spending on reading—in this section, you don't want to just skim over the passage, but read it thoroughly.

Long Passage Problems: If you are getting three or more questions with long passages wrong:

- Reread the Long Passage Section to make sure you understand the basic content and strategies.
- Go back to the questions you answered incorrectly and make sure you didn't make any careless errors. If you did make careless errors, write them down and make a mental note not to make them in the future.

- Practice answering before you answer. The most common error is not understanding the question and/or picking the "trick" answer choice. Read the question carefully, reword it, and then create an answer. Select the choice that most nearly matches your answer.

- Consider your timing. Skim the passage and use most of your time on answering the questions. If you find that you are spending too much time reading and thus rushing through the questions, you may be decreasing your accuracy. Work on adjusting your timing.

- Think about omitting questions that you have difficulty understanding. If you are not able to quickly and clearly paraphrase the question in your own words and provide your own answer then it probably means you don't really understand the question. Often, not understanding the question leads to selecting the wrong answer choice. Questions that seem too dense or answer choices that cannot be narrowed down may be best left blank. You want to spend the time on questions that you will be able to answer with a high level of accuracy and omit those questions that are a time drain and too difficult.

Double Passage Problems: If you are getting three or more questions with long passages wrong:

- Reread the Double Trouble Section to make sure you understand the basic content and strategies.

- Go back to the problems you answered incorrectly and make sure you didn't make any careless errors. If you did make careless errors, write them down and make a mental note not to make them in the future.

- Practice answering before you answer. The most common error is not understanding the question and/or picking the "trick" answer choice. Read the question carefully, reword it, and then create an answer. Select the choice that most nearly matches your answer.

- Consider your timing. Skim the passage and use most of your time on answering the questions. If you find that you are spending too much time reading and thus rushing through the questions, you may be decreasing your accuracy. Work on adjusting your timing.

- Track the order. You should skim the first passage and answer questions that pertain to the first passage. You should then skim the second passage and answer questions relating to that passage. Finally, if you have time, you can look at the questions that refer to both passages. Make sure that you are not wasting time reading both passages and then rushing through the questions.

- Think about omitting questions that you have difficulty understanding. If you are not able to quickly and clearly paraphrase the question in your own words and provide your own answer then it probably means you don't really understand the question. Often, not understanding the question leads to selecting the wrong answer choice. Questions that seem too dense or answer choices that cannot be narrowed down may be best left blank. You want to spend the time on questions that you will be able to answer with a high level of accuracy and omit those questions that are a time drain and too difficult.

Very Long Passage Problems: If you are getting three or more questions with very long passages wrong:

- Reread the Reading Passage Section to make sure you understand the basic content and strategies.
- Go back to the problems you answered incorrectly and make sure you didn't make any careless errors. If you did make careless errors, write them down and make a mental note not to make them in the future.
- Practice answering before you answer. The most common error is not understanding the question and/or picking the "trick" answer choice. Read the question carefully, reword it, and then create an answer. Select the choice that most nearly matches your answer.
- Consider your timing. Skim the passage and use most of your time to answer the questions. If you find that you are spending too much time reading and thus rushing through the questions, you may be decreasing your accuracy. Work on adjusting your timing.
- Think about omitting questions that you have difficulty understanding. If you are not able to quickly and clearly paraphrase the question in your own words and provide your own answer then it probably means you don't really understand the question. Often, not understanding the question leads to selecting the wrong answer choice. Questions that seem too dense or answer choices that cannot be narrowed down may be best left blank.
- The Very Long Passages are tedious and often overwhelmingly boring. Many students have a hard time concentrating and paying attention to the details of these passages. If you found that you made many errors in this type of passage and it was very difficult to stay focused, consider doing drills to sensitize yourself to long, boring reading. Plan on additional practice of especially long passages on topics you do not find interesting.

Question-Type Problems: If the errors you are making are clustered in a question type then you will want to focus your review on question-specific strategies.

General Question Problems: If you are getting two or more general questions wrong:

- Reread the Reading Passage Section to make sure you understand what types of questions fall under the "general" category.

- Hone your skills to be extra alert for general questions.

- Go back to the problems you answered incorrectly and make sure you didn't make any careless errors. If you did make careless errors, write them down and make a mental note not to make them in the future.

- Practice summarizing the passage and make sure to keep in mind the author's tone and gist of the passage.

- Make sure that you are reading the questions slowly and carefully. Pay attention to what the question is asking. Paraphrase the question in your own words or ask yourself: "This question is asking me ...."

- Practice answering before you answer. The most common error is not understanding the question and/or picking the "trick" answer choice. Read the question carefully, reword it, and then create an answer. Select the choice that most nearly matches your answer.

- Think about omitting questions that you have difficulty understanding. If you are not able to quickly and clearly paraphrase the question in your own words and provide your own answer then it probably means you don't really understand the question. Often, not understanding the question leads to selecting the wrong answer choice. Questions that seem too dense or answer choices that cannot be narrowed down may be best left blank.

Specific Question Problems: If you are getting two or more specific questions wrong:

- Reread the Reading Passage Section to make sure you understand what types of questions fall under the "specific" category.

- Hone your skills to be extra alert for specific questions.

- Go back to the problems you answered incorrectly and make sure you didn't make any careless errors. If you did make careless errors, write them down and make a mental note not to make them in the future.

- Make sure that you are not just looking back at the line indicated in the question. Remember to read two lines above and two lines below.

- Practice answering before you answer. The most common error is not understanding the question and/or picking the "trick" answer choice. Read the question carefully, reword it, and then create an answer. Select the choice that most nearly matches your answer.

- Think about omitting questions that you have difficulty understanding. If there is a type of specific question that you are often making errors on (e.g., vocabulary in context), consider leaving that type of question blank.

Verbal Section Score Report (calculate totals for all sentence completion and reading comprehension sections)

1. Total Number Right: _____

2. Total Number Wrong: _____

3. Total Number Wrong ÷ 4: _____

4. Round the number you computed in Step 3 to the nearest whole number: _____

5. Total Number Right – Number from Step 4 = _____ – _____ = _____

6. The number in Step 5 is your Raw Verbal Score. Use the table below to predict your SAT Verbal Section score. **Predicted SAT Verbal Section Score =** _____

Raw Score	Scaled Score
67	800
66	770–800
65	740–800
64	720–800
63	700–800
62	690–790
61	670–770
60	660–760
59	660–740
58	650–730
57	640–720
56	630–710
55	630–710
54	620–700
53	610–690
52	600–680
51	610–670
50	600–660
49	590–650
48	580–640
47	580–640
46	570–630
45	560–620
44	560–620
43	550–610
42	550–610

(Continued)

Raw Score	Scaled Score
41	640–600
40	530–590
39	530–590
38	520–580
37	510–570
36	510–570
35	500–560
34	500–560
33	490–550
32	480–540
31	480–540
30	470–530
29	470–530
28	460–520
27	450–510
26	450–510
25	440–500
24	440–500
23	430–490
22	420–480
21	420–480
20	410–470
19	400–460
18	400–460
17	390–450
16	380–440
15	380–440
14	370–430
13	360–420
12	350–410
11	350–410
10	340–400
9	330–390
8	310–390
7	300–380
6	290–370
5	270–370

(*Continued*)

Raw Score	Scaled Score
4	260–360
3	250–350
2	230–330
1	220–320
0	200–290
-1	200–290
-2	200–270
-3	200–250
-4	200–230
-5	200–210
-6 and below	200

Writing Section

Essay

Use the following rubric to compute your essay score.

Score	Essay Organization	Vocabulary/ Language	Sentence Structure	Grammar/Mechanics	Supporting Details/Evidence
1	Disorganized, no position taken on argument, no coherent flow of ideas	Basic vocabulary, inappropriate word choice, redundancy	Severely flawed sentence structure	Incorrect use of punctuation, fundamental grammatical errors, inappropriate grammar usage interferes with meaning	Severely lacks examples, evidence does not support argument
2	Poorly organized, position taken is unclear, limited flow of ideas	Limited use of vocabulary, word choice errors	Frequent problems with sentence structure	Poor use of punctuation, inconsistency in grammar usage, usage errors interfere with meaning	Inadequate examples, inappropriate evidence
3	Limited organization is present, position demonstrated, lack of consistent coherency	Limited use of vocabulary, poor word choice, demonstrates some variation in vocabulary	Problems with sentence structure, lacks varied sentence structure	Contains many grammatical errors	Insufficient examples, weak evidence

(Continued)

Score	Essay Organization	Vocabulary/ Language	Sentence Structure	Grammar/Mechanics	Supporting Details/Evidence
4	Generally organized, demonstrates position on topic clearly, ideas are focused	Sufficient use of language, displays varied and appropriate use of vocabulary	Sentence structure is varied	Demonstrates developing use of mechanics, contains some grammar errors	Evidence is adequate
5	Well organized, position is taken and clearly developed, flow of ideas is consistent	Demonstrated experienced use of language, appropriate vocabulary use	Good sentence structure	Displays competent use of grammar and mechanics	Evidence is appropriate
6	Well organized, position is taken and clearly developed, outstanding flow of ideas	Displays experienced use of language, vocabulary is appropriate and varied, words chosen accurately	Variety of sentence structure	Skillful use of grammar and mechanics, contains little to no grammatical errors	Evidence is appropriate, examples clearly support position

Essay score: _____

Writing Multiple Choice
Section 6

Improving Sentences						
Problem	Your Answer	Correct Answer	Right	Wrong	Blank	Level of Difficulty
1		B				E
2		A				E
3		A				E
4		D				E
5		A				M
6		A				E
7		D				M
8		B				E
9		B				E
10		C				E
11		A				M

Section 10

Improving Sentences						
Problem	Your Answer	Correct Answer	Right	Wrong	Blank	Level of Difficulty
1		B				E
2		D				E
3		A				E
4		B				M
5		A				H
6		A				E
7		C				M
8		A				E
9		C				E
10		A				M
11		C				M
12		B				M
13		C				M
14		D				H

Compute the following quantities:

1. Total Easy Problems Right: _____
2. Total Medium Problems Right: _____
3. Total Hard Problems Right: _____
4. Total Problems Wrong: _____

(Total Medium Problems Right ÷ 11) * 100 = _____ _____

Compass Tips:

Wrong Answers: If the total number of wrong answers (Step 4) is more than three then you may want to reread the Sentence Improvement Steps section of this book to make sure you have a good understanding of the process. You may also want to review the common grammar errors.

Easy Problems: If you are getting any easy-level problems wrong:

- Reread the Sentence Improvement Section to make sure you understand the basic content and strategies.

- Go back to the problems you answered incorrectly and make sure you didn't make any careless errors. If you did make careless errors, write them down and make a mental note not to make them in the future.

- Find a pattern in the types of grammar errors that you are fixing incorrectly or missing. For example, if you solved all the "ambiguous pronoun" problems incorrectly then go back to that part of the grammar section and carefully reread the rules.

- Continue reviewing basic grammar concepts.

Medium Problems: If the percent calculated in Step 5 is:

- 0 to 60%—Reread the Sentence Improvement Section to make sure you understand the basic content and strategies. Repeat all drills and complete extra practice of Sentence Improvement steps.

- 60 to 80%—Determine whether you can find a pattern in your errors. For medium questions, we suggest that if you are able to narrow down the choices to two (or eliminate three choices) then it is a good idea to guess. However, if you're not able to eliminate one or two choices then you're best off omitting the question. If you're recognizing the error, but having trouble correcting the sentence then go back to grammar review. Leaving problems blank when you aren't completely sure which choice is the correct one is an important strategy. Remember that you lose points for answering a problem incorrectly, but you do not lose points for leaving a problem blank. In other words, it is usually in your favor to *not* guess if you are just randomly guessing. Minimizing the number of problems you get wrong is to your benefit.

- 80 to 100%—Great work. It looks like you have the medium-level problems down pat.

Hard Problems: If you are getting the hard questions wrong:

- While it is possible to practice enough to improve greatly on the hard-level problems, it is extremely difficult to do so. The hard-level questions present the most obscure grammar rules. If you are consistently making errors in the hard questions then we suggest you should consider automatically leaving these questions blank. You will save you several minutes on each section to focus on the easy- and medium-level problems, which you can get right, given a little more time. Remember, colleges never see which level problems you get right. They only see the final score. So it's more important to spend and shift your time wisely to maximize your final score than to worry about answering super-challenging problems.

Section 6

Identifying Sentence Errors						
Problem	Your Answer	Correct Answer	Right	Wrong	Blank	Level of Difficulty
12		D				E
13		C				E
14		D				E
15		E				E
16		E				E
17		A				E
18		B				M
19		E				M
20		D				E
21		E				E
22		A				M
23		B				E
24		B				H
25		E				M
26		D				E
27		B				M
28		C				E
29		D				E

Compute the following quantities:

1. Total Easy Problems Right: _____
2. Total Medium Problems Right: _____
3. Total Hard Problems Right: _____
4. Total Problems Wrong: _____

(Total Medium Problems Right ÷ 5) * 100 = _____

Compass Tips:

Wrong Answers: If the total number of wrong answers (Step 4) is more than two then you may want to reread the Identifying Sentence Errors Steps section of this book to make sure you have a good understanding of the process. You may also want to review the common grammar errors.

Easy Problems: If you are getting any easy-level problems wrong:

• Reread the Identifying Sentence Errors Section to make sure you understand the basic content and strategies.

• Go back to the problems you answered incorrectly and make sure you didn't make any careless errors. If you did make careless errors, write them down and make a mental note not to make them in the future.

• Find a pattern in the types of grammar errors that you are overlooking. Is there a consistent error in the types of problems that you solved incorrectly? Review the appropriate grammar rules.

• Confirm that you are not finding an error in a sentence that is correct. Do not just rely on a sentence sounding "good." Make sure that you work through your "common grammar error" checklist to determine whether the sentence has an error.

• Continue reviewing basic grammar concepts.

Medium Problems: If the percent calculated in Step 5 is:

• 0 to 60%—Reread the Identifying Sentence Errors Section to make sure you understand the basic content and strategies. Repeat all drills and complete extra practice of Sentence Improvement steps.

• 60 to 80%—Determine whether you can find a pattern in your errors. For medium questions, we suggest that if you are able to narrow down the choices to two (or eliminate three choices) then it is a good idea to guess. However, if you're not able to eliminate one or two choices then you're best off omitting the question. Leaving problems blank when you aren't completely sure which choice is the correct one is an important strategy. Remember that you lose points for answering a problem incorrectly, but you do not lose points for leaving a problem blank. In other words, it is usually in your favor to *not* guess if you are just randomly guessing. Minimizing the number of problems you get wrong is to your benefit.

• 80 to 100%—Great work. It looks like you have the medium-level problems down pat.

Hard Problems: If you are getting the hard questions wrong:

• While it is possible to practice enough to improve greatly on the hard-level problems, it is extremely difficult to do so. The hard-level questions present the most obscure grammar rules. If you are consistently making errors in the hard questions then we suggest you should consider automatically leaving these questions blank. You will save you several minutes on each section to focus on the easy- and medium-level problems, which you can get right, given a little more time. Remember, colleges never see which level problems you get right. They only see the final score. So it's more important to spend and shift your time wisely to maximize your final score than to worry about answering super-challenging problems.

Section 6

Improving Paragraphs						
Problem	Your Answer	Correct Answer	Right	Wrong	Blank	Level of Difficulty
30		B				M
31		C				H
32		C				M
33		A				H
34		E				M
35		D				M

Compute the following quantities:

1. Total Medium Problems Right: _____
2. Total Hard Problems Right: _____
3. Total Problems Wrong: _____

Compass Tips:

Wrong Answers: If the total number of wrong answers (Step 3) is more than two then you may want to reread the Identifying Sentence Errors Steps section of this book to make sure you have a good understanding of the process. You may also want to review the common grammar errors.

Medium Problems: If you answered more than one question incorrectly:

• Reread Improving Paragraphs Section to make sure you understand the basic content and strategies.

• Go back to the problems you answered incorrectly and make sure you didn't make any careless errors. If you did make careless errors, write them down and make a mental note not to make them in the future.

• Determine whether you can find a pattern in your errors. For medium questions, we suggest that if you are able to narrow down the choices to 2 (or eliminate 3 choices) then it is a good idea to guess. However, if you're not able to eliminate one or two choices then you're best off omitting the question. Leaving problems blank when you aren't completely sure which choice is the correct one is an important strategy.

Remember that you lose points for answering a problem incorrectly, but you do not lose points for leaving a problem blank. In other words, it is usually in your favor to *not* guess if you are just randomly guessing. Minimizing the number of problems you get wrong is to your benefit.

Hard Problems: If you are getting the hard questions wrong:

- While it is possible to practice enough to improve greatly on the hard-level problems, it is extremely difficult to do so. The hard-level questions present the most obscure grammar rules. If you are consistently making errors in the hard questions then we suggest you should consider automatically leaving these questions blank. You will save you several minutes on each section to focus on the easy and medium level problems, which you can get right, given a little more time. Remember, colleges never see which level problems you get right. They only see the final score. So it's more important to spend and shift your time wisely to maximize your final score than to worry about answering super-challenging problems.

Writing Section Score Report (calculate totals for all writing sections and the essay)

1. Total Number Right: _____
2. Total Number Wrong: _____
3. Total Number Wrong ÷ 4: _____
4. Round the number you computed in Step 3 to the nearest whole number: _____
5. Total Number Right – Number from Step 4 = _____ – _____ = _____
6. Essay Score: _____
7. The number in Step 5 is your Raw Writing Multiple Choice Score (MS Raw Score). Use the table below to predict your SAT Writing Section score by combining the Raw Writing Multiple Choice Score and the Essay Score.

Predicted SAT Writing Section Score = _____

MS Raw Score	Essay Score						
	0	1	2	3	4	5	6
49	650–690	670–720	690–740	710–770	750–780	780–800	800
48	630–690	640–720	660–740	690–770	720–800	760–800	780–800
47	600–690	620–720	640–740	660–770	700–800	730–800	760–800
46	580–690	600–720	620–740	650–770	680–800	710–800	740–800
45	570–690	580–720	600–740	630–770	670–800	700–800	730–800
44	560–680	570–710	590–730	620–760	660–790	690–800	720–800
43	540–660	560–690	580–710	610–740	640–780	670–800	700–800
42	530–660	550–690	570–700	600–730	630–770	660–800	690–800
41	530–650	540–680	560–700	590–720	620–760	660–790	680–800
40	520–640	530–670	550–690	580–710	620–750	650–780	680–800
39	510–630	520–660	540–680	570–710	610–740	640–770	670–800
38	500–620	510–640	540–670	560–700	600–730	630–770	660–790
37	490–610	500–630	530–660	560–690	590–720	620–760	650–780
36	480–600	490–620	520–650	550–680	580–720	610–750	640–770
35	480–590	480–620	510–640	540–670	570–710	610–740	640–770
34	470–590	480–610	500–630	530–660	570–700	600–730	630–760
33	460–580	470–610	490–630	520–650	560–690	590–720	620–750
32	450–570	470–600	490–620	510–640	550–680	580–710	610–740
31	440–560	460–590	480–610	510–640	540–670	570–700	600–730
30	430–550	450–580	470–600	500–630	530–660	560–770	590–720
29	430–540	440–570	460–590	490–620	520–650	560–690	590–710
28	420–530	430–560	450–580	480–610	520–650	550–680	580–700
27	410–520	420–550	440–570	470–600	510–640	540–670	570–700
26	400–520	420–550	430–560	460–590	500–630	530–660	560–690
25	390–510	410–540	430–460	450–580	490–620	520–650	550–680
24	380–500	400–530	420–550	450–570	480–610	510–640	540–670
23	370–490	390–520	410–540	440–570	470–600	500–630	530–660
22	370–480	380–510	400–530	430–560	460–590	500–630	520–650
21	370–480	380–510	400–530	430–560	460–590	500–630	520–650
20	360–470	370–500	390–520	420–550	460–580	490–620	520–640
19	350–460	360–490	380–510	410–540	450–580	480–610	610–630
18	340–450	350–480	370–500	400–530	440–570	470–600	500–630
17	330–450	340–480	360–490	390–520	430–560	460–590	490–620

(Continued)

MS Raw Score	Essay Score						
	0	1	2	3	4	5	6
16	320–440	340–470	360–490	390–510	420–550	450–580	480–610
15	310–430	330–460	540–480	380–510	410–540	440–570	470–600
14	300–420	320–450	340–470	370–500	400–530	430–560	460–590
13	300–410	310–440	330–460	360–490	390–520	430–560	450–590
12	290–400	300–430	320–450	350–480	390–510	420–550	450–570
11	280–390	290–420	310–440	340–470	380–510	410–540	440–570
10	270–390	280–420	300–430	330–460	370–500	400–530	430–560
9	260–380	280–410	290–430	320–450	360–490	390–520	420–550
8	250–370	270–400	290–420	320–450	350–480	380–510	410–540
7	240–360	260–390	280–410	310–440	340–470	370–510	400–530
6	230–350	250–380	270–400	300–430	330–460	360–500	390–520
5	230–340	240–370	260–390	290–420	320–460	360–490	380–520
4	220–340	230–370	250–380	280–410	320–450	350–480	380–510
3	210–330	220–360	240–380	270–400	310–440	340–470	370–500
2	200–320	210–350	230–370	260–400	300–430	330–460	360–490
1	200–300	200–330	220–350	250–380	280–410	310–450	340–470
0	200–290	200–320	210–340	240–370	270–410	300–440	330–470
−1	200–280	200–330	200–330	220–350	250–390	290–420	310–450
−2	200–260	200–290	200–310	200–340	240–370	270–410	300–430
−3	200–240	200–270	200–290	200–320	240–360	270–390	300–420
−4	200–230	200–260	200–280	200–300	240–340	270–370	300–400
−5	200	200–230	200–250	200–280	240–320	270–350	300–370
−6	200	200–220	200–240	200–270	240–310	270–340	300–370
−7	200	200–220	200–230	200–260	240–300	270–330	300–360
−8	200	200–210	200–230	200–250	240–290	270–320	300–350
−9	200	200–210	200–230	200–250	240–290	270–320	300–350
−10	200	200–210	200–230	200–250	240–290	270–320	300–350

chapter **18**

Practice Test II

Answer Sheet

Last Name:_____   First Name:_____

Date:_____   Testing Location:_____

Directions For Test

- Remove these answer sheets from the book and use them to record your answers to this test.
- This test will require 3 hours and 20 minutes to complete. Take this test in one sitting.
- The time allotment for each section is written clearly at the beginning of each section. This test contains
- Six 25-minute sections, two 20-minute sections, and one 10-minute section.
- This test is 25 minutes shorter than the actual sat, which will include a 25-minute "experimental" section that does not count toward your score. That section has been omitted from this test.
- You may take one short break during the test, of no more than 10 minutes in length.
- You may only work on one section at any given time.
- You must stop ALL work on a section when time is called.
- If you finish a section before the time has elapsed, check your work on that section. You may not work on any other section.
- Do not waste time on questions that seem too difficult for you.
- Use the test book for scratchwork, but you will receive credit only for answers that are marked on the answer sheets.
- You will receive one point for every correct answer.
- You will receive no points for an omitted question.
- For each wrong answer on any multiple-choice question, your score will be reduced by ¼ point.
- For each wrong answer on any "numerical grid-in" question, you will receive no deduction.

When you take the real SAT, you will be asked to fill in your personal information in grids as shown below.

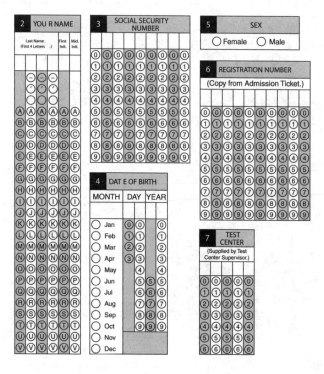

Start with number 1 for each new section. If a section has fewer questions than answer spaces, leave the extra answer spaces blank. Be sure to erase any errors or stray marks completely.

SECTION 2

1 Ⓐ Ⓑ Ⓒ Ⓓ Ⓔ	11 Ⓐ Ⓑ Ⓒ Ⓓ Ⓔ	21 Ⓐ Ⓑ Ⓒ Ⓓ Ⓔ	31 Ⓐ Ⓑ Ⓒ Ⓓ Ⓔ
2 Ⓐ Ⓑ Ⓒ Ⓓ Ⓔ	12 Ⓐ Ⓑ Ⓒ Ⓓ Ⓔ	22 Ⓐ Ⓑ Ⓒ Ⓓ Ⓔ	32 Ⓐ Ⓑ Ⓒ Ⓓ Ⓔ
3 Ⓐ Ⓑ Ⓒ Ⓓ Ⓔ	13 Ⓐ Ⓑ Ⓒ Ⓓ Ⓔ	23 Ⓐ Ⓑ Ⓒ Ⓓ Ⓔ	33 Ⓐ Ⓑ Ⓒ Ⓓ Ⓔ
4 Ⓐ Ⓑ Ⓒ Ⓓ Ⓔ	14 Ⓐ Ⓑ Ⓒ Ⓓ Ⓔ	24 Ⓐ Ⓑ Ⓒ Ⓓ Ⓔ	34 Ⓐ Ⓑ Ⓒ Ⓓ Ⓔ
5 Ⓐ Ⓑ Ⓒ Ⓓ Ⓔ	15 Ⓐ Ⓑ Ⓒ Ⓓ Ⓔ	25 Ⓐ Ⓑ Ⓒ Ⓓ Ⓔ	35 Ⓐ Ⓑ Ⓒ Ⓓ Ⓔ
6 Ⓐ Ⓑ Ⓒ Ⓓ Ⓔ	16 Ⓐ Ⓑ Ⓒ Ⓓ Ⓔ	26 Ⓐ Ⓑ Ⓒ Ⓓ Ⓔ	36 Ⓐ Ⓑ Ⓒ Ⓓ Ⓔ
7 Ⓐ Ⓑ Ⓒ Ⓓ Ⓔ	17 Ⓐ Ⓑ Ⓒ Ⓓ Ⓔ	27 Ⓐ Ⓑ Ⓒ Ⓓ Ⓔ	37 Ⓐ Ⓑ Ⓒ Ⓓ Ⓔ
8 Ⓐ Ⓑ Ⓒ Ⓓ Ⓔ	18 Ⓐ Ⓑ Ⓒ Ⓓ Ⓔ	28 Ⓐ Ⓑ Ⓒ Ⓓ Ⓔ	38 Ⓐ Ⓑ Ⓒ Ⓓ Ⓔ
9 Ⓐ Ⓑ Ⓒ Ⓓ Ⓔ	19 Ⓐ Ⓑ Ⓒ Ⓓ Ⓔ	29 Ⓐ Ⓑ Ⓒ Ⓓ Ⓔ	39 Ⓐ Ⓑ Ⓒ Ⓓ Ⓔ
10 Ⓐ Ⓑ Ⓒ Ⓓ Ⓔ	20 Ⓐ Ⓑ Ⓒ Ⓓ Ⓔ	30 Ⓐ Ⓑ Ⓒ Ⓓ Ⓔ	40 Ⓐ Ⓑ Ⓒ Ⓓ Ⓔ

SECTION 3

1 Ⓐ Ⓑ Ⓒ Ⓓ Ⓔ	11 Ⓐ Ⓑ Ⓒ Ⓓ Ⓔ	21 Ⓐ Ⓑ Ⓒ Ⓓ Ⓔ	31 Ⓐ Ⓑ Ⓒ Ⓓ Ⓔ
2 Ⓐ Ⓑ Ⓒ Ⓓ Ⓔ	12 Ⓐ Ⓑ Ⓒ Ⓓ Ⓔ	22 Ⓐ Ⓑ Ⓒ Ⓓ Ⓔ	32 Ⓐ Ⓑ Ⓒ Ⓓ Ⓔ
3 Ⓐ Ⓑ Ⓒ Ⓓ Ⓔ	13 Ⓐ Ⓑ Ⓒ Ⓓ Ⓔ	23 Ⓐ Ⓑ Ⓒ Ⓓ Ⓔ	33 Ⓐ Ⓑ Ⓒ Ⓓ Ⓔ
4 Ⓐ Ⓑ Ⓒ Ⓓ Ⓔ	14 Ⓐ Ⓑ Ⓒ Ⓓ Ⓔ	24 Ⓐ Ⓑ Ⓒ Ⓓ Ⓔ	34 Ⓐ Ⓑ Ⓒ Ⓓ Ⓔ
5 Ⓐ Ⓑ Ⓒ Ⓓ Ⓔ	15 Ⓐ Ⓑ Ⓒ Ⓓ Ⓔ	25 Ⓐ Ⓑ Ⓒ Ⓓ Ⓔ	35 Ⓐ Ⓑ Ⓒ Ⓓ Ⓔ
6 Ⓐ Ⓑ Ⓒ Ⓓ Ⓔ	16 Ⓐ Ⓑ Ⓒ Ⓓ Ⓔ	26 Ⓐ Ⓑ Ⓒ Ⓓ Ⓔ	36 Ⓐ Ⓑ Ⓒ Ⓓ Ⓔ
7 Ⓐ Ⓑ Ⓒ Ⓓ Ⓔ	17 Ⓐ Ⓑ Ⓒ Ⓓ Ⓔ	27 Ⓐ Ⓑ Ⓒ Ⓓ Ⓔ	37 Ⓐ Ⓑ Ⓒ Ⓓ Ⓔ
8 Ⓐ Ⓑ Ⓒ Ⓓ Ⓔ	18 Ⓐ Ⓑ Ⓒ Ⓓ Ⓔ	28 Ⓐ Ⓑ Ⓒ Ⓓ Ⓔ	38 Ⓐ Ⓑ Ⓒ Ⓓ Ⓔ
9 Ⓐ Ⓑ Ⓒ Ⓓ Ⓔ	19 Ⓐ Ⓑ Ⓒ Ⓓ Ⓔ	29 Ⓐ Ⓑ Ⓒ Ⓓ Ⓔ	39 Ⓐ Ⓑ Ⓒ Ⓓ Ⓔ
10 Ⓐ Ⓑ Ⓒ Ⓓ Ⓔ	20 Ⓐ Ⓑ Ⓒ Ⓓ Ⓔ	30 Ⓐ Ⓑ Ⓒ Ⓓ Ⓔ	40 Ⓐ Ⓑ Ⓒ Ⓓ Ⓔ

SECTION 4

1 Ⓐ Ⓑ Ⓒ Ⓓ Ⓔ	11 Ⓐ Ⓑ Ⓒ Ⓓ Ⓔ	21 Ⓐ Ⓑ Ⓒ Ⓓ Ⓔ	31 Ⓐ Ⓑ Ⓒ Ⓓ Ⓔ
2 Ⓐ Ⓑ Ⓒ Ⓓ Ⓔ	12 Ⓐ Ⓑ Ⓒ Ⓓ Ⓔ	22 Ⓐ Ⓑ Ⓒ Ⓓ Ⓔ	32 Ⓐ Ⓑ Ⓒ Ⓓ Ⓔ
3 Ⓐ Ⓑ Ⓒ Ⓓ Ⓔ	13 Ⓐ Ⓑ Ⓒ Ⓓ Ⓔ	23 Ⓐ Ⓑ Ⓒ Ⓓ Ⓔ	33 Ⓐ Ⓑ Ⓒ Ⓓ Ⓔ
4 Ⓐ Ⓑ Ⓒ Ⓓ Ⓔ	14 Ⓐ Ⓑ Ⓒ Ⓓ Ⓔ	24 Ⓐ Ⓑ Ⓒ Ⓓ Ⓔ	34 Ⓐ Ⓑ Ⓒ Ⓓ Ⓔ
5 Ⓐ Ⓑ Ⓒ Ⓓ Ⓔ	15 Ⓐ Ⓑ Ⓒ Ⓓ Ⓔ	25 Ⓐ Ⓑ Ⓒ Ⓓ Ⓔ	35 Ⓐ Ⓑ Ⓒ Ⓓ Ⓔ
6 Ⓐ Ⓑ Ⓒ Ⓓ Ⓔ	16 Ⓐ Ⓑ Ⓒ Ⓓ Ⓔ	26 Ⓐ Ⓑ Ⓒ Ⓓ Ⓔ	36 Ⓐ Ⓑ Ⓒ Ⓓ Ⓔ
7 Ⓐ Ⓑ Ⓒ Ⓓ Ⓔ	17 Ⓐ Ⓑ Ⓒ Ⓓ Ⓔ	27 Ⓐ Ⓑ Ⓒ Ⓓ Ⓔ	37 Ⓐ Ⓑ Ⓒ Ⓓ Ⓔ
8 Ⓐ Ⓑ Ⓒ Ⓓ Ⓔ	18 Ⓐ Ⓑ Ⓒ Ⓓ Ⓔ	28 Ⓐ Ⓑ Ⓒ Ⓓ Ⓔ	38 Ⓐ Ⓑ Ⓒ Ⓓ Ⓔ
9 Ⓐ Ⓑ Ⓒ Ⓓ Ⓔ	19 Ⓐ Ⓑ Ⓒ Ⓓ Ⓔ	29 Ⓐ Ⓑ Ⓒ Ⓓ Ⓔ	39 Ⓐ Ⓑ Ⓒ Ⓓ Ⓔ
10 Ⓐ Ⓑ Ⓒ Ⓓ Ⓔ	20 Ⓐ Ⓑ Ⓒ Ⓓ Ⓔ	30 Ⓐ Ⓑ Ⓒ Ⓓ Ⓔ	40 Ⓐ Ⓑ Ⓒ Ⓓ Ⓔ

SECTION 6

1 Ⓐ Ⓑ Ⓒ Ⓓ Ⓔ	11 Ⓐ Ⓑ Ⓒ Ⓓ Ⓔ	21 Ⓐ Ⓑ Ⓒ Ⓓ Ⓔ	31 Ⓐ Ⓑ Ⓒ Ⓓ Ⓔ
2 Ⓐ Ⓑ Ⓒ Ⓓ Ⓔ	12 Ⓐ Ⓑ Ⓒ Ⓓ Ⓔ	22 Ⓐ Ⓑ Ⓒ Ⓓ Ⓔ	32 Ⓐ Ⓑ Ⓒ Ⓓ Ⓔ
3 Ⓐ Ⓑ Ⓒ Ⓓ Ⓔ	13 Ⓐ Ⓑ Ⓒ Ⓓ Ⓔ	23 Ⓐ Ⓑ Ⓒ Ⓓ Ⓔ	33 Ⓐ Ⓑ Ⓒ Ⓓ Ⓔ
4 Ⓐ Ⓑ Ⓒ Ⓓ Ⓔ	14 Ⓐ Ⓑ Ⓒ Ⓓ Ⓔ	24 Ⓐ Ⓑ Ⓒ Ⓓ Ⓔ	34 Ⓐ Ⓑ Ⓒ Ⓓ Ⓔ
5 Ⓐ Ⓑ Ⓒ Ⓓ Ⓔ	15 Ⓐ Ⓑ Ⓒ Ⓓ Ⓔ	25 Ⓐ Ⓑ Ⓒ Ⓓ Ⓔ	35 Ⓐ Ⓑ Ⓒ Ⓓ Ⓔ
6 Ⓐ Ⓑ Ⓒ Ⓓ Ⓔ	16 Ⓐ Ⓑ Ⓒ Ⓓ Ⓔ	26 Ⓐ Ⓑ Ⓒ Ⓓ Ⓔ	36 Ⓐ Ⓑ Ⓒ Ⓓ Ⓔ
7 Ⓐ Ⓑ Ⓒ Ⓓ Ⓔ	17 Ⓐ Ⓑ Ⓒ Ⓓ Ⓔ	27 Ⓐ Ⓑ Ⓒ Ⓓ Ⓔ	37 Ⓐ Ⓑ Ⓒ Ⓓ Ⓔ
8 Ⓐ Ⓑ Ⓒ Ⓓ Ⓔ	18 Ⓐ Ⓑ Ⓒ Ⓓ Ⓔ	28 Ⓐ Ⓑ Ⓒ Ⓓ Ⓔ	38 Ⓐ Ⓑ Ⓒ Ⓓ Ⓔ
9 Ⓐ Ⓑ Ⓒ Ⓓ Ⓔ	19 Ⓐ Ⓑ Ⓒ Ⓓ Ⓔ	29 Ⓐ Ⓑ Ⓒ Ⓓ Ⓔ	39 Ⓐ Ⓑ Ⓒ Ⓓ Ⓔ
10 Ⓐ Ⓑ Ⓒ Ⓓ Ⓔ	20 Ⓐ Ⓑ Ⓒ Ⓓ Ⓔ	30 Ⓐ Ⓑ Ⓒ Ⓓ Ⓔ	40 Ⓐ Ⓑ Ⓒ Ⓓ Ⓔ

Start with number 1 for each new section. If a section has fewer questions than answer spaces, leave the extra answer spaces blank. Be sure to erase any errors or stray marks completely.

SECTION 7

1 Ⓐ Ⓑ Ⓒ Ⓓ Ⓔ	11 Ⓐ Ⓑ Ⓒ Ⓓ Ⓔ	21 Ⓐ Ⓑ Ⓒ Ⓓ Ⓔ	31 Ⓐ Ⓑ Ⓒ Ⓓ Ⓔ
2 Ⓐ Ⓑ Ⓒ Ⓓ Ⓔ	12 Ⓐ Ⓑ Ⓒ Ⓓ Ⓔ	22 Ⓐ Ⓑ Ⓒ Ⓓ Ⓔ	32 Ⓐ Ⓑ Ⓒ Ⓓ Ⓔ
3 Ⓐ Ⓑ Ⓒ Ⓓ Ⓔ	13 Ⓐ Ⓑ Ⓒ Ⓓ Ⓔ	23 Ⓐ Ⓑ Ⓒ Ⓓ Ⓔ	33 Ⓐ Ⓑ Ⓒ Ⓓ Ⓔ
4 Ⓐ Ⓑ Ⓒ Ⓓ Ⓔ	14 Ⓐ Ⓑ Ⓒ Ⓓ Ⓔ	24 Ⓐ Ⓑ Ⓒ Ⓓ Ⓔ	34 Ⓐ Ⓑ Ⓒ Ⓓ Ⓔ
5 Ⓐ Ⓑ Ⓒ Ⓓ Ⓔ	15 Ⓐ Ⓑ Ⓒ Ⓓ Ⓔ	25 Ⓐ Ⓑ Ⓒ Ⓓ Ⓔ	35 Ⓐ Ⓑ Ⓒ Ⓓ Ⓔ
6 Ⓐ Ⓑ Ⓒ Ⓓ Ⓔ	16 Ⓐ Ⓑ Ⓒ Ⓓ Ⓔ	26 Ⓐ Ⓑ Ⓒ Ⓓ Ⓔ	36 Ⓐ Ⓑ Ⓒ Ⓓ Ⓔ
7 Ⓐ Ⓑ Ⓒ Ⓓ Ⓔ	17 Ⓐ Ⓑ Ⓒ Ⓓ Ⓔ	27 Ⓐ Ⓑ Ⓒ Ⓓ Ⓔ	37 Ⓐ Ⓑ Ⓒ Ⓓ Ⓔ
8 Ⓐ Ⓑ Ⓒ Ⓓ Ⓔ	18 Ⓐ Ⓑ Ⓒ Ⓓ Ⓔ	28 Ⓐ Ⓑ Ⓒ Ⓓ Ⓔ	38 Ⓐ Ⓑ Ⓒ Ⓓ Ⓔ
9 Ⓐ Ⓑ Ⓒ Ⓓ Ⓔ	19 Ⓐ Ⓑ Ⓒ Ⓓ Ⓔ	29 Ⓐ Ⓑ Ⓒ Ⓓ Ⓔ	39 Ⓐ Ⓑ Ⓒ Ⓓ Ⓔ
10 Ⓐ Ⓑ Ⓒ Ⓓ Ⓔ	20 Ⓐ Ⓑ Ⓒ Ⓓ Ⓔ	30 Ⓐ Ⓑ Ⓒ Ⓓ Ⓔ	40 Ⓐ Ⓑ Ⓒ Ⓓ Ⓔ

SECTION 8

1 Ⓐ Ⓑ Ⓒ Ⓓ Ⓔ	11 Ⓐ Ⓑ Ⓒ Ⓓ Ⓔ	21 Ⓐ Ⓑ Ⓒ Ⓓ Ⓔ	31 Ⓐ Ⓑ Ⓒ Ⓓ Ⓔ
2 Ⓐ Ⓑ Ⓒ Ⓓ Ⓔ	12 Ⓐ Ⓑ Ⓒ Ⓓ Ⓔ	22 Ⓐ Ⓑ Ⓒ Ⓓ Ⓔ	32 Ⓐ Ⓑ Ⓒ Ⓓ Ⓔ
3 Ⓐ Ⓑ Ⓒ Ⓓ Ⓔ	13 Ⓐ Ⓑ Ⓒ Ⓓ Ⓔ	23 Ⓐ Ⓑ Ⓒ Ⓓ Ⓔ	33 Ⓐ Ⓑ Ⓒ Ⓓ Ⓔ
4 Ⓐ Ⓑ Ⓒ Ⓓ Ⓔ	14 Ⓐ Ⓑ Ⓒ Ⓓ Ⓔ	24 Ⓐ Ⓑ Ⓒ Ⓓ Ⓔ	34 Ⓐ Ⓑ Ⓒ Ⓓ Ⓔ
5 Ⓐ Ⓑ Ⓒ Ⓓ Ⓔ	15 Ⓐ Ⓑ Ⓒ Ⓓ Ⓔ	25 Ⓐ Ⓑ Ⓒ Ⓓ Ⓔ	35 Ⓐ Ⓑ Ⓒ Ⓓ Ⓔ
6 Ⓐ Ⓑ Ⓒ Ⓓ Ⓔ	16 Ⓐ Ⓑ Ⓒ Ⓓ Ⓔ	26 Ⓐ Ⓑ Ⓒ Ⓓ Ⓔ	36 Ⓐ Ⓑ Ⓒ Ⓓ Ⓔ
7 Ⓐ Ⓑ Ⓒ Ⓓ Ⓔ	17 Ⓐ Ⓑ Ⓒ Ⓓ Ⓔ	27 Ⓐ Ⓑ Ⓒ Ⓓ Ⓔ	37 Ⓐ Ⓑ Ⓒ Ⓓ Ⓔ
8 Ⓐ Ⓑ Ⓒ Ⓓ Ⓔ	18 Ⓐ Ⓑ Ⓒ Ⓓ Ⓔ	28 Ⓐ Ⓑ Ⓒ Ⓓ Ⓔ	38 Ⓐ Ⓑ Ⓒ Ⓓ Ⓔ
9 Ⓐ Ⓑ Ⓒ Ⓓ Ⓔ	19 Ⓐ Ⓑ Ⓒ Ⓓ Ⓔ	29 Ⓐ Ⓑ Ⓒ Ⓓ Ⓔ	39 Ⓐ Ⓑ Ⓒ Ⓓ Ⓔ
10 Ⓐ Ⓑ Ⓒ Ⓓ Ⓔ	20 Ⓐ Ⓑ Ⓒ Ⓓ Ⓔ	30 Ⓐ Ⓑ Ⓒ Ⓓ Ⓔ	40 Ⓐ Ⓑ Ⓒ Ⓓ Ⓔ

SECTION 9

1 Ⓐ Ⓑ Ⓒ Ⓓ Ⓔ	11 Ⓐ Ⓑ Ⓒ Ⓓ Ⓔ	21 Ⓐ Ⓑ Ⓒ Ⓓ Ⓔ	31 Ⓐ Ⓑ Ⓒ Ⓓ Ⓔ
2 Ⓐ Ⓑ Ⓒ Ⓓ Ⓔ	12 Ⓐ Ⓑ Ⓒ Ⓓ Ⓔ	22 Ⓐ Ⓑ Ⓒ Ⓓ Ⓔ	32 Ⓐ Ⓑ Ⓒ Ⓓ Ⓔ
3 Ⓐ Ⓑ Ⓒ Ⓓ Ⓔ	13 Ⓐ Ⓑ Ⓒ Ⓓ Ⓔ	23 Ⓐ Ⓑ Ⓒ Ⓓ Ⓔ	33 Ⓐ Ⓑ Ⓒ Ⓓ Ⓔ
4 Ⓐ Ⓑ Ⓒ Ⓓ Ⓔ	14 Ⓐ Ⓑ Ⓒ Ⓓ Ⓔ	24 Ⓐ Ⓑ Ⓒ Ⓓ Ⓔ	34 Ⓐ Ⓑ Ⓒ Ⓓ Ⓔ
5 Ⓐ Ⓑ Ⓒ Ⓓ Ⓔ	15 Ⓐ Ⓑ Ⓒ Ⓓ Ⓔ	25 Ⓐ Ⓑ Ⓒ Ⓓ Ⓔ	35 Ⓐ Ⓑ Ⓒ Ⓓ Ⓔ
6 Ⓐ Ⓑ Ⓒ Ⓓ Ⓔ	16 Ⓐ Ⓑ Ⓒ Ⓓ Ⓔ	26 Ⓐ Ⓑ Ⓒ Ⓓ Ⓔ	36 Ⓐ Ⓑ Ⓒ Ⓓ Ⓔ
7 Ⓐ Ⓑ Ⓒ Ⓓ Ⓔ	17 Ⓐ Ⓑ Ⓒ Ⓓ Ⓔ	27 Ⓐ Ⓑ Ⓒ Ⓓ Ⓔ	37 Ⓐ Ⓑ Ⓒ Ⓓ Ⓔ
8 Ⓐ Ⓑ Ⓒ Ⓓ Ⓔ	18 Ⓐ Ⓑ Ⓒ Ⓓ Ⓔ	28 Ⓐ Ⓑ Ⓒ Ⓓ Ⓔ	38 Ⓐ Ⓑ Ⓒ Ⓓ Ⓔ
9 Ⓐ Ⓑ Ⓒ Ⓓ Ⓔ	19 Ⓐ Ⓑ Ⓒ Ⓓ Ⓔ	29 Ⓐ Ⓑ Ⓒ Ⓓ Ⓔ	39 Ⓐ Ⓑ Ⓒ Ⓓ Ⓔ
10 Ⓐ Ⓑ Ⓒ Ⓓ Ⓔ	20 Ⓐ Ⓑ Ⓒ Ⓓ Ⓔ	30 Ⓐ Ⓑ Ⓒ Ⓓ Ⓔ	40 Ⓐ Ⓑ Ⓒ Ⓓ Ⓔ

SECTION 10

1 Ⓐ Ⓑ Ⓒ Ⓓ Ⓔ	11 Ⓐ Ⓑ Ⓒ Ⓓ Ⓔ	21 Ⓐ Ⓑ Ⓒ Ⓓ Ⓔ	31 Ⓐ Ⓑ Ⓒ Ⓓ Ⓔ
2 Ⓐ Ⓑ Ⓒ Ⓓ Ⓔ	12 Ⓐ Ⓑ Ⓒ Ⓓ Ⓔ	22 Ⓐ Ⓑ Ⓒ Ⓓ Ⓔ	32 Ⓐ Ⓑ Ⓒ Ⓓ Ⓔ
3 Ⓐ Ⓑ Ⓒ Ⓓ Ⓔ	13 Ⓐ Ⓑ Ⓒ Ⓓ Ⓔ	23 Ⓐ Ⓑ Ⓒ Ⓓ Ⓔ	33 Ⓐ Ⓑ Ⓒ Ⓓ Ⓔ
4 Ⓐ Ⓑ Ⓒ Ⓓ Ⓔ	14 Ⓐ Ⓑ Ⓒ Ⓓ Ⓔ	24 Ⓐ Ⓑ Ⓒ Ⓓ Ⓔ	34 Ⓐ Ⓑ Ⓒ Ⓓ Ⓔ
5 Ⓐ Ⓑ Ⓒ Ⓓ Ⓔ	15 Ⓐ Ⓑ Ⓒ Ⓓ Ⓔ	25 Ⓐ Ⓑ Ⓒ Ⓓ Ⓔ	35 Ⓐ Ⓑ Ⓒ Ⓓ Ⓔ
6 Ⓐ Ⓑ Ⓒ Ⓓ Ⓔ	16 Ⓐ Ⓑ Ⓒ Ⓓ Ⓔ	26 Ⓐ Ⓑ Ⓒ Ⓓ Ⓔ	36 Ⓐ Ⓑ Ⓒ Ⓓ Ⓔ
7 Ⓐ Ⓑ Ⓒ Ⓓ Ⓔ	17 Ⓐ Ⓑ Ⓒ Ⓓ Ⓔ	27 Ⓐ Ⓑ Ⓒ Ⓓ Ⓔ	37 Ⓐ Ⓑ Ⓒ Ⓓ Ⓔ
8 Ⓐ Ⓑ Ⓒ Ⓓ Ⓔ	18 Ⓐ Ⓑ Ⓒ Ⓓ Ⓔ	28 Ⓐ Ⓑ Ⓒ Ⓓ Ⓔ	38 Ⓐ Ⓑ Ⓒ Ⓓ Ⓔ
9 Ⓐ Ⓑ Ⓒ Ⓓ Ⓔ	19 Ⓐ Ⓑ Ⓒ Ⓓ Ⓔ	29 Ⓐ Ⓑ Ⓒ Ⓓ Ⓔ	39 Ⓐ Ⓑ Ⓒ Ⓓ Ⓔ
10 Ⓐ Ⓑ Ⓒ Ⓓ Ⓔ	20 Ⓐ Ⓑ Ⓒ Ⓓ Ⓔ	30 Ⓐ Ⓑ Ⓒ Ⓓ Ⓔ	40 Ⓐ Ⓑ Ⓒ Ⓓ Ⓔ

Section 1
Essay
Time—25 minutes

> **Write your essay on separate sheets of standard lined paper.**

The essay gives you an opportunity to show how effectively you can develop and express ideas. You should, therefore, take care to develop your point of view, present your ideas logically and clearly, and use language precisely.

Your essay should be written on the lines provided on your answer sheet—you will receive no other paper on which to write. You will have enough space if you write on every line, avoid wide margins, and keep your handwriting to a reasonable size. Remember that people who are not familiar with your handwriting will read what you write. Try to write or print so that what you are writing is legible to those readers.

Important reminders:

- **A pencil is required for the essay.** An essay written in ink will receive a score of zero.
- **Do not write your essay in your test book.** You will receive credit for what you write on your answer sheet.
- **An off-topic essay will receive a score of zero.**
- **If your essay does not reflect your original and individual work, your test scores may be cancelled.**

You have twenty-five minutes to write an essay on the topic assigned below.

Think carefully about the issue presented in the following excerpt and the assignment below.

> We had no external limitations, no overriding authority, no imposed pattern of existence. We created our own links with the world, and freedom was the very essence of our existence.
>
> *Simone de Beauvoir, 1963*

Assignment: Is an individual solely responsible for giving his/her life meaning and living a fulfilling life? Plan and write an essay in which you develop your point of view on this issue. Support your position with reasoning and examples taking from your reading, studies, experiences, or observations.

Begin writing your essay on a separate sheet of paper.

If you finish before time is called, you may check your work on this section only.
Do not turn to any other section in the test.

Section 2
Time—25 Minutes
20 Questions

Directions: For this section, solve each problem and decide which is the best of the choices given. Fill in the corresponding circle on the answer sheet. You may use any available space for scratch work.

Notes

1. The use of a calculator is permitted.
2. All numbers used are real numbers.
3. Figures that accompany problems in this test are intended to provide information useful in solving the problems. They are drawn as accurately as possible EXCEPT when it is stated in a specific problem that the figure is not drawn to scale. All figures lie in a plane unless otherwise indicated.
4. Unless otherwise specified, the domain of any function f is assumed to be the set of all real numbers x for which $f(x)$ is a real number.

Reference Information

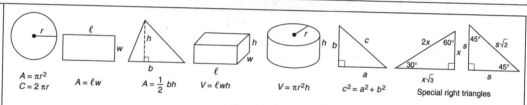

$A = \pi r^2$
$C = 2\pi r$

$A = \ell w$

$A = \frac{1}{2} bh$

$V = \ell wh$

$V = \pi r^2 h$

$c^2 = a^2 + b^2$

Special right triangles

The number of degrees of arc in a circle is 360.
The sum of the measures in degrees of the angles of a triangle is 180.

1.   Let Ω be the set of all positive integers that can be written $s^3 - 4$, where s is a nonzero integer. Which of the following integers is in Ω?

(A) 24
(B) −4
(C) −3
(D) 59
(E) 121

2. If $s^x \cdot s^5 = s^{15}$ and $(s^6)^y = s^{12}$, what is the value of the product xy?

    (A) 9
    (B) 10
    (C) 20
    (D) 16
    (E) 6

3. If j is a positive integer, what is the least value of j for which $\sqrt{\dfrac{7j}{6}}$ is an integer?

    (A) 6
    (B) 7
    (C) 42
    (D) 49
    (E) 168

4.

Number of high school seniors			
Year	2008	2009	2010
Adams High School	300	500	550
Georgian High School	650	550	800

Average number of colleges applied to per student at Georgian High School	
Year	Colleges
2008	5
2009	7
2010	12

The first table above shows the number of high school seniors in Adams High School and Georgian High School in the years 2008 to 2010. The second table shows the average number of colleges to which each student at Georgian High School applied. Based on the information in the tables, which of the following best approximates the total number of college applications generated by the students at Georgian High School during the years 2008 to 2010?

(A) 11,600
(B) 16,700
(C) 32,400
(D) 48,000
(E) 80,400

5. If "every equiangular triangle is an equilateral triangle" is a true statement, which of the following cannot be true?

(A) If a triangle is equilateral, then it is equiangular.
(B) If a triangle is equiangular, then it is equilateral.
(C) If a triangle has three interior angles, each measuring 60°, then it is equilateral.
(D) If a triangle is not equilateral, then it is not equiangular.
(E) If a triangle does not have three equal sides, then no interior angles can be equal.

6.

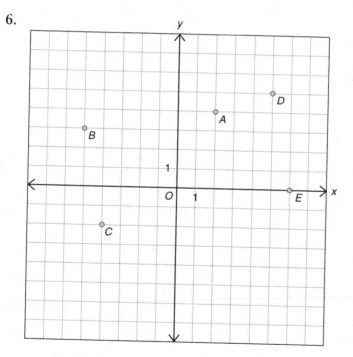

Which of the lettered points on the grid above has coordinates (x, y) such that $|y| - |x| = 2$?

(A) A
(B) B
(C) C
(D) D
(E) E

7. Let $\otimes z$ be defined as $z^2 + z - 12$ for all integral values of z that make the expression sum to zero? If $\otimes z = k$, where k is an integer, which of the following is a possible value of k?

(A) -7
(B) -6
(C) -1
(D) 3
(E) 6

8. Each of the following is equivalent to $\dfrac{xy}{z} + w$ except

(A) $\dfrac{x}{z}\left(y + \dfrac{wz}{x}\right)$

(B) $\dfrac{xy + wz}{z}$

(C) $x\left(\dfrac{y}{z} + \dfrac{w}{x}\right)$

(D) $y\left(\dfrac{xy + wz}{yz}\right)$

(E) $\dfrac{y}{z}\left(y + \dfrac{w}{y}\right)$

9. If $(w - 3)^2 = 64$, then w could be

(A) -11
(B) -5
(C) 3
(D) 5
(E) 8

10. If $0 < x < 1$, then x^2 is how much less than x?

(A) 0

(B) $\dfrac{1}{4}$

(C) x

(D) $x(1-x)$

(E) $(1-x)(1+x)$

11.

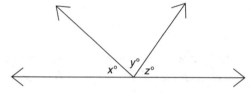

In the figure above, if l is a line, $x + y = 70$ and $y + z = 150$, then what is the value of y?

(A) 30

(B) 40

(C) 50

(D) 70

(E) 80

12.

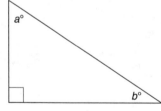

In the triangles above, what is the average (arithmetic mean) of a, b, and c?

(A) 5

(B) 45

(C) 50

(D) 54

(E) 90

13. 20, 4, 9, 18, 11, 10, x

If x is the median of the seven numbers listed above, which of the following could be the value of x?

(A) 9
(B) 9.5
(C) 10
(D) 11.5
(E) 12

14. 5, −1, −7,…

In the sequence above, the first term is 5 and each term after the first is 6 less than the previous term. What is the 14th term of the sequence?

(A) −61
(B) −67
(C) −73
(D) −79
(E) −85

15.

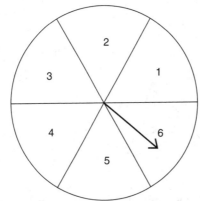

Sheba and her friends are playing a game that uses a disk with a spinner, shown above, to decide if a player will move a space on the game board. Each player spins the arrow twice. The fraction $\frac{x}{y}$ is formed, where x is the number of the sector where the arrow stops after the first spin and y is the number of the sector where the arrow stops after the second spin. On every spin, each of the numbered sectors has an equal probability of being the sector on which the arrow stops. In Sheba's game, a player may only move a space if the fraction $\dfrac{x}{y}$ is less than 1. What is the probability that a player will move a space in Sheba's game?

(A) $\dfrac{6}{36}$

(B) $\dfrac{14}{36}$

(C) $\dfrac{15}{36}$

(D) $\dfrac{16}{36}$

(E) $\dfrac{18}{36}$

16. If x and y are positive integers, what are all the solutions (x, y) of the equation $2x+5y=30$?

(A) $(5, 4)$ only
(B) $(10, 2)$ only
(C) $(5, 4)$ and $(8, 3)$
(D) $(5, 4)$ and $(10, 2)$
(E) $(8, 3)$ and $(10, 2)$

17. The height of a right circular cylinder is 6, and the diameter of its base is 4. What is the distance from the center of one base to a point on the circumference of the other base?

(A) 8
(B) 10
(C) $\sqrt{32}$ (approximately 5.66)
(D) $\sqrt{40}$ (approximately 6.32)
(E) $\sqrt{52}$ (approximately 7.21)

18. Which of the following is a graph of a linear function with a positive slope and a negative y-intercept?

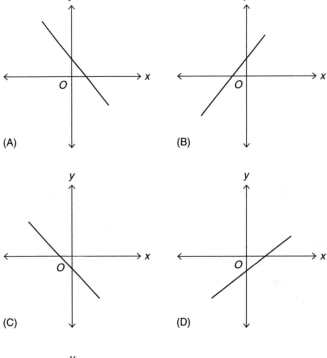

(A)

(B)

(C)

(D)

(E)

19. Which of the following graphs shows the line defined by the equation $\frac{2}{3}y - 6 = x$ in an xy coordinate system?

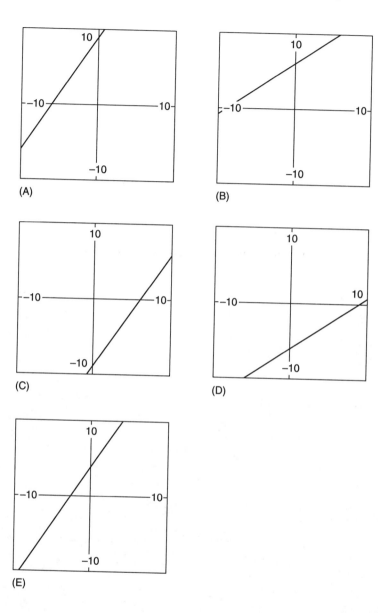

20.

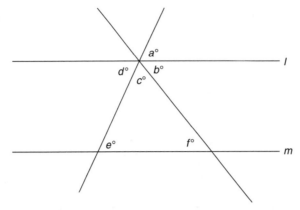

In the figure above, $l \parallel m$. Which of the following must equal 180?

(A) $a+c+d$
(B) $d+e+f$
(C) $a+b+f$
(D) $b+c+f$
(E) $a+c+f$

Section 3
Time—25 minutes
24 questions

Turn to Section 3 (page 426) of your answer sheet to answer the questions in this section.

Directions: For each question in this section, select the best answer from among the answer choices given and fill in the corresponding circle on the answer sheet.

Each sentence below has one or two question blanks, each blank indicating that something has been omitted. Beneath the sentence are five words or sets of words labeled A through E. Choose the word or set of words that, when inserted in the sentence, *best* fits the meaning of the sentence as a whole.

Example:

Susan preferred to be ____, hoping to avoid confusion due to miscommunication.
(A) **direct**
(B) devious
(C) cunning
(D) austere
(E) terse

1. Ben's writing is ____: sentences are fragmented and broken apart by odd use of punctuation.

   (A) disjointed
   (B) embellished
   (C) improvised
   (D) consistent
   (E) novel

2. Failing to focus in math class and ____ to his classmate's distraction resulted in a poor participation grade.

   (A) alerted
   (B) succumbing
   (C) listening
   (D) enjoying
   (E) deviating

3. The final skaters' ____ skills ____ the previous athlete's remarkable talents.

   (A) mediocre...overshadowed
   (B) admirable...amassed
   (C) superior...eclipsed
   (D) aggregate...surpassed
   (E) outlandish...emphasized

4. After their mother promised to take away all privileges, Laura and Max issued ____ and pledges to work together.

   (A) proclamations
   (B) assertions
   (C) sacrifices
   (D) possibilities
   (E) disputes

5. The ____ math solution preoccupied the greatest mathematicians.

   (A) benighted
   (B) indefinable
   (C) denizen
   (D) herculean
   (E) lissome

The passages below are followed by questions based on their content; questions that follow a pair of related passages may also be based on the relationship between the paired passages. Answer the questions on the basis of what is *stated* or *implied* in the passage in any introductory material that may be provided.

Questions 6 through 9 are based on the following passages.

Passage 1

The art of constructing cryptographs or ciphers—intelligible to those who know the key and unintelligible to others—has been studied for
Line   centuries. Their usefulness on certain occasions, especially in time of war, is obvious, while it may be a matter of great importance to those
5   from whom the key is concealed to discover it. But the romance connected with the subject, the not uncommon desire to discover a secret, and the implied challenge to the ingenuity of all from whom the key is hidden, have attracted to the subject the attention of many to whom its utility is a matter of indifference.

6. The passage suggests that cryptographs are

    (A) only useful for conveying insignificant information
    (B) comprehensible to anyone interested in cryptographs
    (C) novel tools for communicating clandestine information
    (D) used primarily during times of war
    (E) recreational and utilitarian by design

7. In line 7 "ingenuity" most nearly means

    (A) extraneousness
    (B) absurdity
    (C) ineptness
    (D) adroitness
    (E) guise

Passage 2

Today we depend for life's necessities almost wholly upon the
activities of others. The work of thousands of human hands and
Line thousands of human brains lies back of every meal you eat, every
journey you take, every book you read, every bed in which you sleep,
5   every telephone conversation, every telegram you receive, every
garment you wear.

And this fellowman of ours has multiplied, since that dim distant
dawn, into almost two billion human beings, with at least one billion
of them after the very things you want, and not a tenth enough to go
10   around!

8.   The primary purpose of this passage is to

(A) persuade people to become self-sufficient
(B) demonstrate the consequences of the global environment
(C) disparage the idea that the world is interconnected
(D) argue that we are living in an overpopulated world
(E) suggest that individuals are no longer able to depend on others for
life's needs

9.   The author of the passage

(A) criticizes a practice
(B) offers an example
(C) proposes a solution
(D) states an opinion
(E) presents a problem

Questions 10 through 18 are based on the following passage.

*This excerpt is from a novel written in 1917. Don and Aurora meet after a long
absence.*

"Mom!" said he. "Mother! I've got a mother, after all—and such a
splendid one! I can't believe it at all—it must all be a dream. To be
Line an orphan all my life—and then to get word that I'm not—that I've a
mother, after all—and you! Why, I'd have known you anyhow, I'm
5   sure, if I'd never seen you, even from the picture I had. It was when

you were a girl. But you've not changed—you couldn't. And it's you who've been my mother all the time. It's fine to be home with you at last. So this is the town where you have lived—that I've never seen. And here are all your friends?"

10   "Yes, Don," said she, "all I have, pretty much." Aurora Lane's speaking voice was of extraordinary sweetness.

"Well, you have lived here all your life."

"Yes," she smiled.

"And they all know you."

15   "Oh, yes," noncommittally. "It was too bad you had to be away from me, Don, boy. You seem like a stranger to me—I can't realize you are here, that you are my own boy, Dieudonné! I'm afraid of you—I don't know you—and I'm so proud and frightened, so surprised, so glad— why, I don't know what to do. But I'd have known you anywhere—

20   I did know you. You're just as I've always dreamed of you—and I'm glad—I'm so very glad!"

"Mom! I loved your little picture, but I never knew how much I loved you till now—why—you're my mother! My mother! And I've never seen you—I've never known you—till right now. You're a ripper,

25   that's what you are!

"And is that where you live, over yonder?" he added quickly, to conceal the catch in his throat, the quick moisture in his eyes. His mother! And never in all his life had he seen her face—this sweet, strange, wistful, wonderful face. His mother! He had not even known

30   she was alive. And now, so overwhelmed was he, he did not as yet even think of unraveling the veil of ignorance or deceit—call it what one might—which had left him in orphanage all his life till now.

"Yes, over yonder," said Aurora, and pointed across the square. "That little house under the shade trees, just at the corner. That's home and

35   workshop for me, Don."

She spoke softly, her eyes still fixed on him, the color of her cheeks deepening.

"Not so much of a house, is it?" laughed the boy, tears on his face, born of his new emotion, so sudden, so tremendous and so strange.

40   "Not so very much," she assented, laughing gayly also, and also in tears, which gave him sudden grief—"but it has served."

"Well, never mind. We're going to do better out West, Mom. We're going to have you with us right away, as soon as I can get started."

"What—what do you say—with us! With us?"

45   She spoke in swift dismay, halting in her walk. "What do you mean, Don—us?"

"I didn't tell you the news," said he, "for I've just got it myself.

"What a week! I heard of you—that you were alive, that you were living here—though why you never told me I can't dream—and now,
50   today, Anne! Two such women—and for me. I can call God kind to me. As if I deserved it!"

He did not see her face as he went on rapidly:

"We didn't know it ourselves much more than an hour or so ago—Anne and I. She came out on the same train with me—we finished
55   school together, don't you see! Anne lives in Columbus, fifty miles west. She's fine! I haven't had time to tell you."

He didn't have time now—did not have time to note even yet the sudden pallor which came upon his mother's face. "Anne?" she began.

10. The passage can best be described as a

    (A) social commentary on reuniting broken families
    (B) nostalgic depiction of a mother and son's meeting
    (C) story of how one individual searches for his family

(D) cautionary story about dividing families

(E) portrayal of the crumbling of an enduring relationship

11. In line 4 the sentence beginning "Why, I'd have known you anyhow..." suggests that

(A) Aurora's physical appearance has not changed since Don saw her last

(B) mother and child are always in some way connected

(C) Don has an uncanny resemblance to his mother and is able to easily recognize Aurora

(D) Don and Aurora were destined to meet

(E) Don could only recognize Aurora from the photos that were sent to him

12. Aurora's feelings at meeting her adult son can best be described as

(A) overt joy

(B) lively anticipation

(C) restrained elation

(D) weary surprise

(E) careful hesitation

13. In the context of the passage, the statement "he did not as yet even think of unraveling the veil of ignorance or deceit" (lines 30–31) suggests that Don

(A) has been unaware of the extent of his emotional vulnerability

(B) is frustrated that he was deluded by those closest to him

(C) is too overcome with emotion of the reunion to consider the circumstances

(D) feels guilty about how much she resented his mother

(E) is amazed that he could be mislead by his family

14. In line 15 "noncommittally" most nearly means

(A) excitedly

(B) calmly

(C) indistinctively

(D) impassively

(E) nervously

15. Aurora's observation in lines 33–37 ("That little house… cheeks deepening.") suggests that Aurora

(A) is worried that Don will feel insulted about being invited to her scant home
(B) is embarrassed that she cannot provide a more luxurious setting for Don
(C) is proud of what she has achieved at work and at home
(D) does not want Don to compare her home to his lavish dwellings
(E) is appalled by Don's reaction to her home

16. Don mentions, "We're going to do better out West…" (line 42) in order to

(A) demonstrate that he will provide for his wife
(B) suggest a new location for the family to live together
(C) demand that his mother understand that she can live an improved life
(D) express his yearning to reunite his family
(E) share his aspirations with his mother

17. In lines 47–56, Don's reaction to his mother's response suggests that he

(A) is apathetic to his mother's feelings
(B) trusts that he can persuade his mother to align with his plan
(C) has not contemplated any alternative
(D) does not consider that his mother could disagree with his plan
(E) believes the plan he has formulated is optimal for the family

18. The final sentence, lines 57–58, suggests that Aurora is

(A) disappointed that she will not be able to spend time with Don
(B) resentful that Don met Anne
(C) apprehensive about the future
(D) overjoyed that she will be sharing her travels with Don and Anne
(E) overwhelmed by Don's enthusiasm

Questions 19 through 24 are based on the following passage.

The text is excerpted from a book on myths and legends of Ancient Greece and Rome.

We will now return to Zeus and his brothers, who, having gained a
complete victory over their enemies, began to consider how the
world, which they had conquered, should be divided between them.
At last it was settled by lot that Zeus should reign supreme in
Heaven, whilst Aïdes governed the Lower World, and Poseidon had
full command over the Sea, but the supremacy of Zeus was
recognized in all three kingdoms, in heaven, on earth (in which of
course the sea was included), and under the earth. Zeus held his court
on the top of Mount Olympus, whose summit was beyond the clouds;
the dominions of Aïdes were the gloomy unknown regions below the
earth; and Poseidon reigned over the sea. It will be seen that the
realm of each of these gods was enveloped in mystery. Olympus was
shrouded in mists, Hades was wrapt in gloomy darkness, and the sea
was, and indeed still is, a source of wonder and deep interest. Hence
we see that what to other nationswere merely strange phenomena,
served this poetical and imaginative people as a foundation upon
which to build the wonderful stories of their mythology.

The division of the world being now satisfactorily arranged, it would
seem that all things ought to have gone on smoothly, but such was
not the case. Trouble arose in an unlooked-for quarter. The Giants,
those hideous monsters (some with legs formed of serpents) who had
sprung from the earth and the blood of Uranus, declared war against
the triumphant deities of Olympus, and a struggle ensued, which, in
consequence of Gæa having made these children of hers invincible as
long as they kept their feet on the ground, was wearisome and
protracted. Their mother's precaution, however, was rendered
unavailing by pieces of rock being hurled upon them, which threw
them down, and their feet being no longer placed firmly on their
mother-earth, they were overcome, and this tedious war (which was
called the Gigantomachia) at last came to an end. Among the most
daring of these earth-born giants were Enceladus, Rhoetus, and the
valiant Mimas, who, with youthful fire and energy, hurled against
heaven great masses of rock and burning oak-trees, and defied the
lightnings of Zeus. One of the most powerful monsters who opposed

35 Zeus in this war was called Typhon or Typhoeus. He was the youngest
son of Tartarus and Gæa, and had a hundred heads, with eyes which
struck terror to the beholders, and awe-inspiring voices frightful to
hear. This dreadful monster resolved to conquer both gods and men,
but his plans were at length defeated by Zeus, who, after a violent
40 encounter, succeeded in destroying him with a thunderbolt, but not
before he had so terrified the gods that they had fled for refuge to
Egypt, where they metamorphosed themselves into different animals
and thus escaped.

19. The sentence beginning "We will now return to Zeus..." (lines 1–3)
    implies that

    (A) the world was previously not divided into heaven, earth, and Lower
         world
    (B) Zeus and his brothers defeated incumbent rulers to control the
         world
    (C) Zeus and his brothers sought to divide control of the world into
         sovereign bodies
    (D) the preceding rulers fought intensely to maintain authority of
         the world
    (E) Zeus and his brothers wanted to regain control of the world

20. According to the first paragraph, Greek mythology is based on

    (A) the division of the world into heaven, earth, and Lower world
    (B) a structured belief system rooted on supernatural phenomena
    (C) the mysterious nature of the earth and how it served human
         imagination
    (D) the human-like gods who gained control to rule the earth
    (E) a warring family that holds militant control over the heaven, earth,
         and Lower world

21. In line 23 "triumphant deities of Olympus" refers to

    (A) Zeus and his brothers
    (B) Zeus alone
    (C) the gods of heaven
    (D) people living on Olympus
    (E) Gæa and her children

22. According to paragraph 2, the Giants were defeated because

    (A) they were immune to Zeus's lighting bolt
    (B) their major defense mechanism was compromised
    (C) they were able to protect themselves by firing thunderbolts
    (D) they were not equipped to protect themselves from a large army
    (E) they were not able to adapt to the new environment

23. In line 23 "ensued" most nearly

    (A) terminated
    (B) urbanized
    (C) commenced
    (D) concluded
    (E) settled

24. It can be inferred from lines 41–42 that the gods left for Egypt because

    (A) Zeus was defeated and the gods retreated for safety
    (B) they heard the voice of Typhoeus encourage them to leave Mount Olympus
    (C) Mount Olympus was destroyed during the war Gigantomachia
    (D) they were scared off by Typhoeus
    (E) they were able to morph into animals and thus flee to Egypt

STOP
If you finish before time is called, you may check your work on this section only.
Do not turn to any other section in the test.

Section 4
Time—25 Minutes
18 Questions

Directions: This section contains two types of questions. You have 25 minutes to complete both types. For questions 1–8, solve each problem and decide which is the best of the choices given. Fill in the corresponding circle on the answer sheet. Questions 9–18 require that you solve the problem and record your answers on a grid. A problem may have more than one solution, but only one solution of your choosing may be recorded. No Student-Produced Response question may have a negative solution. You may use any available space for scratch work and for registering your answer.

1. The use of a calculator is permitted.
2. All numbers used are real numbers.
3. Figures that accompany problems in this test are intended to provide information useful in solving the problems. They are drawn as accurately as possible EXCEPT when it is stated in a specific problem that the figure is not drawn to scale. All figures lie in a plane unless otherwise indicated.
4. Unless otherwise specified, the domain of any function f is assumed to be the set of all real numbers x for which $f(x)$ is a real number.

Reference Information

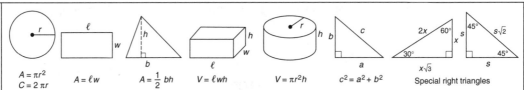

$A = \pi r^2$
$C = 2\pi r$

$A = \ell w$

$A = \frac{1}{2} bh$

$V = \ell w h$

$V = \pi r^2 h$

$c^2 = a^2 + b^2$

Special right triangles

The number of degrees of arc in a circle is 360.
The sum of the measures in degrees of the angles of a triangle is 180.

1. What is the greatest possible area of a triangle with one side of length 8 and another side of length 10?

   (A) 18
   (B) 24
   (C) 40
   (D) 80
   (E) 160

2.

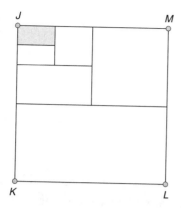

In the figure above, square *JKLM* is made up of six non-overlapping rectangles. The two smallest rectangles have the same area. Each of the other rectangles has twice the area of the next smaller rectangle. The area of the shaded rectangle is what fraction of the area of rectangle *JKLM*?

(A) $\dfrac{1}{4}$

(B) $\dfrac{1}{6}$

(C) $\dfrac{1}{8}$

(D) $\dfrac{1}{32}$

(E) $\dfrac{1}{64}$

3.

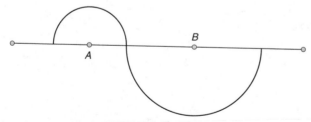

The two semicircles in the figure have centers *A* and *B*, respectively. If *AB* = 18, what is the total length of the darkened curve?

(A) 3π
(B) 6π
(C) 12π
(D) 18π
(E) 36π

4.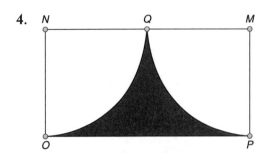

In rectangle *MNOP* above, arcs *QO* and *QP* are quarter circles with centers at *N* and *M*, respectively. If the radius of each quarter circle is 2, what is the area of the shaded region?

(A) $4-2\pi$
(B) $8-2\pi$
(C) $2-4\pi$
(D) $8-4\pi$
(E) $8-8\pi$

5. Grover the dog lives in a dog house. His 1000-foot-long leash is attached to the dog house, allowing him to move freely within a 1000-foot radius of the dog house. Grover walks 700 feet due south. From that point, he walks due west and stops at the maximum range of the leash. In which of the following directions can Grover walk while still attached to his leash?

    I. Due north
   II. Due west
  III. Due south

(A) I only
(B) II only
(C) III only
(D) I and II only
(E) I and III only

6.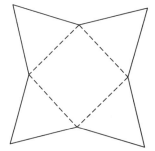

If the area of the square in the figure above is 121 and the perimeter of each of the four triangles is 28, what is the perimeter of the figure outlined by the solid line?

(A) 17
(B) 34
(C) 51
(D) 68
(E) 112

7.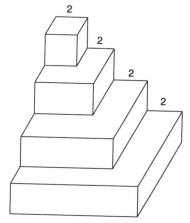

The figure above shows the dimensions of a pedestal constructed of four layers of marble. Each layer is a rectangular solid that is 2 feet high and has a square base. How many cubic feet of marble make up the pedestal?

(A) 36
(B) 72
(C) 128
(D) 240
(E) 248

8. If $w, x, y,$ and z are four nonzero numbers, then all of the following proportions are equivalent except

    (A) $\dfrac{w}{x} = \dfrac{y}{z}$

    (B) $\dfrac{z}{y} = \dfrac{x}{w}$

    (C) $\dfrac{1}{xy} = \dfrac{1}{wz}$

    (D) $\dfrac{w}{z} = \dfrac{y}{x}$

    (E) $1 = \dfrac{xy}{wz}$

9. If a pie is cut into fourths and each fourth is cut into fifths, how many pieces of cake are there?

10.

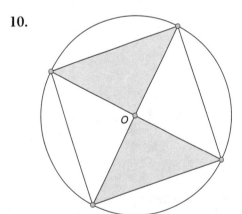

If the shaded region above has a perimeter of $20 + 10\sqrt{2}$ inches, what is the area, in square inches, of the inscribed square?

11. If the distance from $(4, 7)$ to $(5, y)$ is d, and $d = (|-1| + 25)^{1/2}$, what is one possible value of y?

12.

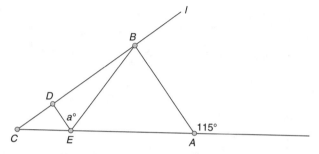

In the figure above, $\overline{DE} \perp \overline{BC}$ and $\overline{BA} \perp \overline{BC}$. If the lengths of $\overline{BA}$ and $\overline{BE}$ are equal, what is the value of a?

13. If $y = \dfrac{k}{x}$, where k is a constant, and if $y = 5$ when $x = 8$, what does y equal when $x = 4$?

14.

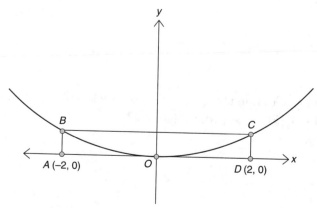

In the figure above, $ABCD$ is a rectangle, and points B and C lie on the graph of $y = cx^2$, where c is a constant. If the perimeter of $ABCD$ is 12, what is the value of c?

15. If $8(a + b)(a - b) = 48$ and $x - y = 2$, what is the value of $x - y$?

16. The average (arithmetic mean) of the test scores of a class of x students is 74, and the average of the test scores of a class of y students is 88. When the scores of both classes are combined, the average score is 83. What is the value of $\dfrac{x}{y}$?

17. If $a^2 - b^2 = 40$ and $a - b = 5$, what is the value of a?

18. Let the function g be defined by $g(x) = x^2 + 32$. If k is a positive number such that $g(2k) = 3g(k)$, what is the value of k?

Section 6
Time—25 minutes
35 questions

Turn to Section 6 (page 426) of your answer sheet to answer the questions in this section.

Directions: For each question in this section, select the best answer from among the answer choices given and fill in the corresponding circle on the answer sheet.

The following sentences test correctness and effectiveness of expression. Part of each sentence or the entire sentence is underlined; beneath each sentence are five ways of phrasing the underlined material. Choice A repeats the original phrasing; the other four choices are different. If you thing the original phrasing produces a better sentence than any of the alternatives, select choice A; if not, select one of the other choices.

In making your selection, follow the requirements of standard written English; that is, pay attention to grammar, choice of words, sentence construction, and punctuation. Your selection should result in the most effective sentence—clear and precise, without awkwardness or ambiguity.

Example:

The numerous biographies published about Roosevelt's life <u>are testament to his great achievements</u>.

(A) are testament to his great achievements
(B) is testament to his great achievements
(C) **stand as a testament for his great achievement**
(D) full of achievement, the books are testament
(E) are testaments to his great achievements

---

1. Bobby <u>has nearly annoyed every babysitter he has had</u>.

   (A) has nearly annoyed every babysitter he has had.
   (B) has every babysitter annoyed
   (C) has annoyed nearly every babysitter he has had
   (D) annoyed every babysitter nearly who he has had
   (E) has had every babysitter annoyed

2. The beloved teacher always had enthusiastic students in his classroom <u>and they asked many questions</u>.

   (A) and they asked many questions
   (B) who asked many questions
   (C) with whom they asked many questions
   (D) and many questions were asked
   (E) asked about many questions

3. Her terror of vampires <u>kept her out of the dark basement</u>.

   (A) kept her out of the dark basement
   (B) keeps him out of the dark basement
   (C) has kept her out of the dark basement
   (D) had kept her out of her the dark basement
   (E) has been keeping her out of the dark basement

4. The keys Larry <u>looked at are</u> under the sofa.

   (A) looked at are
   (B) looked for are
   (C) was looking for
   (D) looking at are
   (E) has been looking are

5. <u>As I had studied for the test with my teacher, I</u> was confident that I would do well.

   (A) As I had studied for the test with my teacher, I
   (B) As I had studied for the test with my teacher I
   (C) As I studied for the test with my teacher, I
   (D) Because I studied for the test with my teacher I
   (E) Since I had studied for the test with my teacher I

6. In today's class we'll discuss different types of statistical analysis, <u>suggest useful techniques for recognizing mathematical patterns, providing you with sample calculations to try</u>.

   (A) suggest useful techniques for recognizing mathematical patterns, providing you with sample calculations to try
   (B) suggesting useful techniques for recognition of mathematical patterns, providing you with sample calculations to try

(C) suggest useful techniques for recognizing mathematical patterns, and provide you with sample calculations to try

(D) suggest useful techniques in recognition of mathematical patterns, and provide you with sample calculations to try

(E) suggesting useful techniques for recognizing mathematical patterns, providing you with sample calculations to try

7. <u>It is normal for tourists to visit Pushkar from all over India</u>, especially in the fall, to participate in the camel fair.

(A) It is normal for tourists to visit Pushkar from all over India

(B) Normally, tourists from all over India visit Pushkar

(C) Tourists visit Pushkar normally from all over India

(D) All over India, tourists normally visit Pushkar

(E) It is normal for Indian tourists to visit Pushkar

8. Everybody <u>was enjoying their vacation</u>.

(A) was enjoying their vacation

(B) enjoyed their vacations

(C) had enjoyment in their vacations

(D) was enjoying his/her vacation

(E) had enjoys his/her vacation

9. The famous musician visited our school <u>and performed with the band</u> at the holiday concert.

(A) and performed with the band

(B) with the band's performance

(C) and would perform with the band

(D) and with the band performed

(E) in order to perform with the band

10. <u>A born scientist who trained with the best researchers in biology, Dr. Lauren's groundbreaking discoveries</u> brought her international fame and praise.

(A) A born scientist who trained with the best researchers in biology, Dr. Lauren's groundbreaking discoveries

(B) A born scientist; who trained with the best researchers in biology, Dr. Lauren's groundbreaking discoveries

(C) A born scientist, having trained with the best researchers in biology, Dr. Lauren's groundbreaking discoveries

(D) Dr. Lauren's training, in addition to being a born scientist, resulted in grounding breaking discoveries that

(E) Dr. Lauren's training, in addition to being a born scientist, resulted in grounding breaking discoveries which

11. In this <u>example, if you understand how to derive the variable, you know</u> enough information to solve the problem.

(A) example, if you understand how to derive the variable, you know

(B) example if you understand how to derive the variable you know

(C) example if you understand how to derive the variable, you know

(D) example, if you understand how to derive the variable than you know

(E) example, if you understood how to derive the variable, you know

---

The following sentences test your ability to recognize grammar and usage errors. Each sentence contains either a single error or no error at all. No sentence contains more than one error. The error, if there is one, is underlined and lettered. If the sentence contains an error, select the one underlined part that must be changed to make the sentence correct. If the sentence is correct, select choice E. In choosing answers, follow the requires of standard written English.

Example:

<u>The other boys</u> and <u>him quickly</u> agreed <u>to meet</u> at the nearby pizza parlor.
    A   B   C   D

<u>No error.</u>
  E

---

12. Although the local airport <u>remains closed</u> to air traffic, <u>nearly</u> half a
                               A   B   C
million visitors <u>somehow make</u> their way to the historic city each year.
              D

<u>No error.</u>
  E

13. Paula, <u>whose</u> the president of the <u>club, was</u> the <u>first</u> to speak. <u>No error</u>.
     A   B   C   D   E

14. <u>Sizzling on the skillet</u>, Laurie <u>could not resist</u> the smell of her <u>mother's</u>
     A   B   C   D
delicious cooking. <u>No error</u>.
                   E

15. Lauren <u>thinks that</u> she <u>is allergic to</u> apples and <u>raw</u> peanuts. <u>No error</u>.
            A   B C   D   E

16. I wonder <u>if</u> you would <u>be willing</u> to dress up <u>as</u> an angel or a devil <u>for</u>
           A   B   C   D
Halloween. <u>No error</u>.
        E

17. The ultimate <u>effect</u> of all of the false-alarm calls <u>to</u> the fireman <u>were</u> to
             A   B   C
make them suspicious of the <u>callers</u>. <u>No error</u>.
                         D   E

18. The contract <u>had</u> to <u>be signed</u> by <u>both</u> Thomas and <u>me</u>. <u>No error</u>.
         A   B   C   D   E

19. Ben, <u>along with</u> his <u>younger</u> sister, <u>are</u> coming to the party at <u>Glen's</u>
          A   B   C   D
house. <u>No error</u>.
      E

20. <u>The kidnapping</u> scene <u>from</u> the horror movie <u>scared her</u> and <u>me</u>. <u>No error</u>.
        A   B   C   D   E

21. <u>Each of</u> the children <u>have</u> to carry their <u>own</u> books <u>and lunches</u>. <u>No error</u>.
     A   B   C   D   E

22. <u>To keep</u> them from <u>fighting</u>, each dog <u>has been</u> given its <u>own</u> set of toys.
     A   B   C   D
<u>No error</u>.
  E

23. I want to travel to either India or France, but I have neither the time and
   A   B   C
the money I need. No error.
           D   E

24. Although Clair was not aloud to watch television on most school days,
                        A   B
she was permitted to watch her favorite show on Wednesdays. No error.
    C   D   E

25. If I would have known about the homework, I would have completed it.
  A   B   C   D
No error.
  E

26. I never would of thought that our small puppy would grow up to a
         A   B   C   D
150 pound behemoth. No error.
                  E

27. After he joined the team, Wilson appears at all the practices and never
     A   B   C
missed a game. No error.
  D   E

28. As a young girl, she heard her mother tell stories of her years as a circus
    A   B   C   D
clown. No error.
     E

29. My brothers or my sisters come every day to help me with homework.
          A   B   C   D
No error.
  E

> **Directions:** The following passage is an early draft of an essay. Some parts of the passage need to be rewritten.
>
> Read the passage carefully and select the best answers for the questions that follow. Some questions are about particular sentences or parts of sentences and ask you to improve sentence structure or word choice. Other questions ask you to consider organization and development. In choosing answers, follow the requirements of standard written English.

(1) Throughout one's life love and emotional attachment may affect how the person behaves. (2) In the novel *The Great Gatsby*, by F. Scott Fitzgerald, there is a character named Jay Gatsby and his emotions drive his actions. (3) He is a very wealthy man who makes his money through illegal activity. (4) The characters of the book do not know this. (5) Although, it's for a good cause in his life, it does not serve him well. (6) His main motivation for earning money is to entice his one true love, Daisy Buchanan. (7) Jay ignores Daisy's shortcomings: he does not notice her obsession of money or her single-mindedness. (8) Lastly, Jay loses responsibility for everything, he throws parties without knowing any of the guests and he allows people to take control of his life, mainly Daisy. (9) Daisy on the other hand just falls in love with who the person that has the most amount of money. (10) She has no care for anyone except herself. (11) Gatsby tries so hard to get Daisy back in his hands that he completely destroys his life.

30. In context, which is the best way to revise sentence 2 (reproduced below)?

    In the novel The Great Gatsby, *by F. Scott Fitzgerald, there is a character named Jay Gatsby and his emotions drive his actions.*

    (A) In the novel *The Great Gatsby*, by F. Scott Fitzgerald, there is a character named Jay Gatsby who shows us how his emotions drive his actions.
    (B) In the novel *The Great Gatsby*, F. Scott Fitzgerald introduces to us the character named Jay Gatsby and shows us how his emotions drive his actions.
    (C) In the novel, *The Great Gatsby*, by F. Scott Fitzgerald, the character of Jay Gatsby demonstrates how emotions may drive actions.
    (D) F. Scott Fitzgerald in his novel *The Great Gatsby* demonstrates how emotions may drive actions through the character of Jay Gatsby.
    (E) Jay Gatsby of F. Scott Fitzgerald's novel *The Great Gatsby* is an example of how emotions drive actions.

31. What should be done with sentence 4 (reproduced below)?

    The characters of the book do not know this.

    (A) (as is now)
    (B) Delete it
    (C) Insert "is" after sentence 5
    (D) Add the word "information" after the word "this"
    (E) Add the word "However" to the beginning of the sentence

32. In context, which of the following is the best way to revise sentences 5 and 6 in order to combine the sentences?

    (A) Although, it's for a good cause in his life, the enticement of his one true love, Daisy Buchanan, it does not serve him well to earn money.
    (B) Although, his main motivation for earning money is for the good cause of enticing his one true love, Daisy Buchanan, it does not serve him well.
    (C) Gatsby's main motivation for earning money is to entice his one true love, Daisy Buchanan and this does not serve him well.
    (D) Gatsby is motived to earn money to entice his one true love, Daisy Buchanan, however, this does not serve him well.
    (E) Gatsby is not served well by trying to entice his one true love, Daisy Buchanan, with the money he earns.

33. In context, which of the following is the best way to revise sentence 8 (reproduced below)?

    Lastly, Jay let's go of responsibility for everything, he throws parties without knowing any of the guests and he allows people to take control of his life, mainly Daisy.

    (A) Lastly, Jay let's go of responsibility for everything, he starts to throw parties without knowing any of the guests and he allows people to take control of his life, mainly Daisy.
    (B) Finally, Jay let's go of responsibility for everything, he throws parties without knowing any of the guests and he allows people to take control of his life, mainly Daisy.
    (C) Lastly, Jay let's go of control over his life: he throws parties without knowing the guests and allows other people, especially Daisy, to control his life.

(D) Ultimately, Jay surrenders responsibility for his actions: he throws parties without knowing the guests and allows other people, especially Daisy, to control his life.

(E) The ultimate letting go of responsibility happens when Jay throws parties without knowing the guests and allows other people, especially Daisy, to control his life.

34. In context, what is the best revision for sentence 4 (reproduced below)?

Daisy on the other hand just falls in love with who the person that has the most amount of money.

(A) Daisy on the other hand just falls in love with who the person who has the most amount of money.

(B) Daisy, on the other hand, just falls in love with who the person that has the most amount of money is.

(C) Unlike other characters, Daisy falls in love with the person who has the most amount of money.

(D) Daisy, unlike Jay, just falls in love with the person that has amassed the most amount of money.

(E) Unlike Jay, Daisy just falls in love with the person who has the most amount of money.

35. What should be done with sentence 11 (reproduced below)?

Gatsby tries so hard to get Daisy back in his hands that he completely destroys his life.

(A) (as is now)
(B) Insert it after sentence 7
(C) Insert it before sentence 9
(D) Delete it
(E) Add "On the other hand" at the beginning of the sentence

STOP
If you finish before time is called, you may check your work on this section only.
Do not turn to any other section in the test.

Section 7
Time—25 minutes
24 questions

Turn to Section 7 (page 427) of your answer sheet to answer the questions in this section.

Directions: For each question in this section, select the best answer from among the answer choices given and fill in the corresponding circle on the answer sheet.

Each sentence below has one or two question blanks, each blank indicating that something has been omitted. Beneath the sentence are five words or sets of words labeled A through E. Choose the word or set of words that, when inserted in the sentence, best fits the meaning of the sentence as a whole.

Example:

Susan preferred to be _____, hoping to avoid confusion due to miscommunication.
(A) **direct**
(B) devious
(C) cunning
(D) austere
(E) terse

1. The conference produced _____ results, including agreements on the curriculum and information on how to improve literacy in elementary school children.

    (A) concrete
    (B) stimulating
    (C) innovative
    (D) conflicting
    (E) primeval

2. The record-breaking heat wave tried the _____ and _____ of those who dared to venture outside.

    (A) fortitude...serenity
    (B) tolerance...pushiness

    (C) patience... resilience
    (D) resolve...outcome
    (E) interest...beseech

3. Although the detectives battled to collect evidence, the ____ piece of the puzzle could not be found and the case remained unsolved.

    (A) elusive
    (B) intangible
    (C) palpable
    (D) important
    (E) inconsequential

4. Samantha ____ agreed to attend the performance even though she ____ classical music.

    (A) reluctantly...loathed
    (B) hesitantly...adored
    (C) enthusiastically...abhorred
    (D) amiably...revered
    (E) credulously...enjoyed

5. After months of searching for employment, only one opportunity ____.

    (A) aggrandized
    (B) ruminated
    (C) materialized
    (D) receded
    (E) perished

6. The grandfather's ____ startled his grandson who was used to a more ____ attitude from the patriarch of the family.

    (A) injunction...blithe
    (B) inattention...agreeable
    (C) imprudence...austere
    (D) consideration...ubiquitous
    (E) squabble...raucous

7. Years of past successes help explain the team's _____ optimism, even as it struggled in today's tournament.

    (A) unrelenting
    (B) fleeting
    (C) stamina
    (D) recalcitrant
    (E) hapless

8. Because Paul Cèzanne's work was a catalyst for the abstract art of the 20th century and paved the way for later modern artists, he is considered the _____ of that style.

    (A) connoisseur
    (B) revivalist
    (C) beneficiary
    (D) disparager
    (E) progenitor

The passages below are followed by questions based on their content; questions that follow a pair of related passages may also be based on the relationship between the paired passages. Answer the questions on the basis of what is *stated* or *implied* in the passage in any introductory material that may be provided.

Questions 9 through 12 are based on the following passages.

Passage 1

In no country have women reached a mobilization so complete and systematized as in Great Britain. This mobilization covers the whole

Line field of war service—in industry, business and professional life, and in government administration. Women serve on the Ministry of Food

5   and are included in the membership of twenty-five of the important government committees, not auxiliary or advisory, but administrative committees, such as those on War Pensions, on Disabled Officers and Men, on Education after the War, and the Labor Commission to Deal with Industrial Unrest.

10   In short, the women of Great Britain are working side by side with
     men in the initiation and execution of plans to solve the problems
     which confront the nation.

     Four committees, as for instance those making investigations and
     recommendations on Women's Wages and Drink Among Women, are
15   entirely composed of women, and great departments, such as the
     Women's Land Army, the Women's Army Auxiliary Corps, are
     officered throughout by them. Hospitals under the War Office have
     been placed in complete control of medical women; they take rank
     with medical men in the army and receive the pay going with their
     commissions.

9.   The primary purpose of this passage is to

   (A) give a brief history of women's role in government administration
   (B) place female labor in the context of the war
   (C) detail women's fight for labor equality
   (D) establish that women are capable of working alongside men
   (E) demonstrate the wide inclusion of women in the workforce

10.   In line 11 "initiation" most nearly means

   (A) training
   (B) admittance
   (C) formulation
   (D) implementation
   (E) supervision

Passage 2

     You have had your first glimpse of Prague, and it was beautiful, so
     you set about endeavouring to enter into the spirit of the place, to
Line absorb its atmosphere and to study its character. For every ancient
     city that has stood up against adversity and overcome it has a very
5   definite character of its own. And it is a mysterious, wonderful thing
     this character, this cachet of a great city; the charm of Paris or the
     grandeur of London, the glittering stillness of Venice or the insistent
     glory of eternal Rome.

The character of a city, as is that of man, is formed by experience,
10 chiefly adverse, and is made evident by the work the city has done for
humanity, its creator and its care. From the study of a city's character
may you look into its future and presage whether it be likely to
achieve success or doomed to failure. For there have been failures
among cities as among men, some pathetic owing to inherent
15 weakness, others as a consequence of their own misdeeds.

11. The sentence beginning "And it is a mysterious…" (line 5 is used to demonstrate the

    (A) parallels between Prague and Paris
    (B) idiosyncratic nature of a city's character
    (C) importance of Rome's history
    (D) distinctiveness of Prague
    (E) common attributes of various great cities

12. It can be inferred from this passage that the future of a city can be predi-
cated based on

    (A) understanding the city's history
    (B) comparing the city to other great cities
    (C) calculating the demographic make-up of the city
    (D) reviewing the city's past success
    (E) knowing who designed the city's architecture

Questions 13 through 24 are based on the following passages.

The following passages consider the experience of war nurses. Passage 1 is an account of a hospital environment during the Civil War. In Passage 2 a nurse recounts her time at a French field hospital during WWI.

Passage 1

The first thing I met was a regiment of the vilest odors that ever
assaulted the human nose, and took it by storm. Cologne, with its
Line seven and seventy evil savors, was a posy-bed to it; and the worst of
this affliction was, every one had assured me that it was a chronic
5 weakness of all hospitals, and I must bear it. I did, armed with
lavender water, with which I so besprinkled myself and premises, that,
like my friend Sairy, I was soon known among my patients as "the

nurse with the bottle." Having been run over by three excited
surgeons, bumped against by migratory coal-hods, water-pails, and
10   small boys, nearly scalded by an avalanche of newly-filled tea-pots,
and hopelessly entangled in a knot of colored sisters coming to wash,
I progressed by slow stages up stairs and down, till the main hall was
reached, and I paused to take breath and a survey. There they were!
"our brave boys," as the papers justly call them, for cowards could
15   hardly have been so riddled with shot and shell, so torn and shattered,
nor have borne suffering for which we have no name, with an
uncomplaining fortitude, which made one glad to cherish each as a
brother. In they came, some on stretchers, some in men's arms, some
feebly staggering along propped on rude crutches, and one lay stark
20   and still with covered face, as a comrade gave his name to be recorded
before they carried him away to the dead house. All was hurry and
confusion; the hall was full of these wrecks of humanity, for the most
exhausted could not reach a bed till duly ticketed and registered; the
walls were lined with rows of such as could sit, the floor covered with
25   the more disabled, the steps and doorways filled with helpers and
lookers on; the sound of many feet and voices made that usually quiet
hour as noisy as noon; and, in the midst of it all, the matron's
motherly face brought more comfort to many a poor soul, than the
cordial draughts she administered, or the cheery words that
30   welcomed all, making of the hospital a home.

The sight of several stretchers, each with its legless, armless, or
desperately wounded occupant, entering my ward, admonished me
that I was there to work, not to wonder or weep; so I corked up my
feelings, and returned to the path of duty, which was rather "a hard
35   road to travel" just then. The house had been a hotel before hospitals
were needed, and many of the doors still bore their old names; some
not so inappropriate as might be imagined, for my ward was in truth
a ball-room, if gun-shot wounds could christen it. Forty beds were
prepared, many already tenanted by tired men who fell down
40   anywhere, and drowsed till the smell of food roused them. Round the
great stove was gathered the dreariest group I ever saw—ragged,
gaunt and pale, mud to the knees, with bloody bandages untouched
since put on days before; many bundled up in blankets, coats being
lost or useless; and all wearing that disheartened look which

45   proclaimed defeat, more plainly than any telegram of the Burnside
      blunder. I pitied them so much, I dared not speak to them, though,
      remembering all they had been through since the rout at
      Fredericksburg, I yearned to serve the dreariest of them all. Presently,
50   Miss Blank tore me from my refuge behind piles of one-sleeved shirts,
      odd socks, bandages and lint…

Passage 2

      THIS is how it was. It is pretty much always like this in a field
      hospital. Just ambulances rolling in, and dirty, dying men, and the
Line guns off there in the distance! Very monotonous, and the same, day
      after day, till one gets so tired and bored. Big things may be going on
5   over there, on the other side of the captive balloons that we can see
      from a distance, but we are always here, on this side of them, and
      here, on this side of them, it is always the same. The weariness of
      it—the sameness of it! The same ambulances, and dirty men, and
      groans, or silence. The same hot operating rooms, the same beds,
10   always full, in the wards. This is war. But it goes on and on, over and
      over, day after day, till it seems like life. Life in peace time. It might be
      life in a big city hospital, so alike is the routine. Only the city hospitals
      are bigger, and better equipped, and the ambulances are smarter, and
      the patients don't always come in ambulances—they walk in
15   sometimes, or come in street cars, or in limousines, and they are of
      both sexes, men and women, and have ever so many things the matter
      with them—the hospitals of peace time are not nearly so stupid, so
      monotonous, as the hospitals of war. Bah! War's humane compared to
      peace! More spectacular, I grant you, more acute,—that's what
20   interests us,—but for the sheer agony of life—oh, peace is way ahead!

      War is so clean. Peace is so dirty. There are so many foul diseases in
      peace times. They drag on over so many years, too. No, war's clean! I'd
      rather see a man die in prime of life, in war time, than see him
      doddering along in peace time, broken hearted, broken spirited, life
25   broken, and very weary, having suffered many things,—to die at last, at
      a good, ripe age! How they have suffered, those who drive up to our
      city hospitals in limousines, in peace time. What's been saved them,
      those who die young, and clean and swiftly, here behind the guns. In
      the long run it dots up just the same. Only war's spectacular, that's all.

13. The tone of Passage 1 is

    (A) reflective anticipation
    (B) anxious compassion
    (C) unrestrained excitement
    (D) detached analysis
    (E) incomprehensible fear

14. The narrator of Passage 1 uses the phrase "a hard road to travel" (lines 34–35) to demonstrate that

    (A) nursing is a dreadful profession
    (B) hospitals are not connected by dependable roads
    (C) attending to patients is a arduous responsibility
    (D) it is difficult to contain one's emotions and return to work
    (E) soldiers have a hard time locating hospitals

15. As described in lines 8–13 of Passage 1, atmosphere in the hospital is most nearly one of

    (A) excitement
    (B) commotion
    (C) urgency
    (D) sanctity
    (E) devastation

16. In line 50 of Passage 1, "tore" most nearly means

    (A) ripped
    (B) snatched
    (C) charged
    (D) injured
    (E) removed

17. Passage 2 is narrated from the point of view of

    (A) a historian and an expert on hospital environments
    (B) an apathetic observer
    (C) an administrator at a war hospital
    (D) an observer who is familiar with the routines of war and civilian hospitals
    (E) a soldier at a war hospital who has previously experienced a civilian hospital

18. The narrator of Passage 2 states that "Big things…always the same" (lines 4–7) to

    (A) underscore the isolated experience of the hospital
    (B) illustrate the exciting nature of battle
    (C) contrast the relative exhilaration of the operating room and battle field
    (D) elicit sympathy from the reader for the boredom that nurses experience
    (E) communicate her desire to be on the other side

19. The narrator of Passage 2 suggests that war is like life (lines 6–12) because both

    (A) are cyclical and routine
    (B) are made up of life and death
    (C) have surgeons working in hospitals
    (D) are dirty and disappointing
    (E) have suffering

20. In Passage 2, line 25 the word "weary" most closely means

    (A) pained
    (B) worn down
    (C) sleepy
    (D) sardonic
    (E) exultant

21. The narrator's tone in Passage 2 is

    (A) judiciously impartial
    (B) bitterly apologetic
    (C) jubilantly frank
    (D) scathingly intolerant
    (E) positively supportive

22. The primary purpose of Passage 2 is to

    (A) romanticize wartime medicine
    (B) cultivate patriotism
    (C) offer an interpretation of military experience
    (D) juxtapose treatment procedures of different hospitals
    (E) recount the experiences of a hospital nurse

23. With which of the following statements would authors of BOTH passages most likely agree?

    (A) The transition from peacetime to wartime medicine is tedious
    (B) During and after the war, patients benefited from advances in medicine
    (C) Illness and injury are unjust
    (D) Nurses are primarily necessary during time of war
    (E) Hospitals are by nature repressive environments

24. The narrator of Passage 1 would most likely interpret the description of war medicine by the narrator of Passage 2 in lines 21–29 ("War is so clean…") as being

    (A) disturbing, because of the suffering that soldiers endure
    (B) one-sided, since the second narrator has not worked in a hospital
    (C) astonishing, because almost nothing can be done for wounded soldiers
    (D) disheartening, because fewer people die during peace time than war time
    (E) accurate, because injuries that occur during war are consistent

STOP
If you finish before time is called, you may check your work on this section only.
Do not turn to any other section in the test.

Section 8
Time—20 Minutes
16 Questions

Directions: For this section, solve each problem and decide which is the best of the choices given. Fill in the corresponding circle on the answer sheet. You may use any available space for scratch work.

---

1. The use of a calculator is permitted.
2. All numbers used are real numbers.
3. Figures that accompany problems in this test are intended to provide information useful in solving the problems. They are drawn as accurately as possible EXCEPT when it is stated in a specific problem that the figure is not drawn to scale. All figures lie in a plane unless otherwise indicated.
4. Unless otherwise specified, the domain of any function f is assumed to be the set of all real numbers x for which $f(x)$ is a real number.

Reference Information

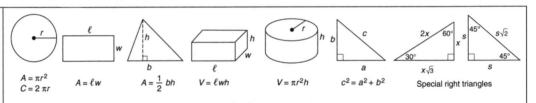

$A = \pi r^2$
$C = 2\pi r$

$A = \ell w$

$A = \frac{1}{2} bh$

$V = \ell wh$

$V = \pi r^2 h$

$c^2 = a^2 + b^2$

Special right triangles

The number of degrees of arc in a circle is 360.
The sum of the measures in degrees of the angles of a triangle is 180.

---

1. If x is 50% greater than y, and y is 40% less than 400, what is the value of $x - y$?

   (A) 60
   (B) 80
   (C) 120
   (D) 240
   (E) 280

2. If $z = \dfrac{3x^3}{y}$, what happens to the value of z when both x and y are doubled?

   (A) z is halved.
   (B) z is doubled.

(C) *z* is tripled.

(D) *z* is multiplied by 4.

(E) *z* is multiplied by 12.

3. If the domain of *f* is given by *x* = {0, 2, 3}, what is the range of the function $f(x) = x^2 - 5x + 6$?

(A) $f(x) = \{0, 6\}$

(B) $f(x) = \{-6, 0, 6\}$

(C) $-6 \le f(x) \le 6$

(D) $0 \le f(x) \le 6$

(E) $f(x) = \{12\}$

4. A certain population of animal *M* loses one-third of its inhabitants every 12 years. If animal *M* has a population of 243,000 animals, how large a population will *M* have after 36 years?

(A) 0

(B) 72,000

(C) 81,000

(D) 108,000

(E) 162,000

5.

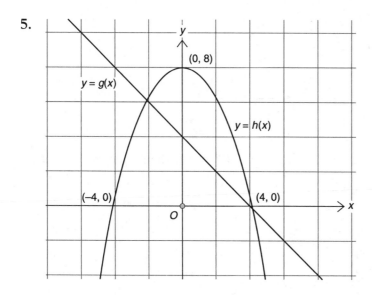

Based on the portions of the graphs of the functions *g* and *h* shown above, what are all values of *x* between −5 and 5 for which $g(x) > h(x)$?

(A) $-4 < x < -2$ only
(B) $-1 < x < 4$ only
(C) $-2 < x < 4$ only
(D) $-5 < x < -1$ and $4 < x < 5$
(E) $-5 < x < -2$ and $4 < x < 5$

6. If x and y are positive integers, which of the following is equivalent to $(3y)^{4x} + (3y)^{x}$?

(A) $(3y)^{3x}$
(B) $3^{x}(y^{4} + y^{x})$
(C) $(3y)^{x}[(3y)^{3x} + 1]$
(D) $(3y)^{x}(27y^{x} + 1)$
(E) $(3y)^{x}[(3y)^{4} + 1]$

7.

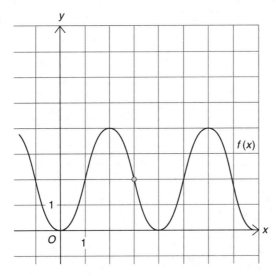

In the figure above, if the value of $f(1) = c$, then what is the value of $f(2c)$?

(A) 0
(B) 1
(C) 2
(D) 3
(E) 4

8.   If the function h is defined by $h(x) = ax^2 + bx + c$, and a is negative while c is positive, which of the following could be the graph of the function h?

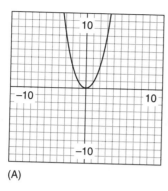

(A)

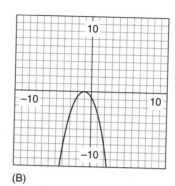

(B)

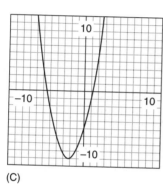

(C)

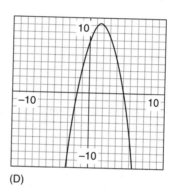

(D)

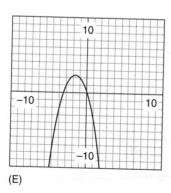

(E)

9. If j, k, and z are consecutive even integers such that $0 < j < k < z$ and the units (ones) digit of the product jz is 6, what is least possible value of k?

    (A) 4
    (B) 10
    (C) 15
    (D) 16
    (E) 20

10. If m and n are positive integers and $3(9^m) = 3^n$, what is m in terms of n?

    (A) $2n + 1$
    (B) $n - 1$
    (C) $\dfrac{1}{2}n - \dfrac{1}{2}$
    (D) $n + 1$
    (E) $\dfrac{1}{2}n - 1$

11. If $w = x^{-\frac{3}{4}}$ and $x = y^2$, what is the value of w in terms of y?

    (A) $\sqrt{y^3}$

    (B) $\dfrac{1}{\sqrt[3]{y^2}}$

    (C) $-\sqrt{y^3}$

    (D) $\sqrt[3]{y^2}$

    (E) $\dfrac{1}{\sqrt{y^3}}$

12.

Dish	Total Population	Population Density
X	1,200,000	800 bacteria per square millimeter
Y	4,500,000	900 bacteria per square millimeter

The table above shows populations of two bacteria and their population densities on two different culture dishes. The number of square millimeters in the area of Dish X is approximately how much less than the number of square millimeters in the area of Dish Y?

(A) 1500
(B) 1950
(C) 3350
(D) 3500
(E) 5000

13. Set U has j members and set V has k members. Set W is the union of sets U and V and two additional members that are not in U or V. Sets U and V have m common members. Which of the following represents the number of elements in set W?

(A) $j + k + 2 + m$
(B) $2m + 2 - j - k$
(C) $j + 2 + k - m$
(D) $j + k - 2 + 2m$
(E) $j + k - 2 - m$

14. Let $w \cup x \cup y$ be defined by the equation $w \cup x \cup y = wxy - \dfrac{wy}{x}$ for all non-zero numbers w, x, y. Which of the following is equal to an odd integer?

(A) $6 \cup 3 \cup 2$
(B) $5 \cup 7 \cup 9$
(C) $14 \cup 2 \cup 3$
(D) $4 \cup 2 \cup 5$
(E) $9 \cup 3 \cup 6$

15. If a, b, and c are positive numbers greater than 1, and $\dfrac{ab + bc}{a^2 + c^2} = \dfrac{b^2}{a + c}$ then $b =$

(A) 1
(B) $2ac$
(C) $\dfrac{a^2 + c^2}{a + c}$
(D) $a + c$
(E) $\dfrac{(a + c)^2}{a^2 + c^2}$

16.

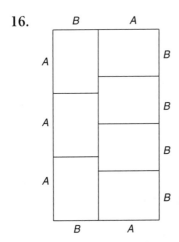

The pattern shown above is composed of rectangles. This pattern is used repeatedly to completely cover a rectangular region 14*A* units wide and 15*A* units long. How many rectangles of dimension *A* by *B* are needed?

(A) 35
(B) 40
(C) 70
(D) 210
(E) 280

Section 9
Time—20 minutes
19 questions

Turn to Section 9 (page 427) of your answer sheet to answer the questions in this section.

Directions: For each question in this section, select the best answer from among the answer choices given and fill in the corresponding circle on the answer sheet.

Each sentence below has one or two question blanks, each blank indicating that something has been omitted. Beneath the sentence are five words or sets of words labeled A through E. Choose the word or set of words that, when inserted in the sentence, <u>best</u> fits the meaning of the sentence as a whole.

Example:

Susan preferred to be ____, hoping to avoid confusion due to miscommunication.
(A) **direct**
(B) devious
(C) cunning
(D) austere
(E) terse

1. The aspiring actress was ____ to be at a school where creativity was encouraged.

     (A) servile
     (B) fortunate
     (C) pilfered
     (D) luminous
     (E) flagrant

2. Dr. Butler, a renowned scientist whose work ____ significant changes in environmental policy, was honored by the President.

     (A) formed
     (B) instigated
     (C) debased
     (D) jaded
     (E) accommodated

3. Eleanor's enthusiasm for modern art led her to _____ an important collection that rivaled those of many museums.

   (A) amass
   (B) formulate
   (C) experience
   (D) decimate
   (E) curate

4. Like many linguists, Peter has a/an _____ memory, and can quickly summon into consciousness the words of famous speakers.

   (A) formidable
   (B) sporadic
   (C) tremulous
   (D) undulating
   (E) verdant

5. Many of the art works that are stored in the basement are so decayed that their once _____ colors have become washed out.

   (A) opaque
   (B) resplendent
   (C) lackluster
   (D) dense
   (E) stagnate

6. The reform bill that Congress appears ready to pass is not the _____ for the crises that some hoped for or wanted.

   (A) panacea
   (B) auspices
   (C) coterie
   (D) élan
   (E) respite

The passages below are followed by questions based on their content; questions that follow a pair of related passages may also be based on the relationship between the paired passages. Answer the questions on the basis of what is *stated* or *implied* in the passage in any introductory material that may be provided.

Questions 7 through 19 are based on the following passages.

The following excerpt is from a historical work that examines the customs and beliefs of Native American peoples.

Faith in the revelations of astrology was a deeply rooted superstition with the Aztecs. It pervaded the whole structure of society, affecting the most intelligent and well-informed, as well as the humblest and most ignorant individual. In this case, the prophetic wailings of the
5   priestly oracle rolled, like a long funereal knell, through the magnificent halls of the imperial palace, and fell upon the ear of the monarch, as if it had been a voice from the unseen world. Montezuma was reclining on a splendidly embroidered couch, in his private apartment, anxiously awaiting the response of the celestial
10   oracle. He was magnificently arrayed in his royal robes of green, richly ornamented with variegated feather-work, and elaborately inwrought with gold and silver. His sandals were of pure gold, with ties and anklets of gold and silver thread, curiously interwoven with a variegated cotton cord. On his head was a rich fillet of gold, with a
15   beautiful plume bending gracefully over one side, casting a melancholy shade over his handsome but naturally pensive features. A few of the royal princes sat, in respectful silence, at the farther end of the chamber, waiting, with an anxiety almost equal to that of the monarch, the return of the royal messenger.

20   The emperor leaned pensively on his hand, seemingly oppressed with some superstitious melancholy forebodings. Perhaps the shadow of that mysterious prophecy, which betokened the extinction of the Aztec dynasty, and the consequent ruin of his house, was passing athwart the troubled sky of his mind, veiling the always doubtful
25   future in mists of tenfold dimness. Whatever it was that disturbed his royal serenity, his reverie was soon broken by the sound of an approaching footstep. For a moment, nothing was heard but the measured tread of the trembling messenger, pacing with unwilling

step the long corridor, that led to the royal presence. With his head
30 bowed upon his breast, his eyes fixed upon the pavement, his person
veiled in a coarse cloth, and his feet bare, he stood before the
monarch, dumb as a statue.

"What response bring you," eagerly enquired the emperor, "from the
burning oracles of heaven? How reads the destiny of my new-born
35 infant?"

"The response be to the enemies of the great Montezuma," replied
the messenger, without lifting his eyes from the floor, "and the destiny
it foreshadows to the children of them that hate him."

"Speak," exclaimed the monarch, "What message do you bring from
40 the priest of the stars?"

"Alas! my royal master, my message is full of woe—my heart faints,
and my tongue refuses its office to give it utterance. The old prophet
bade me say, that the celestial influences are all unpropitious; that the
destiny of the infant princess is a life of sorrow, with a gleam of more
45 than earthly brightness in its evening horizon. And then, prostrating
himself upon the great altar, he groaned out one long, deep, heart-
rending wail for the imperial House of Tenochtitlan, and the golden
realm of Anahuac."

A deeper shade came over the brow of Montezuma, and heaving a
50 sigh from the very depths of a soul that had long been agitated by
melancholy forebodings of coming evil, he raised his eyes to heaven,
and said, "the will of the gods be done." Then, waving his hand to his
attendants, they bowed their heads, and retired in silence from the
apartment.

55 "It has come at last," inwardly groaned the monarch, as soon as he
found himself alone—"it has come at last—that fearful prophecy,
that has so long hung, like the shadow of a great cloud, over my
devoted house, is now to be fulfilled. The fates have willed it, and
there is no escape from their dread decrees. I must make ready for the
60 sacrifice."

Nerved by the stern influence of this dark fatalism, Montezuma brushed a tear from his eye, and putting a royal restraint upon the turbulent sorrows and fears of his paternal heart, hastened to the apartments of the queen, to break to her, with all the gentleness and
65 caution which her delicate and precarious circumstances required, the mournful issue of their inquiries at the court of heaven, into the future destiny and prospects of their new-born babe.

A deep gloom hung over the palace and the city. Every heart, even the most humble and unobserved, sympathized in the disappointment,
70 and shared the distress, of their sovereign. And the day, which should have been consecrated to loyal congratulations, and general festivities, became, as by common consent, a sort of national fast, a season of universal lamentation.

7. It can be inferred from the passage that the Aztec people viewed the "priestly oracle" (line 5) as

    (A) supercilious
    (B) exotic
    (C) capricious
    (D) redoubtable
    (E) lucky

8. The statement "Affecting the most intelligent..." (lines 2–3) is made in order to

    (A) suggest the lasting relevance of religious belief
    (B) establish a contrast between religions followed by the Aztecs
    (C) draw a parallel between the citizens and monarchy
    (D) present the diversity of the population
    (E) explain the all-encompassing nature of the Aztec belief system

9. As described in lines 17–19, the atmosphere in the imperial palace is most nearly one of

    (A) deference
    (B) emptiness
    (C) inviolability
    (D) urgency
    (E) anticipation

10. The prophecy delivered by the "priest of the stars" (line 40) is primarily concerned with the

    (A) realization of the people's greatest superstition
    (B) gender of the monarch's newborn child
    (C) destiny of the civilization
    (D) news that Montezuma must bring to the queen
    (E) coronation of the monarch

11. In line 24 "troubled sky" refers to the

    (A) revelations of astrology
    (B) emperor's thoughts
    (C) impending storm
    (D) disturbing news of the messenger
    (E) court's expectations

12. The phrase "my tongue refuses its office" (line 42) suggests that the messenger

    (A) is paralyzed and unable to communicate
    (B) cannot bring himself to relinquish his position
    (C) does not have control over his words
    (D) is distraught over the implication of his message
    (E) has not been trained to complete his task

13. The word "unpropitious" (line 43) most nearly means

    (A) buoyant
    (B) inauspicious
    (C) jovial
    (D) encouraging
    (E) ambiguous

14. The paragraph beginning "It has come..." (lines 55–60) suggests that

    (A) Montezuma's forecasting abilities rival that of the priest
    (B) the monarch did everything possible to avoid the fulfillment of the prophecy
    (C) Montezuma remained stoic while with his advisors
    (D) the royal family is prepared to do what is necessary to protect the newborn child
    (E) a successor will be immediately selected for Montezuma

15. The emperor's remark in line 52, "the will of the gods be done" suggests the

 (A) infallibility of the emperor's beliefs
 (B) absolute credence of the messenger
 (C) irrevocability of the belief system
 (D) emperor's inherent omniscience
 (E) overbearing sadness of the news

16. In line 64, "break" most nearly means to

 (A) divulge
 (B) decipher
 (C) breach
 (D) contravene
 (E) crack

17. The phrase "as by common consent" (line 72) suggests that the "future destiny and prospects of [the] new-born babe" mentioned in lines 66–67 is

 (A) something that was approved by all citizens
 (B) the concern of only the monarch and the queen
 (C) an event that was foreshadowed by the most humble citizens
 (D) distressing to the citizens of the city
 (E) an occasion marked by city-wide celebration

18. The narrator's presentation is most like that of a/an

 (A) novelist depicting an account based on true events
 (B) historian describing an Aztec custom and tradition
 (C) sympathetic storyteller recounting an ancient people's burden
 (D) raconteur delivering a refrain
 (E) religious leader explaining an ancient belief system

STOP
If you finish before time is called, you may check your work on this section only.
Do not turn to any other section in the test.

Section 10
Time—10 minutes
14 questions

Turn to Section 10 (page 427) of your answer sheet to answer the questions in this section.

Directions: For each question in this section, select the best answer from among the answer choices given and fill in the corresponding circle on the answer sheet.

The following sentences test correctness and effectiveness of expression. Part of each sentence or the entire sentence is underlined; beneath each sentence are five ways of phrasing the underlined material. Choice A repeats the original phrasing; the other four choices are different. If you thing the original phrasing produces a better sentence than any of the alternatives, select choice A; if not, select one of the other choices.

In making your selection, follow the requirements of standard written English; that is, pay attention to grammar, choice of words, sentence construction, and punctuation. Your selection should result in the most effective sentence—clear and precise, without awkwardness or ambiguity.

Example:

The numerous biographies published about Roosevelt's life <u>are testament to his great achievements</u>.
(A)   are testament to his great achievements
(B)   is testament to his great achievements
(C)   **stand as a testament for his great achievement**
(D)   full of achievement, the books are testament
(E)   are testaments to his great achievements

1.   Pool rules necessitate swimmers to <u>present a membership card before entry into</u> the pool area.

     (A)   present a membership card before entry into
     (B)   presentation of a membership card before entering
     (C)   present a membership card prior to, entering
     (D)   present a membership card before entering
     (E)   present a membership card prior to entering into

2. Mary's dinner <u>was so delicious; it had</u> all of the dinner guests stuffed.

   (A) was so delicious; it had
   (B) was such a deliciously; it had
   (C) was so delicious, it had
   (D) was so deliciousness that it had
   (E) was so delicious, had

3. <u>The rooms on the fifth floor are smaller than the first floor</u>.

   (A) The rooms on the fifth floor are smaller than the first floor
   (B) The rooms on the fifth floor are smaller then the first floor
   (C) The rooms on the fifth floor are smaller than those on the first floor
   (D) The rooms on the first floor are bigger than the fifth floor
   (E) Those rooms which are on the fifth floor are smaller than the first

4. <u>The window was broken by the ball</u>.

   (A) The window was broken by the ball
   (B) The window broke because of the ball
   (C) The ball broke the window
   (D) The broken window was caused by the ball
   (E) Because of the ball, the window was broken

5. <u>Adam was adept at working in small spaces: he could create</u> a five-course meal in a tiny kitchen.

   (A) Adam was adept at working in small spaces: he could create
   (B) Adam was adept at working in small spaces, he could create
   (C) Adam can be adept at working in small spaces: he could create
   (D) Adept at working in small spaces Adam could create
   (E) Because of his adaptability to working in small spaces, Adam could

6. The rain was <u>devastating and lasted three months, which duration made it</u> seem never-ending.

   (A) devastating and lasted three months, which duration made it
   (B) devastating, and because it lasted three months, made it
   (C) devastating and lasted three months, this made it seem
   (D) devastating and lasted a duration of three months, which made it
   (E) devastating, and lasting three months made it

7. The dog's floppy ears and shining eyes <u>give it a cartoonish look</u>.

   (A) give it a cartoonish look
   (B) gives it a cartoonish look
   (C) makes it look cartoonish
   (D) give the appearance of a cartoon
   (E) gives it a look of a cartoon

8. Suzy desperately <u>wanted to win the contest and pushes her go-cart to the breaking point</u>.

   (A) wanted to win the contest and pushes her go-cart to the breaking point
   (B) wants to win the contest and pushing her go-cart to the breaking point
   (C) wanted to win the contest and pushed her go-cart to the breaking point
   (D) wanted to win pushing her go-cart to the breaking point
   (E) wanted to win and pushed her go-cart to it's breaking point

9. Even though Katie tries to prepare for her <u>exams, you still worries</u> about not doing well.

   (A) exams, you still worries
   (B) exams, you still worry
   (C) exams it results in her worrying
   (D) exams, she still worries
   (E) exams, she still is worried

10. <u>Every word of the study guide was read by us</u>.

    (A) Every word of the study guide was read by us
    (B) We read every word of the study guide
    (C) The study guide's every word was ready by us
    (D) Having read every word of the study guide by us
    (E) We have the guides' every word

11. Just as cameras and recording devices <u>was prohibited in the museum, as were food and drinks</u>.

    (A) was prohibited in the museum, as were food and drinks
    (B) was prohibited in the museum, food and drinks were prohibited too

(C) were prohibited in the museum, so too were food and drinks

(D) were prohibited in the museum, and so was food and drinks

(E) were prohibited in the museum; as were food and drinks

12. Of the many school districts represented at the conference, <u>the principal of Public School 13 was the only one to suggest</u> plans for improving the lagging math standards.

(A) the principal of Public School 13 was the only one to suggest

(B) the principal in Public School 13 was the only one to suggest

(C) suggests by the principal of Public School 13 for

(D) Public School 13's principal was the only one to suggest

(E) Public School 13's principal only suggested

13. The bed bug epidemic has traveled across the <u>entire country, and it has changed</u> the way that people sleep, shop, and travel.

(A) entire country, and it has changed

(B) entire country, which has changed

(C) entire country and it has changed

(D) entire country, and they have changed

(E) entire country; it has, therefore changed

14. Last year our high school defeated the rival school in the district's final <u>game, even so, they did not</u> win the championship.

(A) game, even so, they did not

(B) game, however, they did not

(C) game, but they still did not

(D) game, but it did not

(E) game, nevertheless, it was not able to

Exam 2   Answer Key

Section 2 Math	Section 3 Verbal	Section 4 Math	Section 6 Writing Multiple Choice
1. E	1. A	1. C	1. C
2. C	2. B	2. D	2. B
3. D	3. C	3. D	3. A
4. B	4. A	4. B	4. B
5. E	5. B	5. A	5. A
6. A	6. E	6. D	6. C
7. B	7. D	7. D	7. A
8. E	8. B	8. D	8. D
9. B	9. E	9. 20	9. A
10. D	10. B	10. 50	10. A
11. B	11. B	11. 2, 12	11. A
12. C	12. C	12. 50	12. E
13. C	13. C	13. 10	13. A
14. C	14. C	14. ½	14. A
15. C	15. B	15. 3	15. E
16. D	16. A	16. $\dfrac{5}{9}$	16. E
17. D	17. D		17. C
18. D	18. C	17. $\dfrac{13}{2}$	18. E
19. A	19. B		19. C
20. E	20. C	18. 8	20. E
	21. A		21. B
	22. B		22. E
	23. C		23. C
	24. D		24. A
			25. B
			26. A
			27. B
			28. E
			29. E
			30. C
			31. B
			32. E
			33. D
			34. E
			35. B

Section 7 Verbal	Section 8 Math	Section 9 Verbal	Section 10 Writing
1. A	1. C	1. B	1. D
2. C	2. D	2. B	2. A
3. A	3. A	3. A	3. C
4. A	4. B	4. A	4. C
5. C	5. E	5. B	5. A
6. A	6. C	6. A	6. E
7. A	7. A	7. D	7. A
8. E	8. D	8. E	8. C
9. E	9. B	9. E	9. D
10. B	10. C	10. C	10. B
11. B	11. E	11. B	11. C
12. A	12. D	12. D	12. D
13. B	13. C	13. B	13. A
14. D	14. C	14. C	14. D
15. B	15. E	15. C	
16. E	16. E	16. A	
17. D		17. D	
18. E		18. C	
19. A			
20. B			
21. D			
22. C			
23. C			
24. A			

chapter 19

Practice Test III

Answer Sheet

Last Name:_____   First Name:_____

Date:_____   Testing Location:_____

Directions For Test

- Remove these answer sheets from the book and use them to record your answers to this test.
- This test will require 3 hours and 20 minutes to complete. Take this test in one sitting.
- The time allotment for each section is written clearly at the beginning of each section. This test contains
- Six 25-minute sections, two 20-minute sections, and one 10-minute section.
- This test is 25 minutes shorter than the actual sat, which will include a 25-minute "experimental" section that does not count toward your score. That section has been omitted from this test.
- You may take one short break during the test, of no more than 10 minutes in length.
- You may only work on one section at any given time.
- You must stop ALL work on a section when time is called.
- If you finish a section before the time has elapsed, check your work on that section. You may not work on any other section.
- Do not waste time on questions that seem too difficult for you.
- Use the test book for scratchwork, but you will receive credit only for answers that are marked on the answer sheets.
- You will receive one point for every correct answer.
- You will receive no points for an omitted question.
- For each wrong answer on any multiple-choice question, your score will be reduced by ¼ point.
- For each wrong answer on any "numerical grid-in" question, you will receive no deduction.

When you take the real SAT, you will be asked to fill in your personal information in grids as shown below.

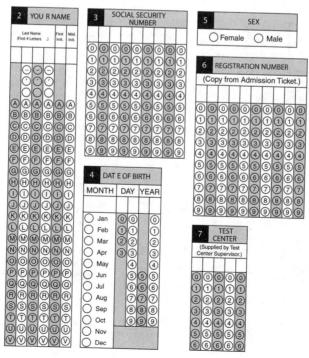

Start with number 1 for each new section. If a section has fewer questions than answer spaces, leave the extra answer spaces blank. Be sure to erase any errors or stray marks completely.

SECTION 2

1	A B C D E	11	A B C D E	21	A B C D E	31	A B C D E
2	A B C D E	12	A B C D E	22	A B C D E	32	A B C D E
3	A B C D E	13	A B C D E	23	A B C D E	33	A B C D E
4	A B C D E	14	A B C D E	24	A B C D E	34	A B C D E
5	A B C D E	15	A B C D E	25	A B C D E	35	A B C D E
6	A B C D E	16	A B C D E	26	A B C D E	36	A B C D E
7	A B C D E	17	A B C D E	27	A B C D E	37	A B C D E
8	A B C D E	18	A B C D E	28	A B C D E	38	A B C D E
9	A B C D E	19	A B C D E	29	A B C D E	39	A B C D E
10	A B C D E	20	A B C D E	30	A B C D E	40	A B C D E

SECTION 3

1	A B C D E	11	A B C D E	21	A B C D E	31	A B C D E
2	A B C D E	12	A B C D E	22	A B C D E	32	A B C D E
3	A B C D E	13	A B C D E	23	A B C D E	33	A B C D E
4	A B C D E	14	A B C D E	24	A B C D E	34	A B C D E
5	A B C D E	15	A B C D E	25	A B C D E	35	A B C D E
6	A B C D E	16	A B C D E	26	A B C D E	36	A B C D E
7	A B C D E	17	A B C D E	27	A B C D E	37	A B C D E
8	A B C D E	18	A B C D E	28	A B C D E	38	A B C D E
9	A B C D E	19	A B C D E	29	A B C D E	39	A B C D E
10	A B C D E	20	A B C D E	30	A B C D E	40	A B C D E

SECTION 4

1	A B C D E	11	A B C D E	21	A B C D E	31	A B C D E
2	A B C D E	12	A B C D E	22	A B C D E	32	A B C D E
3	A B C D E	13	A B C D E	23	A B C D E	33	A B C D E
4	A B C D E	14	A B C D E	24	A B C D E	34	A B C D E
5	A B C D E	15	A B C D E	25	A B C D E	35	A B C D E
6	A B C D E	16	A B C D E	26	A B C D E	36	A B C D E
7	A B C D E	17	A B C D E	27	A B C D E	37	A B C D E
8	A B C D E	18	A B C D E	28	A B C D E	38	A B C D E
9	A B C D E	19	A B C D E	29	A B C D E	39	A B C D E
10	A B C D E	20	A B C D E	30	A B C D E	40	A B C D E

SECTION 5

1	A B C D E	11	A B C D E	21	A B C D E	31	A B C D E
2	A B C D E	12	A B C D E	22	A B C D E	32	A B C D E
3	A B C D E	13	A B C D E	23	A B C D E	33	A B C D E
4	A B C D E	14	A B C D E	24	A B C D E	34	A B C D E
5	A B C D E	15	A B C D E	25	A B C D E	35	A B C D E
6	A B C D E	16	A B C D E	26	A B C D E	36	A B C D E
7	A B C D E	17	A B C D E	27	A B C D E	37	A B C D E
8	A B C D E	18	A B C D E	28	A B C D E	38	A B C D E
9	A B C D E	19	A B C D E	29	A B C D E	39	A B C D E
10	A B C D E	20	A B C D E	30	A B C D E	40	A B C D E

Start with number 1 for each new section. If a section has fewer questions than answer spaces, leave the extra answer spaces blank. Be sure to erase any errors or stray marks completely.

SECTION 7

1 Ⓐ Ⓑ Ⓒ Ⓓ Ⓔ	11 Ⓐ Ⓑ Ⓒ Ⓓ Ⓔ	21 Ⓐ Ⓑ Ⓒ Ⓓ Ⓔ	31 Ⓐ Ⓑ Ⓒ Ⓓ Ⓔ
2 Ⓐ Ⓑ Ⓒ Ⓓ Ⓔ	12 Ⓐ Ⓑ Ⓒ Ⓓ Ⓔ	22 Ⓐ Ⓑ Ⓒ Ⓓ Ⓔ	32 Ⓐ Ⓑ Ⓒ Ⓓ Ⓔ
3 Ⓐ Ⓑ Ⓒ Ⓓ Ⓔ	13 Ⓐ Ⓑ Ⓒ Ⓓ Ⓔ	23 Ⓐ Ⓑ Ⓒ Ⓓ Ⓔ	33 Ⓐ Ⓑ Ⓒ Ⓓ Ⓔ
4 Ⓐ Ⓑ Ⓒ Ⓓ Ⓔ	14 Ⓐ Ⓑ Ⓒ Ⓓ Ⓔ	24 Ⓐ Ⓑ Ⓒ Ⓓ Ⓔ	34 Ⓐ Ⓑ Ⓒ Ⓓ Ⓔ
5 Ⓐ Ⓑ Ⓒ Ⓓ Ⓔ	15 Ⓐ Ⓑ Ⓒ Ⓓ Ⓔ	25 Ⓐ Ⓑ Ⓒ Ⓓ Ⓔ	35 Ⓐ Ⓑ Ⓒ Ⓓ Ⓔ
6 Ⓐ Ⓑ Ⓒ Ⓓ Ⓔ	16 Ⓐ Ⓑ Ⓒ Ⓓ Ⓔ	26 Ⓐ Ⓑ Ⓒ Ⓓ Ⓔ	36 Ⓐ Ⓑ Ⓒ Ⓓ Ⓔ
7 Ⓐ Ⓑ Ⓒ Ⓓ Ⓔ	17 Ⓐ Ⓑ Ⓒ Ⓓ Ⓔ	27 Ⓐ Ⓑ Ⓒ Ⓓ Ⓔ	37 Ⓐ Ⓑ Ⓒ Ⓓ Ⓔ
8 Ⓐ Ⓑ Ⓒ Ⓓ Ⓔ	18 Ⓐ Ⓑ Ⓒ Ⓓ Ⓔ	28 Ⓐ Ⓑ Ⓒ Ⓓ Ⓔ	38 Ⓐ Ⓑ Ⓒ Ⓓ Ⓔ
9 Ⓐ Ⓑ Ⓒ Ⓓ Ⓔ	19 Ⓐ Ⓑ Ⓒ Ⓓ Ⓔ	29 Ⓐ Ⓑ Ⓒ Ⓓ Ⓔ	39 Ⓐ Ⓑ Ⓒ Ⓓ Ⓔ
10 Ⓐ Ⓑ Ⓒ Ⓓ Ⓔ	20 Ⓐ Ⓑ Ⓒ Ⓓ Ⓔ	30 Ⓐ Ⓑ Ⓒ Ⓓ Ⓔ	40 Ⓐ Ⓑ Ⓒ Ⓓ Ⓔ

SECTION 8

1 Ⓐ Ⓑ Ⓒ Ⓓ Ⓔ	11 Ⓐ Ⓑ Ⓒ Ⓓ Ⓔ	21 Ⓐ Ⓑ Ⓒ Ⓓ Ⓔ	31 Ⓐ Ⓑ Ⓒ Ⓓ Ⓔ
2 Ⓐ Ⓑ Ⓒ Ⓓ Ⓔ	12 Ⓐ Ⓑ Ⓒ Ⓓ Ⓔ	22 Ⓐ Ⓑ Ⓒ Ⓓ Ⓔ	32 Ⓐ Ⓑ Ⓒ Ⓓ Ⓔ
3 Ⓐ Ⓑ Ⓒ Ⓓ Ⓔ	13 Ⓐ Ⓑ Ⓒ Ⓓ Ⓔ	23 Ⓐ Ⓑ Ⓒ Ⓓ Ⓔ	33 Ⓐ Ⓑ Ⓒ Ⓓ Ⓔ
4 Ⓐ Ⓑ Ⓒ Ⓓ Ⓔ	14 Ⓐ Ⓑ Ⓒ Ⓓ Ⓔ	24 Ⓐ Ⓑ Ⓒ Ⓓ Ⓔ	34 Ⓐ Ⓑ Ⓒ Ⓓ Ⓔ
5 Ⓐ Ⓑ Ⓒ Ⓓ Ⓔ	15 Ⓐ Ⓑ Ⓒ Ⓓ Ⓔ	25 Ⓐ Ⓑ Ⓒ Ⓓ Ⓔ	35 Ⓐ Ⓑ Ⓒ Ⓓ Ⓔ
6 Ⓐ Ⓑ Ⓒ Ⓓ Ⓔ	16 Ⓐ Ⓑ Ⓒ Ⓓ Ⓔ	26 Ⓐ Ⓑ Ⓒ Ⓓ Ⓔ	36 Ⓐ Ⓑ Ⓒ Ⓓ Ⓔ
7 Ⓐ Ⓑ Ⓒ Ⓓ Ⓔ	17 Ⓐ Ⓑ Ⓒ Ⓓ Ⓔ	27 Ⓐ Ⓑ Ⓒ Ⓓ Ⓔ	37 Ⓐ Ⓑ Ⓒ Ⓓ Ⓔ
8 Ⓐ Ⓑ Ⓒ Ⓓ Ⓔ	18 Ⓐ Ⓑ Ⓒ Ⓓ Ⓔ	28 Ⓐ Ⓑ Ⓒ Ⓓ Ⓔ	38 Ⓐ Ⓑ Ⓒ Ⓓ Ⓔ
9 Ⓐ Ⓑ Ⓒ Ⓓ Ⓔ	19 Ⓐ Ⓑ Ⓒ Ⓓ Ⓔ	29 Ⓐ Ⓑ Ⓒ Ⓓ Ⓔ	39 Ⓐ Ⓑ Ⓒ Ⓓ Ⓔ
10 Ⓐ Ⓑ Ⓒ Ⓓ Ⓔ	20 Ⓐ Ⓑ Ⓒ Ⓓ Ⓔ	30 Ⓐ Ⓑ Ⓒ Ⓓ Ⓔ	40 Ⓐ Ⓑ Ⓒ Ⓓ Ⓔ

SECTION 9

1 Ⓐ Ⓑ Ⓒ Ⓓ Ⓔ	11 Ⓐ Ⓑ Ⓒ Ⓓ Ⓔ	21 Ⓐ Ⓑ Ⓒ Ⓓ Ⓔ	31 Ⓐ Ⓑ Ⓒ Ⓓ Ⓔ
2 Ⓐ Ⓑ Ⓒ Ⓓ Ⓔ	12 Ⓐ Ⓑ Ⓒ Ⓓ Ⓔ	22 Ⓐ Ⓑ Ⓒ Ⓓ Ⓔ	32 Ⓐ Ⓑ Ⓒ Ⓓ Ⓔ
3 Ⓐ Ⓑ Ⓒ Ⓓ Ⓔ	13 Ⓐ Ⓑ Ⓒ Ⓓ Ⓔ	23 Ⓐ Ⓑ Ⓒ Ⓓ Ⓔ	33 Ⓐ Ⓑ Ⓒ Ⓓ Ⓔ
4 Ⓐ Ⓑ Ⓒ Ⓓ Ⓔ	14 Ⓐ Ⓑ Ⓒ Ⓓ Ⓔ	24 Ⓐ Ⓑ Ⓒ Ⓓ Ⓔ	34 Ⓐ Ⓑ Ⓒ Ⓓ Ⓔ
5 Ⓐ Ⓑ Ⓒ Ⓓ Ⓔ	15 Ⓐ Ⓑ Ⓒ Ⓓ Ⓔ	25 Ⓐ Ⓑ Ⓒ Ⓓ Ⓔ	35 Ⓐ Ⓑ Ⓒ Ⓓ Ⓔ
6 Ⓐ Ⓑ Ⓒ Ⓓ Ⓔ	16 Ⓐ Ⓑ Ⓒ Ⓓ Ⓔ	26 Ⓐ Ⓑ Ⓒ Ⓓ Ⓔ	36 Ⓐ Ⓑ Ⓒ Ⓓ Ⓔ
7 Ⓐ Ⓑ Ⓒ Ⓓ Ⓔ	17 Ⓐ Ⓑ Ⓒ Ⓓ Ⓔ	27 Ⓐ Ⓑ Ⓒ Ⓓ Ⓔ	37 Ⓐ Ⓑ Ⓒ Ⓓ Ⓔ
8 Ⓐ Ⓑ Ⓒ Ⓓ Ⓔ	18 Ⓐ Ⓑ Ⓒ Ⓓ Ⓔ	28 Ⓐ Ⓑ Ⓒ Ⓓ Ⓔ	38 Ⓐ Ⓑ Ⓒ Ⓓ Ⓔ
9 Ⓐ Ⓑ Ⓒ Ⓓ Ⓔ	19 Ⓐ Ⓑ Ⓒ Ⓓ Ⓔ	29 Ⓐ Ⓑ Ⓒ Ⓓ Ⓔ	39 Ⓐ Ⓑ Ⓒ Ⓓ Ⓔ
10 Ⓐ Ⓑ Ⓒ Ⓓ Ⓔ	20 Ⓐ Ⓑ Ⓒ Ⓓ Ⓔ	30 Ⓐ Ⓑ Ⓒ Ⓓ Ⓔ	40 Ⓐ Ⓑ Ⓒ Ⓓ Ⓔ

SECTION 10

1 Ⓐ Ⓑ Ⓒ Ⓓ Ⓔ	11 Ⓐ Ⓑ Ⓒ Ⓓ Ⓔ	21 Ⓐ Ⓑ Ⓒ Ⓓ Ⓔ	31 Ⓐ Ⓑ Ⓒ Ⓓ Ⓔ
2 Ⓐ Ⓑ Ⓒ Ⓓ Ⓔ	12 Ⓐ Ⓑ Ⓒ Ⓓ Ⓔ	22 Ⓐ Ⓑ Ⓒ Ⓓ Ⓔ	32 Ⓐ Ⓑ Ⓒ Ⓓ Ⓔ
3 Ⓐ Ⓑ Ⓒ Ⓓ Ⓔ	13 Ⓐ Ⓑ Ⓒ Ⓓ Ⓔ	23 Ⓐ Ⓑ Ⓒ Ⓓ Ⓔ	33 Ⓐ Ⓑ Ⓒ Ⓓ Ⓔ
4 Ⓐ Ⓑ Ⓒ Ⓓ Ⓔ	14 Ⓐ Ⓑ Ⓒ Ⓓ Ⓔ	24 Ⓐ Ⓑ Ⓒ Ⓓ Ⓔ	34 Ⓐ Ⓑ Ⓒ Ⓓ Ⓔ
5 Ⓐ Ⓑ Ⓒ Ⓓ Ⓔ	15 Ⓐ Ⓑ Ⓒ Ⓓ Ⓔ	25 Ⓐ Ⓑ Ⓒ Ⓓ Ⓔ	35 Ⓐ Ⓑ Ⓒ Ⓓ Ⓔ
6 Ⓐ Ⓑ Ⓒ Ⓓ Ⓔ	16 Ⓐ Ⓑ Ⓒ Ⓓ Ⓔ	26 Ⓐ Ⓑ Ⓒ Ⓓ Ⓔ	36 Ⓐ Ⓑ Ⓒ Ⓓ Ⓔ
7 Ⓐ Ⓑ Ⓒ Ⓓ Ⓔ	17 Ⓐ Ⓑ Ⓒ Ⓓ Ⓔ	27 Ⓐ Ⓑ Ⓒ Ⓓ Ⓔ	37 Ⓐ Ⓑ Ⓒ Ⓓ Ⓔ
8 Ⓐ Ⓑ Ⓒ Ⓓ Ⓔ	18 Ⓐ Ⓑ Ⓒ Ⓓ Ⓔ	28 Ⓐ Ⓑ Ⓒ Ⓓ Ⓔ	38 Ⓐ Ⓑ Ⓒ Ⓓ Ⓔ
9 Ⓐ Ⓑ Ⓒ Ⓓ Ⓔ	19 Ⓐ Ⓑ Ⓒ Ⓓ Ⓔ	29 Ⓐ Ⓑ Ⓒ Ⓓ Ⓔ	39 Ⓐ Ⓑ Ⓒ Ⓓ Ⓔ
10 Ⓐ Ⓑ Ⓒ Ⓓ Ⓔ	20 Ⓐ Ⓑ Ⓒ Ⓓ Ⓔ	30 Ⓐ Ⓑ Ⓒ Ⓓ Ⓔ	40 Ⓐ Ⓑ Ⓒ Ⓓ Ⓔ

Section 1
Essay
Time—25 minutes

Write your essay on separate sheets of standard lined paper.

The essay gives you an opportunity to show how effectively you can develop and express ideas. You should, therefore, take care to develop your point of view, present your ideas logically and clearly, and use language precisely.

Your essay should be written on the lines provided on your answer sheet—you will receive no other paper on which to write. You will have enough space if you write on every line, avoid wide margins, and keep your handwriting to a reasonable size. Remember that people who are not familiar with your handwriting will read what you write. Try to write or print so that what you write is legible to those readers.

Important reminders:

- **A pencil is required for the essay.** An essay written in ink will receive a score of zero.
- **Do not write your essay in your test book.** You will receive credit for what you write on your answer sheet.
- **An off-topic essay will receive a score of zero.**
- **If your essay does not reflect your original and individual work, your test scores may be cancelled.**

You have twenty-five minutes to write an essay on the topic assigned below.

Think carefully about the issue presented in the following excerpt and the assignment below.

> I have not failed. I've just found 10,000 ways that won't work.
>
> *Thomas A. Edison*

Assignment: Does ultimate failure exist or is every failed attempt an opportunity? Plan and write an essay in which you develop your point of view on this issue. Support your position with reasoning and examples taking from your reading, studies, experiences, or observations.

Begin writing your essay on a separate sheet of paper.

If you finish before time is called, you may check your work on this section only. Do not turn to any other section in the test.

Section 2
Time—25 minutes
24 questions

Turn to Section 2 (page 500) of your answer sheet to answer the questions in this section.

Directions: For each question in this section, select the best answer from among the answer choices given and fill in the corresponding circle on the answer sheet.

Each sentence below has one or two question blanks, each blank indicating that something has been omitted. Beneath the sentence are five words or sets of words labeled A through E. Choose the word or set of words that, when inserted in the sentence, *best* fits the meaning of the sentence as a whole.

Example:

Susan preferred to be ____, hoping to avoid confusion due to miscommunication.
(A) **direct**
(B) devious
(C) cunning
(D) austere
(E) terse

1. The rationale offered for acquiring new team jerseys was that new uniforms would ____ team morale and lead to a victorious season.

    (A) undermine
    (B) soak
    (C) bolster
    (D) allocate
    (E) curtail

2. Peter ____ his summer to working full-time at the museum, ____ himself in the technical aspects of art restoration.

    (A) dedicated...immersing
    (B) devoted...ordaining
    (C) bequeathed...surrendering
    (D) maximized...focusing
    (E) donated...establishing

3. Although the psychologist Carl Jung had ____ access to his manuscript of *Red Book* to the public, his grandson ____ Jung's wishes and published the book in 2009.

   (A) implied...publicized
   (B) stipulated...repealed
   (C) denied...disregarded
   (D) revealed...executed
   (E) insisted...honored

4. Ben was a/an ____ supporter of free education and often contributed to scholarship funds.

   (A) ardent
   (B) lackadaisical
   (C) averse
   (D) indifferent
   (E) acute

5. Although Lauren tried to persuade her father to allow her to borrow the car, he would not ____ to her pleas.

   (A) acquiesce
   (B) endure
   (C) objurgate
   (D) deviate
   (E) forfeit

6. The chef, known for his tumultuous reign of the kitchen, placed a/an ____ stamp on the culinary world through ownership of many restaurants and publication of several cookbooks.

   (A) enduring
   (B) strenuous
   (C) equivocal
   (D) overbearing
   (E) laggard

7. It was clear by the judge's probing questions that Rob's ____ argument
    would not convince the jury of his innocence.

    (A) belated
    (B) candid
    (C) beseeching
    (D) disingenuous
    (E) abhorrent

8. Annoyed by the student's excessively ____ manner, the teacher advised
    him that such fawning was inappropriate.

    (A) obsequious
    (B) argumentative
    (C) enigmatic
    (D) lethargic
    (E) aggressive

The passages below are followed by questions based on their content;
questions that follow a pair of related passages may also be based on the
relationship between the paired passages. Answer the questions on the
basis of what is *stated* or *implied* in the passage in any introductory
material that may be provided.

Questions 9 through 12 are based on the following passages.

Passage 1

Elfride Swancourt was a girl whose emotions lay very near the
surface. Their nature more precisely, and as modified by the creeping
Line   hours of time, was known only to those who watched the
circumstances of her history.

5   Personally, she was the combination of very interesting particulars,
whose rarity, however, lay in the combination itself rather than in the
individual elements combined. As a matter of fact, you did not see
the form and substance of her features when conversing with her; and
this charming power of preventing a material study of her lineaments
10 by an interlocutor, originated not in the cloaking effect of a well-
formed manner (for her manner was childish and scarcely formed),

but in the attractive crudeness of the remarks themselves. She had
lived all her life in retirement—the monstrari gigito of idle men had
not flattered her, and at the age of nineteen or twenty she was no
15 further on in social consciousness than an urban young lady of fifteen.

9. In line 12, "crudeness" most nearly means

(A) simplicity
(B) vulgarity
(C) thoughtfulness
(D) mystery
(E) rudeness

10. The sentence beginning "She had lived all…" (lines 12–15) suggests that
Elfridge is

(A) unattractive
(B) obtuse
(C) elderly
(D) naive
(E) unaware

Passage 2

Line I never thought that I should be guilty of writing a book. I did not,
however, do this with malice aforethought. My son is responsible for
5 whatever sin I may have committed in presenting this to the public.
He and I have been good friends ever since we became acquainted,
and he has always insisted upon my telling him all that I know. When
he was about three years old he discovered that I had been a soldier
in Lee's army from 1861 to 1865, and, although he is of Quaker
10 descent and a loyal member of the Society of Friends, and I am half
Quaker, yet he loved war stories and I loved to tell them. This
accounts for the production of the book. After I had told him these
stories over and over, again and again, when he was grown he insisted
upon my starting at the beginning and giving him the whole of my
15 experience in the Confederate army. Then he wanted it published.
I yielded to his request, and here is the book. This is not, however, an
exact copy of the typewritten manuscript which he has. The original
manuscript is more personal. I thought the change would make it
more acceptable to the general reader.

11. Based on the information in the passage, Hopkins's decision to publish his stories can best be described as

   (A) deeply cynical
   (B) overly spontaneous
   (C) without regret
   (D) careful surrender
   (E) above reproach

12. In context, "more acceptable" (line 19) is best understood as

   (A) satisfactory
   (B) tolerable
   (C) gratifying
   (D) interesting
   (E) personal

Questions 13 through 24 are based on the following passages.

Passage 1 is from a novel published in 1847 that satirizes society in 19th century Britain. Passage 2 is excerpted from a novel published in 1838 is an early example of a social novel that calls attention to social issues of the time.

Passage 1

   MADAM,

   —After her six years' residence at the Mall, I have the honour and
Line   happiness of presenting Miss Amelia Sedley to her parents, as a young
   lady not unworthy to occupy a fitting position in their polished and
5   refined circle. Those virtues which characterize the young English
   gentlewoman, those accomplishments which become her birth and
   station, will not be found wanting in the amiable Miss Sedley, whose
   INDUSTRY and OBEDIENCE have endeared her to her instructors,
   and whose delightful sweetness of temper has charmed her AGED
10   and her YOUTHFUL companions.

   In music, in dancing, in orthography, in every variety of embroidery
   and needlework, she will be found to have realized her friends'
   fondest wishes. In geography there is still much to be desired; and a
   careful and undeviating use of the backboard, for four hours daily
15   during the next three years, is recommended as necessary to the
   acquirement of that dignified DEPORTMENT AND CARRIAGE, so
   requisite for every young lady of FASHION.

In the principles of religion and morality, Miss Sedley will be found worthy of an establishment which has been honoured by the

20 presence of THE GREAT LEXICOGRAPHER, and the patronage of the admirable Mrs. Chapone. In leaving the Mall, Miss Amelia carries with her the hearts of her companions, and the affectionate regards of her mistress, who has the honour to subscribe herself,

Madam, Your most obliged humble servant,

25 BARBARA PINKERTON

Passage 2

For the next eight or ten months, Oliver was the victim of a systematic course of treachery and deception. He was brought up by

Line hand. The hungry and destitute situation of the infant orphan was duly reported by the workhouse authorities to the parish authorities.

5 The parish authorities inquired with dignity of the workhouse authorities, whether there was no female then domiciled in "the house" who was in a situation to impart to Oliver Twist, the consolation and nourishment of which he stood in need. The workhouse authorities replied with humility, that there was not.

10 Upon this, the parish authorities magnanimously and humanely resolved, that Oliver should be "farmed," or, in other words, that he should be dispatched to a branch-workhouse some three miles off, where twenty or thirty other juvenile offenders against the poor-laws, rolled about the floor all day, without the inconvenience of too much

15 food or too much clothing, under the parental superintendence of an elderly female, who received the culprits at and for the consideration of sevenpence-halfpenny per small head per week. Sevenpence-halfpenny's worth per week is a good round diet for a child; a great deal may be got for sevenpence-halfpenny, quite enough to overload

20 its stomach, and make it uncomfortable. The elderly female was a woman of wisdom and experience; she knew what was good for children; and she had a very accurate perception of what was good for herself. So, she appropriated the greater part of the weekly stipend to her own use, and consigned the rising parochial generation to even a

25 shorter allowance than was originally provided for them. Thereby finding in the lowest depth a deeper still; and proving herself a very great experimental philosopher.

13. The purpose of Passage 1 is to

   (A) cast aspersions on the nature of education
   (B) communicate a complimentary appraisal of Miss Sedley
   (C) convey the affections of a teacher for her student
   (D) outline the achievements and standards of a boarding school
   (E) suggest the areas of weakness of a particular student

14. In line 4 in Passage 1, "polished" most nearly means

   (A) deserving
   (B) practiced
   (C) smooth
   (D) skillful
   (E) sophisticated

15. In Passage 1, the phrase "Those virtues which characterize" (line 5) indicates that

   (A) the standards of the educational system have changed over the years
   (B) Miss Sedley did not learn much at the Mall because she was born into good manners and skills
   (C) the success of the Mall is demonstrated by its instructors and students
   (D) charm and social graces are the most important accomplishments
   (E) the primary purpose of education is to prepare the pupil for her position in life

16. Passage 1 implies that Miss Amelia Sedley requires additional training in

   (A) geography
   (B) religion
   (C) dancing
   (D) orthography
   (E) needlework

17. Passage 1 mentions "her aged and her youthful companions" (lines 9–10) in order to make the point that Amelia

   (A) was respected by younger and older staff members of the mall
   (B) focused more on addressing social issues than educational ones
   (C) was appreciated only by those in her social position
   (D) was adept at manipulating friends
   (E) was equally liked by diverse groups of people

18. In Passage 2, the phrase "brought up by hand" (lines 2–3) implies that Oliver was

   (A) mistreated by his caretakers
   (B) expected to work with his hands
   (C) carefully observed by the authorities
   (D) treated like a small child
   (E) raised by someone other than his mother

19. The narrator of Passage 2 suggests that "parish authorities" (line 4) and "workhouse authorities" (line 4) are

   (A) working together to create solutions for orphans
   (B) problematic government institutions
   (C) the result of national distaste for adoption
   (D) potential solutions to childcare crisis
   (E) equally responsible for the abuse of orphans

20. In line 8, the term "consolation" most nearly means

   (A) support
   (B) relief
   (C) succor
   (D) caretaking
   (E) sustenance

21. The "elderly female" steward introduced in Passage 2 could most closely be described as

   (A) altruistic
   (B) judicious
   (C) selfish
   (D) concerned
   (E) mean spirited

22. In Passage 2 the attitude of the author toward the treatment of children is

    (A) open-mindedness and staunch advocacy
    (B) alarm and disapproving concern
    (C) indifference and grudging acceptance
    (D) outrage and resentful disappointment
    (E) skepticism and qualified admiration

23. The narrator of Passage 2 would most likely argue that individuals who "occupy a fitting position" (line 4) illustrated in Passage 1

    (A) are raised in poverty and work their way up
    (B) look down on wealth and riches
    (C) learn to fit in through training
    (D) are not deserving of their high status
    (E) are born into their station

24. Based on the description of Oliver's and Amelia's childhoods it can be inferred that

    (A) the government created formal academic institutions for children
    (B) lower-class children often did not have the same opportunities as upper-class children
    (C) education was mandatory for all children in England
    (D) an individual's social position depended solely on his or her birth and upbringing
    (E) orphans could not raise their status regardless of education and behavior

STOP
**If you finish before time is called, you may check your work on this section only.
Do not turn to any other section in the test.**

Section 3
Time—25 Minutes
20 Questions

Directions: For this section, solve each problem and decide which is the best of the choices given. Fill in the corresponding circle on the answer sheet. You may use any available space for scratch work.

Reference Information

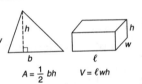
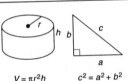
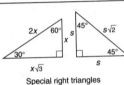

$A = \pi r^2$ $A = \ell w$ $A = \frac{1}{2} bh$ $V = \ell wh$ $V = \pi r^2 h$ $c^2 = a^2 + b^2$ Special right triangles
$C = 2\pi r$

The number of degrees of arc in a circle is 360.
The sum of the measures in degrees of the angles of a triangle is 180.

1. The ones digit of the number that results when a positive integer is squared cannot be which of the following?

(A) 9
(B) 6
(C) 5
(D) 0
(E) 2

2. If k is a positive integer, which of the following is not equal to $(4^3)^k$?

   (A) $\dfrac{(4^6)^k}{(4^3)^k}$

   (B) 3^{4k}

   (C) $4^k(4^{2k})$

   (D) 8^{2k}

   (E) 4^{3k}

3. If $\dfrac{\sqrt{x}}{5} = 2\sqrt{3}$, what is the value of x?

   (A) 10

   (B) 30

   (C) $100\sqrt{3}$

   (D) 300

   (E) $20\sqrt{3}$

4.

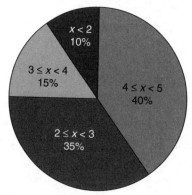

Survey results

The chart above shows the results when 500 people were asked, "How many times do you exercise each week?" The number of times they exercise each week is represented by x. How many people said that they exercise less than four times per week?

   (A) 75

   (B) 125

   (C) 200

   (D) 225

   (E) 300

5. The members of set A are all the numbers divisible by three between 0 and 59. The members of set B are all the numbers divisible by 15 between 0 and 74. If set C is the intersection of sets A and B, how many members does set C contain?

    (A) 0
    (B) 1
    (C) 2
    (D) 3
    (E) 4

6.

    If $v, w, x, y,$ and z are coordinates of the indicated points on the number line above, which of the following is greatest?

    (A) $|v+z|$
    (B) $|v-z|$
    (C) $|x+y|$
    (D) $|w-y|$
    (E) $|v+w|$

7. For all real values of s and t, let $s \boxtimes t$ be defined by the equation $s \boxtimes t = st - t$. If $0 < s \leq 1$ and $1 < t < 2$, then which of the following must be true?

    (A) $-1 < s \boxtimes t < 2$
    (B) $-1 < s \boxtimes t \leq 0$
    (C) $-2 < s \boxtimes t < 0$
    (D) $-2 < s \boxtimes t \leq 0$
    (E) $0 < s \boxtimes t \leq 2$

8. Four college students plan to rent an apartment together. The monthly rent is m dollars, and the total cost is to be shared equally among the four students. If one of the students decides not to rent at the last minute, how much more money, in terms of m, will each of the three remaining students have to pay each month?

   (A) $\dfrac{m-1}{3}$

   (B) $\dfrac{m}{3}$

   (C) $\dfrac{m}{4}$

   (D) $\dfrac{m}{12}$

   (E) $\dfrac{5m}{12}$

9. If 5 times a number is equal to $\dfrac{5}{6}$, what is the number?

   (A) $\dfrac{1}{6}$

   (B) $\dfrac{6}{5}$

   (C) $\dfrac{1}{30}$

   (D) 5

   (E) 6

10. If $0 < a < 1$, which of the following gives the correct ordering of $\sqrt{a}$, a, and a^4?

    (A) $\sqrt{a} < a < a^4$
    (B) $a^4 < \sqrt{a} < a$
    (C) $a^4 < a < \sqrt{a}$
    (D) $a < \sqrt{a} < a^4$
    (E) $a < a^4 < \sqrt{a}$

11. If $3x + 2z = y$ and $3x + 2y + 2z = 18$, what is the value of y?

(A) 3
(B) 6
(C) 9
(D) 18
(E) It cannot be determined from the information given

12. $7.5 - n, 7.5, 7.5 + n$

What is the average (arithmetic mean) of the three quantities above?

(A) 2.5
(B) 7.5
(C) 11.25
(D) $2.5 + \dfrac{n}{3}$
(E) $7.5 + \dfrac{n}{3}$

13.

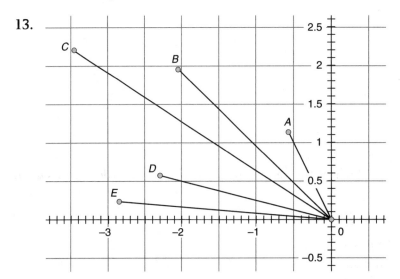

In the figure above, each of the five line segments has a particular slope. In terms of the slopes of the line segments, which of the following line segments represents the median slope?

(A) $\overline{OA}$
(B) $\overline{OB}$

(C) $\overline{OC}$

(D) $\overline{OD}$

(E) $\overline{OE}$

14. After the first term, each term in a sequence is 4 greater than $\frac{1}{4}$ of the preceding term. If x is the first term of the sequence and $x \neq 0$, what is the ratio of the second term to the first term?

   (A) $\frac{x}{4}$

   (B) $\frac{3x + 16}{4}$

   (C) $\frac{x + 4}{4}$

   (D) $\frac{4x + 16}{x}$

   (E) $\frac{x + 16}{4x}$

15. There are 80 marbles in an urn. If a marble is chosen at random, the probability that it will be red is $\frac{7}{16}$. How many red marbles must be added to the jar so that the probability of choosing a red marble is $\frac{1}{2}$?

   (A) 1
   (B) 5
   (C) 8
   (D) 10
   (E) 20

16. The point (a, b) is reflected over the y-axis, and then the reflected point is reflected over the line $y = x$. If a and b are both positive, which of the following represents the coordinates of the point after the second reflection?

   (A) (a, b)
   (B) (b, a)
   (C) (lb, a)
   (D) $(b, -a)$
   (E) $(lb, -a)$

17.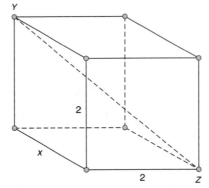

In the rectangular box above with dimensions 2 by 2 by x, what is the length of diagonal $\overline{YZ}$ in terms of x?

(A) $2\sqrt{2+x^2}$

(B) $\sqrt{8+x^2}$

(C) $2\sqrt{2}+x$

(D) $\sqrt{8x}$

(E) $\sqrt{4x}$

18.

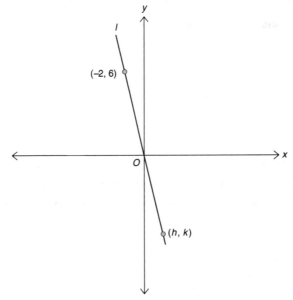

In the figure above, line l passes through the origin. What is the value of $\dfrac{k}{h}$?

(A) 6

(B) 3

(C) $\dfrac{1}{3}$

(D) $-\dfrac{1}{3}$

(E) -3

19.

x	2	3	4	5
y	4	7	10	13

The table above represents a relationship between x and y. Which of the following linear equations describes the relationship?

(A) $y = x + 2$
(B) $y = 2x$
(C) $y = 2x + 1$
(D) $y = 3x - 2$
(E) $y = 4x - 4$

20.

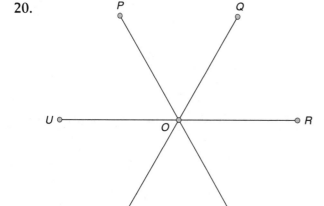

In the figure above (not drawn to scale), $\overline{UR}$, $\overline{PS}$, and $\overline{QT}$ intersect at point O. If the measure of $\angle UOT$ is 70° and $\overline{SP}$ bisects $\angle TOR$, what is the measure of $\angle SOR$?

(A) 45°
(B) 55°
(C) 65°
(D) 70°
(E) 75°

Section 4
Time—25 minutes
24 questions

Turn to Section 4 (page 500) of your answer sheet to answer the questions in this section.

Directions: For each question in this section, select the best answer from among the answer choices given and fill in the corresponding circle on the answer sheet.

Each sentence below has one or two question blanks, each blank indicating that something has been omitted. Beneath the sentence are five words or sets of words labeled A through E. Choose the word or set of words that, when inserted in the sentence, *best* fits the meaning of the sentence as a whole.

Example:

Susan preferred to be ____, hoping to avoid confusion due to miscommunication.
(A) **direct**
(B) devious
(C) cunning
(D) austere
(E) terse

1. Although she couldn't see him clearly, she caught a ____ of his red shirt and blue cap.

    (A) glimpse
    (B) landscape
    (C) preview
    (D) glance
    (E) panorama

2. The teacher's ____ to make literature more relevant led her to form a literature club, start the school theater and begin a program to help struggling readers.

    (A) quest
    (B) entreat
    (C) disinterest
    (D) malaise
    (E) foment

3. She seemed to communicate with her hands, ____ wildly as she spoke.

    (A) lacerating
    (B) allaying
    (C) gesticulating
    (D) projecting
    (E) effacing

4. The explorers returned from the long expedition ____ and fatigued.

    (A) unsullied
    (B) rejuvenated
    (C) haggard
    (D) ephemeral
    (E) victorious

5. The otherwise well-mannered boy had the ____ insolence to avoid shaking hands with his opponent after a devastating loss.

    (A) culpable
    (B) granular
    (C) gratuitous
    (D) infatuated
    (E) anticipated

The passages below are followed by questions based on their content; questions that follow a pair of related passages may also be based on the relationship between the paired passages. Answer the questions on the basis of what is *stated* or *implied* in the passage in any introductory material that may be provided.

Questions 6 through 9 are based on the following passages.

Passage 1

It has already been pointed out that the animal has a very important share of the endowment which we call mind. Only recently has he been
Line getting his due. He was formerly looked upon, under the teachings of a dualistic philosophy and of a jealous humanity, as a soulless machine, a
5 mere automaton which was moved by the starting of certain springs to run on until the machine ran down. There are two reasons that this view has been given up, each possibly important enough to have accomplished the revolution and to have given rise to Animal Psychology.

6. The author of this passage would most likely agree with all of the following EXCEPT

   (A) the awe-inspiring nature of the mind
   (B) the importance of studying animals
   (C) animals are creatures to be protected, loved, and nurtured
   (D) animals are not robotic in their thinking
   (E) humans have long misunderstood animals

7. In line 4, the description of "jealous humanity" establishes

   (A) human envy of an animal's superior mental facilities
   (B) the author's distrust of earlier approaches to understanding the animal mind
   (C) human inability to trust the judgment of animals
   (D) the lack of thoroughness in the scientific study of animals
   (E) science's failure to reconcile different philosophies

Passage 2

The seasons are indeed only of value to primitive man because they
are related, as he swiftly and necessarily finds out, to his food supply.
Line   He has, it would seem, little sensitiveness to the aesthetic impulse of
the beauty of a spring morning, to the pathos of autumn. What he
5   realizes first and foremost is, that at certain times the animals, and
still more the plants, which form his food, appear, at certain others
they disappear. It is these times that become the central points, the
focuses of his interest, and the dates of his religious festivals. These
dates will vary, of course, in different countries and in different
10   climates. It is, therefore, idle to attempt a study of the ritual of a
people without knowing the facts of their climate and surroundings.
In Egypt the food supply will depend on the rise and fall of the Nile,
and on this rise and fall will depend the ritual and calendar of Osiris.
… The Nile regulates the food supply of Egypt, the monsoon that of
15   certain South Pacific islands; the calendar of Egypt depends on the
Nile, of the South Pacific islands on the monsoon.

8.   The reference to the monsoon in line 16 is to

(A) provide an example of severe weather
(B) contrast the behavior of rivers and storms
(C) support the passage's central argument
(D) explain the importance of a consistent water source
(E) introduce an example of distinct religious festival

9.   Which of the following, if true, would undermine the validity of the
author's assumption about the impact of climate on primitive man?

(A) the discovery of a shrine to the sun
(B) a religious festival marking the end of the harvest period
(C) a holy day associated with seasons
(D) a decorative vase depicting ritual prayer for water
(E) a primitive ode to the beauty of summer

Questions 10 through 15 are based on the following passage.

This excerpt is from a letter written from Abraham Lincoln to his stepbrother.

DEAR JOHNSTON,

—Your request for eighty dollars I do not think it best to comply with
Line   now. At the various times when I have helped you a little you have said to
me, 'We can get along very well now'; but in a very short time I find you
5   in the same difficulty again. Now, this can only happen by some defect in
your conduct. What that defect is, I think I know. You are not lazy, and
still you are an idler. I doubt whether, since I saw you, you have done a
good whole day's work in any one day. You do not very much dislike to
work, and still you do not work much, merely because it does not seem to
10   you that you could get much for it. This habit of uselessly wasting time is
the whole difficulty; and it is vastly important to you, and still more so to
your children, that you should break the habit. It is more important to
them, because they have longer to live, and can keep out of an idle habit
before they are in it easier than they can get out after they are in. You are
15   now in need of some money; and what I propose is that you shall go to
work, 'tooth and nail,' for somebody who will give you money for it. Let
father and your boys take charge of things at home, prepare for a crop,
and make the crop, and you go to work for the best money-wages, or in
discharge of any debt you owe, that you can get; and, to secure you a fair
20   reward for your labor, I now promise you, that, for every dollar you will,
between this and the first of next May, get for your own labor, either in
money or as your own indebtedness, I will then give you one other
dollar. By this, if you hire yourself at ten dollars a month, from me
you will get ten more, making twenty dollars a month for your work.
25   In this I do not mean you shall go off to St. Louis, or the lead-mines,
or the gold-mines in California; but I mean for you to go at it, for the
best wages you can get, close to home, in Coles County. Now, if you
will do this you will soon be out of debt, and, what is better, you will
have a habit that will keep you from getting in debt again.

30   But if I should now clear you out of debt, next year you would be in
just as deep as ever. You say you would almost give your place in
heaven for $70 or $80. Then you value your place in heaven very
cheap; for I am sure you can, with the offer I make, get the seventy or
eighty dollars for four or five months' work. You say, if I will furnish

35 you the money, you will deed me the land, and if you don't pay the
money back, you will deliver possession.

Nonsense! If you can't now live with the land, how will you then live
without it? You have always been kind to me, and I do not mean to be
unkind to you. On the contrary, if you will but follow my advice, you
40 will find it worth more than eighty times eighty dollars to you.

10. The primary purpose of this passage is to

    (A) provide practical recommendations
    (B) rebuke a hasty demand
    (C) express severe frustration
    (D) refute an irresponsible request
    (E) send a stern warning

11. The sentence beginning "Your request for eighty dollars..." (line 1) suggests that the author of this passage

    (A) is unable to provide financial support
    (B) does not understand the purpose of the request
    (C) needs a great deal of persuasion to make a loan
    (D) does not believe it is prudent to consent to the request
    (E) disagrees with the conditions of the loan

12. "Charge" in line 17 most nearly means

    (A) accountability
    (B) responsibility
    (C) safekeeping
    (D) indictment
    (E) hurtle

13. The author suggests that Johnston is

    (A) lazy and disinterested
    (B) rigorous in his ambitions
    (C) a ruthless farm worker
    (D) unable to find employment
    (E) lethargic because of habit

14. The author can best be described as

   (A) concerned and patient
   (B) logical and stern
   (C) thoughtful and anxious
   (D) empathetic and stingy
   (E) distressed and reckless

15. The author suggests that Johnston should alter his behavior because

   (A) nobody else can take care of the farm responsibilities
   (B) the children are in need of a better role model
   (C) too much time has already been wasted
   (D) there are no more loans available
   (E) the land deed must be transferred

Questions 16 through 24 are based on the following passage.

The following passage is adapted from a novel. In this except, Buck, a domesticated dog who is kidnapped into the wild, is now part of a team of dogs who pulls the sled.

He swiftly lost the fastidiousness which had characterized his old life.
A dainty eater, he found that his mates, finishing first, robbed him of
his unfinished ration. There was no defending it. While he was
fighting off two or three, it was disappearing down the throats of the
5 others. To remedy this, he ate as fast as they; and, so greatly did
hunger compel him, he was not above taking what did not belong to
him. He watched and learned. When he saw Pike, one of the new
dogs, a clever malingerer and thief, slyly steal a slice of bacon when
Perrault's back was turned, he duplicated the performance the
10 following day, getting away with the whole chunk. A great uproar was
raised, but he was unsuspected; while Dub, an awkward blunderer
who was always getting caught, was punished for Buck's misdeed.

This first theft marked Buck as fit to survive in the hostile Northland
environment. It marked his adaptability, his capacity to adjust himself
15 to changing conditions, the lack of which would have meant swift and
terrible death. It marked, further, the decay or going to pieces of his
moral nature, a vain thing and a handicap in the ruthless struggle for
existence. It was all well enough in the Southland, under the law of
love and fellowship, to respect private property and personal feelings;

20   but in the Northland, under the law of club and fang, whoso took
      such things into account was a fool, and in so far as he observed them
      he would fail to prosper.

      Not that Buck reasoned it out. He was fit, that was all, and
      unconsciously he accommodated himself to the new mode of life. All
25   his days, no matter what the odds, he had never run from a fight. But
      the club of the man in the red sweater had beaten into him a more
      fundamental and primitive code. Civilized, he could have died for a
      moral consideration, say the defence of Judge Miller's riding-whip;
      but the completeness of his decivilization was now evidenced by his
30   ability to flee from the defence of a moral consideration and so save
      his hide. He did not steal for joy of it, but because of the clamor of
      his stomach. He did not rob openly, but stole secretly and cunningly,
      out of respect for club and fang. In short, the things he did were done
      because it was easier to do them than not to do them.

35   His development (or retrogression) was rapid. His muscles became
      hard as iron, and he grew callous to all ordinary pain. He achieved an
      internal as well as external economy. He could eat anything, no
      matter how loathsome or indigestible; and, once eaten, the juices of
      his stomach extracted the last least particle of nutriment; and his
40   blood carried it to the farthest reaches of his body, building it into
      the toughest and stoutest of tissues. Sight and scent became
      remarkably keen, while his hearing developed such acuteness that in
      his sleep he heard the faintest sound and knew whether it heralded
      peace or peril. He learned to bite the ice out with his teeth when it
45   collected between his toes; and when he was thirsty and there was a
      thick scum of ice over the water hole, he would break it by rearing
      and striking it with stiff fore legs. His most conspicuous trait was an
      ability to scent the wind and forecast it a night in advance. No
      matter how breathless the air when he dug his nest by tree or bank,
50   the wind that later blew inevitably found him to leeward, sheltered
      and snug.

      And not only did he learn by experience, but instincts long dead
      became alive again. The domesticated generations fell from him. In
      vague ways he remembered back to the youth of the breed, to the
55   time the wild dogs ranged in packs through the primeval forest and
      killed their meat as they ran it down. It was no task for him to learn

to fight with cut and slash and the quick wolf snap. In this manner
had fought forgotten ancestors. They quickened the old life within
him, and the old tricks which they had stamped into the heredity of
60   the breed were his tricks. They came to him without effort or
discovery, as though they had been his always. And when, on the still
cold nights, he pointed his nose at a star and howled long and
wolflike, it was his ancestors, dead and dust, pointing nose at star and
howling down through the centuries and through him. And his
65   cadences were their cadences, the cadences which voiced their woe
and what to them was the meaning of the stiffness, and the cold,
and dark.

16.   The primary purpose of this passage is to suggest that the

   (A)   property and personal feelings are respected in the wild
   (B)   lives that animals lead are much more violent than humans
         imagine
   (C)   only necessary element to survival is instinct
   (D)   behavior must be modified to the demands of the environment
   (E)   human pursuit to domesticate animals is futile

17.   The statement "There was no defending it" (line 3) refers to the

   (A)   food that is distributed to the dogs
   (B)   territory that the dogs are given protect
   (C)   lifestyle that Buck finds himself in
   (D)   despicable rules that govern the behavior of the dogs
   (E)   Perrault's bacon

18.   The sentence beginning "To remedy this…" (line 5) suggests that Buck's
behavior was

   (A)   acquired through exhaustive practice
   (B)   an instinctual response to the environment
   (C)   learned during his stay with Judge Miller
   (D)   a result of deep cogitation
   (E)   necessary to conceal his true intentions

19. Buck's metamorphosis shows that

    (A) moral concerns of human civilization have no place in the world of the wild
    (B) new breeds of animals evolve only in domestic environments
    (C) every species is able to evolve when necessary
    (D) pilfering is necessary for survival
    (E) physical changes must take place to adjust to new surroundings

20. In line 24, "accommodated" most closely means

    (A) familiarized
    (B) acclimated
    (C) obliged
    (D) trained
    (E) ameliorated

21. Upon entering life in Northland, Buck must learn to

    (A) find his way back to his old lifestyle and escape the pack
    (B) adjust his work ethic and become self-reliant
    (C) tap into his instinctual skills and steal consistently from his pack
    (D) suppress his memories and alter his expectations
    (E) domesticate the other members of his pack

22. As used in line 47, "conspicuous" most nearly means

    (A) zealous
    (B) prominent
    (C) subtle
    (D) notorious
    (E) smell

23. The primary purpose of the final paragraph of the passage is to suggest that

(A) when man leaves civilization and its trappings, he becomes like his ancestors
(B) the reappearance of familial traits is necessary for success in the wild
(C) the theory of survival of the fittest is based on scientific evidence
(D) establishing a link with one's ancestors is important for self-discovery
(E) man is not truly fit for the world of the wild

24. The sentence beginning "They quickened the old life within him..." (lines 58–59) suggests that

(A) primitive instincts do not fade away in the civilized world
(B) old habits are difficult to resurrect
(C) instincts always re-emerge in the wild environment
(D) morality can only exist in the human species
(E) impulses can be honed through careful training

STOP
If you finish before time is called, you may check your work on this section only.
Do not turn to any other section in the test.

Section 5
Time—25 Minutes
18 Questions

Directions: This section contains two types of questions. You have 25 minutes to complete both types. For questions 1–8, solve each problem and decide which is the best of the choices given. Fill in the corresponding circle on the answer sheet. Questions 9–18 require that you solve the problem and record your answers on a grid. A problem may have more than one solution, but only one solution of your choosing may be recorded. No Student-Produced Response question may have a negative solution. You may use any available space for scratch work and for registering your answer.

Notes

1. The use of a calculator is permitted.
2. All numbers used are real numbers.
3. Figures that accompany problems in this test are intended to provide information useful in solving the problems. They are drawn as accurately as possible EXCEPT when it is stated in a specific problem that the figure is not drawn to scale. All figures lie in a plane unless otherwise indicated.
4. Unless otherwise specified, the domain of any function f is assumed to be the set of all real numbers x for which $f(x)$ is a real number.

Reference Information

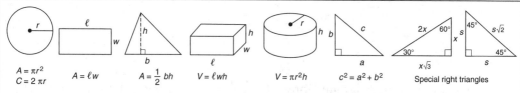

$A = \pi r^2$
$C = 2\pi r$

$A = \ell w$

$A = \frac{1}{2} bh$

$V = \ell wh$

$V = \pi r^2 h$

$c^2 = a^2 + b^2$

Special right triangles

The number of degrees of arc in a circle is 360.
The sum of the measures in degrees of the angles of a triangle is 180.

1.

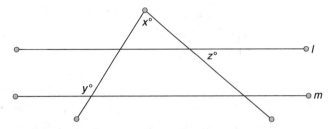

In the figure above, if $l \parallel m$, what does z equal in terms of x and y?

(A) $y - x$
(B) $x - y$
(C) $180 - y + x$
(D) $180 + y - x$
(E) $180 - (x + y)$

2.

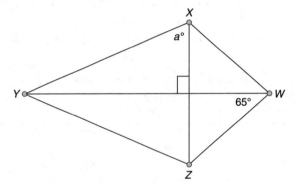

In the quadrilateral above (not drawn to scale), $YX = YW = YZ$. If $WX = WZ$, then what is the value of a?

(A) 25
(B) 30
(C) 35
(D) 40
(E) 45

3.

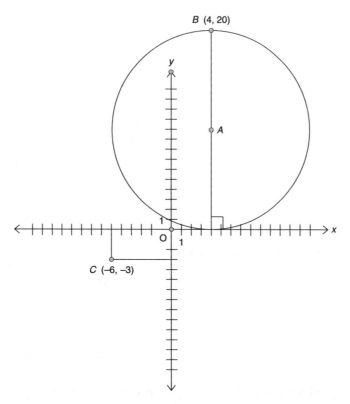

In the *xy*-plane above, point *A* lies in the center of a circle which is tangent to the *x*-axis. What is the measurement of $\overline{AC}$ (not shown)?

(A) 23
(B) $13\sqrt{2}$
(C) $10\sqrt{13}$
(D) $\sqrt{269}$
(E) It cannot be determined from the information given

4.

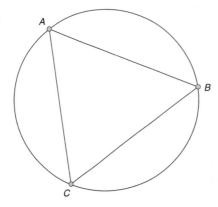

In the figure above, equilateral triangle ABC is inscribed in the circle. What is the degree measure of arc AB?

(A) 30°
(B) 60°
(C) 90°
(D) 120°
(E) 150°

5.   What is the maximum number of points of intersection between a circle and a rectangle that lie in the same plane?

(A) 4
(B) 6
(C) 8
(D) 9
(E) 10

6.

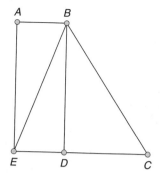

In equilateral triangle *EBC* above (not drawn to scale), *EC* = 10. If *m*∠*BDC* = 90°, what is the area of rectangle *ABED*?

(A) $10\sqrt{3}$
(B) 25
(C) 50
(D) $25\sqrt{3}$
(E) 100

7.   If the volume of a cube is e^3, what is the shortest distance from the center of the cube to the base of the cube?

(A) $\sqrt[3]{e}$

(B) $\sqrt{e}$

(C) $\dfrac{\sqrt{e}}{2}$

(D) $\dfrac{e}{2}$

(E) $2e$

8.

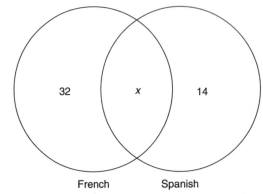

French   Spanish

The Venn diagram above shows the distribution of students who are in French class, Spanish class, or both classes. If the ratio of the number of students in French class to the number of students in Spanish class is 5:3, then what is the value of x?

(A) 3
(B) 5
(C) 8
(D) 13
(E) 26

9. If $x + 3y$ is equal to 120 percent of 5y, what is the value of $\frac{y}{x}$?

10. The measures of the four angles in a quadrilateral have a ratio of 3:4:8:9. What is the measure, in degrees, of the largest of these angles?

11. Point P lies on the line with equation $y - 6 = \dfrac{4}{5}(x - 10)$. If the x-coordinate of P is 15, what is the y-coordinate of P?

12. To solve a treasure hunt, Beatrice and Howard must compare the lengths of their strides. Beatrice and Howard start standing back to back, and then walk 8 steps in opposite directions away from each other. Beatrice turns around, walks toward Howard, and reaches him in 13 steps. The length of one of Beatrice's steps is how many times the length of one of Howard's steps. (Assume that Beatrice's strides are always the same length and Howard's steps are always the same length.)

13. On a test worth a total of 150 points, Roger lost 8 percent of those points because he answered one of the questions incorrectly, but he got 7 points added back to his score for answering the extra credit question correctly. If Roger answered all of the other test corrections correctly, how many points did he earn on the test?

14. $x, 2x, \ldots$

The first term in the sequence above is x, and each term after the first term is two times the preceding term. If the sum of the first six terms is 315, what is the value of x?

15. If x is chosen at random from the set $\{3, 4, 5\}$ and y is chosen at random from the set $\{9, 10, 11, 12\}$, what is the probability that the product of x and y is divisible by 3?

16. $a + b + 5c = 210$
$a + b + 3c = 150$

In the system of equations above, what is the value of $a + b$?

17. If $(f + g)^2 = 25$ and $fg = 10$, what is the value of $f^2 + g^2$?

18. Maybelline drove to work in the morning at an average speed of 44 miles per hour. She returned home in the evening along the same route and averaged 77 miles per hour. If Maybelline spent a total of 2 hours commuting to and from work, how many miles did Maybelline drive to work in the morning?

Section 7
Time—25 minutes
35 questions

Turn to Section 7 (page 501) of your answer sheet to answer the questions in this section.

Directions: For each question in this section, select the best answer from among the answer choices given and fill in the corresponding circle on the answer sheet.

The following sentences test correctness and effectiveness of expression. Part of each sentence or the entire sentence is underlined; beneath each sentence are five ways of phrasing the underlined material. Choice A repeats the original phrasing; the other four choices are different. If you thing the original phrasing produces a better sentence than any of the alternatives, select choice A; if not, select one of the other choices.

In making your selection, follow the requirements of standard written English; that is, pay attention to grammar, choice of words, sentence construction, and punctuation. Your selection should result in the most effective sentence—clear and precise, without awkwardness or ambiguity.

Example:

The numerous biographies published about Roosevelt's life <u>are testament to his great achievements</u>.
(A) are testament to his great achievements
(B) is testament to his great achievements
(C) **stand as a testament for his great achievement**
(D) full of achievement, the books are testament
(E) are testaments to his great achievements

---

1. By accident, he hit <u>his teammate with the ball in the eye</u>.

   (A) his teammate with the ball in the eye
   (B) his teammate in the eye with the ball
   (C) the eye of his teammate with the ball
   (D) the teammate's eye with his ball
   (E) the ball into the eye of his teammate

2. Both Dr. Kahn and Dr. Sherman being widely known for his pioneering work in alternative medical treatments.

   (A) Both Dr. Kahn and Dr. Sherman being widely known for his pioneering work

   (B) Both Dr. Kahn and Dr. Sherman being widely known for their pioneering work

   (C) Widely known are Dr. Kahn and Dr. Sherman, for their pioneering work

   (D) Both Dr. Kahn and Dr. Sherman are widely known for their pioneering work

   (E) As a result of their pioneering work Dr. Kahn and Dr. Sherman are widely known

3. The hardworking student spent his time perfecting his Spanish, volunteering at the hospital, and he also coached the junior varsity soccer team.

   (A) perfecting his Spanish, volunteering at the hospital, and he also coached the junior

   (B) perfecting his Spanish, volunteering at the hospital, and coaching the junior

   (C) by perfecting his Spanish, by volunteering at the hospital, and by coaching the junior

   (D) in perfection of his Spanish, volunteered at the hospital, and also coached the junior

   (E) perfecting his Spanish, while also volunteering at the hospital and coaching the junior

4. I wanted to buy a new couch, but they didn't have the one I could afford.

   (A) couch, but they didn't have

   (B) couch but they didn't have

   (C) couch but the store didn't have

   (D) couch, but the store didn't have

   (E) couch, but the store doesn't have

5. The infamous author visited our writer's <u>workshop and participated with</u> the weekly editorial meeting.

   (A) workshop and participated with
   (B) workshop to participate with
   (C) workshop, and participated in
   (D) workshop and participated in
   (E) workshop and participates in

6. The movie's colorful images and its humorous language <u>give the viewer pleasure</u>.

   (A) give the viewer pleasure
   (B) please the one who is viewing
   (C) give on pleasure in viewing it
   (D) please the viewer of the film
   (E) gives pleasure to those who view it

7. School regulations require students to <u>not only passing all final exams but also to submit</u> a portfolio.

   (A) not only passing all final exams but also to submit
   (B) not only passing all final exams, but also to submit
   (C) not only to pass all final exams but also, to submit
   (D) not only the passing of all final exams, but also submission to
   (E) not only pass all final exams but also to submit

8. Between <u>you and I, the green</u> textbook is better than the yellow textbook.

   (A) you and I, the green
   (B) you and me, the green
   (C) you and us, the green
   (D) us the green
   (E) you and me, that green

9. Since Lauren <u>was talking during the entire swim practice, making it</u> impossible for anyone to concentrate, the coach demanded that Lauren swim extra laps.

    (A) was talking during the entire swim practice, making
    (B) talked during the entire practice and thus made it
    (C) has talked during the entire swim practice, making it
    (D) was talking during the entire swim practice; and made it
    (E) talked all of the entire swim practice, it made it

10. <u>I can go to New York or Boston. I wonder which is best.</u>

    (A) I can go to New York or Boston. I wonder which is best.
    (B) I can go to New York or Boston; I wonder which is best.
    (C) I am able go to New York or Boston. I wonder which is best.
    (D) I can go to New York or Boston. I wonder which is better.
    (E) I can go to New York or Boston and am wondering which is best.

11. <u>Although she was a great storyteller</u>, Lindsay is extremely imaginative and skilled at describing her ideas.

    (A) Although she was a great storyteller
    (B) A great storyteller
    (C) Because of her storytelling
    (D) In being a great storyteller
    (E) Known, as a great storyteller

The following sentences test your ability to recognize grammar and usage errors. Each sentence contains either a single error or no error at all. No sentence contains more than one error. The error, if there is one, is underlined and lettered. If the sentence contains an error, select the one underlined part that must be changed to make the sentence correct. If the sentence is correct, select choice E. In choosing answers, follow the requires of standard written English.

Example:

The other boys and him quickly agreed to meet at the nearby pizza parlor.
    A   B   C   D

No error.
    E

12.   Noreen, together with Billy, are representing JKF High School in the
                  A   B   C   D
final round of the Empire State games. No error.
                                    E

13.   Although Shelly allows her dog to run loose, she has never tried to run
      A   B   C   D
away. No error.
      E

14.   In today's English class we learned how to take notes and outline
         A   B   C
and we also practiced various reading comprehension strategies. No error.
      D   E

15.   We studied for an hour; than we took a break and went to the movies.
         A   B   C   D
No error.
    E

16.   Both Bobby and I had to agree to the terms of the agreement. No Error.
    A   B   C   D   E

17.   Sam either wanted to play soccer on the junior varsity team or play
          A   B   C
basketball on the varsity team. No error.
           D   E

18. A central part of my test preparation have been to read all the books in
     A   B   C   D
     the public library. No error.
                        E

19. The teacher said that our reports are due at the end of the week and
          A   B
     be sure to include your bibliography. No error.
       C   D   E

20. He insisted that he was able to complete all of the math homework,
        A   B
     which was not considered difficult by him. No error.
                     C   D   E

21. Anita and Susan are each others best friend. No error.
                     A   B   C   D   E

22. This is well written and thoughtfully organized; however, the draft
     A   B
     should be proofread carefully. No error.
       C   D   E

23. Please be aware that there is no changes for the students. No error.
       A   B   C   D   E

24. If an athlete wants to succeed in sports, they must dedicate a lot of
       A   B   C   D
     time to rigorous practice. No error.
                                E

25. The students read books on nature to learn about the flora, and fauna of
                   A   B C   D
     the country. No error.
                   E

26. The doctor prescribed a stronger medicine, however, it is not helping.
                A   B   C   D
     No error.
     E

27. <u>I took myself</u> out <u>to a</u> fancy dinner <u>on my</u> birthday. <u>No error.</u>
    A   B   C   D   E

28. The <u>values of</u> A and B <u>were found</u> to be 99.8 and 16.9, <u>respectively.</u>
        A   B   C   D

    <u>No error.</u>
      E

29. My cousin <u>John,</u> <u>who</u> <u>lives</u> in New Hampshire, <u>is visiting in</u> two weeks.
           A   B   C   D

    <u>No error.</u>
      E

Directions: The following passage is an early draft of an essay. Some parts of the passage need to be rewritten.

Read the passage carefully and select the best answers for the questions that follow. Some questions are about particular sentences or parts of sentences and ask you to improve sentence structure or word choice. Other questions ask you to consider organization and development. In choosing answers, follow the requirements of standard written English.

---

(1) Some people believe that what doesn't kill you makes you stronger. (2) Although silly to think about it literally, there is certainly truth to it. (3) As one who has learned from difficult experiences. (4) I can say firsthand that difficult experiences make people stronger and give people an ability to learn. (5) Because of my experiences I have seen and felt how a challenge teaches me and thus makes me stronger. (6) Even in the instance when an experience does not make you stronger you still learn from it. (7) For example, when I decided to run the marathon, I thought I would "die" during training. (8) However, I worked tirelessly, received help from my trainer, and ultimately not only become a stronger run, but also learned a lot about the sport of running. (9) For example, when I finished the marathon, I was not strong (because I was so tired) but I still felt that I had learned a lot about myself. (10) I remember my coach telling me, "Joan, you gain wisdom every time you run." (11) Such trail and tribulation is necessary for growth. (12) If all that we do is sit around

do the same thing we usually do then we will never grow, we will never get stronger, and we will never learn. (13) It is important to challenge ourselves, to feel pain, in order to get stronger. (14) What does not kill us will make us stronger, smarter, and allow us to grow. (15) What do you believe?

30. In context, what is the best version of the underlined portion of sentence 2 (reproduced below)?

    Although silly to think about it literally, <u>there is certainly truth to it</u>.

    (A) (as is now)
    (B) there is certain truth to it
    (C) there is certainly truth to the saying
    (D) there has to be truth to the saying
    (E) there is certainly truth in it

31. In context, which of the following is the best way to revise sentences 3 and 4 in order to combine the sentences?

    (A) (as is now)
    (B) As an individual who has learned from difficult experiences, I can say first hand that challenging circumstances give people an ability to learn.
    (C) From difficult circumstances comes much learning and I can say this based on my own personal experiences.
    (D) My personal experiences have shown me how to have the ability to learn from challenges.
    (E) Based on personal experiences, I believe that difficult circumstances present opportunity for growth and learning.

32. What should be done with sentence 6 (reproduced below)?

    Even in the instance when an experience does not make you stronger you still learn from it.

    (A) (as is now)
    (B) insert it before sentence 9
    (C) delete it
    (D) combine it with sentence 5
    (E) insert it after sentence 11

33. In context, which is the best revision for sentence 12 (reproduced below)?

    If all that we do is sit around do the same thing we usually do then we will never grow, we will never get stronger, and we will never learn.

    (A) change "then" to a comma
    (B) remove "we will never" before "get stronger" and "learn"
    (C) change "same" to "consistent"
    (D) change "If all that we do is sit around do the same thing we usually do then" to "If we do not challenge ourselves then"
    (E) change "we will never grow, we will never get stronger, and we will never learn" to "we will never make any change"

34. What should be done with sentence 14 (reproduced below)?

    What does not kill us will make us stronger, smarter, and allow us to grow.

    (A) (as is now)
    (B) delete it
    (C) insert "will" before "allow"
    (D) Add an exclamation point at the end of the sentence
    (E) Insert it at the end of the passage

35. All of the following strategies are used by the writer of the passage EXCEPT

    (A) background explanation
    (B) direct quotation
    (C) rhetorical questions
    (D) imaginative description
    (E) personal narration

STOP
If you finish before time is called, you may check your work on this section only.
Do not turn to any other section in the test.

Section 8
Time – 20 minutes
19 questions

Turn to Section 8 (page 501) of your answer sheet to answer the questions in this section.

Directions: For each question in this section, select the best answer from among the answer choices given and fill in the corresponding circle on the answer sheet.

Each sentence below has one or two question blanks, each blank indicating that something has been omitted. Beneath the sentence are five words or sets of words labeled A through E. Choose the word or set of words that, when inserted in the sentence, *best* fits the meaning of the sentence as a whole.

Example:

Susan preferred to be _____, hoping to avoid confusion due to miscommunication.
(A) **direct**
(B) devious
(C) cunning
(D) austere
(E) terse

1. The coach was called a visionary and a giant because he took a _____ group of players and changed the team's destiny.

   (A) avid
   (B) degenerate
   (C) struggling
   (D) promising
   (E) victorious

2. The company principal owner and chairman _____ authority to his sons when he decided to dedicate his time to philanthropic works.

   (A) amplified
   (B) dedicated
   (C) ceded
   (D) seized
   (E) conveyed

3. After a display of poor sportsmanship the coach ____ his players for their ____ behavior.

    (A) admonished...deplorable
    (B) lamented...terrible
    (C) emboldened...animated
    (D) commended...exultant
    (E) extolled...perilous

4. He was ____ by his fellow bunkmates when his underwear was hung on the flag pole for the whole camp to see.

    (A) disintegrated
    (B) revered
    (C) abased
    (D) appreciated
    (E) disdained

5. The valley is ____ with vegetation because of ____ rainfall.

    (A) lush...abundant
    (B) sumptuous...verdant
    (C) ripe...scarce
    (D) overflowing...insufficient
    (E) profuse...average

6. The usually ____ child was behaving in an uncharacteristically ____ and quiet way.

    (A) introverted...timid
    (B) garrulous...diffident
    (C) inhibited...reticent
    (D) outgoing...insecure
    (E) gregarious...convivial

The passages below are followed by questions based on their content; questions that follow a pair of related passages may also be based on the relationship between the paired passages. Answer the questions on the basis of what is *stated* or *implied* in the passage in any introductory material that may be provided.

Questions 7 through 19 are based on the following passages.

The following passage is adapted from a novel published in 1818 and is one of the earliest examples of science fiction writing.

After days and nights of incredible labour and fatigue, I succeeded in discovering the cause of generation and life; nay, more, I became
Line   myself capable of bestowing animation upon lifeless matter.

The astonishment which I had at first experienced on this discovery
5   soon gave place to delight and rapture. After so much time spent in painful labour, to arrive at once at the summit of my desires was the most gratifying consummation of my toils. But this discovery was so great and overwhelming that all the steps by which I had been progressively led to it were obliterated, and I beheld only the result.
10   What had been the study and desire of the wisest men since the creation of the world was now within my grasp. Not that, like a magic scene, it all opened upon me at once: the information I had obtained was of a nature rather to direct my endeavours so soon as I should point them towards the object of my search than to exhibit that
15   object already accomplished. I was like the Arabian who had been buried with the dead and found a passage to life, aided only by one glimmering and seemingly ineffectual light.

I see by your eagerness and the wonder and hope which your eyes express, my friend, that you expect to be informed of the secret with
20   which I am acquainted; that cannot be; listen patiently until the end of my story, and you will easily perceive why I am reserved upon that subject. I will not lead you on, unguarded and ardent as I then was, to your destruction and infallible misery. Learn from me, if not by my precepts, at least by my example, how dangerous is the acquirement
25   of knowledge and how much happier that man is who believes his native town to be the world, than he who aspires to become greater than his nature will allow.

When I found so astonishing a power placed within my hands, I
hesitated a long time concerning the manner in which I should employ
30   it. Although I possessed the capacity of bestowing animation, yet to
prepare a frame for the reception of it, with all its intricacies of fibres,
muscles, and veins, still remained a work of inconceivable difficulty and
labour. I doubted at first whether I should attempt the creation of a
being like myself, or one of simpler organization; but my imagination
35   was too much exalted by my first success to permit me to doubt of my
ability to give life to an animal as complex and wonderful as man. The
materials at present within my command hardly appeared adequate to
so arduous an undertaking, but I doubted not that I should ultimately
succeed. I prepared myself for a multitude of reverses; my operations
40   might be incessantly baffled, and at last my work be imperfect, yet
when I considered the improvement which every day takes place in
science and mechanics, I was encouraged to hope my present attempts
would at least lay the foundations of future success. Nor could I
consider the magnitude and complexity of my plan as any argument of
45   its impracticability. It was with these feelings that I began the creation
of a human being. As the minuteness of the parts formed a great
hindrance to my speed, I resolved, contrary to my first intention, to
make the being of a gigantic stature, that is to say, about eight feet in
height, and proportionably large. After having formed this
50   determination and having spent some months in successfully collecting
and arranging my materials, I began.

No one can conceive the variety of feelings which bore me onwards,
like a hurricane, in the first enthusiasm of success. Life and death
appeared to me ideal bounds, which I should first break through, and
55   pour a torrent of light into our dark world. A new species would bless
me as its creator and source; many happy and excellent natures would
owe their being to me. No father could claim the gratitude of his child
so completely as I should deserve theirs. Pursuing these reflections, I
thought that if I could bestow animation upon lifeless matter, I might
60   in process of time (although I now found it impossible) renew life
where death had apparently devoted the body to corruption.

7.   The imagery in lines 1–3 ("After days and nights of incredible labour and fatigue...") functions to

(A)   elucidate how arduously the narrator worked
(B)   illustrate the passage of time
(C)   position the creation of a new being
(D)   foreshadow a crucial discovery
(E)   contrast the distinct speed of shaping the creation

8.   It can be inferred from the second paragraph (lines 4–17) that the narrator's initial reaction to his discovery was of

(A)   elated surprise
(B)   genuine distress
(C)   aggressive resolve
(D)   underwhelming progress
(E)   solemn conceit

9.   The effect of the narrator's obsessive efforts toward the "discovery" (line 4) results in his

(A)   being buried under his work
(B)   engaging in questionable scientific inquiry
(C)   not being able to undo what he has created
(D)   being uninterested in the final result
(E)   creating the first effective light

10.   In line 21, "perceive" most nearly means

(A)   observe
(B)   sense
(C)   understand
(D)   distinguish
(E)   identify

11. The narrator refuses to reveal the "secret" with which he is "acquainted" (lines 19–20) because

(A) he believes that his friend is too eager for the information
(B) he does not want the same injury to come to his friend as has plagued him
(C) he is concerned that others will use him as an example
(D) he wants his friend to learn from his careful teachings
(E) he wants to divulge the formula to happiness

12. The narrator's remarks in lines 24–27 ("how dangerous... nature will allow.") reveal that the narrator believes that

(A) with knowledge comes great social responsibility
(B) man should not aspire to eminence
(C) knowledge brings great misery
(D) man should not leave the land where he is born
(E) nature determines our path in life

13. It can be inferred from the passage that the narrator's decision to build the creation is based on all of the following EXCEPT

(A) he is encouraged by what he has already accomplished
(B) he believes that his efforts will form the underpinning for further advancement
(C) he does not deem the challenge insurmountable
(D) he feels he can prepare even without sufficient materials
(E) he wants to create a new human of enormous stature

14. The purpose of the statement "hesitated a long time" in lines 28–29 is to

(A) to dispel any doubts about the narrator's abilities to reach a thoughtful conclusion
(B) to emphasize the narrator's particular point of view
(C) to illustrate the limits of scientific knowledge
(D) to underscore that significance of the narrator's abilities
(E) to suggest that the narrator's main concern is to expand the reach of science

15. The narrator mentions the size of his creation (lines 46–49) in order to

    (A) demonstrate his surgical acumen
    (B) explain why he intended to build a human-sized frame
    (C) give the reader an understanding of the construction
    (D) illustrate the great complexity of building the body
    (E) reveal the extent of his ambition

16. "Dark world" in line 55, refers to

    (A) people's powerlessness over death
    (B) the underworld
    (C) human inability to create new life
    (D) people's innate ignorance about life and death
    (E) science's failure to produce new species

17. The narrator's remarks in lines 55–57 ("A new species would bless me as its creator and source; many happy and excellent natures would owe their being to me. ") suggests that the narrator

    (A) is a humble man yearning to extend his life
    (B) is a curious scientist striving to tackle biology's greatest question
    (C) believes he will take over the role of god
    (D) is an egotistical man who believes he will be revered by his creations
    (E) yearns to become a father although he cannot have children

18. In line 58, "reflections" most nearly means

    (A) likeness
    (B) signs
    (C) considerations
    (D) cogitations
    (E) ideas

19. Line 61 (last line) primarily encourages the reader to view death as a/an

   (A) source of great distress for humans
   (B) opportunity for industrious scientific research
   (C) depressing fact of human existence
   (D) force that science will never able to impede
   (E) condition that extends into the afterlife

STOP
If you finish before time is called, you may check your work on this section only.
Do not turn to any other section in the test.

Section 9
Time—20 Minutes
16 Questions

Directions: For this section, solve each problem and decide which is the best of the choices given. Fill in the corresponding circle on the answer sheet. You may use any available space for scratch work.

Notes

1. The use of a calculator is permitted.
2. All numbers used are real numbers.
3. Figures that accompany problems in this test are intended to provide information useful in solving the problems. They are drawn as accurately as possible EXCEPT when it is stated in a specific problem that the figure is not drawn to scale. All figures lie in a plane unless otherwise indicated.
4. Unless otherwise specified, the domain of any function f is assumed to be the set of all real numbers x for which $f(x)$ is a real number.

Reference Information

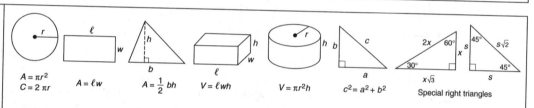

$A = \pi r^2$
$C = 2\pi r$

$A = \ell w$

$A = \frac{1}{2} bh$

$V = \ell wh$

$V = \pi r^2 h$

$c^2 = a^2 + b^2$

Special right triangles

The number of degrees of arc in a circle is 360.
The sum of the measures in degrees of the angles of a triangle is 180.

1. At Happy Home Appliances, the regular price of a washing machine is $800. How much money is saved by buying this refrigerator at 30 percent off the regular price rather than buying it on sale at 15 percent off the regular price with an additional discount of 15 percent off the sale price?

(A) $12
(B) $16
(C) $18
(D) $22
(E) No money is saved

2. If $y = \dfrac{2x^3}{3z}$, what happens to the value of y when both x and z are doubled?

    (A) y is halved

    (B) y is multiplied by $\dfrac{8}{3}$

    (C) y is multiplied by $\dfrac{4}{3}$

    (D) y is multiplied by 4

    (E) y is multiplied by 16

3.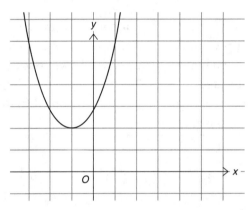

    The figure above shows the graph of a quadratic function g that has a minimum at the point $(-1, 2)$. If $g(m) = g(1)$, which of the following could be the value of m?

    (A) −3
    (B) −2
    (C) −1
    (D) 0
    (E) 6

4. Six hundred dollars was invested at a yearly simple interest rate of y percent. If at the end of one year the investment had grown to 870 dollars, what is the value of y?

    (A) 25
    (B) 30
    (C) 35
    (D) 45
    (E) 50

5.

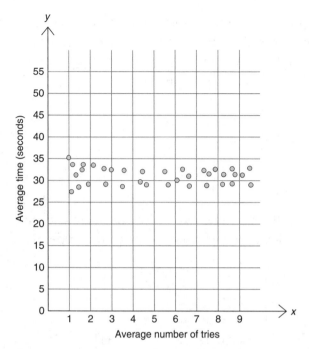

Meredith is preparing for a race. Each day she runs a certain distance a certain number of times. The values on the x-axis represent Meredith's average number of tries per week at a particular distance. The values on the y-axis represent Meredith's average time needed to run the particular distance. Based on the data, which of the following functions best models the relationship between y, Meredith's average time (in seconds), and x, Meredith's average number of tries (per week)?

(A) $y(x) = 30$
(B) $y(x) = x$
(C) $y(x) = 30x$
(D) $y(x) = \dfrac{x}{30}$
(E) $y(x) = x + 30$

6. If b and c are constants and $x^2 + bx + 8$ is equivalent to $(x + 4)(x + c)$, what is the value of b?

(A) 0
(B) 2
(C) 4
(D) 6
(E) It cannot be determined from the information given

7. The total weekly profit k, in dollars, from producing and selling m units of a particular sweater is given by the function $k(m) = 15m - (7m + c)$, where c is a constant. If 400 units were produced and sold last week for a total profit of $2,700, what is the value of c?

(A) −600
(B) −500
(C) 0
(D) 500
(E) 600

8. If the function g is defined by $g(x) = ax^2 + bx + c$, where a, b, and c are positive constants, which of the following could be the graph of g?

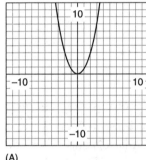

(A)

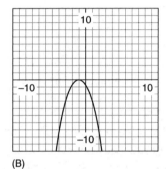

(B)

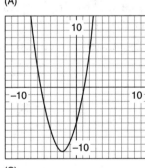

(C)

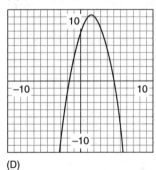

(D)

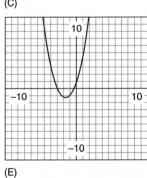

(E)

9. If x is a positive integer and $x > 1$, which of the following represents the least odd integer that is the sum of two consecutive integers?

(A) $2x + 1$
(B) $4x + 2$
(C) $2x$
(D) $2x + 2$
(E) $2x + 3$

10. If $(x + 2y)^{1/3} = (x - 2y)^{-1/3}$, which of the following must be true?

(A) $x = 0$
(B) $x + 2y = 1$
(C) $x - 2y = 1$
(D) $x^2 + 4y^2 = 1$
(E) $x^2 - 4y^2 = 1$

11. If x is a positive integer, and $8 = 16 - \sqrt{2x}$, which of the following could be the value of x?

(A) 8
(B) 16
(C) 32
(D) 64
(E) $\sqrt{32}$

12.

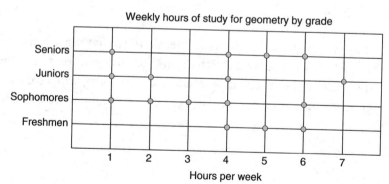

When asked how many hours they study each week for geometry, each of the 16 students surveyed at Urban High School responded, and their answers are recorded in the grid above. It shows the number of hours each student in a particular grade level studies per week. According to the data in the grid, which of the following is true?

(A) More students study five hours per week than two hours per week
(B) Of the students who study more than six hours per week, at least one is a junior
(C) More than half the students study less than four hours per week
(D) The students who study five hours per week are all juniors or sophomores
(E) The average number of hours freshmen study per week is four hours

13. Georgina's bank account password consists of three two-digit numbers. The password satisfies the three conditions below.

   I. One number is a multiple of 3
   II. One number is even
   III. One number is the month Georgina was born

If each number satisfies exactly one of the conditions above, which of the following could be Georgina's bank account password?

(A) 27-12-10
(B) 11-15-14
(C) 12-14-15
(D) 9-12-11
(E) 11-12-14

14. At Happy Reading Bookstore, club members receive $5 off their first purchase, $4 off their second purchase, and $2 off every purchase thereafter. If a member has made more than two purchases, which of the following functions describes his or her total savings, in dollars, for b purchases?

(A) $s(b) = 11b$
(B) $s(b) = 9 + 2b$
(C) $s(b) = 9b + 2(b-2)$
(D) $s(b) = 9 + 2(b-1)$
(E) $s(b) = 9 + 2(b-2)$

15.

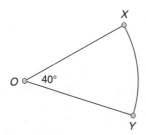

In the figure above, XY is the arc of a circle with center O. If the length of arc XY is 8π, what is the area of sector OXY?

(A) 288π
(B) 144π
(C) 136π
(D) 81π
(E) 72π

16. For all numbers x and y, let $x \bowtie y$ be defined by $x \bowtie y = x - xy + y$. For all numbers m and n, which of the following must be true?

I. $m \bowtie n = n \bowtie m$

II. $(n+1) \bowtie (m+n) = (m+n) \bowtie n$

III. $(m+1) \bowtie n = [(m+1) \bowtie (m+n)] + m^2$

(A) I only
(B) II only
(C) III only
(D) I and III only
(E) I, II, and III

Section 10
Time—10 minutes
14 questions

Turn to Section 10 (page 501) of your answer sheet to answer the questions in this section.

Directions: For each question in this section, select the best answer from among the answer choices given and fill in the corresponding circle on the answer sheet.

The following sentences test correctness and effectiveness of expression. Part of each sentence or the entire sentence is underlined; beneath each sentence are five ways of phrasing the underlined material. Choice A repeats the original phrasing; the other four choices are different. If you thing the original phrasing produces a better sentence than any of the alternatives, select choice A; if not, select one of the other choices.

In making your selection, follow the requirements of standard written English; that is, pay attention to grammar, choice of words, sentence construction, and punctuation. Your selection should result in the most effective sentence—clear and precise, without awkwardness or ambiguity.

Example:

The numerous biographies published about Roosevelt's life <u>are testament to his great achievements</u>.
(A) are testament to his great achievements
(B) is testament to his great achievements
(C) stand as a testament for his great achievement
(D) full of achievement, the books are testament
(E) are testaments to his great achievements

1. Between <u>you and I, the SAT</u> is a really difficult test.

   (A) you and I, the SAT
   (B) you and I the SAT
   (C) you and me, the SAT
   (D) you and me the SAT
   (E) us the SAT

2. Bill's performance <u>was so exciting, it had</u> the entire audience in awe.

   (A) was so exciting, it had
   (B) was such an excitement that it has
   (C) was so exciting that it has had
   (D) was so exciting; it had
   (E) was so exciting: it had

3. <u>She did good on the test</u>.

   (A) She did good on the test
   (B) She done good on the test
   (C) She done well on the test
   (D) She did well on the test
   (E) She tested good

4. Every one of the girls in Ms. Kim's class <u>is trying to do their best</u> in Ms. Kim's competition.

   (A) is trying to do their best
   (B) will try to do their best
   (C) has tried to do their best
   (D) is trying to do her best
   (E) tried to do her best

5. <u>The pink headband is better than the yellow</u>.

   (A) the pink headband is better than the yellow
   (B) the pink headband was better than the yellow
   (C) the pink headband is better than the yellow headband
   (D) the pink headband were better than the yellow headband
   (E) the pink one is better than the yellow headband

6. <u>It is hot at the beach today, I need a hat</u>.

   (A) It is hot at the beach today, I need a hat
   (B) Since it is hot at the beach today, I need a hat
   (C) It is hot at the beach today; I need a hat
   (D) Because of the hotness at the beach today, I need a hat
   (E) I need a hat: it is hot at the beach today

7. When Joanie was a <u>toddler, she was so uncoordinated that she often falls down</u>.

   (A) toddler, she was so uncoordinated that she often falls down
   (B) toddler; she had been so uncoordinated that she often falls down
   (C) toddler, she was so uncoordinated that she often falls down
   (D) toddler she often fell down because of her uncoordination
   (E) toddler, she was so uncoordinated that she often fell down

8. After the sun had set behind the trees, the <u>dusk brings a relief from</u> the sweltering heat.

   (A) dusk brings a relief from
   (B) dusk brought a relief from
   (C) dusk has brought a relief from
   (D) dusk brings a relief to
   (E) dusk brought a relief of

9. Since <u>Jackie was passing notes during the entire class, making it impossible for her friends to concentrate the</u> teacher kept Jackie after school.

   (A) Jackie was passing notes during the entire class, making it impossible for her friends to concentrate the
   (B) Jackie was passing notes during the entire class: making it impossible for her friends to concentrate the
   (C) Jackie was passing notes during the entire class, making it impossible for her friends to concentrate, the
   (D) Jackie passed notes during the entire class and made it impossible for her friends to concentrate the
   (E) Jackie's friends were not able to concentrate, because of her passing notes during the entire class

10. The <u>Sputnik, launched on October 4, 1957, sent</u> the first human-made object to orbit the Earth.

   (A) Sputnik, launched on October 4, 1957, sent
   (B) On October 4, 1957 the Sputnik was launched and sent
   (C) Sputnik which was launched on October 4, 1957 sent
   (D) Sputnik, launched on October 4, 1957, sends
   (E) Launched on October 4, 1957 the Sputnik, sent

11. <u>Being that he is a great gourmand</u>, Ben is expert at selecting the best restaurants in town.

   (A) Being that he is a great gourmand
   (B) In being a great gourmand
   (C) Although Ben is a great gourmand
   (D) A great gourmand
   (E) Because he was a great gourmand

12. First novels are often <u>their writer's most</u> imaginative works.

   (A) their writer's most
   (B) their writers' most
   (C) it's writers' more
   (D) it's writers most
   (E) the writers's most

13. Kim and Sami will represent Kennedy High School in the state track and field <u>championships, their work in this having been excellent this year</u>.

   (A) championships, their work in this having been excellent this year
   (B) championships as this is an excellent year for their work
   (C) championships, for their results as athletes have been excellent this year
   (D) championships; in what has been an excellent year for the athletes
   (E) championships, her work in this having been excellent this year

14. Maybe Jon was working at the computer on his <u>homework; on the other hand, he could have been playing</u> video games.

   (A) homework; on the other hand, he could have been playing
   (B) homework, on the other hand, he could have been playing
   (C) homework on the other hand, he could have been playing
   (D) homework; he could have been, on the other hand,
   (E) homework: on the other hand, he could have been playing

Exam 3   Answer Key

Section 2 Verbal	Section 3 Math	Section 4 Verbal	Section 5 Math
1. C	1. E	1. A	1. A
2. A	2. B	2. A	2. D
3. C	3. D	3. C	3. D
4. A	4. E	4. C	4. D
5. A	5. D	5. C	5. C
6. A	6. B	6. C	6. D
7. D	7. D	7. B	7. D
8. A	8. D	8. C	8. D
9. A	9. A	9. E	9. $\frac{1}{3}$
10. D	10. C	10. A	10. 135
11. D	11. B	11. D	11. 10
12. D	12. B	12. B	12. $\frac{8}{5}$
13. B	13. C	13. E	13. 145
14. E	14. E	14. A	14. 5
15. E	15. D	15. B	15. $\frac{2}{3}$
16. A	16. D	16. D	16. 60
17. E	17. B	17. A	17. 5
18. A	18. E	18. B	18. 56
19. E	19. D	19. A	
20. D	20. B	20. B	
21. C		21. B	
22. B		22. B	
23. E		23. A	
24. B		24. A	

Section 7 Writing	Section 8 Verbal	Section 9 Math	Section 10 Writing
1. B	1. C	1. C	1. C
2. D	2. C	2. D	2. D
3. B	3. A	3. A	3. D
4. D	4. C	4. D	4. D
5. D	5. A	5. A	5. C
6. A	6. B	6. D	6. B
7. E	7. C	7. D	7. E
8. B	8. A	8. E	8. B
9. A	9. C	9. A	9. C
10. D	10. C	10. E	10. A
11. B	11. B	11. C	11. D
12. B	12. C	12. B	12. B
13. D	13. E	13. B	13. C
14. D	14. D	14. E	14. A
15. C	15. E	15. B	
16. E	16. A	16. D	
17. A	17. D		
18. C	18. D		
19. D	19. C		
20. D			
21. C			
22. A			
23. C			
24. C			
25. D			
26. B			
27. B			
28. E			
29. E			
30. C			
31. E			
32. E			
33. D			
34. B			
35. D			

Appendix

Test Checklist
* * * * * * *

Week Before

☐ Understand all trouble spot topics

☐ Answer the "not so sure" questions

☐ Complete at least 2 practice exams

☐ Familiarize yourself with the exam layout

☐ Review exam instructions

☐ Start making a "night before exam hint sheet"

Night Before

☐ Read over your Logs

☐ Pack your bag (remember pens, pencils, ID, etc.)

☐ Go to sleep at a reasonable time

Morning of

☐ Don't stress; you are prepared

☐ Eat something (you want to be concentrating on the test, not what's for lunch after the test!)

Good Luck!!

Math Formula Sheet the Formulas You're Not Given That You Ought to Know

Arithmetic Operations

$$ab + ac = a(b + c)$$

$$a\left(\frac{b}{c}\right) = \frac{ab}{c}$$

$$\frac{\left(\frac{a}{b}\right)}{c} = \frac{a}{bc}$$

$$\frac{a}{\left(\frac{b}{c}\right)} = \frac{ac}{b}$$

$$\frac{a}{b} + \frac{c}{d} = \frac{ad + bc}{bd}$$

$$\frac{a}{b} - \frac{c}{d} = \frac{ad - bc}{bd}$$

$$\frac{a - b}{c - d} = \frac{b - a}{d - c}$$

$$\frac{a + b}{c} = \frac{a}{c} + \frac{b}{c}$$

$$\frac{ab + ac}{a} = b + c, \, a \neq 0$$

$$\frac{\left(\frac{a}{b}\right)}{\left(\frac{c}{d}\right)} = \frac{ad}{bc}$$

Exponent Rules

$$a^n a^m = a^{n+m}$$

$$\frac{a^n}{a^m} = a^{n-m} = \frac{1}{a^{m-n}}$$

$$(a^n)^m = a^{nm}$$

$$a^0 = 1, \, a \neq 0$$

$$(ab)^n = a^n b^n$$

$$\left(\frac{a}{b}\right)^n = \frac{a^n}{b^n}$$

$$a^{-n} = \frac{1}{a^n}$$

$$\frac{1}{a^{-n}} = a^n$$

$$\left(\frac{a}{b}\right)^{-n} = \left(\frac{b}{a}\right)^n = \frac{b^n}{a^n}$$

$$a^{\frac{n}{m}} = \left(a^{\frac{1}{m}}\right)^n = (a^n)^{\frac{1}{m}}$$

Linear Functions

$$y = mx + b \text{ or } f(x) = mx + b$$

Graph is a line with point $(0, b)$ and slope m.

Distance Formula

If $P_1 = (x_1, y_1)$ and $P_2 = (x_2, y_2)$ are two points the distance between them is

$$d(P_1, P_2) = \sqrt{(x_2 - x_1)^2 + (y_2 - y_1)^2}$$

Constant Function

$$y = a \text{ or } f(x) = a$$

Graph is a horizontal line passing though the point $(0, a)$.

Factoring Formulas

$$x^2 - a^2 = (x + a)(x - a)$$
$$x^2 + 2ax + a^2 = (x + a)^2$$
$$x^2 - 2ax + a^2 = (x - a)^2$$

Slope

Slope of the line containing the two points (x_1, y_1) and (x_2, y_2) is

$$m = \frac{y_2 - y_1}{x_2 - x_1} = \frac{\text{rise}}{\text{run}}$$

Slope–Intercept Form

The equation of the line with slope m and y-intercept $(0, b)$ is

$$y = mx + b$$

Point–Slope Form

The equation of the line with slope m and passing through the point (x_1, y_1) is

$$y - y_1 = m(x - x_1)$$

Common Mistakes You Need to Avoid

Error	Correction
$\dfrac{3}{0} \neq 0$ and $\dfrac{3}{0} \neq 3$	You can never divide by 0. Division by 0 is undefined.
$-4^2 \neq 16$	$-4^2 = -16$ and $(-4)^2 = 16$. Be careful how you use parentheses.
$(x^3)^4 \neq x^7$	$(x^3)^4 = x^{12}$. Raising a power to a power means you have to multiply, not add.
$\dfrac{x}{y+z} \neq \dfrac{x}{y} + \dfrac{x}{z}$	$\dfrac{3}{4} = \dfrac{3}{3+1} \neq \dfrac{3}{3} + \dfrac{3}{1} = 1 + 3 = 4$. You can only divide monomials (not binomials) into a numerator.
$\dfrac{x+cy}{x} \neq 1 + cy$	$\dfrac{x+cy}{x} = 1 + \dfrac{cy}{x}$. If you divide a monomial into one piece of the numerator, you need to divide it into all the pieces.
$-b(y-1) \neq -by - b$	$-b(y-1) = -by + b$. Make sure you distribute to each piece inside the parentheses.
$(x+m)^2 \neq x^2 + m^2$	$(x+m)^2 = (x+m)(x+m) = x^2 + 2xm + m^2$. When raising a binomial to a power, make sure you FOIL! You may never "distribute" a power over a + or a − sign.

Night Before Exam Hint Sheet

✷ ✷ ✷ ✷ ✷ ✷ ✷ ✷ ✷ ✷ ✷ ✷ ✷ ✷ ✷ ✷

Use this page to write down any words, dates, and formulas that you have had trouble remembering. Don't fill it up with every one you need to know—just the information that doesn't seem to stick. Begin reviewing a few nights before the exam.

Math Log

✶ ✶ ✶ ✶ ✶ ✶

Problem	What You Did in Words to Solve It—Step by Step!!!

(Continued)

Problem	What You Did in Words to Solve It—Step by Step!!!

Verbal Log

✳ ✳ ✳ ✳ ✳ ✳

Vocabulary Notes

Reading Comp Notes

Writing Log

✻ ✻ ✻ ✻ ✻ ✻

Essay Notes

Multiple-Choice Notes

My Strategy Log

ENGLISH STRATEGY

MATH STRATEGY